A GRAMMAR
OF THE
ARABIC LANGUAGE

A GRAMMAR
OF THE
ARABIC LANGUAGE

**INTENDED MORE ESPECIALLY
FOR THE USE OF YOUNG MEN PREPARING FOR THE EAST
INDIA CIVIL SERVICE; AND ALSO FOR THE USE OF
SELF-INSTRUCTING STUDENTS IN GENERAL.**

BY

DUNCAN FORBES, LL.D.
LATE PROFESSOR OF ORIENTAL LANGUAGES IN KING'S
COLLEGE, LONDON; MEMBER OF THE ROYAL ASIATIC
SOCIETY OF GREAT BRITAIN AND IRELAND AND AUTHOR
OR EDITOR OF SEVERAL WORKS ON THE PERSIAN,
HINDUSTANI AND BENGALI LANGUAGES.

GYAN

Published by

GYAN

Gyan Publishing House
5, Ansari Road
Daryaganj, New Delhi-110002
Phone: 011-47034999, 9811692060
E-mail: books@gyanbooks.com

Distribution Network
gyanbooks.com
India, USA, Canada, UK, Australia, France

ISBN : 978-81-212-2170-2 (HB)
First Published, 1863

2nd Impression 2021

Printed at: Gyan Press, Delhi.

A Grammar of the Arabic Language
Author: Duncan Forbes

A

GRAMMAR

OF THE

ARABIC LANGUAGE:

INTENDED MORE ESPECIALLY

FOR THE USE OF YOUNG MEN PREPARING FOR THE EAST INDIA CIVIL SERVICE; AND ALSO FOR THE USE OF SELF-INSTRUCTING STUDENTS IN GENERAL.

BY

DUNCAN FORBES, LL.D.,

LATE PROFESSOR OF ORIENTAL LANGUAGES IN KING'S COLLEGE, LONDON; MEMBER OF THE ROYAL ASIATIC SOCIETY OF GREAT BRITAIN AND IRELAND; AND AUTHOR OR EDITOR OF SEVERAL WORKS ON THE PERSIAN, HINDŪSTĀNĪ, AND BENGĀLĪ LANGUAGES.

LONDON:
WM. H. ALLEN & Co., 13, WATERLOO PLACE, S.W.
1863.

PREFACE.

THERE exist, at the present day, at least half a hundred works on Arabic Grammar,—composed chiefly in the Latin, French, or German languages. The reader may, then, not unreasonably ask—Why add one more to the number? My answer to this question is, that I believe the subject to be susceptible of a far plainer and more methodical mode of treatment than what I have yet met with in any of the works to which I have just alluded; and this desideratum I have endeavoured to supply, in the following pages, to the best of my ability.

As I lay no claim to originality in this work, with the exception of the first and last Sections, and the general arrangement of the subject throughout, it is but fair that I should name the sources from which I have drawn my materials. These are—1st, Dr. Lumsden's Arabic Grammar, Vol. I. comprising the System of Inflection—(all that has been published). folio. Calc. 1813. pp. 705; and 2nd, De Sacy's Grammaire Arabe, 2nd ed. 2 vols. 8vo. Paris, 1831. pp. 608+697. Both of these Grammars are invaluable as works of reference, but they are utterly unadapted for the use of beginners. Dr. Lumsden's Grammar, so far as it extends, is copious even to the exhaustion of the subject. De Sacy's is equally copious, but exceedingly defective with regard to methodical arrangement, as I have occasionally pointed out in the following pages. This drawback in De Sacy, however, is in a great measure compensated by the copious Indices given at the end of each of his volumes. Such Arabic Grammars as appeared before the days of Lumsden and De Sacy, are of course superseded by those of the latter; and Grammars that have been published since the time of the last-mentioned masters, contain little or nothing that is new. I must, however, express my obligations to Rosenmüller's Grammar, 4to. Lipsiæ, 1818, which is a very judicious condensation of De Sacy's first edition. It has, at the same time, the faults of De Sacy on the score of arrangement; and besides, it abounds in errors of the press; still, with all its defects, it is the only work of the kind that I could have hitherto conscientiously recommended to my pupils when *commencing* the study of Arabic.

In compiling the following Grammar, I have, upon the whole, adopted the same scale, with regard to copiousness, as that used by Rosenmüller; my object, like that of the latter, being to give the student a fair condensation of all that is important in De Sacy's and Lumsden's works. In the disposal of my materials I have ventured to differ entirely from my predecessors, as may be seen by a glance at my Table of Contents. I hold, that in works of this nature, methodical arrangement is of very great importance in assisting the student's memory. Nor is this object difficult of attainment; all that a writer has to do, is to discuss plainly and concisely every part of the subject under treatment, *at the right time and in the proper place.*

As the following work is intended for the use of self-instructing students of the Arabic language, a few plain directions for the guidance of all such may not be deemed irrelevant. In the first place, then, I would advise the learner to peruse such parts only of this Grammar as are printed in the larger type, for his elementary study; and I think he may even omit Sections IV. and IX. altogether. After that let him exercise himself in reading and translating the first seven pages of Mr. Schalch's Arabic Selections, 4to. East India College, 1830; or the first Tale in the Chrestomathia Arabica of Kosegarten, 8vo. Lipsiæ, 1828. Both of these works are furnished with copious vocabularies, and the extracts I have mentioned are pointed in full. Secondly, let him, after that, read over *the whole* of this Grammar, including of course, all the portions of it printed in smaller type, and marked *a*, *b*, etc.; after which let him finish the perusal of the two reading-books above mentioned. This we may call a fair elementary course, or *Little-go*, in the study of the language; and it has this solid advantage, that it does not encroach very heavily on the learner's finances.

The preceding economical course will prove highly serviceable to three classes of self-instructing students.—First, To young and middle-aged clergymen, stationed throughout the country, who may wish to acquire a moderate knowledge of Arabic, as a valuable auxiliary to the study of Hebrew; for it is now an acknowledged fact, that a man can no more be a thorough Hebrew scholar without Arabic, than he can be a Latin scholar without Greek. Secondly, To young men preparing for the East India Civil Service, to whom the above course ought to suffice for passing their examination in this country. Thirdly and lastly, To all those who intend to visit any of the extensive regions where the Muḥammadan religion prevails, or wherever the modern Arabic is generally spoken.

The Modern Arabic differs from the Ancient or Classical, chiefly in this, that the former has undergone a process of simplification, such as the rejection of the *nūnation*, and of the final short vowels in general; also the rejection of the dual number both in nouns and verbs. In fact, the Modern is to the Ancient Arabic, what the Greek of the present day is to that of Thucydides. An elementary knowledge of the Classical Arabic will enable a traveller to acquire, with ease, and in a very short time, every dialect of the Modern Tongue spoken between the Atlantic and the Tigris.

For a second and finishing course of reading, let the student procure, in the first place, one or other of the following Dictionaries, viz.—Freytagii (Georgii Wilhelmi) Lexicon

Arabico-Latinum, præsertim ex Jauharì Fīrusabādīque et aliorum Arabum operibus desumtum, etc.; accedit Index Vocum Latinarum locupletissimus. 4 vols. 4to. Halis Saxonum, 1830-1838. This is an enlarged and vastly improved edition of the far-famed Arabic Lexicon of Golius, which used to sell for ten guineas. For ordinary purposes, the abridged edition of this work will suffice, viz.—Freytagii (G. W.) Lexicon Arabico-Latinum ex opere suo majore in usum Tironum excerptum. 4to. Halis Saxonum, 1837. By the aid of either of these Lexicons the learner may peruse such of the following works as he may find convenient; viz. —Arabic Reader, 8vo. Calcutta, 1828. Ikhwānu-ṣ-Ṣafā, royal 8vo. 1812. History of Tīmūr, by Ibn 'Arab Shāh, royal 8vo. 1817. Ḳur,ān, Flügel's edition, 4to. no date—about 1840. Concordantiæ Corani, etc., diligenter disposuit Gustavus Flügel, 4to. Lipsiæ, 1842.

To the above we may add the following works edited by M. De Sacy, viz,—Calila et Dimna en Arabe, 4to. Paris, 1816. Chrestomathie Arabe, three thick volumes 8vo. 2nd edition, Paris, 1826. This last work is invaluable on account of its numerous critical notes, and illustrations of the text. Les Seances de Hariri en Arabe avec un Commentaire, fol. Paris, 1821. To these, again, we may add several valuable works printed at Calcutta in the course of the present century, viz.—Nafhatu-l-Yaman, a Selection of Easy Stories in Prose and Verse from the best Authors. 4to. 1811. Ḥadīḳatu-l-Afrāḥ, A Miscellany, from the Writings of the most distinguished Arabian Poets, Orators, and Historians. Royal 4to. 1813. Alf Lailah, or, Book of the Thousand and One Nights, (Arabian Nights' Entertainment). Edited by Sir W. H. Macnaghten, assisted by learned Moulavies. 4 vols. royal 8vo. Calc. 1839-42. This is the most complete edition of the work. The first Fifty Nights have been translated very literally into English by H. Torrens. 8vo. London, 1838. There are two other editions of the Alf Lailah, viz.—Alf Lailah: oder Tausend und eine Nacht, Arabisch, nach eine, Handschrift aus Tunis, herausg. von M. Habicht, 12 vols. 12mo. Breslau, 1825-1843. Also, Alf Lailah, the Būlāḳ edition, from different Arabic MSS., very carefully edited by some of the most learned natives of Egypt. 2 vols. 4to. Cairo, 1830. Finally, the learner should add to his Arabian library the Mu'allaḳāt, with commentary. royal 8vo. Calc. 1823.

To complete his knowledge of Arabic Grammar, the student should procure, if possible, the following works by M. De Sacy, viz.—Grammaire Arabe, two thick volumes 8vo. 1831. Anthologie Grammaticale Arabe, 8vo. 1829. Alfiya, by Ibn Malik, roy. 8vo. 1833. To these he may add—Lumsden's Arabic Grammar, already alluded to; and Lockett's Mi,at 'Âmil, 4to. Calcutta, 1814. The man who has gone through this second course, or even a moiety of it, may be safely left thenceforth to his own guidance.

With regard to the importance of the Arabic language to the Hebrew student, it is sufficient for me to refer him to the following works, viz.—1st. Dissertatio de Origine, etc. Linguæ Arabicæ, ejusque intima Affinitate et Convenientiâ cum Linguâ Hebraicâ, 8vo. Edin. 1769, by Dr. James Robertson, of the Edinburgh University, the soundest, if not the *only* sound, Semitic scholar, that Scotland had till then produced. —2nd. Clavis dialecti Arabicæ, etc. sm. 4to. Lugduni Batavorum, 1733, by Albert Schultens. The most complete work of this nature, however, is the Origines Hebrææ, by Albert Schultens. Folio, Lugd. Batt. 1761, pp. 648, cum Indicibus. All of these are first-rate works on this particular subject; and they ought long ago to have been translated into our own vernacular, if, in our country, Semitic studies had met with that attention which their importance demands. As a valuable guide in this department I would strongly recommend the Arabic Grammar recently published by my friend William Wright, Esq., of the British Museum, formerly Professor of Arabic in the University of Dublin. 2 vols. 8vo. Leipzig and London, 1859 and 1862.

To the general scholar, the Arabic language recommends itself as the vehicle of science and civilization, between the brilliant æra of Grecian literature, and the not less brilliant dawn of the Reformation in modern Europe. This has been so well expressed by an old and esteemed pupil of mine, H. B. Beresford, Esq., late of the Bengal Civil Service, that I cannot here do better than reproduce his very words. Mr. Beresford, in the preface to a translation by him of a work on Arabic Syntax, entitled, Hidāyatu-n-Naḥwi, 8vo. London, 1843, says,—"In whatever point of view we regard the

Arabic Language, whether as the language of a people who in the Middle Ages contributed so materially to the literature and refinement of Europe, or as the language of a religion which numbers upwards of 100,000,000 followers, and at the present day affects greater numbers of mankind than Christianity itself; or whether it be regarded as the medium for communicating sound European knowledge to the whole body of the *learned* Muḥammadans of India, and as *one* of the inexhaustible fountains for enriching some of the Indian vernaculars, so as to render them competent vehicles of European science and literature to the great mass of the Muḥammadan population throughout British India; under all the above, and various other points of view, Arabic may be said to be an object of deep and peculiar interest."

In conclusion, I have to acknowledge my deep obligations to my friends, Professor Francis Johnson, late of Haileybury College, Herts; and Dr. Charles Rieu, of the British Museum, Professor of Arabic in University College, London. The kindness shewn to me by these gentlemen in perusing and correcting the sheets of this work as they passed through the press, is more than I can ever adequately repay.

D. FORBES.

58, Burton Crescent,
August, 1863.

TABLE OF CONTENTS.

SECTION I.

WHICH TREATS OF THE LETTERS AND SYMBOLS USED IN WRITING.

SECTION II.

WHICH TREATS OF THE ARTICLE, THE SUBSTANTIVES, NUMERALS, ADJECTIVES, AND PRONOUNS.

SECTION III.

WHICH TREATS OF THE VERB.

SECTION IV.

WHICH TREATS OF THE INFIRM OR IMPERFECT VERBS, ETC.

SECTION V.

WHICH TREATS OF THE INDECLINABLE PARTICLES.

SECTION VI.

WHICH TREATS OF THE DERIVATION AND FORMATION OF NOUNS.

SECTION VII.

WHICH TREATS OF THE SYNTAX OF THE ARTICLE, SUBSTANTIVES, ADJECTIVES, & PRONOUNS.

SECTION VIII.

WHICH TREATS OF THE SYNTAX OF VERBS AND PARTICLES.

SECTION IX.

WHICH TREATS OF THE PROSODY.

ERRATA.

PAGE	LINE	
17	25	*for* "on," *read* "under."
21	6	*for* "of vowel," *read* "of the vowel."
29	15	*for* "as," *read* "thus."
36	16	*for* "begin," *read* "begin with."
39	11	*for* قابليّت *read* قابليّة
42	19	*for* مَشْيُوخا "an old man," *read* مَشْيُوخآءُ "old men."
48, last line but one,		*for* اَوَائِبْ *read* عِيَابٌ
50	6	*for* اَسْكِيفْ *read* اَسَاكِيفُ
50	13	*for* "quiescent," *read* "inert."
55	11	*for* "participles," *read* "particles."
57	17	*for* "in other," *read* "their other."
58	25	*omit* the two words, "عَشَرَة or."
64	19	*for* "positive," *read* "comparative."
66	17 and 20,	*omit* the word "both."
68	21	*for* اِيَّاسَكُمَا *read* اِيَّاكُمَا
86	7	*for* "future," *read* "Aorist."
96	19	*for* "Grammar," *read* "Grammars."
102	24	*for* "indefinite," *read* "Aorist."
129	17	*for* يَسِيرُ *read* سَيْرُ
165	14	*omit* the two words, "or اِلَّا"
215	19	*for* "a distribution of individuality," *read* "distribution or individuality."
284	24	*for* "conjunction لِ" *read* "particle لِ"

ARABIC GRAMMAR.

SECTION I.

Of the Letters and Symbols used in Writing.

1. THE Arabs, like the ancient Phœnicians, the Jews and Samaritans, write and read their letters from right to left; hence their books *begin* at what we should call the *end*. The Arabic Alphabet* consists of twenty-eight letters, all of which are considered as consonants. Most of these assume different forms (some three, and a few others four), according as they are situated at the commencement, middle, or end of a combined group of letters, as may be seen in the following Table, Column V. Thus, in a combination of three or more letters, the first of the group, on the right-hand side, will have the form marked *Initial;* the letter or letters between the first and last will have the form marked *Medial;* and the last, on the left, will have the *Final* form. Observe, also, that in this Table, Column I. contains the names of the letters in the Arabic character; II. the same in the Roman character; III. the detached form of the letters, which should be learned first; and IV. the corresponding English letters.

* The Alphabet here described is used, generally speaking, by all those nations who have adopted the religion of Muhammad; viz., the people inhabiting the North-west, the North, and the East of Africa, the Turks, the Arabs, the Persians, the Afghāns, and the Musalmān portion of the people of India and Malacca.

THE ARABIC ALPHABET.

I. NAME.	II. NAME.	III. DETACHED FORM.	IV. POWER.	V. COMBINED FORM. Final.	V. Med.	V. Initial	VI. EXEMPLIFICATIONS. Final.	VI. Medial.	VI. Initial.
الِف	*alif*	ا	*a, etc.*	ا	ا	ا	تا	بار	اب
با	*bā*	ب	*b*	ـب	ـبـ	بـ	طلب	صبر	بَدَر
تا	*tā*	ت	*t*	ـت	ـتـ	تـ	بنت	ستر	تبر
ثا	*thā*	ث	*th*	ـث	ـثـ	ثـ	خبث	بثر	ثُور
جِيم	*jīm*	ج	*j*	ـج	ـجـ	جـ	شلج	شجر	جبر
حا	*ḥā*	ح	*ḥ*	ـح	ـحـ	حـ	صبح	بحر	حرّ
خا	*kh̲ā*	خ	*kh̲*	ـخ	ـخـ	خـ	سلخ	تخْم	خبر
دال	*dāl*	د	*d*	ـد	ـد	د	جِلد	فِدا	دبر
ذال	*dhāl*	ذ	*dh*	ـذ	ـذ	ذ	كاغَذ	نَذر	ذكر
را	*rā*	ر	*r*	ـر	ـر	ر	مرّ	فرْد	رشد
زا	*zā*	ز	*z*	ـز	ـز	ز	عجز	بزم	زجر
سِين	*sīn*	س	*s*	ـس	ـسـ	سـ	لبس	فسق	سِرّ
شِين	*shīn*	ش	*sh*	ـش	ـشـ	شـ	جيش	تشدّ	شِد
صاد	*ṣād*	ص	*ṣ*	ـص	ـصـ	صـ	شخص	قصْد	صدر

THE ARABIC ALPHABET—*Continued.*

I. NAME.	II.	III. DETACHED FORM.	IV. POWER.	V. COMBINED FORM. Final.	Med.	Initial	VI. EXEMPLIFICATIONS. Final.	Medial.	Initial.
ضاد	*ḍād*	ض	*ḍ*	ـض	ـضـ	ضـ	بعض	خِضر	ضِدّ
طا	*ṭā*	ط	*ṭ*	ـط	ـطـ	طـ	خطّ	بطن	طبق
ظا	*ẓā*	ظ	*ẓ*	ـظ	ـظـ	ظـ	حِفظ	نظر	ظفر
عَين	*'ain*	ع	*'a, etc.*	ـع	ـعـ	عـ	صنع	بُعّد	عسل
غَين	*ghain*	غ	*gh*	ـغ	ـغـ	غـ	صبغ	بغِي	غُسل
فا	*fā*	ف	*f*	ـف	ـفـ	فـ	صنف	سفر	فِكر
قاف	*ḳāf*	ق	*ḳ*	ـق	ـقـ	قـ	سفق	سقر	قدر
كاف	*kāf*	ك	*k*	ـك	ـكـ	كـ	ملك	يكُن	كلم
لام	*lām*	ل	*l*	ـل	ـلـ	لـ	اكل	عِلْم	لفظ
مِيم	*mīm*	م	*m*	ـم	ـمـ	مـ	سِتم	يُمن	منع
نُون	*nūn*	ن	*n*	ـن	ـنـ	نـ	صحن	بنت	نبض
واو	*wāw*	و	*w, etc.*	ـو	ـو	و	أبُو	ثور	وجد
ها	*hā*	ه	*h*	ـه	ـهـ	هـ	بِهِ	بِها	هجر
يا	*yā*	ي	*y, etc.*	ـي	ـيـ	يـ	ابِي	حيث	يدّ

2. Besides the foregoing twenty-eight letters there are five additional marks or symbols used in writing, viz. (ـَ), (ـِ), (ـُ), (ـْ), and (ـّ), with which the student may here at once familiarise himself. The first is called *Fatḥa* (ـَ) which when placed over a letter indicates the presence of the short vowel *a*, thus, فَلَك *falak*. 2nd. *Kasra* (ـِ) placed under a letter and indicating a short *i*, as in بِهِ *bihi*. 3rd. *Ḍamma* (ـُ), which when placed over a letter indicates the presence of a short *u*, as in the word كُتُب *kutub*. 4th. *Jazm* (ـْ), which when placed over a letter denotes that none of the three short vowels immediately follows; thus, فَرْد *fard*. 5th. *Tash-dīd* (ـّ), which when placed over a letter indicates that such letter is doubled, as in the word حَرّ *ḥarr*.

3. Perhaps the best mode of learning the Alphabet, is, First, to write out several times the detached or full forms of the letters in Column III. Secondly, to observe what changes (if any) these undergo, when combined in the formation of words, as exhibited in Column V. Lastly, to endeavour to transfer, into their corresponding English letters, the words given as exemplifications in Column VI. These words are three in number, and are to be read, of course, from right to left. They shew at once the various phases assumed by the leading letter, whether *initial*, *medial*, or *final*. At the same time, as an exercise for the student we have given a sprinkling of the five symbols above noticed.

Of the Sounds of the Letters.

4. The following twelve letters require very little notice

as their respective sounds are sufficiently represented by the English letters opposite to each in Column IV. The letter ب *b* has the sound of our *b* in "ball;" ث *th*, that of our *th* in "thin;" ج *j*, that of our *j* in "jar;" ر *r*, as in "river;" ز *z*, as in "zeal;" س *s*, as in "sin;" ش *sh*, as in "shin;" ف *f*, as in "fin;" ك *k*, as in "kin;" ل *l*, as in "land;" م *m*, as in "man;" ه *h*, as in "hand." To these we may add the consonants و and ي when beginning a word or syllable; the sound of و *w* being that of our *w* in "war," and that of ي *y*, our *y* in "yard." These last, however, when not initial, contribute to the formation of long vowels and diphthongs, of which we shall treat hereafter, in their proper place.

a. There are some instances in which the letter ل *lām* of the article الْ *al*, "the," changes its proper sound in accordance with the initial letter of the substantive to which the article is prefixed (See § 46).

5. We shall now endeavour to give a concise description of such Arabic letters as have no exact corresponding sound in our own language; premising, at the same time, that it is rather a difficult task to convey in writing, in such cases, a correct idea of the pronunciation of foreign letters. We can only do so approximately, by having recourse to such languages, among our neighbours, as happen to have the requisite sounds. It is highly probable, however, that the majority of students may be unacquainted with the languages employed by us as illustrations: hence, it clearly follows, as a general rule, that the correct sounds of such letters as differ from our own, must be learned *by the ear*—we may say, by a *good ear*;

and, consequently, a long description is needless. The remark applies in particular to the letters ث, ح, خ, ذ, ص, ض, ع, غ, ق, and the various sounds assumed by the letter ن.

6. At the beginning of a word or syllable, the letter ا *alif*, like any other consonant, depends for its sound on the accompanying vowel: of itself, it is a very weak aspirate, like our *h* in the words *herb*, *honour*, and *hour*. It is still more closely identified with the *spiritus lenis* of the Greek, in such words as ἀπὸ, ἐπὶ, ὀρθός, where the apostrophe (ʼ) represents the *alif*. In fact, when we utter the syllables *ab*, *ib*, and *ub*, there is a slight movement of the muscles of the throat at the commencement of utterance; and the part where that movement takes place, the Oriental grammarians consider to be the *makhraj*, or "place of utterance" of the *consonant* ا, as in the words اَبْ *ab*, اِبْ *ib*, and اُبْ *ub*, just the same as the lips form the *makhraj* of *b*, in the syllables بَدْ *bad*, بِدْ *bid*, and بُدْ *bud*. Finally, the ا may be considered as the *spiritus lenis*, or weak aspirate of the letter ه.

a. Strictly speaking, the initial *alif* in the above examples ought to have been accompanied with the symbol called *hamza* (See § 35) as well as the essential vowel mark; thus, أَبْ *ab*, إِبْ *ib*, and أُبْ *ub*. It would be quite preposterous, however, to perplex the student at the present stage of his progress, by carrying along with us this cumbersome and useless symbol. The very best Arabic Grammar in our language, that of Dr. Lumsden, eschews throughout the use of the *hamza* in combination with the *initial alif*.

b. The term مَخْرَج *makhraj* denotes "the place of emission," or "place of utterance" of a syllable consisting of a consonant and a vowel. Thus, in the syllable بَ *bă*, بِ *bĭ*, and بُ *bŭ*, or of مَ *mă*, مِ *mĭ*, and مُ *mŭ*, the place of utterance is between the lips: so the *makh-raj* of the letters ح *ḥā*, and ع *'ain* is in the lower part of the throat, and their true sounds can be acquired only from the mouth of an Arab.

7. ت *t*. The sound of this letter is softer and more dental than that of the English *t*. It corresponds with the Sanskrit त; or with the *t* of the Italians in the words "*sotto*" and "*petto*."

8. ث *th* is sounded, as has been said § 4, like our *th* in "thin," or the *θ theta* of the Greeks; but the natives of Egypt and Syria frequently confound it with the letter ت *t*, just described. The Turks, Persians, and other Musalmān people to the eastward, give it the sound of *s*. In fact, it would appear that most nations have an aversion to the aspirate *th*, which to us seems such an easy sound.

9. ح *ḥ* is a very strong aspirate, somewhat like our *h* in the word "haul," but uttered by compressing the lower muscles of the throat. It will be represented in the Roman character by *ḥ*.

10. خ *kh* has a sound like the *ch* in the word "loch" as pronounced by the Scotch and Irish; or the final German *ch*, in the word "buch." It will be represented in the Roman character by *kh*.

a. In an Arabic Grammar published at Vienna, in 4to. 1813, by a reverend gentleman named Antonio Aryda, who styles himself "Tripolis Syriæ Archipresbyter," we are told, sensibly enough, that "خ pronunciatur uti χ Græcorum, seu potius veluti Germanicum *ch* vocalem *a* subsequens." As if this, however, were not sufficiently explicit, the author adds, "ad amussim congruit cum sono quem, ad spuendum se præparans, elicet; uti *chrr*" *!!!*

11. د *d* has a softer and more dental sound than our *d*. It corresponds to the Sanskrit द, or the *d* of most European languages except the English.

12. ذ *dh* is sounded like our soft *th* in the words "thy" or "thine." In Egypt and Syria it is sometimes sounded like *d*, and in Turkey, Persia, etc., like *z*. It bears the same relation to د *d*, that ث *th* has to ت *t*. In the Roman character we shall uniformly represent it by *dh*.

a. It is a curious fact that the Anglo-Saxon Alphabet had two distinct characters corresponding exactly to the ث *th* and ذ *dh* of the Arabs, viz. þ *tha*, and ð *edh*, respectively, which, it might have been as well if we had still retained.

13. ص *ṣ* has a stronger or more hissing sound than our *s*. According to Dr. Lumsden it is formed by the tip of the tongue pressed against the upper gums. We represent it in the Roman character by *ṣ*.

14. ض *ḍ* is pronounced by the Arabs like a hard *d*, by pressing the tongue against the upper teeth on one side of the mouth, generally the left. In the Roman character we use for it *ḍ*. The Persians, etc., sound it like *z*.

15. ط *ṭ* and ظ *ẓ*. These letters are sounded somewhat like ت and ز, or very nearly so. We represent them in the Roman character by *ṭ* and *ẓ* respectively.

16. ع *'a*, etc. The consonant ع has the same relation to

the strong aspirate ح, that ا has to ه; that is, the ع, like the ا, is a *spiritus lenis* or weak aspirate; but the *makhraj*, or place of utterance, of the ع is lower down in the muscles of the throat than that of the *alif*. With this distinction, its sound, if we may use the expression, depends as in the case of the letter ا, on the accompanying vowel, as عَب *'ab*, عِب *'ib*, عُب *'ub*, which, in the mouth of an Arab, are different from اَب *ab*, اِب *ib*, and اُب *ub*. In the Roman character the *'ain* will be represented by the *spiritus lenis* ('). At the same time, it is impossible to explain in writing the true sound of this letter; as it is not to be found in any European language, so far as we know. The student who has not the advantage of a competent teacher, may treat the ع as he does the ا, until he has the opportunity of learning its true sound by the ear, from the mouth of a native.

a. Some grammarians have favoured us with descriptions, most amusingly absurd, of this *indescribable* letter. Meninski says that the sound of it is "instar vocis vituli matrem vocantis." Vriemoet, a Dutch *savant*, in his Arabic Grammar published at Tranequer, 1733, calls it an "adspiratio fortissima," and represents it by *hhh!!!* which I suppose means *h to the third power*. Most grammarians tell us that it is the same as the Hebrew ע *ain;* but then the Hebrew *ain* itself is a very disputed point, even among the Jews; and most assuredly one of the sounds given to it by the latter, viz. *ṅg*, is not that of the Arabs.

17. غ *gh* has a sound somewhat like *g* in the German word "*sagen*." About the banks of the Tweed, the natives sound what they fancy to be the letter *r*, very like the Eastern غ, a peculiarity well known as the Northumbrian *burr*, or the

r of the French when "*grasseyé.*" We shall represent it in the Roman character by *gh*.

18. ق *ḳ* bears some resemblance to our *c* hard, in the words "calm," "cup;" with this difference, that the ق is uttered from the lower muscles of the throat. In the Roman character it will be represented by *ḳ*.

19. ن *n*. This letter is variously sounded according to circumstances. 1st. When followed by a vowel or a guttural consonant, that is, by ا, ح, خ, ع, غ, or ه, it is sounded exactly as in English. 2nd. When followed by any of the fifteen letters, ت, ث, د, ذ, ز, س, ش, ص, ض, ط, ظ, ق, ف, or ك, it has a nasal sound like that of the French *n* in the words "entrez," and "rendre." 3rd. When followed by the letter ب it naturally becomes *m*, as is the case in Latin and Greek; for example, the word عَنْبَر *'anbar*, "amber," is pronounced as if written *'ambar;* so instead of مِن بَيْتِ *min-baiti*, "from the house," they say *mim-baiti.* 4th. When the letter ن *n* is followed by any of the four liquids ر *r*, ل *l*, م *m*, or ن *n*, the two letters coalesce as in Latin and Greek; thus مِن رَبِّي *min-rabbī*, "from my lord," is pronounced *mirrabbī;* so مِن لَيْلَة *min-lailati* becomes مِنْلَيْلَة *mil-lailati*, etc. Lastly, when a word ending in ن *n* is followed by a word beginning with و *w* or ي *y*, the sound of the ن *n* is scarcely perceptible, but the و and ي are doubled, thus مِن وَالِدِي *min-wālidī*, "from my father," becomes *miwwālidī;* so ان يَتَقَدَّم *an-yataḳaddama* becomes *ayyataḳaddama.* When, however, ن *n* in the middle of a word is followed by the con-

sonants و w or ي y it retains its natural sound; as in the words قِنْوانٌ *ḳinwānu* and دُنْيا *dunyā*.

20. ة *t*. The letter ه *h*, at the end of a word, is frequently marked with two dots above it, in which case it is sounded exactly like the letter ت *t*. It is then what is called a servile letter, and is chiefly used to denote the feminine gender of substantives and adjectives as we shall see hereafter.

21. لا or لا *lā*, a peculiar form of *lām* and *alif*, is in many grammars stuck in at the end of the table of letters, with a view apparently to puzzle the student. Its purport, I believe, is to shew that the *alif* is a long *ā* or letter of prolongation (see § 27), but then any other consonant followed by *alif*, such as با *bā*, تا *tā*, etc., would have answered the purpose equally well; or it may be intended to exhibit the ordinary mode of combining the ل and ا in writing and printing.

Of the Primitive or Short Vowels—اَلْحَرَكَاتُ.

22. The Primitive Vowels as we briefly noticed in § 2, are three in number, which are indicated by the following simple notation. The first of the primitive vowels is called فَتْحَة *fatḥa*, and is writen thus, (ـَ) over the consonant to which it belongs. Its sound is that of a short *a*, such as we have in the word "calamus," which is of Eastern origin, and of which the first two syllables or root, *calam* or *ḳalam*, are thus written, قَلَم. Dr. Lumsden and several eminent Oriental scholars, have considered the *fatḥa* as equivalent to our short *u* in the words "sun" and "summer." We have no hesitation, however, in saying that (in the Arabic language especially) our short

u is not generally a true representation of *fatḥa*. In pronouncing the short *u* of *sun*, the mouth *is more shut* than in pronouncing the *a* in the words *calamus* and *calendar;* and it so happens, moreover, that the very signification of the term *fatḥa* is, "open." In such Arabic words, therefore, as we may have occasion to write in Roman characters, the *a* unmarked is understood always to represent the vowel *fatḥa*, and to have no other sound than that of *a* in "calamus" or "calendar."

23. The second is called *kasra* كَسْرة, and is thus (ـِ) written under the consonant to which it belongs. Its sound is generally that of our short *i* in the words "sin" and "fin," which in Arabic would be written سِن and فِن. Occasionally it has a sound like our short *e* in the words "bed" and "fed," which words would be most nearly represented in Arabic as بِد and فِد. In general, however, the *kasra* has the sound of our short *i:* the unmarked *i*, therefore, in the course of this work is understood to have the sound of *i* in "sin" and "fin," in all Oriental words written in the Roman character.

24. The third is called *ḍamma* ضَمّة, which is thus (ـُ) written over its consonant. Its sound is like that of our short *u* in the words "bull" and "bush," which in Arabic would be written بُل and بُش: we have its sound also in the words "foot" and "hood," which would be written فُت and هُد. Sometimes in the modern Arabic the *ḍamma* has a sound approaching our short *o* in the word "solemn;" for example the word شُغْل "labour," is pronounced *shog͟hl* in-

stead of *shughl*. We shall, however, in this work uniformly represent the *ḍamma* by the unmarked *u*, which, in all Oriental words in the Roman character, is understood to have the sound of *u* in "bull" and "bush;" but never that of our *u* in such words as "usage" and "perfume," or such as our *u* in "sun" and "fun."

Of Tanwīn or Nūnation—اَلتَّنوِين.

25. Sometimes the preceding short vowels are, in a peculiar manner, employed for a particular purpose on the last letter of a word, which process is called *tanwīn* or *nūnation*, that is, the use or application of the letter ن *n*. The *tanwīn*, which in Arabic grammar serves to mark the inflexions of a noun, is formed by doubling the vowel-point of the last letter, which indicates at once its presence and its sound; the last syllable thus becoming *uṇ*, *iṇ*, or *aṇ*, as in the words بابٌ *bābuṇ*, بابٍ *bābiṇ*, بابًا *bābaṇ*. The last form, that of the vowel *fatḥa*, requires the letter ا, which does not, however, prolong the sound of the final syllable. The ا is not required when the noun ends with a *hamza* or the letter ة, as شَيْءً *shai-aṇ*, حِكْمَةً *ḥikmataṇ;* or when the word ends in ي *ya*, surmounted by ا (in which case the ا only is pronounced), as هُدًي *hudaṇ*. As a general rule the termination ٌ denotes the Nominative case; ٍ the Genitive, Dative, or Ablative; and اً, ءً, or ةً the Accusative. In words ending in ي, surmounted by ا, without the *tanwīn* or *nūnation*, the *alif* is sounded like the *alif* of prolongation, § 27, as تعالي *ta'ālā*, عُقْبي *'ukbā*, etc. Of this, however, we shall have more to say further on.

a. In some Arabic Grammars recently printed the *tanwīn* is said to be a *nasal n!* This is simply misleading the learner. The *tanwīn* has precisely the sound of the letter *nūn* ن when final (See § 19), and is subject to exactly the same modifications as the latter under similar circumstances. In the Roman character we shall represent the *nūnation* by *n̲*.

Of the Symbol جَزْم *Jazm, or Amputation.*

26. When a consonant is accompanied by one of the three primitive vowels, it is said to be مُتَحَرِّك *mutaḥarrik*, that is, *moving* or *moveable* by that vowel. Arabian grammarians consider a syllable as a *step* or *move* in the formation of a word or sentence; and, in their language, the first letter of a word is always accompanied, or moveable, by a vowel; but with regard to the remaining letters of the word there is no certain rule. When, in the middle or end of a word, a consonant is not accompanied by a vowel, it is said to be سَاكِن *sākin*, "resting" or "inert;" and the mark (ـْـ) called جَزْم *jazm*, which signifies "amputation," is placed over such consonant to shew when this is the case.

a. For example let us take the word كَتَبْتُمْ *katabtum*, "you wrote," or "you have written," the letters *kāf* and *tā* are moveable by *fatḥa*; the letter *bā* is *sākin* or *inert;* then the following *tā* is moveable by *ḍamma*, and the final letter *mīm* is *inert*. In most Arabic Grammars a letter not followed by a vowel is called *quiescent:* now, I object to the latter term, as it is apt to mislead the beginner, it being already applied in English Grammar in the sense of *not sounded*. For instance, the letter *g* is *quiescent* in the word *phlegm;* we cannot, however, say that *m* is *quiescent* in the same word, though we may say that it is *inert*. The student will be pleased to bear in mind, then, that in this work a letter is said to be *inert* when it is not followed by a vowel; when we call it *quiescent*, we mean that it is not sounded at all.

Of the Symbol Tashdīd—اَلتَّشْدِيدُ.

27. When a letter is doubled, the mark (ّ) called *tashdīd*, which signifies corroboration, is placed over it. Thus, in the word شِدَّت *shid-dat*, where the first syllable ends with د *d* and the next begins with د *d*, instead of following the natural mode of writing, as, شِدْدَت, the two *dāls* are united, and the mark ّ indicates this union. Hence, whenever we see a letter followed by the same one, we may rest assured that there is a vowel between them; thus the word مَدَّت with the *tashdīd* on the *dāl* is sounded *maddat*, but the word مَدَد is pronounced *madad*.

a. In certain instances the symbol *tashdīd* is employed for the sake of euphony, when an inert letter is followed by a different letter having a cognate sound, or one which is capable of coalescing with the former, thus مَدَدْتُ is pronounced, not *madadtu*, but *madattu*, and written مَدَدتُّ in which case the final ت *t* is marked with the *tashdīd* to shew that it has coalesced with the preceding د *d;* so لَبِثتُّ *labitta* for *labithta*. In like manner the ل *l* of the definite article اَلْ, "the," coalesces with the initial letter of the substantive following when it is what is technically called a *solar* letter, as will be noticed hereafter when we come to treat of the *Article*. We have already pointed out (§ 19) the changes in sound to which the final ن *n* inert is subject, and the same rule applies to the *nūnation* (See § 25). In some instances the final *nūn* is changed into that which follows, as مِمَّن *mim-man* for *min-man*; اِلّا *illā* for *in-lā*, etc. It is needless to say that this is a general rule in the composition of words in Latin and Greek.

Of the Letters of Prolongation—حُرُوفُ المَدِّ.

28. The letters ا, و, and ي, when *inert*, serve to prolong the preceding vowel, as follows: when ا *inert* is preceded by a letter moveable by *fatḥa*, the *fatḥa* and *alif* together form a long sound like our *a* in "war," or *au* in "haul," which in Arabic might be written وَار and حَال. On a similar principle, we may consider the unaspirated *h* as a letter of prolongation in the German words "wahr" and "zahl." We may also consider the second *a* as *inert* in the words "aachen" and "waal."

29. When the letter و *inert* is preceded by a consonant moveable by the vowel *ḍamma*, the *ḍamma* and و joined together form a sound like our *oo* in "tool;" which in Arabic might be written طُول, or, which is the same thing, like our *u* in "rule," which the Arabs would write رُول. If the letter و be preceded by a consonant moveable by *fatḥa*, the *fatḥa* and و united will form a diphthong, nearly like our *ou* in "sound," or *ow* in "town," but more exactly like *au* in the German word "kaum," which in Arabic might be written قَوم. If the و be preceded by the vowel *kasra*, no union takes place, and the و preserves its natural sound as a consonant, as in the word سِوَا *siwā*. In English, the *w* is a letter of prolongation in many words, as "draw," "crow," etc.; it also contributes to the formation of a diphthong, as in "town," "gown," etc.

30. When the letter ي *inert* is preceded by a consonant moveable by *kasra*, the *kasra* and the ي unite, and form a long vowel, like our *ee* in "feel," which in Arabic might be written فِيل; or, which is the same thing, like our *i* in "machine," which would be written مَشِين. When the letter ي *inert* is preceded by a consonant, moveable by *fatḥa*, the *fatḥa* and the ي unite, and form a diphthong, like *ai* in the german word *Kaiser*, which in Arabic is written قَيْصَر. This sound is really that of our own *i* in "wise," "size," which we are pleased to call a vowel, but which, in reality, is a diphthong. When the ي is preceded by *ḍamma*, no union takes place, and the ي retains its usual sound as a consonant, as in the word مُيَسَّر *muyassar*. In English the letter *y* is a letter of prolongation in the words "say" and "key;" it also contributes to the formation of a diphthong in the word "buy," which in Arabic might be written بَيْ.

a. The three letters of prolongation ا, و, and ي, are occasionally liable to certain deviations from the rules above laid down. This subject will be more fully explained hereafter when we come to treat of the permutation of the *infirm letters*. Suffice it for us to say at present that the letters of prolongation ا, و, and ي, are said to possess their *homogeneous* or *natural* vowels, when *fatḥa* is placed over the consonant that precedes ا, *ḍamma* over that which precedes و, and *kasra* on that which precedes ي; when this is not the case, the vowels and letters of prolongation are said to be *heterogeneous* or *dissimilar*. When a heterogeneous vowel precedes those letters, the two together either form a diphthong as we have just shown, thus, لَيْلٌ *lailun*, جَوْهَرٌ *jauharun*, or the last letter may remain silent, as

رَمَي *ramā* and صَلٰوة *salāt;* in which two last words the ي and و are really *quiescent* or not *sounded.*

31. It appears then, from what we have stated in the six preceding paragraphs, that the vocal sounds in Arabic are eight in number, viz., 1. three short; 2. the same three long; and 3. two diphthongs, as may be seen in the following table:

	1. SHORT.			2. LONG.			3. DIPHTHONG.	
1.	*fun*	*fin*	*foot*	*fall*	*feel*	*fool*	*file*	*foul*
2.	فَن	فِن	فُت	فَال	فِيل	فُول	فَيْل	فَوْل
3.	*fan*	*fin*	*fut*	*fāl*	*fīl*	*fūl*	*fail*	*faul*

Here the upper line (1) contains eight English words of common occurrence, the sounds of each of which fairly represent those of the respective Arabic words underneath. The lowest line (3) exhibits the system uniformly adhered to in the course of this work for representing Arabic words in the Roman character.

32. We have now, we trust, fully explained how the vowels are to be represented when they *follow* an audible consonant, such as the letter ف *f* in the foregoing list of words. In order to represent the vowels as initial or commencing a word, it will at once occur to the student that we have merely to annihilate or withdraw the letter ف *f* from the above words, leaving everything else as it stands, and the object is effected. This is precisely what we do *in reality,* though not *in appearance.* The Arabian grammarians have taken into their heads a most subtle crotchet on this point, which is, *that no word or syllable can begin with a vowel.*

Therefore, to represent what we call an initial vowel, that is, a vowel commencing a word or syllable, they employ the letter ا *alif* (otherwise called *hamza*) as a fulcrum for the vowel. We have already stated (§ 6) that they consider the ا as a very weak aspirate or *spiritus lenis;* hence its presence supports the above theory, at least to the eye, if not to the ear. In order, then, to exhibit the vowels in the preceding paragraph as initial, we must, after taking away the letter ف *f*, substitute ا in its place, which ا being *nothing*, or *very nearly so*, the process amounts *in reality* to the withdrawal of the letter ف *f*, and the substitution of what may be considered as *next to nothing*, thus—

	1. SHORT.			2. LONG.			3. DIPHTHONG.	
1.	*un*	*in*	*ŏŏt*	*all*	*eel*	*óól*	*aisle*	*owl*
2.	اَن	اِن	اُت	آال	اِيل	اُول	اَيل	اَول
3.	*an*	*in*	*ut*	*āl*	*īl*	*ūl*	*ail*	*aul*

33. If, instead of ا in the above series, we substitute the letter ع, we shall have virtually the same sounds, only that they must be uttered from the lower muscles of the throat, thus—

1. SHORT.			2. LONG.			3. DIPHTHONG.	
عَن	عِن	عُت	عَال	عِيل	عُول	عَيل	عَول
'an	*'in*	*'ut*	*'āl*	*'īl*	*'ūl*	*'ail*	*'aul*

a. It appears, then, that when in Arabic a word or syllable begins with what we consider to be a vowel, such word or syllable must have the letter ا or ع to start with. Throughout this work, when we have occasion to write such words in the Roman character, the corresponding place of the ع will be indicated by an apostrophe or *spiritus lenis;* thus, عَسَل *'asal,* عَابِد *'ābid,* بَعْد *ba'd,* to distinguish the same from اَسَل *asal,* آبِد *abid,* بَد *bad* or بَاد *bād.* In other respects the reader may view the ا and ع in any of the three following lights. 1st. He may consider them of the same value as the *spiritus lenis* (') in such Greek words as ἀν, ἐν, etc. 2ndly. He may consider them as equivalent to the letter *h* in the English words "hour," "herb," "honour," etc. Lastly. He may consider them as mere pegs whereupon to fix or hang the vowels requisite to the formation of the syllable. Practically speaking, then, ا and ع *when initial,* and the و and ي *when not initial,* require the beginner's strictest attention, as they all contribute in such cases to the formation of several vocal sounds.

b. In concluding our account of the general pronunciation of the Arabic consonants and vowels we are bound to acknowlege that the rules laid down are merely *approximate* not *absolute.* Composed as the language is of the dialects of various tribes, and diffused along with the Muḥammadan religion, over so many regions, "omnibus in terris quae sunt a Gadibus usque Gangen et Auroram," through Mauritania, Egypt, Turkey, Persia, India, and other countries in the East, where it forms a principal branch in the education of the higher classes, it can be no wonder if a considerable disagreement should be found in the pronunciation which those nations give, in their respective tongues, to particular letters and combinations; or that an Arab of Yaman should consequently consider as barbarous those modes of pronunciation which prevail at Fez, Cairo, Aleppo, Constantinople, Ispahān, and Delhī. The rules which have been followed in general by European Lexicographers and Translators, are such as have been laid down by old Arabian Grammarians and Scholiasts; from whom, however, it is not easy to form a standard consistent in every point, as they differ in many respects from one another, and often give several opposite pronunciations to the same word, owing to the reasons we have just stated. It must be confessed, at the same time, that both the scholiasts and grammarians have laid down many a puerile and tedious rule, and added much perplexity to a language, not naturally easy, by enlarging on the minute, intricate, and unsatisfactory theory of the moveable powers of vowel points, making trifles. serious, embarrassing the learner's mind, and consuming, in pursuit of objects comparatively uninteresting, that time which might be more usefully employed in smoothing the way to the essential difficulties of the study. Out of this mass of pedantry and confusion however it is but fair to state that the eminent Silvestre de Sacy has, in the First Book of his *Grammaire Arabe* elicited all the light and clearness that the student can desire.

Of the Symbol Madda—مَدَّة.

34. Instead of writing two *alifs* at the beginning of a word, to expresss the long *ā*, as in اادَ *ād*, it is usual, (except in Dictionaries), to write one *alif*, and according to some grammarians to lay the other curved over the former; thus, آد. This symbol (ٓ) is called مَدَّة *madda*, "extension," and denotes that the *alif* is sounded long, like our *a* in "water." M. de Sacy considers the mark *madda* as simply the letter م *mīm*, (the initial of the word), in a recumbent posture. Either theory is plausible, and after all the matter is of no great importance. The *madda*, however, is not necessarily confined to the beginning of a word; it occurs both in the middle and end of words in those instances where otherwise two *alifs* would come together, thus, السَّمَآء for السَّمَاا; جَآءَ for جَاا and يتَسَآءَلُون for يتَسَاالُون.

a. The symbol *madda* is also inscribed over arithmetical signs, and likewise over certain abbreviations, said to be expressive of some mystery. A single word is represented by the first letter; as صٓ for صَدِيقٌ "just;" if there are two words, the initial letter of the first and the final of the second are used, عمٓ for عَلَيْهِ ٱلسَّلَامُ "Peace be upon him;" if three, the initial of the first, a medial of the second, and the final of the third are generally taken, as الٓمٓ for أَنَا ٱللّٰهُ أَعْلَمُ "I am the most wise God." But when there are several words, their initials are most commonly made use of.

Of the Symbol Hamza—هَمْزٌ *or* هَمْزَةٌ.

35. Among Arabian grammarians the consonant *alif* is more commonly known by the name of *hamza*, which denotes "pressure" or "puncture." In books and manuscripts where the vowel-points are employed, the *hamza* always accompanies the vowel which attends ا, and is thus marked أَ, أُ, إِ, over or under the latter, as أَبْيَضُ *abyaḍu*, إِتِّفَاقٌ *ittifāḳun*, and أُبْهَتُ *ubhatu;* without a vowel it shows ا to be a radical letter, as يَأْمَنُ *yāmanu*. At the end of a word it supplies the place of ا after the letters of prolongation ا, و, and ي, as مَاءٌ *mā* or *māa* شَيْءٌ *shaia*, سُوءٌ *sūa*, instead of مَاآ, شَيَا, سُوا, as also in the middle, after an inert letter, as يَسْئَلُ *yesalo*, for يَسْأَلُ; or following another ا, as أَنْذَرَ *andhara* for أَأْنْذَرَ. When written over و or ي it denotes that these letters are put for moveable ا, as أُوْمُلٌ for أُأْمُلٌ *umul*, إِيْزِرٌ *īzir* for إِأْزِرٌ.

a. In the following pages we intend to employ the symbol *hamza* only in those instances where it is essential, or where its omission would be improper. Such is the plan adopted by Dr. Lumsden in his profound and excellent work.

Of the Symbol Waṣla—وصل, *or* وصلة.

36. *Wasla* (ـٱ) implies conjunction, and is only inscribed over ا at the beginning of certain words to denote that such word is united with the preceding one, ا being then silent, as بيتُ ٱلمقدّس *baitu-l-mukaddas*, "the holy house;" in which expression the initial *alif* of the second word is not sounded, or we may say, practically, that it adopts the sound of the vowel terminating the preceding word.

a. The *waṣla*, as a matter of course, does not occur at the beginning of a sentence or after a pause. In other respects it is always used in the following instances, viz.—1. With the article ال "the" (see § 46). 2. With the imperative of the primitive form of the verb. 3. In the preterite active, imperative, and infinitive of derived forms of the verb of the second and third class. 4. In the following ten nouns, امرا *imrā*, "a man;" امرأة *imrāt*, "a woman;" ابن *ibn* or ابنم *ibnam*, "a son;" ابنة *ibnat*, "a daughter;" اثنان *ithnān*, "two" (masculine); اثنتان *ithnatān*, "two" (feminine); اسم *ism*, "a name;" است *ist*, "buttocks;" ايمن *aimun*, "an oath;" in all which cases, unless when beginning a sentence, or following the article, the initial ا is not pronounced, the subsequent letter being always inert, and united in pronunciation to the vowel with which the preceding word ends, as يد امراة *yad-umrātin*, "the hand of a woman;" ا being sometimes even altogether omitted, as حدث الحارث بن همام *Ḥaddatha-l-ḥārithu-bnu Hammāmin*, "Harith the son of Hammam related." It is also dropped when the subsequent letter has a vowel, as مُدّ for امدّ "extend thou." If any word, whose final letter is naturally inert, precedes ٱ, such letter is then pronounced generally with *kasra*, as ضربت *ḍarabat*, "she whipped;" ضربتِ الام *ḍarabati-l-ummu*, "the mother whipped." The affixed pronouns كم and هم, also the verbal terminations تُمْ and تُوا take *damma*. The preposition مِنْ "from," takes *fatha*. Any of the letters ا, و, and ي, terminating the preceding word, does not prevent the union, and the nūnation is rarely pronounced when *wasla* follows. The *alif of union* naturally takes *kasra* when beginning a sentence, or after the article; excepting in the imperative, which sometimes takes *damma*, and in the article, which assumes *fatha*, as does the single noun ايمن "an oath."

Classification of the Letters.

37. Arabian grammarians arrange the letters under the following heads or classes, viz.—1. *Pronunciation.*—Six letters are called *gutturals*, ا, ح, خ, ع, غ, ه; four *labials*, ب, ف, م, و; four *palatials*, ج, ق, ك, ي; eight *dentals*, ت, ث, د, ذ, ط, ظ, ل, ن; and six *linguals*, ر, ز, س, ش, ص, ض. The *dentals* and *linguals* are called *solar* letters, the rest *lunar*. Of these more hereafter when we come to treat of the Article. 2. *Strength.*—The three letters ا, و, ي, are called *infirm* or *weak*, being considered as having no sound but what they receive from the accompanying short vowels either attending themselves or the preceding letters. All others are styled *firm* or *robust*.. 3. *Affinity.*—Some letters are *permutable*, being such in general as are formed by the same organs, as ص with س, د with ت, but particularly ا, و, ي, which are often substituted one for another. 4. *Office.*—Some are denominated *radical*, others *servile*. The *radicals* are twenty-one in number, ب, ث, ج, ح, خ, د, ذ, ر, ز, ش, ص, ض, ط, ظ, ع, غ, ف, ق, ك, ل, and ه. They are so called, because they are never found excepting in the roots or primitive forms of Arabic words. The remaining seven are called *serviles*, because they are employed

in forming the *derivatives* and various inflections resulting from the roots. The *servile* letters, however, are often employed as *radicals*, particularly in the *imperfect* verbs; but the *radicals* are never used as *serviles*, excepting ط and د which are sometimes substituted for ت. 5. *Association.*— Some are *compatible*, which may follow one another in the same radical or primitive word. The others cannot, and are therefore called *incompatible*. These consist of the *gutturals* ح, خ, ع, غ, ه (though ه is sometimes subjoined to ع); to which add the following, viz., ب with ف and م; ث with ت, س, ص, ض, ط, and ظ; ج with غ, ق, and ك; خ with ظ, ق, and ك; د with ذ; ذ with ص, ض, ط, and ظ; ر with ل; ز with ص, ض, and ظ; س with ص and ض; ش with ض; ص with ض, ط, and ظ; ض with ط and ظ; ط with ظ and ك; ظ with غ and ق; ع with ق and ك; ق with ك; ل with ن except لَن "by no means," and عَلَن "he manifested."

a. The *infirm* letters ا, و, and ي, are often liable to be used for each other, especially in verbs; these permutations being considered as an *infirmity* or *imperfection*. In the beginning of a word, however, they usually retain their original sounds already described, except when, by the influence of certain prefixed inseparable particles, they virtually cease to be initial. This, however, we shall more fully discuss hereafter; to treat of the subject, as most grammarians do, at this early stage of the student's progress would be altogether out of place.

b. The *servile* letters properly so called, are really seven in number, viz., ا, ت, س, م, ن, و, and ي; these letters and none else are employed in the inflections of nouns and verbs, except that occasionally د and ط are substituted for ت. They are all included in the word

يَتَسَمَّنُوا literally "they fatten." We may here observe, in passing, that the final ا is not sounded in the third person plural of the preterite and of the aorist; neither is it sounded in the second person plural of the imperative. The four letters ب, ف, ك, and ل, included in the word بِفَلْكٍ though reckoned by grammarians as serviles, are merely inseparable particles prefixed to other words; and the ه or ة is simply a supplementary letter added to the end of words to indicate such words to be of the feminine gender, and as a general rule mere derivatives. In fact the ة is equivalent to ت into which it is frequently changed.

c. The servile letters alluded to in the preceding paragraphs are included as incompatibles only when they constitute part of the *root* of any word; for when acting as serviles, they may be joined with any letter, as بِفِضَّةٍ "in silver;" كَقَوْلِكَ "according to thy statement." These observations may be of some use in manuscripts, where the diacritical points are either neglected, or irregularly placed; as also in fixing ambiguous meanings; and in distinguishing pure Arabic words from such as are either corrupted or derived from foreign sources. For example, the occurrence of the letters ر and ل accompanying each other in the word وَرَلٌ (*Lacerta Nilotica*) leads us to suspect that the term is not of Arabian origin.

Of the Various Arabic Handwritings.

38. The oldest Arabic handwriting with which we are at all familiar is, 1st, the Kūfic, though we read of a still more ancient character, called the Himyaric. The Kūfic was used about the time of Muḥammad and during some four centuries after. It is evidently derived from the Syriac Estrangelo, which itself was apparently derived from the ancient Phœnician, the source of the Greek alphabet of Cadmus. 2nd. In

the second or third centuries after Muḥammad, the Kūfic alphabet was simplified and rounded into the *Naskhī*, the form in which we now have it. At the same time it long maintained its ground in the inscriptions on coins, and in the headings of literary compositions. For instance, the author possesses a unique copy of Ḥakīm Sanāyī, written in A.D. 1281, in which all the headings are in the finest Kūfic. In a still more recent work in his possession, the Dīwāni Kātibī transcribed in A.D. 1486, the titles or headings of the various poetical pieces are all in the Kūfic character. Of the various handwritings used in the East, however, we may say that the نَسْخِي *Naskhī* (of which our extract in the larger type, § 43, of the present work, is a fair imitation), is that in which most Arabic manuscripts, and particularly those of the Ḳurān, are written. Owing to its round and compact form it is generally used in Europe for printing books in the Arabic, Persian, Turkish, and Hindūstānī languages. The *Ta'līḳ* تَعْلِيق, is also a beautiful hand, used chiefly by the Persians in disseminating copies of their more esteemed authors. We occasionally meet with some fine Arabic MSS. written in this hand chiefly transcribed in Persia.

a. There are several other hands more or less used, such as the ثُلْثِي *Thulthī* or ثُلُث *Thuluth,* adopted in the titles of books, royal edicts, diplomas, or letters of great men; answering among those nations much the same purpose as capitals amongst us, or the flourished letters in illuminated manuscripts. The *Tughrā* is another ornamental hand, employed like the *Thulthī* in expressing the titles of their princes in ceremonial letters and solemn deeds. To these we may add the مغْرِبي *Maghribī* or *Mauritanic,* which is used by the Moors of North-western Africa, who are descendants of the Arabians. This hand differs in many respects from those above mentioned, resembling the Kūfic more than any of the others. Lastly, the *Shikasta* شِكَسْتَه, or *broken* hand, which is used in correspondence. It is quite irregular, and unadapted for printing; but not inelegant in appearance when properly written. For a more ample account of this subject, see "Essai de Calligraphie Orientale," in the Appendix to Herbin's "Développements des Principes de la Langue Arabe," 4to. Paris, 1803. Also the 1st volume of de Sacy's "Grammaire Arabe," 2 vols. 8vo., Paris, 1831, in both of which works specimens of the various hands are given.

b. The term *Shikasta* is generally applied to the cursive or running hand used by the people of Persia and Hindūstān; but the Arabs also have their own *Shikasta*, as well as their co-religionists to the eastward, as the student will find to his cost when he comes to decypher ordinary letters on business.

Of the Numerical Value of the Letters.

39. We may here mention that the twenty-eight letters of the Arabic language are also used for the purpose of Numerical computation. The Numerical order of the Letters, however, in this case differs from that given in the Alphabet; being, in fact, the identical arrangement of the Phœnician, the Samaritan, the Syriac, and the Hebrew, so far as their alphabets extend, viz., to the letter ت, 400. The following is the order of the Numerical Alphabet with the corresponding number placed above each letter; the whole being grouped into eight unmeaning words, to serve as a *memoria technica*.

1000 900 800	700 600 500	400 300 200 100	90 80 70 60	50 40 30 20	10 9 8	7 6 5	4 3 2 1
ضظغ	ثخذ	قرشت	سعفص	كلمن	حطي	هوز	ابجد

Where ا denotes one, ب two, ج three, د four, etc.

a. The Arabs of Mauritania arrange their ابجد with the following slight differences, viz., they have صعفض instead of سعفص ; قرست instead of قرشت ; and ظغش instead of ضظغ. In all other respects the two schemes agree. About or soon after the time of Muḥammad the Arabs received from the Hindūs the decimal scale of numeration, which in time they imported into Europe. The ten figures or cyphers are written from left to right and applied exactly like our own; thus—

١,	٢,	٣,	٤,	٥,	٦,	٧,	٨,	٩,	١٠,	١١,	١٢,	١٣.
1,	2,	3,	4,	5,	6,	7,	8,	9,	10,	11,	12,	13.

For example the Christian year 1862 is ١٨٦٢ ; the last half of which corresponds with the Muslim year 1279 as ١٢٧٩.

b. The ابجد is used chiefly as a "memoria technica" for recording the dates of historical events, or the decease of illustrious personages, etc. The plan is to compose a brief sentence or verse of such a nature that the sum of all the letters shall amount to the year of the *Hijra* in which the event took place. In Europe, during the middle ages, when Latin was the language of literature, such memorial verses were common. The Latin, however, laboured under this disadvantage, that its alphabet contained only seven numerical letters, viz., I, V, X, L, C, D, and M; whereas every one of the letters in Arabic counts for something. A curious coincidence of this kind is to be found in a line from Ovid, written more than fifteen centuries before the event to which it is applied, viz.—

"F I L I V s ante DIeM patrIos, InqVIrIt In annos."
"The son prematurely makes inquiry into the years of his father."
It will be found that the sum of the numerical letters of the above line amount to 1568, the year in which Prince Charles of Spain was put to death, by the command of his stern father, Philip II., for plotting treason and rebellion. The following effusion in commemoration of the restoration of our Second Charles is the latest of the kind with which I am acquainted: "CeDant arMa oLeæ, paX regna serenat et agros;" where C, D, M, L, and X amount to 1660.

Of the Accent.

40. The rules respecting the accent in the Arabic language are much the same as those we apply to the Latin and Greek. In words of two syllables, if both short or both long, the accent is on the first; but if one be short and the other long, the long syllable naturally takes the accent. In words of three or more syllables, if the penult be long, it takes the accent, otherwise the ante-penult syllable takes it. By a long syllable we here mean one which contains a letter of prolongation, *i.e.*, ا, و, or ي inert, or a short vowel followed by two consonants of which the first is inert.

a. The greater part of the words in Arabic generally end in a short vowel, except before a *pause* (§ 41) as we shall immediately shew; hence as a general rule the accent seldom falls on the very last syllable of a word. Most grammarians, apparently following each other like a string of sheep, tell us that "the accent *never* falls on the last syllable." The assertion is too sweeping; for example, in the first verse of the Ḳurān, as I have often heard it read by the

Mullas, viz., بِسْمِ ٱللهِ ٱلرَّحْمٰنِ ٱلرَّحِيمِ *bism Illāhi-r-Raḥmani-r-Raḥīm*, the accent of the last word *raḥīm* is most assuredly on the last syllable.

Of the Pause.

41. The pause وَقْفٌ, which takes place after a word, being the last of a period, of a phrase, or of a proposition, makes in the manner of reading or pronouncing that word, some alterations necessary to be noticed. In general, when a pause occurs, the vowel or nūnation of the last letter is suppressed; thus, instead of saying ضَرَبَنِي زَيْدٌ "Zaid has struck me," and جَاءَنِي عَبْدُ ٱلْحَمِيدِ "'Abd ul Ḥamīd has come to me," pronouncing in the first example the nūnation of زَيْدٌ, and in the second the final *Kasrah* of ٱلْحَمِيدِ, we say only زَيْد "Zaid," and ٱلْحَمِيد "al Ḥamīd." If, however, the nūnation is اً as in this example لَمْ نَرَا مُحَمَّدًا "We have not seen Muḥammad," the ن of the nūnation is only dropped, and the *fatḥa* followed by ا is preserved, thus مُحَمَّدَا.

a. Analogous to the preceding rule there are certain forms of the Aorist and Imperative of verbs, which, under the influence of certain particles, terminate in ن *inert*, in which case the ن before the pause is withdrawn in pronunciation, and the word is pronounced as if the vowel immediately preceding the ن were followed by its homogeneous letter of prolongation, thus يَكْتُبَا for يَكْتُبَنْ; تَكْتُبِي for تَكْتُبِنْ; يَكْتُبُوا for يَكْتُبُنْ; اُكْتُبَا for اُكْتُبَنْ; اُكْتُبُوا for اُكْتُبُنْ; اُكْتُبِي for اُكْتُبِنْ. Of this, however, we shall treat more fully hereafter, as the discussion at the present stage of the student's progress would be altogether premature.

42. Marks or symbols corresponding to our full stops,

commas, etc., are seldom to be found in any manuscript, excepting in the Ḳurān and a few other books, where they are expressed by marks similar to ۞ . : ∴ ∵ .: :: etc.

a. Poetic quotations are generally distinguished by having certain words prefixed, as نَظْم "poetry," بَيْت "distich," مِصْرَاع "hemistich," قِطْعَة "strophe," etc., the verses being closed by little curve lines resembling inverted commas, ،،.

b. In the present work a system of punctuation will be adopted such as I advantageously employed in my Persian and Hindūstānī publications. The *comma* and *semicolon* will be represented by a small dash, thus, ـ; the full stop by a star, thus, *; and the symbols of interrogation and admiration by those we use in the European languages, as may be seen from the following extract to which is subjoined a transcript in the Roman character. Before trying to decypher the text, however, the student is requested to peruse what we have said on the Article, § 46.

43. The following Fable from Luḳmān, the Oriental Æsop, will serve both as an exercise in reading and as an illustration of our mode of punctuation; also of the system we have adopted for representing the Arabic character in Roman letters. It will at the same time exemplify most of the principles of orthography already discussed.

الْاِنْسَانُ وَٱلْخِنْزِيرُ

اِنْسَانٌ مَرَّةً حَمَلَ عَلَي بَهِيمَةٍ كَبْشًا وَعَنْزًا وَخِنْزِيرًا ـ وَتَوَجَّهَ اِلَي ٱلْمَدِينَةِ لِيَبِيعَ ٱلْجَمِيعَ * فَالْكَبْشُ وَٱلْعَنْزُ فَلَمْ يَكُونَا يَضْرِبَانِ

عَلَي ٱلْبَهِيمَةِ ـ وَامَّا ٱلْخَنْزِيرُ فَانَّهُ كَانَ يُعَرِّضُ دَايِمًا وَلَا يَهْدَي *
فَقَالَ لَهُ ٱلْاِنْسَانُ ـ يَا اشَرَّ ٱلْوُحُوشِ! لِمَاذَا ٱلْكَبْشُ وَٱلْعَنْزُ
سَكُوتٌ * لَا يَضْرِبَانِ وَانْتَ لَا تَهْدَي وَلَا تَسْتَقِرُّ ؛ قَالَ لَهُ
ٱلْخِنْزِيرُ ـ انَا اعْلَمُ انَّ ٱلْكَبْشَ يُطْلَبُ لِصُوفِهِ وَٱلْعَنْزَ لِلَبَنِهَا ـ وَانَا
ٱلشَّقِيُّ لَا صُوفَ لِي وَلَا لَبَنَ * انَا عِنْدَ وُصُولِي اِلَي ٱلْمَدِينَةِ
أُرْسَلُ اِلَي ٱلْمَسْلَخِ لَا مَحَالَةَ *

Al-insānu wa-l-Khinzīru.

Insānun marratan ḥamala 'ala bahīmatin kabshan wa 'anzan wa khinzīran; wa tawajjaha ila-l madīnati li-yabī'a-l-jamī'a. Fa-l-kabshu wa-l-'anzu fa-lam yakūnā yadribāni 'ala-l-bahīmati; wa amma-l-khinzīru fa-innahu kāna yu'arridu dāiman, wa lā yahda. Fa-ḳāla la-hu-l-insānu, yā asharra-l-wuhūshi! limā-dhā-l-kabshu wa-l'anzu sakūtun? lā yadribāni, wa anta lā tahdā wa lā tastaḳirru. Ḳāla la-hu-l-khinzīru, anā a'lamu anna-l-kabsha yuṭlabu li-ṣūfihi, wa-l-'anzu li-labanihā; wa anā-sh-shaḳīyu lā ṣūfa lī wa lā labana. Anā 'inda wuṣūlī ila-l-madīnati ursalu ila-l-maslakhi, lā maḥālata.

THE MAN AND THE HOG.

A man once upon a time was conveying on his quadruped a lamb, a she-goat, and a hog; and he was proceeding towards the city with a view to sell the lot. Now the lamb and the she-goat molested not the quadruped; but the pig constantly resisted, and would not be quiet. Then the man said to him, "O you most vicious of beasts! How comes it that the lamb and the goat are quiet? They give no annoyance; but you neither keep quiet nor take repose." The pig said to him, "I know that the lamb is sought after for its wool, and the goat for her milk; but I, wretched, have neither wool nor milk. On my arrival in the city I shall undoubtedly be sent to the shambles."

a. The learner is particularly requested to study the foregoing Section with the utmost attention before he proceeds further. A thorough knowledge of the elements of the language, which are here, it is to be hoped, fully and clearly explained, will enable him to advance boldly through the rest of the work both with pleasure and with profit.

SECTION II.

OF THE ARTICLE, THE SUBSTANTIVES, NUMERALS, ADJECTIVES, AND PRONOUNS.

44. According to the Grammarians of Arabia, as well as those of ancient Greece, there are only Three Parts of Speech—the Noun اِسْمٌ *Ism*, the Verb فِعْلٌ *Fi'l*, and the Particle حَرْفٌ *Ḥarf*. Under the term Noun, they include Substantives, Adjectives, Pronouns, to which I think we may add the Numerals, Participles, and Infinitives. Their Verb agrees in its nature with ours; and their Particle includes the Article اَلْ "the," Adverbs, Prepositions, Conjunctions, and Interjections. They consider the Verb as the first part of speech, and the third person singular masculine of the preterite tense as the root or origin from which the other parts of speech are derived. There appears, however, to be no impropriety in following the mode generally practised in teaching the Greek, Latin, and other European languages, which I have therefore here adopted.

a. We shall hereafter see the propriety of having discussed the Noun and Pronoun, especially the latter, before we come to the Verb. Certainly the verb has no claim *in nature* to rank as the *leading* part of speech. The vocabulary of very young children, and of savages, who are little else than in a state of nature, consists entirely of nouns and probably a few particles, in the Oriental sense of the terms. The absurdity of deriving *all nouns* from verbs is most glaring in the instance of اَللّٰه "God," said to be derived from أَلَهَ "he worshipped or adored"!!! As if the name of God did not exist before the verb "to worship."

45. The Parts of Speech in Arabic, as in English, are nine in number, viz., the Article, the Substantive, the Adjective, the Pronoun, the Verb, the Adverb, the Preposition, the Conjunction, and the Interjection.

Of the Article—اَلْمَعْرِفَةُ.

46. The Arabs, like the Greeks, have only the Definite Article اَلْ *al*, "the," which, however, is not, as in Greek, liable to any change on account of gender or number. If the substantive to which the article is prefixed happens to begin any one of the *solar* letters, viz., ت, ث, د, ذ, ر, ز, س, ش, ص, ض, ط, ظ, ل, or ن (see § 37), the ل of the article assumes the sound of the initial letter of the noun, which is then marked with *tashdīd;* thus, اَلنُّور "the light," pronounced *an-nūru*, not *al-nūru*. But in these instances, although the ل has altered its own sound, it must always be written in its own form. Of course, when the noun begins with ل, the ل of the article coincides with it without alteration, as in the words اَللَّيْلَةُ *al-lailatu*, "the night;" and in this latter case the ل of the article is sometimes improperly omitted, and the initial *lām* of the noun marked by *tashdīd*, as اَلَّيْلَةُ *al-lailatu*.

a. The ل of the article is always omitted in the masculine singular of the relative pronoun ٱلَّذِي "the (man) who;" the feminine singular of the same ٱلَّتِي, and the plural masculine ٱلَّذِينَ being so written in the place of ٱللَّذِي, etc., but never in the Dual of the same pronoun. When the particle لِ is prefixed to a noun beginning with ل, which, when definite, ought to have the article; the *alif* of the latter disappears, and in order to avoid the meeting of three *lāms*, the *lām* of the article is dispensed with, or, in other words, represented by *tashdīd*, as لِلَّيْلِ for لِللَّيْلِ, "to or for the night," so, لِلّٰهِ for لِاللّٰهِ, as in the following ejaculation, لِلّٰهِ ٱلْحَمْدُ وَ ٱلْمِنَّةُ *Li-llāhi-l-ḥamdu wa-l-minnatu,* "To God be praise and glory." But, when prefixed to nouns not beginning with ل, the *alif* alone is dropped, as لِلْقَمَرِ *li-l-ḳamari,* "to the moon."

b. In the modern dialects of Egypt and Syria the ل of the article retains its natural sound before all letters, whether *solar* or *lunar,* thus they say ٱلنُّور *al-nūr,* "the light," ٱلشَّمْس *al-shams,* "the sun." The fanciful classification of the letters of the alphabet into fourteen *solar* and as many *lunar,* arose perhaps from the accidental circumstance that شَمْسٌ "the sun," begins with one of the former class, and قَمَرٌ "the moon," with one of the latter. Of course the captious critic might find a thousand equally valid reasons for calling them by any other terms, such as "gold" and "silver," "blue" and "black," etc.

Of the Substantive—ٱلْإِسْمُ.

47. Arabic Substantives have only two Genders أَجْنَاسٌ, the Masculine ٱلْمُذَكَّرُ, and the Feminine ٱلْمُؤَنَّثُ. There are also several words of the common gender ٱلْمُسْتَوِي. They have

three Numbers أَعْدَادٌ, the Singular أَلْفَرْدُ, the Dual أَلْمُثَنَّي, and the Plural أَلْجَمْعُ. They have generally three Cases حَالَاتٌ in the singular, and in some of the irregular plurals, viz., the Nominative أَلرَّفْعُ, the Genitive أَلْجَرُّ (which also serves for the Dative and Ablative of the Latin by the addition of the particles لِ, "to," and مِنْ, "from") and the Accusative أَلنَّصْبُ. There are, however, many nouns that have only two cases, or rather only two case terminations in the singular, which we may specify as the Nominative and the Oblique. The Dual, as in Greek, is invariably a Diptote, as we shall see when we come to the Declension. The Vocative case is either the same as the Nominative, or as the Accusative.

Of the Forms and Measures of Nouns.

48. The radical words of the Arabic language generally consist of three letters; a few there are consisting of four, and a still smaller number of five letters. The greater portion of the triliteral roots are Verbs, the rest Substantives or Adjectives. There are a few verbal roots of four letters, but none of five, the latter being all Substantives. The mode adopted for the development of the triliteral roots of the Arabic language is highly ingenious and philosophic. This consists not only in adding terminations to the simple root, but also in expanding it by means of certain letters, either prefixed or inserted somewhere between the beginning and end of a word, so as to produce certain *forms*, bearing in general a definite relation to the original root; and for that

reason they are called *servile letters.* The letters thus employed are seven in number. These are, as we have already stated, ا, ت (or ة), س, م, ن, و, and ي, all contained in the technical word يَتَسَمَّنُوا, literally, "they fatten." The serviles ا and ت may occur either at the beginning, or in the interior, or, lastly at the end of a word (ة being always found at the end), the ن and ي, either in the interior or at the end; the م always at the beginning; the و, is employed in the interior of a word; and the س always as the second letter of a word, and it is preceded either by ا or م, and followed by ت. For example, let us take the verbal root قبل, which signifies "accepting;" we thence, by means of the servile ا alone, deduce the forms اقبال, قابل, قِبال, and قَبَلاءُ. Then the various forms تقبيل, مقبول, قبلتين, قابليت, استقبال, and مستقبل, exhibit a few of the other serviles in their mode of application, of which more hereafter.

a. It is evident, then, as a general rule, that if we strip every Arabic word of its servile letters, we at once come to the *root*: thus, in the words انفعال, متفارق, and استغفار, we see at once that the roots are فعل, فرق, and غفر respectively. We must observe, however, that the seven serviles, conjointly or severally, may be employed as radical letters of the triliteral root. Thus the word مَفْتون, "tried," or "tested" (as gold in the fire), contains no fewer than four servile letters, and only one letter strictly radical, viz., ف. Now, out of these four serviles, two *must* belong to the root. We see, however, that the word is of the form مقبول, already cited; hence we infer that the root is فتن, just as that of مَقْبُول is قبل. A little practice, however, will enable the learner to get over difficulties of this sort; at the same time had it been possible for the Arabs, when manufacturing their very artificial language, to have excluded the servile letters altogether from the primitive triliteral roots, Arabic would have been the most perfect of human tongues.

49. With a view to precision, I adopt the term *form* to denote the mere outward appearance of a word as consisting of so many consonants, independent of the short vowels by which such consonants may become moveable. The various modifications or changes which a *form* may undergo by the application of the short vowels, together with the *jazm*, I call the *measures* of such *form*. For example, the primitive *form* قبل is susceptible of twelve different *measures*, according as we apply the three short vowels and the *jazm*. Supposing then the student meets with the root قبل for the first time, in a book without vowel-points, he has the comfort of knowing that the word may be pronounced in twelve different ways or *measures*, though it remains all along under one and the same *form*. Thus it may be قَبْلٌ, قِبْلٌ, or قُبْلٌ, by using the *jazm* on the middle letter; or it may be any of the following nine measures as trisyllables, viz., قَبَلٌ, قَبِلٌ, قَبُلٌ, with *fatḥa* on the first letter; also قِبَلٌ, قِبِلٌ, قِبُلٌ, with *kasra* for the first vowel; or, lastly, it may be قُبَلٌ, قُبِلٌ, or قُبُلٌ, with *ḍamma* on the first letter. We may at the same time observe that the measures قِبُلٌ and قُبِلٌ are here inserted as a matter of *theory*, for they do not occur in the *practice* of the language.

50. The Semitic Grammarians, both Arabs and Jews, have adopted, *as a special favourite*, the triliteral root فَعَلَ, with a

view to exemplify the various *forms* and *measures* of their words. This root, however, is not the best adapted for Europeans, not one in a thousand of whom ever can realize the true sound of the letter ع as the middle consonant. I notwithstanding retain it as my model, generally speaking, when the object intended is merely to exemplify the *form* or *measure* of a word to the *eye;* but not when the word is intended to be *pronounced* to the *ear*, as in the rules of Prosody, etc. Another cogent reason for retaining it will be found in § 94 *a.* when we come to the Verb. But the student must not suppose that فعل or any other root in the language furnishes us with *all* the *forms* and *measures* we are about to detail. Some roots furnish us with a certain number of forms and measures which must be determined merely by *prescription;* others may give out different forms and measures, to be determined in like manner; but no single root in the language has ever furnished *all* the forms and measures assigned by the Grammarians to the root فَعَلَ. A similar instance occurs in the Greek Grammar, in the case of the verb τυπτω, where we are treated to some hundred different moods and tenses, etc., whilst it is perfectly understood that no single Greek verb ever exhibited the *whole* of them.

Of Gender—أَلْجِنْس.

51. In the Arabic there are, as we have already stated, only two genders, the masculine and the feminine; together with some words that are of the common gender, such as the

names of the letters of the alphabet, and some adjectives of a certain form. There are certain characteristics by which we may infer that a noun is feminine. These are to be distinguished either by signification or termination. Nouns are feminine by signification, 1st—Names of women and female appellatives, as مَرْيَمُ "Mary," أُمٌّ "a mother," عَرُوبٌ "a woman who loves her husband." This is simply the good old rule of the Latin Grammar, viz., "Esto femineum quod femina sola reposcat." 2ndly—The double members of the body, as أُذُنٌ "the ear," يَدٌ "the hand," عَيْنٌ "the eye," كَتِفٌ "the shoulder." 3rdly—Names of countries, towns, and winds, as مِصْرُ "Egypt," قُبْرُسُ "Cyprus," مُخَا "Mokhā," قَبُولٌ "the east wind," جَنُوبٌ "the south wind."

52. Such nouns are feminine by termination as fall under the following heads: 1st—Those ending in ة, as جَلَالَةٌ "magnificence," جَنَّةٌ "a garden," ظُلْمَةٌ "darkness," a very few excepted, which we shall immediately notice. 2ndly—Those ending in ا servile, as كِبْرِيَاءُ "pride," حَمْرَاءُ "red," except مَشْيُوخَا "an old man." 3rdly—In ي servile, quiescent and pronounced like ا, as ذِكْرَى *dhikrā*, "remembrance;" أُولَى *ūlā*, "first;" طُولَى *ṭūlā*, "longest;" this termination is adopted by many comparatives and superlatives.

a. To these may be added some eighty words that are feminine neither by signification nor by termination, such as أَرْضٌ "the earth," خَمْرٌ "wine," بِئْرٌ "a well," نَارٌ "fire," سَعِيرٌ "blazing fire," سَقَرٌ "hell-fire," دَارٌ "a house," دَلْوٌ "a bucket," حَرْبٌ "war," عَصًا "a staff," كَأْسٌ "a cup," نَعْلٌ "a shoe," رِيحٌ "the wind," نَفْسٌ "the soul," شَمْسٌ "the sun," together with the rest which are to be learnt by practice and observation. (See De Sacy, Tome i., p. 347.)

53. All substantives and adjectives not comprised under the foregoing heads are understood to be masculine; as قَمَرٌ "the moon," بَيْتٌ "a house." There are, however, a few words having the feminine termination ة, which are of the masculine gender, as خَلِيفَةٌ "a Khalif;" also some verbal adjectives to which ة is added, so that they become of more emphatic or intensive signification, such as عَلَّامَةٌ "very learned;" ضُحَكَةٌ "habituated to laugh;" رَاوِيَةٌ "relating from memory." Verbal adjectives of the forms فَعَّالَةٌ, فِعَالَةٌ, فَعُولَةٌ, فُعَلَةٌ, مِفْعَلَةٌ, though ending in ة, are of both genders.

54. There are some forty-five words which are of the common gender; amongst the number are إِزَارٌ "a veil or anything that covers nakedness;" حَالٌ "state, condition;" جَنَاحٌ "a wing;" سَبِيلٌ "a path;" سِكِّينٌ "a knife" (Gaelic *scian*); سِلَاحٌ "a weapon," "armour;" سِلْمٌ "peace;" سُلَّمٌ "a ladder;" سَمَاءٌ "heaven;" صُلْحٌ "peace;" طَرِيقٌ "a path or way;" عُقَابٌ "an eagle;" فَرَسٌ "a horse;" قَوْسٌ "a bow;" لَيْلٌ "night;" مِلْحٌ "salt," etc. (See De Sacy, p. 349.)

Of the Formation of Feminine from Masculine Nouns.

55. Feminines are formed from masculines by the addition, transposition, or changing of letters; but chiefly by the

addition of ة, as رَجُلٌ "a man," رَجُلَةٌ "a woman," مَلِكٌ "a king," مَلِكَةٌ "a queen," كَبِيرٌ "great," كَبِيرَةٌ. فَتًي *fatan*, "a young man," changes ي to ا before ة, فَتَاةٌ "a young woman," as do many other nouns of this form. Some adjectives, when in the positive degree, follow the second termination (in ا servile) in forming the feminine, transposing the initial ا to the end, as بَيْضَآءُ from ابَيضُ "white" or "splendid." In the comparative and superlative degree, however, the initial ا is changed to ي final, quiescent and pronounced like ا, as اطوَلُ *atwalu*, طُولَي *tūla*, "longer," "longest." Some other adjectives also form their feminine in ي servile, as سَكْرَانُ, سَكْرَي "intoxicated;" اوَّلُ أُولَي "first;" آخَرُ, أُخْرَي "another;" whilst some change ان into ي, as غَضْبَانُ, غَضْبَي "irritated." أَحَدٌ "one," makes اِحْدَي in the feminine; but وَاحِدٌ "one," has وَاحِدَةٌ.

a. Numbers of adjectives are used both as masculines and feminines without any alteration, as صَبُورٌ "patient," مِعْطَارٌ "odoriferous," مِغْشَمٌ "rash," مِسْكِينٌ "poor" (making also in the feminine مِسْكِينَةٌ), قَتِيلٌ "slain" (which, when used substantively, is written likewise قَتِيلَةٌ "she that is slain"); with many others of the same forms. Nouns implying anything divisible into parts assume often the feminine gender to express such parts, as ذَهَبَةٌ "a piece of gold," from ذَهَبٌ "gold." As the Arabs have no neuter gender, neutral adjectives or such as are common to either gender, when used indefinitely as substantives, are expressed by the feminine, as وَاحِدَةٌ تَعْوَزُكَ "one is wanting to you."

b. On this subject the reader is referred to the excellent "Grammaire

Arabe" of M. De Sacy, page 343–352 of the first volume. The limits assigned to us in the present work do not permit us to translate De Sacy's account at full length.

Of Numbers.

56. In Arabic the nouns have three numbers (as we have already stated), viz., the Singular, the Dual, and the Plural. The Dual is invariably a *diptote*, i.e., consisting of two cases, and is generally formed by suppressing the nūnation of the singular, and adding ـَانِ for the nominative, and ـَيْنِ for the oblique cases; thus دَارٌ "a house," dual دَارَانِ "two houses," دَارَيْنِ "of, to, or in two houses."

a. When the singular noun ends in ة the latter is changed in the dual to ت, as مَدِينَةٌ *madīnatun*, "a city;" مَدِينَتَانِ *madīnatāni*, "two cities." Where و and ي, (or ا officiating for them,) are final, and quiescent, after *fatḥa* in the singular, they become what grammarians call *moveable*, receiving some alteration, either in the final letter or vowel-points, as فَتًى *fatan*, "a youth;" فَتَيَانِ *fatayāni*, "two youths;" عَصًا *'aṣan*, "a staff;" عَصَوَانِ *'aṣawāni*, "two staffs" (or staves). If ا servile terminates the singular, it is changed to و as صَفْرَآءُ *ṣafrā,u*, "yellow;" صَفْرَوَانِ *ṣafrawāni*, "two yellow objects;" but if radical, it remains, as جُزْءٌ *juz,un*, "a part;" جُزْآنِ *juz,āni*, "two parts;" unless, when under the form of *hamza* ء, it supplies the place of و or ي, in which case it either discretionally remains, or is changed to و, as رِدَآءٌ *ridā,un*, "a garment;" رِدَآءَانِ *ridā,āni*, or رِدَاوَانِ *ridāwāni* "two garments."

57. The regular masculine plural is formed by suppressing the nūnation of the singular, and adding ـُونَ for the nominative and ـِينَ for the oblique cases; thus وَالِدٌ "a father," وَالِدُونَ "fathers," وَالِدِينَ "of, to, or by fathers;" نَاصِرٌ "assisting," نَاصِرُونَ; فَرِحٌ "glad," فَرِحُونَ; نَبِيٌّ "a prophet," نَبِيُّونَ. The regular feminine plural is formed by suppressing the final ةٌ of the singular, and substituting ـَاتٌ for the nominative, and ـَاتٍ for the oblique; thus وَالِدَةٌ "a mother," وَالِدَاتٌ "mothers," وَالِدَاتٍ "of, to, or by mothers;" so فَرِحَةٌ "a cheerful woman," فَرِحَاتٌ "cheerful women," نَبِيَّةٌ "a prophetess," نَبِيَّاتٌ.

a. If a masculine noun terminates in ي inert after *kasra*, it is thrown away, while *kasra* is changed to *ḍamma*, as قَاضِي "a judge," قَاضُونَ; if in ي after *fatḥa* it is also dropped, *fatḥa* forming a diphthong with و, as مُصْطَفَي *Muṣṭafa*, مُصْطَفَوْنَ. Perfect feminine substantives (that is, not derived from imperfect verbs) whether simple, or augmented only by ةٌ, whose middle radical is inert, change in the plural the *jazm* (ْ) to the vowel of the first radical, as جُمْرٌ *Jumrun*, "a woman's name," جُمُرَاتٌ *Jumarātun*; قَصْعَةٌ *ḳaṣ'atun*, "a saucer," قَصَعَاتٌ *ḳasa'ātun*, "saucers;" those, however, whose first radical takes *kasra* or *ḍamma*, may either retain the *jazm* or change it to *fatḥa*.

Of the Irregular or Broken Plurals.

58. Besides the regular plurals exemplified in the words وَالِدٌ and وَالِدَةٌ, the Arabs have adopted several modes of

forming *artificial*, or, as they call them, *broken plurals*, of which the following are a few specimens: 1st—From the triliteral root a plural may be formed of the measure اَقْبَالٌ, by means of two *alifs*, thus حُكْمٌ "an order," plural اَحْكَامٌ "orders;" so مِلْكٌ "property," plural اَمْلَاكٌ "goods" or "chattels." 2nd—From a triliteral root, with or without the additional ة, may be formed a broken plural of the measure قِبَالٌ; thus, جَبَلٌ "a mountain," plural جِبَالٌ "mountains;" so رَجُلٌ "a man," رِجَالٌ "men;" خَصْلَةٌ "disposition," خِصَالٌ "dispositions." 3rd—From the triliteral root another plural, of frequent occurrence, may be formed on the measure قُبُولٌ; thus مَلِكٌ "a king," plural مُلُوكٌ "kings;" so عِلْمٌ "science," plural عُلُومٌ "sciences." 4th—Another broken plural, of frequent occurrence, is formed on the measure قُبَلَاءُ; thus, حَكِيمٌ "a sage," حُكَمَاءُ "sages;" so شَاعِرٌ "a poet," plural شُعَرَاءُ "poets." This form of plural arises from singular nouns of the measure قَابِلٌ or قَبِيلٌ. There are several other modes of forming broken plurals, which shall be fully detailed hereafter, when we come to our Section on the Derivation and Formation of Nouns.

a. De Sacy enumerates thirty-one forms of broken plurals, but several of these, especially the last seven, are of rare occurrence. In the meanwhile we subjoin a useful table of twenty-four forms of *broken plurals* with examples of such singulars as usually produce them.

No.	Form of Plural.	Singular.	Plural.	No.	Form of Plural.	Singular.	Plural.
1	فَعَل	عُلْبَة a milk pail,	عُلَب	14	اَفْعَال	مَطَر rain,	اَمْطَار
2	فُعُل	كِتَاب a book,	كُتُب	15	اَفْعِلَة	قِلَادَة a necklace,	اَقْلِدَة
3	فُعْل	اَحْمَر red,	حُمْر	16	فَوَاعِل	طَابِق a frying pan,	طَوَابِق
4	فِعَل	كِسْرَة a fragment,	كِسَر	17	فَعَائِل	شِمَال the left hand,	شَمَائِل
5	فِعَال	رَجُل a man,	رِجَال	18	فِعْلَان	غُلَام a boy,	غِلْمَان
6	فُعُول	بَيْت a house,	بُيُوت	19	فُعْلَان	سَقْف a roof,	سُقْفَان
7	فُعَّل	حَاكِم a judge,	حُكَّم			بَلَد a country,	بُلْدَان
8	فُعَّال		حُكَّام	20	فُعَلَاء	شَرِيف noble,	شُرَفَاء
9	فَعَلَة	كَامِل perfect,	كَمَلَة			شَاعِر a poet,	شُعَرَاء
10	فُعَلَة	قَاضٍ a Ḳādhī,	قُضَاة for قُضَيَة	21	اَفْعِلَاء	حَبِيب a friend,	اَحِبَّاء for اَحْبِبَاء
11	فِعَلَة	قِرْد an ape,	قِرَدَة	22	فَعْلَي	جَرِيح wounded,	جَرْحَي
12	فِعَلَة	غُصْن a branch,	غِصَنَة	23	فَعَالِي	صَحْرَاء a desert,	صَحَارِي
13	اَفْعُل	وَجْه the face,	اَوْجُه	24	فَعَالَي	سَكْرَان intoxicated,	سَكَارَي

b. It may be observed here, at the same time, that some nouns have various forms of plural,—sometimes a regular plural, and besides that one or more of the broken forms; thus from نَفْس "the soul," are formed the plural نُفُوس and اَنْفُس ; from غُلَام "a boy," plu. غِلْمَة and غِلْمَان ; from عَيْن "the eye," اَعْيَان , عُيُون ; from عَيْب "a fault or vice," عُيُوب and اَوَائِب ; from سُور "a wall," اَسْوَار , سِيرَان ; from عَبْد "a slave," عِبَاد , عَبِيد , عُبْدَان ; and also from بَحْر "the sea," بِحَار ,

بُحُرٌ , أَبْحُرٌ ; from شَاهِدٌ "a witness," شُهُودٌ , شَاهِدُونَ , شَوَاهِدُ . The student is not to infer, however, that a singular employs indifferently all the plurals of which its *form* is susceptible; thus نَفْسٌ does not admit نِفَاسٌ , نِفْسَةٌ , نِفَسَةٌ , نُفْسَانٌ ; nor does عَبْدٌ adopt the plurals أَعْبَادٌ , عِبْدَةٌ , عَبَدَةٌ , etc. Sometimes one only is formed, as from رَجُلٌ "a man," the only plural is رِجَالٌ , and أَمْرٌ "an affair," "a command," makes only أُمُورٌ . These, however, are best learnt by practice. When a singular, having several meanings, admits several plurals, it will be generally found that certain plurals are peculiarly, or exclusively attached to certain specific meanings of the singular; for example, عَيْنٌ signifies "the eye," "a fountain," "the substance or essence of a thing," and "a person of rank." In the plural it has عُيُونٌ , أَعْيُنٌ and أَعْيَانٌ . The two first of these forms answer to the two first meanings of the singular respectively, and the third only to the two last. The regular plurals, and those of the twelfth, thirteenth, fourteenth, and fifteenth forms, are called جُمُوعُ قِلَّةٍ "plurals of paucity," in contradistinction to the other forms, which are called جُمُوعُ كَثْرَةٍ "plurals of multitude." This observation applies, however, only to nouns having several forms of plural: when the plural of one of these four forms is its only one, it is employed indiscriminately like those of the other forms.

c. With regard to the quadriliteral nouns, all the simple ones, and many of those which are augmented, together with their feminines, form their plurals by inserting ا after the second letter (the first having *fatha*, and the third *kasra*), as كَوَاكِبُ from كَوْكَبٌ "a star." When ة happens to be the final letter of the singular, it is dropped in forming the plural, as مَزْبَلَةٌ "a dunghill," مَزَابِلُ . When the last radical is preceded by ا , و and ي without a vowel, ي remains in the plural, as

قَنْدِيلٌ "a candle," قَنَادِيلُ ; but ا and و are changed to ي (on account of the preceding *kasra*), as سُلْطَانٌ , سَلَاطِينُ ; عُرْقُوبٌ "the heel," عَرَاقِيبُ ; some words, at the same time, not only follow this rule, but have another plural formed by dropping the ي and taking ة at the end, as إِبْلِيسٌ "the devil," أَبَالِيسُ and أَبَالِسَةٌ ; إِسْكَافٌ "a shoemaker," أَسَاكِيفُ and أَسَاكِفَةٌ : تِلْمِيذٌ "a disciple," تَلَامِيذُ and تَلَامِذَةٌ . A few other words form also their plurals in this manner, as أُسْقُفٌ "a bishop," أَسَاقِفُ and أَسَاقِفَةٌ . Some plurals of triliteral words may be comprehended under this form; another plural being formed from them in the same manner, as ظُفْرٌ "the nail of the finger," 1st plural أَظْفَارٌ, 2nd plural أَظَافِيرُ ; عِرْقٌ "an artery," 1st plural عُرُوقٌ , 2nd plural عَرَائِقُ .

d. Nouns consisting of five or more letters (ة and ا , و , ي quiescent not being numbered as such) follow the same mode, throwing away at the same time either the last radical or the penult, as سَفَرْجَلٌ "a pomegranate," سَفَارِجُ ; عَنْكَبُوتٌ "a spider," عَنَاكِبُ ; فَرَزْدَقٌ "a piece of bread," "crumb," فَرَازِدُ and فَرَازِقُ . If the penult is و or ي forming a diphthong after *fatḥa*, both the last letter and the penult remain, و being changed to ي on account of the preceding *kasra*, as فِرْعَوْنٌ "a crocodile," فَرَاعِينُ . Augmented words throw away the serviles, excepting م when servile along with ن or ست, as مُنْطَلِقٌ "loosed," مَطَالِقُ ; مُسْتَخْرِجٌ "a leader," مَخَارِجُ .

e. Some words form their plural in a manner exceedingly irregular, as أُمٌّ "a mother," أُمَّهَاتٌ ; فَمٌ "the mouth," أَفْوَاهٌ ; مَاءٌ "water," أَمْوَاهٌ and مِيَاهٌ ; إِمْرَأَةٌ "woman," نِسَآءٌ , نِسْوَةٌ and نِسْوَانٌ ; إِنْسَانٌ "man," أَنَاسٌ for أَنَاسِيُّ, the final ي being cut off on account of the frequent use made of this word.

Of the Declension of Nouns.

59. Some grammarians divide the Arabic nouns into two, if not more, declensions. I think it much better to view them under one declension, reducible to five heads or classes, according as they consist in the singular or plural, or both, of *diptotes*, i.e., two cases, or of *triptotes*, i.e., three cases. The dual is always a *diptote*, so that we need only to direct our attention to the singular and plural.

CLASS I.

60. Under this class I include all substantives, masculine and feminine, which form their plurals *regularly*, as described in § 57. They all are, as may be seen, *triptotes* in the singular and *diptotes* in the plural; thus وَالِدٌ "a father."

SINGULAR.	DUAL.	PLURAL.
Nom. وَالِدٌ a father.	وَالِدَانِ two fathers.	وَالِدُونَ fathers.
Gen. وَالِدٍ of a father.	وَالِدَيْنِ of two fathers.	وَالِدِينَ of fathers.
Acc. وَالِدًا a father.	وَالِدَيْنِ two fathers.	وَالِدِينَ fathers.

As an example of a regular feminine noun we subjoin وَالِدَةٌ "a mother."

SINGULAR.	DUAL.	PLURAL.
Nom. وَالِدَةٌ a mother.	وَالِدَتَانِ two mothers.	وَالِدَاتٌ mothers.
Gen. وَالِدَةٍ of a mother.	وَالِدَتَيْنِ of two mothers.	وَالِدَاتٍ of mothers.
Acc. وَالِدَةً a mother.	وَالِدَتَيْنِ two mothers.	وَالِدَاتٍ mothers.

a. Under this class are included—1st. All participles, both active and passive, masculine and feminine, derived from regular verbs (which are generally employed as substantives), as نَاصِرٌ "assisting" or "assistant;" مَنْصُورٌ "assisted," also a man's name. All such nouns form their feminines by changing their final *nūnation* into ـَةٌ as نَاصِرَةٌ, etc., and are declined like وَالِدَةٌ. 2nd. Nouns of the measures فَعَّالٌ and فَعِلٌ as مَلَّاحٌ "a mariner," نَجَّارٌ "a carpenter;" plural مَلَّاحُونَ, etc. 3rd. Nouns ending in ـِيٌّ which are generally patronymic or possessive adjectives, as بَغْدَادِيٌّ "a man of Bagdad," سَوْدَاوِيٌّ "a man given to melancholy," "a hypochondriac;" plural بَغْدَادِيُّونَ, etc. 4th. Diminutive nouns of the measure فُعَيْلٌ, as رُجَيْلٌ "a mannikin" or "insignificant little man;" plural رُجَيْلُونَ, etc. To these we might add several others which cannot be reduced under specific heads; and must be left entirely to practice.

CLASS II.

61. Nouns of this class, like the preceding, are *triptotes* in the singular and *diptotes* in the plural, with this difference, that the plural is *broken* or *irregular;* thus, مَسْجِدٌ "a mosque."

SINGULAR.	DUAL.	PLURAL.
N. مَسْجِدٌ a mosque.	مَسْجِدَانِ two mosques.	مَسَاجِدُ mosques.
G. مَسْجِدٍ of, to, or in a mosque.	مَسْجِدَيْنِ of two mosques	مَسَاجِدَ of mosques.
A. مَسْجِدًا a mosque.	——— two mosques.	——— mosques.

CLASS III.

62. Nouns of this class are *triptotes* both in the singular and plural; thus, بَيْتٌ "a house."

SINGULAR.	DUAL.	PLURAL.
N. بَيْتٌ a house.	بَيْتَانِ two houses.	بُيُوتٌ houses.
G. بَيْتٍ of, etc. a house.	بَيْتَيْنِ of two houses.	بُيُوتٍ of houses.
A. بَيْتًا a house.	—— two houses.	بُيُوتًا houses.

a. Of Classes II. and III. we may say in general that they include such substantives as have not been already specified under Class I.; but it is very difficult, if not impossible, to subject them to any specific rules. The student must be guided by practice alone.

CLASS IV.

63. This class consists of such adjective nouns (not being comparatives or superlatives) as are *diptotes* in the singular and *triptotes* in the plural; thus, أَحْمَرُ "red."

SINGULAR.		DUAL.	PLURAL.	
Nom.	أَحْمَرُ	أَحْمَرَانِ	حُمْرٌ	Nom.
Gen. & Acc.	أَحْمَرَ	أَحْمَرَيْنِ	حُمْرٍ	Gen.
			حُمْرًا	Acc.

CLASS V.

64. This class consists of a few substantives and such adjectives (comparatives and superlatives) as are *diptotes* both in the singular and plural; thus أَصْغَرُ "less."

SINGULAR.		DUAL.	PLURAL.	
Nom.	أَصْغَرُ	أَصْغَرَانِ	أَصَاغِرُ	Nom.
Gen. & Acc.	أَصْغَرَ	أَصْغَرَيْنِ	أَصَاغِرَ	Gen. & Acc.

a. Classes IV. and V. consist chiefly of adjectives; those of the former being in the positive degree though under the form of comparatives and superlatives; Class V. consists of *bonâ fide* comparatives and superlatives.

65. When the last letter of a noun is و preceded by *fatḥa*, or ا, or ي, also preceded by *fatḥa*, and called *short alif*, أَلِفٌ مَقْصُورَةٌ, the three cases are alike; if it be ي preceded by *kasra*, the nominative and the genitive alone are alike;

in this case the ي not bearing either *ḍamma* or *kasra*. Thus in the three cases عَصًى "a staff," is written for عَصَوٌ, عَصَوٍ, عَصَوًا and رَحًى "a mill," for رَحَيٌ, رَحَيٍ, رَحَيًا which are of the first class, or triptotes. قَاضٍ "a Ḳāḍī" or "judge," in the nominative and genitive for قَاضِيٌ and قَاضِيٍ, of the same class, بُشْرَى "good news," for بُشْرَيُ in the nominative, and بُشْرَيَ, in the genitive and accusative of the last class, or diptotes. صَحَارٍ "deserts," for صَحَارِيُ in the nominative, and صَحَارِيَ in the genitive and accusative, irregular quadriliteral plural of the second class.

66. Six words have a variation of case peculiar to themselves, when in construction either with a noun or an affixed possessive pronoun, viz., أَبٌ "a father," أَخٌ "a brother," حَمٌ "a father-in-law," هَنٌ "a thing," فَمٌ or فُو "the mouth," and ذُو "having," "possessed of," "endowed with," which are declined as follows:

Nom.	أَبُو زَيْدٍ the father of Zaid.	أَخُوهُ his brother.
Gen.	أَبِي زَيْدٍ of the father of Zaid.	أَخِيهِ of his brother.
Acc.	أَبَا زَيْدٍ the father of Zaid.	أَخَاهُ his brother.

Nom.	فُمُ عُمَرَ the mouth of 'Umar.	حَمُوكَ thy father-in-law.
Gen.	فِي عُمَرَ of the mouth of 'Umar.	حَمِيكَ of thy father-in-law.
Acc.	فَا عُمَرَ the mouth of 'Umar.	حَمَاكَ thy father-in-law.

Nom.	ذُو رَحْمَةٍ endowed with compassion.	هَنُوكِ thy thing.
Gen.	ذِي رَحْمَةٍ of one who is compassionate.	هَنِيكِ of thy thing.
Acc.	ذَا رَحْمَةٍ compassionate.	هَنَاكِ thy thing.

a. When these words, however, are prefixed to the pronoun of the first person there is no change of case, as أَبِي "my father," أَبِي "of my father," etc. When فَمٌ is followed by an affixed pronoun, it varies only in the vowel-points, as فَمُكَ "your mouth," فَمِكَ "of your mouth," فَمَكَ "your mouth." أَبو has sometimes a peculiar idiom, similar in sense to ذُو as in the following epithet, which the lion in the fable gives to the fox, لِمَاذَا لا تَدْخُلُ يَا ابا ٱلْحِصْنِ "Why do you not enter, O father of the stronghold?" *i.e.* "O thou endowed with strength."

b. The accusative is substituted for the nominative when certain participles go before, as إِنَّ "indeed," "certainly," أَنَّ "that," كَأَنَّ "as if," لَكِنَّ "but," لَيْتَ "would to God," لَعَلَّ "perhaps;" as إِنَّ رَجُلاً يَقُومُ "indeed a man will stand;" لَكِنَّ ٱلْمَلِكَ قَدِيرٌ "but the king is powerful;" no other word must intervene, however, excepting a preposition with its case, as إِنَّ فِي ٱلدَّارِ رَجُلاً "certainly there is a man in the house." The word لا signifying "is not," when immediately preceding any appellative, gives it, in general, the accusative termination, as لَا رَيْبَ فِيهِ "there is no doubt of it" (or "in it"). In this case the accusative loses the nūnation, but the noun must not be definite, either as a noun proper, or as an appellative limited by the article ٱل, or by a word which it governs.

67. The vocative is expressed by the nominative without nūnation, with يا prefixed, as, يَا عُثْمَانُ "O 'Uthmān!" يَا أَمِيرُ "O prince!" except when followed by a genitive, where the

accusative is employed in place of the nominative, as يا عَبْدَ ٱللّٰه "O servant of God."

a. The nominative thus employed is naturally pronounced with rapidity. Hence it is that the nūnation is always dropped, and that the affixed pronoun ـِي is sometimes cut off, as يَا قَوْمِ "O my people!" رَبِّ "O my Lord!" Some words, chiefly proper names in frequent use, throw off a whole syllable at the end, as يَا صَاحِ for يَا صَاحِبِي "O my friend!" يَا مَنْصُ "O Manṣūr!" يَا مَرْوَ "O Marvān!" for مَنْصُور, etc.

b. On the other hand, when placed at the end of a sentence, and pronounced more strongly, the vowel is prolonged, and receives a kind of aspirate, as يَا غُلَامِيَه for غُلَامِ "O my boy!" Sometimes this appears as final *ā*, as يَا غُلَامَا or *āh*, as يَا غُلَامَاه or غُلَامَه for غُلَامِي.

c. When the name invoked, however, bears the article اَلْ, the pronoun هَذَا, or one of these words, اَيُّهَا, اَيَّتُهَا, اَيُّهَذَا, always comes between the name and the particle يَا, as يَا اَيُّهَا ٱلنَّاسُ "O men!"

d. In calling for help, لَ is often prefixed to the genitive, as يَا لَصَلَاحِ ٱلدِّينِ "help, O Saladin!" and sometimes اه is added for the same purpose, as يا صديقاه "help, O friend!" اَبَتَ is however sometimes used for ابي "O my father!" and أُمَّتَ for أُمِّي "O my mother."

68. The dual and the perfect masculine plurals in ن drop that letter when followed by a noun in the genitive case, or by the affixed pronouns, as غَزَالَانِ "two fawns, غزالا يُوسُف "the

two fawns of Joseph;" قَدَمَانِ "two feet," قَدَمَاهُ "his two feet;" مُسْلِمُونَ "Musulmans," مُسْلِمُو ٱلْبَلَدِ "the Musulmans of the town," بَنُونَ "sons," بَنُوهُ "his sons."

a. When a noun is rendered *definite* by prefixing the article أَلْ the *nūnation*, which appears at the end of some of the cases, is dropped and the simple short vowel retained; thus, Nom. الْوَالِدُ "the father;" Gen. الْوَالِدِ "of the father;" Acc. الْوَالِدَ "the father;" so الْوَالِدَةُ "the mother;" الْوَالِدَةِ "of the mother;" الْوَالِدَةَ "the mother." In like manner, the nūnation is rejected when one noun governs a noun following in the genitive; thus, امِيرُ ٱلْمُومِنِينَ "Commander of the Faithful;" اِقْبَالُ ٱلدَّوْلَةِ "Prosperity of the State." The article changes the substantives singular, and irregular plurals, which are diptotes, into triptotes, as Nom. ٱلْاَسْوَدُ "the black;" Gen. ٱلْاَسْوَدِ; Acc. ٱلْاَسْوَدَ; so Nom. الْبَيْضَآءُ "the white;" Gen. الْبَيْضَآءِ; Acc. الْبَيْضَآءَ.

b. The nūnation is affected in the same manner as ن when under the above circumstances. It is also rejected by all those nouns called *invariable*, which form their nominative in ـُ and in other cases in ـَ, as may be observed with regard to the plurals of the 2nd and 5th classes of nouns.

Of the Numerals—اَسْمَآءُ ٱلْعَدَدِ.

69. The Arabic Numerals hold a sort of middle rank between the Substantives and Adjectives; consequently this is the proper place wherein to introduce them. Several of them, as we shall see hereafter, are *bonâ fide* substantives, others adjectives. Our object here is simply to exhibit them such as they are; the application and use of them belong to the Syntax. The following are

THE CARDINAL NUMBERS.

	FEMININE.	MASCULINE.			FEMININE.		MASCULINE.	
5	خَمْسٌ	خَمْسَةٌ	٥	1	وَاحِدَةٌ اِحْدَى	or	وَاحِدٌ اَحَدٌ	١
6	سِتٌّ	سِتَّةٌ	٦					
7	سَبْعٌ	سَبْعَةٌ	٧	2	اِثْنَتَانِ ثِنْتَانِ		اِثْنَانِ	٢
8	ثَمَانٍ	ثَمَانِيَةٌ	٨					
9	تِسْعٌ	تِسْعَةٌ	٩	3	ثَلَاثٌ		ثَلَاثَةٌ	٣
10	عَشْرٌ	عَشَرَةٌ	١٠	4	اَرْبَعٌ		اَرْبَعَةٌ	٤

a. From three to ten inclusive, the termination ةٌ, the usual sign of the feminine gender, here marks the masculine. All these numbers are triptotes, except اِثْنَانِ and اِثْنَتَانِ, both of which are diptotes, having for their inflexions اِثْنَيْنِ and اِثْنَتَيْنِ for the genitive and accusative, like all the duals. From three to ten, the cardinal numbers are employed either as adjectives or substantives; in the first case, they are placed after the thing numbered, and agree with it in gender and case; if employed as substantives, they govern the genitive of the thing numbered, and then of course lose their nūnation, as ثَلَاثَةُ رِجَالٍ "three men," literally, "three of men," or as we might say, "a trio of men." When ثَمَانٍ "eight," loses its nūnation, it recovers the ي, which had disappeared according to the rule, § 65, for ثَمَانٍ is for ثَمَانِيٌ; we then write ثَمَانِي in the nominative and genitive, and ثَمَانِيَ in the accusative.

70. From eleven to nineteen inclusive, the cardinal numbers are composed of units, and of the number ten, which in the masculine is عَشَرَ, and in the feminine عَشْرَةَ or عَشَرَةَ, the smaller number being always put first, thus—

	MASC.	FEM.	
١١	أَحَدَ عَشَرَ	إِحْدَي عَشْرَةَ	11
١٢	إِثْنَا عَشَرَ	إِثْنَتَا عَشْرَةَ	12
١٣	ثَلَاثَةَ عَشَرَ	ثَلَاثَ عَشْرَةَ	13
١٤	أَرْبَعَةَ عَشَرَ	أَرْبَعَ عَشْرَةَ	14
١٥	خَمْسَةَ عَشَرَ	خَمْسَ عَشْرَةَ	15
١٦	سِتَّةَ عَشَرَ	سِتَّ عَشْرَةَ	16
١٧	سَبْعَةَ عَشَرَ	سَبْعَ عَشْرَةَ	17
١٨	ثَمَانِيَةَ عَشَرَ	ثَمَانِي عَشْرَةَ	18
١٩	تِسْعَةَ عَشَرَ	تِسْعَ عَشْرَةَ	19

71. The Decades from twenty upwards are,

20.	عِشْرُونَ	50.	خَمْسُونَ	80.	ثَمَانُونَ	200.	مِائَتَانِ
30.	ثَلٰثُونَ	60.	سِتُّونَ	90.	تِسْعُونَ	1000.	أَلْفٌ
40.	أَرْبَعُونَ	70.	سَبْعُونَ	100.	مِائَةٌ	2000.	أَلْفَانِ

a. In the numbers composed of decades and of units from twenty to ninety-nine inclusive, the conjunction وَ is inserted between the two numbers; the smallest number is put first, and both are declined, as عِشْرُونَ وَ أَحَدٌ ; genitive عِشْرِينَ وَ أَحَدٍ ; accusative عِشْرِينَ وَ أَحَدًا.

b. The numbers for the hundreds are of both genders; thus مِائَةٌ 100; مِائَتَانِ 200; ثَلَاثُ مِائَةٍ 300; أَرْبَعُ مِائَةٍ 400; خَمْسُ مِائَةٍ 500; سِتُّ مِائَةٍ 600; سَبْعُ مِائَةٍ 700; ثَمَانِ مِائَةٍ or ثَمَانِي مِائَةٍ 800; تِسْعُ مِائَةٍ 900.

c. The numbers for the thousands are as follows: أَلْفٌ 1,000; أَلْفَانِ 2,000; ثَلَاثَةُ آلَافٍ 3,000; أَرْبَعَةُ آلَافٍ 4,000; and so on up to ten thousand. Beyond ten thousand they are, أَحَدَ عَشَرَ أَلْفًا 11,000; إِثْنَا عَشَرَ أَلْفًا 12,000; and so on up to ninety-nine thousand. After that they are مِائَةُ أَلْفٍ 100,000; مِائَتَا أَلْفٍ 200,000; ثَلٰثُمِائَةِ أَلْفٍ 300,000, etc.

ORDINAL NUMBERS.

72. The ordinal numbers up to ten inclusive, have (with the exception of the first) the measure فَاعِلٌ for the masculine, and فَاعِلَةٌ for the feminine. The compound numbers from the 11th to the 19th inclusive are made up of the corresponding ordinals of their units with the addition of عَشَرَ for the masculine, and عَشْرَةَ for the feminine. When these nine compounds are indeterminate, they both end in a *fatḥa* and are not subject to declension. If, however, they have the article prefixed, the units are regularly declined like a noun of the first class, and the decades remain unaltered; thus, Nom. اَلثَّالِثُ عَشَرَ; Gen. اَلثَّالِثِ عَشَرَ; Acc. اَلثَّالِثَ عَشَرَ; and the same rule is observed with regard to the feminine; thus, اَلثَّالِثَةُ عَشْرَةَ, and so on.

FEM.	MASC.		FEM.	MASC.	
حَادِيَةَ عَشْرَةَ	حَادِيَ عَشَرَ	11th	أُولَي	أَوَّل	1st
ثَانِيَةَ عَشْرَةَ	ثَانِيَ عَشَرَ	12th	ثَانِيَةٌ	ثَانٍ	2nd
ثَالِثَةَ عَشْرَةَ	ثَالِثَ عَشَرَ	13th	ثَالِثَةٌ	ثَالِثٌ	3rd
رَابِعَةَ عَشْرَةَ	رَابِعَ عَشَرَ	14th	رَابِعَةٌ	رَابِعٌ	4th
خَامِسَةَ عَشْرَةَ	خَامِسَ عَشَرَ	15th	خَامِسَةٌ	خَامِسٌ	5th
سَادِسَةَ عَشْرَةَ	سَادِسَ عَشَرَ	16th	سَادِسَةٌ	سَادِسٌ	6th
سَابِعَةَ عَشْرَةَ	سَابِعَ عَشَرَ	17th	سَابِعَةٌ	سَابِعٌ	7th
ثَامِنَةَ عَشْرَةَ	ثَامِنَ عَشَرَ	18th	ثَامِنَةٌ	ثَامِنٌ	8th
تَاسِعَةَ عَشْرَةَ	تَاسِعَ عَشَرَ	19th	تَاسِعَةٌ	تَاسِعٌ	9th
عِشْرُونَ	عِشْرُونَ	20th	عَاشِرَةٌ	عَاشِرٌ	10th

73. The twentieth and all the decades above, are expressed by the cardinal numbers; and the intermediate ones are formed by prefixing the ordinals of the units with the conjunction وَ between, thus—

FEM.	MASC.	
حَادِيَةٌ وَ عِشْرُونَ or	حَادِي وَ عِشْرُونَ or	21st.
وَاحِدَةٌ وَ عِشْرُونَ	وَاحِدٌ وَ عِشْرُونَ	

FRACTIONAL NUMBERS.

74. In Arabic fractional numbers from one-third to one-tenth inclusive are expressed by certain words modified from the corresponding radical numbers; thus, نِصْفٌ "a half," ثُلُثٌ "a third," رُبْعٌ "a fourth," خُمْسٌ "a fifth," سُدْسٌ "a sixth," سُبْعٌ "a seventh," ثُمْنٌ "an eighth," تُسْعٌ "a ninth," عُشْرٌ "a tenth." Beyond the fraction $\frac{1}{10}$ recourse is had to a kind of periphrasis: thus, to express the fraction "three-twentieths" they say ثَلَاثَةُ اجْزَآءٍ مِنْ عِشْرِينَ جُزْءًا literally, "three parts out of twenty parts."

DISTRIBUTIVE NUMBERS.

75. Distributive numbers are expressed either by twice repeating the ordinal number, as وَاحِدًا وَاحِدًا "one by one," or (from one to ten) by words of the measure فُعَالُ or مَفْعَلُ derived from the radical number. These may be used singly or by repetition; thus, أُحَادُ or أُحَادُ أُحَادُ, or مَوْحَدُ مَوْحَدُ "one by one," so رُبَاعُ رُبَاعُ or مَرْبَعُ مَرْبَعُ "four by four." All such numerals are diptotes.

RELATIVE NUMERALS.

76. These embrace such adjectives as denote "relating to" or "consisting of" such or such a number from one to ten; thus ثُنَائِيٌّ "containing two," ثُلَاثِيٌّ "containing three," رُبَاعِيٌّ "containing four," خُمَاسِيٌّ "containing five," etc. In like manner from the cardinal numbers are formed relative adjectives from one to ten; these present no difficulty. It must be remarked, however, that from اِثْنَانِ "two," a dual of which the singular, if it could have one, would be اِثْنٌ for ثَنَوٌ; the relative adjective is formed by recurring to the form of the singular اِثْنِيٌّ and ثَنَوِيٌّ, like اِسْمِيٌّ. From eleven to nineteen, the numeratives composed of two indeclinable words, form their relative adjectives from the first word only, wholly suppressing the second; whence it follows that these adjectives exactly resemble those derived from numeratives from one to nine; thus ثَنَوِيٌّ is the relative adjective of اِثْنَانِ "two," and of اِثْنَا عَشَرَ "twelve;" خَمْسِيٌّ is that of خَمْسَةٌ "five," and of خَمْسَةَ عَشَرَ "fifteen." From مِائَةٌ "one hundred," is formed the relative adjective مِئَوِيٌّ or مِئِيٌّ; and from أَلْفٌ "a thousand," أَلْفِيٌّ.

PERIODIC NUMERALS.

77. Numerative words denoting a periodical return, are of the measure فِعْلٌ. They are put in the accusative with or without an article, as اَلثِّلْثَ or ثِلْثًا "every three (days, months, etc.)," so ثِمْنًا or اَلثِّمْنَ "every eight (days, months, etc.)." When for the sake of precision the *days*, etc. must

be specified they express the same in the following manner: يَشْرَبُ الخَمْرَ مَرَّةً آلثَّلٰثَ سَنَةً "he drinks wine once every three years."

a. Numerative words denoting "simple" or "single," "double," "triple," etc., are expressed thus, مُفْرَدٌ "single," مُضَاعَفٌ "double," ثَلَاثَةَ أَضْعَافٍ "triple," أَرْبَعَةَ أَضْعَافٍ "quadruple," etc.

NUMERAL ADVERBS.

78. Words corresponding to our "once," "twice," "thrice," etc., are generally expressed by a word denoting "time" or "turn" in the accusative case preceded by the requisite numeral, thus "once" is expressed by مَرَّةً or تَارَةً or دَفْعَةً; "twice" by مَرَّتَيْنِ; "thrice" by ثَلَاثَ مَرَّاتٍ, etc.

79. The Arabs have a curious idiom in expressing their dates and other large numbers, placing, generally, the units before the tens, the tens before the hundreds, and the hundreds before the thousands. This rule obtains strictly when the number consists of only two figures, decades and units; but if thousands and hundreds are employed, the thousands may optionally come first, then the hundreds, then the decades, and lastly the units, though the former mode is the more common. Thus in expressing in words the year 1862 they say "two and sixty and eight hundred and one thousand." This idiom is probably owing to the circumstance that the numerical cyphers of the Arabs, which they borrowed or adopted from the Hindūs, read contrariwise to their alphabetic characters, *i.e.* from right to left; so that

when an Arab, in reading, comes to such a number as 1862 for example, he naturally decyphers the group of figures from right to left, for the reasons we have just stated.

Of the Adjective—اَلصِّفَةُ.

80. The Adjective has two genders and generally three numbers like the substantive, but the explanation of its concord with the latter belongs more appropriately to our Section on Syntax. At present we shall confine ourselves to the mode of forming the Comparative and Superlative Degrees of Comparison.

81. The comparative is formed from the positive by prefixing أ, as خَيْرٌ "good," اَخْيَرُ "better," and takes in general مِنْ "than," after it; thus اَنْتَ اَعْظَمُ مِنَ ٱلْمَلِكِ "thou art greater than the king." Sometimes the mere positive with مِنْ is used to express the comparative, as in the following line from Elnawabig; وَيَوْمِي خَيْرٌ مِنْ اَمْسِي "the present day is better than the past." The particle فِي, however, and some others often follow the comparative in place of مِنْ, so as to express either a positive or superlative degree according to circumstances; as اَشْهَرُ فِي ٱلْحَرْبِ "more or most intrepid in war." In the feminine of the comparative ي quiescent after *fatha* is added in place of ا prefixed, as كَبِيرٌ "great," اَكْبَرُ "greater" (masc.), كُبْرَي "greater" (fem.). The particle مِن does not always immediately follow the comparative; as in the following example: اعزّ عِنْدِي مِن بُوبُو عَينِي "Dearer to me than the apple of mine eye."

82. Without مِن the form اَفْعَل when followed by a genitive expresses the superlative degree, as اَحْسَنُ آلنَّاسِ "the best of men." It becomes superlative also where the substantive precedes the adjective, as سَعْدِي اَعْلَمُ "Sa'dī is most wise." It has likewise a superlative sense when placed absolutely with a substantive or pronoun in construction, as هُمَا الاَعْدَلَانِ "they two are the most upright;" هُمْ آلْاَفْضَلُونَ بَينَ آلنَّاسِ "they are the most excellent among human beings." Of the comparative and superlative we shall treat more fully in our Section on Syntax.

Of the Pronoun—اَلضَّمِيرُ.

PERSONAL PRONOUNS.

83. These consist of two classes, viz., the *Isolated* and the *Affixed.* The Isolated are the following, viz.:—

1st Pers. Sing. اَنَا "I." (No Dual). 1st Pers. Plur. نَحْنُ "we."
2nd Pers. Sing. Masc. اَنْتَ, Fem. اَنْتِ "thou." Dual comm. اَنْتُمَا "you two." Plur. Masc. اَنْتُمْ, Fem. اَنْتُنَّ "you."
3rd Pers. Sing. Masc. هُوَ "he," Fem. هِيَ "she." Dual comm. هُمَا "they both." Plur. Masc. هُمْ, Fem. هُنَّ "they."

a. We may here observe that the third person masculine هُوَ loses its first vowel *damma,* and the third feminine its *kasra,* when preceded by either of the conjunctions وَ and فَ, which both denote "and;" thus, instead of وَهُوَ, they say وَهْوَ; so for وَهِيَ they say وَهْيَ. We may also observe that the Personal, Demonstrative, and Relative Pronouns have the same variation of gender and number as nouns, but they have no difference of case, with the exception of the duals of the Demonstratives and Relatives, which follow the mode of other duals, as we shall immediately see. The first person is naturally of the common gender, and wants the dual number.

84. We now come to the Affixed Pronouns, which occur almost in every line, and are always annexed to a verb, a noun, or a preposition. When added to verbs they are generally in the accusative case, though often in the dative, especially when another accusative comes immediately after. When joined to nouns they are possessive or relative. When affixed to a preposition they have a personal and sometimes a relative sense. The Affixed Pronouns are the following:

1st Pers. Sing. ـِي or نِي "of me" or "me." (No Dual). 1st Pers. Plur. نَا "of us" or "us."

2nd Pers. Sing. Masc. كَ, Fem. كِ, "of thee" or "thee." Dual (comm.) كُمَا "of you both," etc. Plur. Masc. كُمْ; Fem. كُنَّ "of you both," etc.

3rd Pers. Sing. هُ "of him" or "him;" هَا "of her" or "her." Dual هُمَا "of them both," etc. Plur. Masc. هُمْ; Fem. هُنَّ "of them both."

a. We here add a few examples to illustrate the use of the affixed pronouns, premising that in all nouns the nunation disappears when the affixed ـِي is added; thus, كِتَابٌ "a book; كِتَابِي "my book." The other affixes also displace the *nunation,* but the simple vowel remains; thus, دَارٌ "a house;" دَارُهُ "his house." We must also notice a few changes or modifications which take place both in the termination of the words to which the pronoun is affixed, and also in the initial syllable of the affixes themselves.

b. The affixes هُ, هُمَا, هُمْ, and هُنَّ, turn the *ḍamma* of the ه into *kasra* when another *kasra* immediately precedes; as, مِنْ رَبِّهِ "from his master," or when following the ـِي of prolongation; as, فِيهِ "in him" or "it." The pronoun of the first person ي in the case of *kasra* preceding it, takes *fatḥa* above it, when annexed to any word ending with ا, و, or ي, without vowels; as, خَطَايَا "sins," خَطَايَايَ "my sins;" مُسْلِمِيَّ "of my faithful (people);" عَصًا "a staff," عَصَايَ "my staff;" رَامٍ "an archer," رَامِيَّ "my archer." After *kasra* ي is frequently omitted in the vocative case; as, رَبِّ "my lord!" or when another ي (officiating for *hamza* ء) precedes; as, أَحِبَّائِي "my friends;" آبَائِي "my fathers." For the verbal affix نِي, only نِ is sometimes used; as, أُنْصُرُونِ "assist me," for أُنْصُرُونِي.

c. Not only the nūnation vowels, as we have already stated, but also the ن in the duals and in the perfect masculine plurals, are dropped when followed by the affixed pronouns; as, كِتَابَانِ "two books," كِتَابَاهُ "his two books," etc. When affixed to words ending in ة, they change the latter into ت; as, عَمَّةٌ "an aunt," عَمَّتُكَ "thy aunt." In the 3rd person plural masculine of the preterites of verbs, also in the 2nd person plural masculine of the imperatives, the quiescent *alif* after و is rejected; as, نَصَرُوا "they assisted," نَصَرُونَا "they assisted us;" and after the verbal termination تُمْ they add ـُو; as, نَصَرْتُمْ "you assisted," نَصَرْتُمُوهُ "you assisted him." When following verbs or nouns ending in ي quiescent after *fatḥa*, ي either remains, or is changed to ا; as, رَمَي "he threw," رَمَيهُ or رَمَاهُ "he threw him." فَتَي "a boy," فَتَاهُ and فَتَيهُ "his boy." In particles final ي forms a diphthong with the preceding *fatḥa*; as, إِلَي "to," إِلَيهِ "to him." In books where no vowel points are used ي is sometimes added to the 2nd person feminine singular to distinguish it from the masculine; thus, كِي for كِ.

d. The affix نِي in place of ـِي, is used when joined to verbs, and also to particles ending in ن, such as أَنَّ, إِنَّ, مِنْ, عَنْ, etc.; as, أَنَّنِي "that I;" مِنِّي for مِنْنِي "from me;" the two *nūns* of the latter, however, always coalesce, as مِنِّي. The affixed pronouns, when the particle لِ is prefixed, have often a possessive signification similar to the Latin idiom, *mihi est, tibi est, illi est*, etc., as لِي in this phrase from our fable, § 43, where the pig says, أَنَا ٱلشَّقِيُّ لَا صُوفَ لِي وَلَا لَبَنَ "*ego miser, non est lana mihi, neque lac;*" "I wretched have neither wool nor milk."

e. Two affixes may be annexed to one word, when that of the first person is always placed before the second, and the second before the third; as, اَعْطَانِيهُ "he gave it to me" يَكْفِيكَهُمْ "he or it will, or may, or can suffice thee against them," *i.e.*, "will protect thee from them."

f. These pronouns may also be put separately after verbs to denote the accusative case, but with the particle إِيَّا prefixed to them; as, ضَرَبَ إِيَّاكَ "he beat you;" or they may be placed before the verb in the same sense as in the following passage from the *Kurān:* إِيَّاكَ نَعْبُدُ وإِيَّاكَ نَسْتَعِينُ "Thee we adore, and thee we call to our aid." In like manner the other affixes, as, إِيَّايَ "me;" إِيَّانَا "us;" إِيَّاكِ "thee" (fem.); إِيَّاكُمَا "you two;" إِيَّاكُمْ "you" (masc.); إِيَّاكُنَّ "you" (fem.); إِيَّاهُ "him;" إِيَّاهَا "her;" إِيَّاهُمَا "them" (two); إِيَّاهُمْ "them" (masc.); إِيَّاهُنَّ "them" (fem.).

THE DEMONSTRATIVE PRONOUNS.

85 The Demonstrative pronoun, implying an object near

at hand, is expressed ذَا "this" (*hic*), and is declined as follows:

PLURAL.		DUAL. OBLIQUE.	DUAL. NOM.	SINGULAR.	
أُولَى or	أُولَآءِ	ذَيْنِ	ذَانِ	ذَا	Masc.
				تَا تِهِ تِهِي تِي	Fem.
—	—	تَيْنِ	تَانِ	ذِهِ ذِهِي ذِي	

The remote demonstrative, "that" (*ille*) is formed from the above by adding كَ.

PLURAL.		DUAL. OBLIQUE.	DUAL. NOM.	SINGULAR.	
أُولَاكَ	أُولَآئِكَ	ذَيْنِكَ	ذَانِكَ	ذَاكَ	Masc.
—	—	تَيْنِكَ	تَانِكَ	تَاكَ	Fem.

لِ is often inserted before كَ, as ذَالِكَ or ذٰلِكَ ; تَالِكَ or تِلْكَ, (for تَالِكَ, etc.) هَا is frequently prefixed to ذَا and ذَاكَ, the ا being generally dropped, and represented in pointed books by ~ or a perpendicular *fatḥa*; thus

PLURAL.	DUAL. OBLIQUE.	DUAL. NOM.	SINGULAR.	
هٰؤُلَاءِ	هٰذَيْنِ	هٰذَانِ	هٰذَا	Masc.
—	هٰتَيْنِ	هٰتَانِ	هٰذِهِ	Fem.

هٰذَا "this," is sometimes used for the personal pronoun "thou" or "you," though it is then in general expressive of contempt or detestation, as يَا هٰذَا "O thou."

THE RELATIVE PRONOUNS.

86. The Relative "who," "which," "that," is compounded of the article اَلْ and لَذِي, the ل of the article being omitted in the singular and masculine plural, and the initial ل of the pronoun marked by *tashdīd*, as formerly observed under the article (§ 46 *a*). It is declined as follows:

PLURAL. OBLIQUE.	PLURAL. NOM.	DUAL. OBLIQUE.	DUAL. NOM.	SINGULAR.	
اَلَّذِينَ	اَلَّذُونَ	اَللَّذَيْنِ	اَللَّذَانِ	اَلَّذِي	Masc.
اَللَّائِي اَللَّاءِ اَللَّوَاتِي اَللَّاءُ	اَللَّاتِي	اَللَّتَيْنِ	اَللَّتَانِ	اَلَّتِي	Fem.

This relative does not admit of any of the servile letters being prefixed, excepting فَ, كَ, لَ, and وَ, which, as we have already observed, we consider to be inseparable particles *not* serviles. The oblique cases are seldom used, and it is often construed with the affixed pronouns annexed to the subsequent word, as اَلَّذِي بِهِ "in which," for بِالَّذِي ; اَلَّذِي مِنْهُ "from which," for مِنَ ٱلَّذِي ; اَلَّذِي رَأَيْتُهُ "whom I saw," for اَلَّذِي رَأَيْتُ ; or, sometimes with a word intervening, as اَلَّتِي فِيهَا يُتَوَلَّدُ "(the land, etc.) in which he was born."

87. The Pronouns مَنْ "he who," "those who," "whoever," and مَا "that which," or "whatsoever," "whatever," are also relatives including the antecedent, the former referring to rational beings and the latter to brutes or lifeless objects, as in the proverb: مَنِ ٱسْتَرْعَى ٱلذِّئْبَ ٱلْغَنَمَ فَقَدْ ظَلَمَ "He who commits (has committed) to the care of the wolf (the pasturing of) the sheep, certainly does (has done) an injustice."

Whereupon Al Damīrī in his "History of Animals," shrewdly observed that there was a greater injustice done to the wolf than to the sheep; because, says he, "they employed him to do that which was not in his nature."

a. مَنْ employed interrogatively, also receives the genders, numbers, and cases; but nothing must then be added after this word. For example, should a person say to another, "Some one is come," or "I have seen somebody;" if the other should simply ask "Who?" or "Whom?" the proper word in Arabic is مَنُو, etc.

PLURAL.	DUAL.	SINGULAR.	MASCULINE.
Who? مَنُونْ	What two? مَنَانْ	Who? مَنُو	Nom.
مَنِينْ	Of what two? مَنَيْنْ	Of whom? مَنِي	Gen.
Of whom? etc.		Whom? مَنَا	Accus.
مَنَاتْ	مَنْتَانْ	مَنَتْ, مَنْتْ, مَنَهْ	Fem.
for all cases.	Gen. and Acc. مَنْتَيْنْ	for all cases.	

INTERROGATIVE PRONOUNS.

88. أَيٌّ feminine أَيَّةٌ "who?" "which?" "what?" "of what kind?" etc., is generally used interrogatively, governing the substantive in the genitive, as أَيُّ كِتَابٍ "what book?" When it is employed alone, without a substantive, it receives all the numbers and cases; thus dual, أَيَّانِ, fem. أَيَّتَانِ, plural أَيُّونَ, fem. أَيَّاتٌ. The singular, as well as the plural, are declined as triptotes. It is often joined with مَنْ and مَا, as أَيُّمَنْ "whoever;" "whosoever;" أَيَّمَا "whatever;" "whatso-

ever;" and sometimes plurally, أَيُّهُم masc. أَيُّهُنَّ fem. "which of them?" dual أَيُّهُمَا, etc.

RECIPROCAL PRONOUNS.

89. Reciprocal actions are expressed by the noun نَفْسٌ "soul," "self," with the affixes, as اَحْبَبْتُ نَفْسِي "I pleased myself;" or in the following remarkable anecdote of the despotic influence which Baitina, the famous chief of the assassins, so celebrated in the history of the Crusades by the name of "the Old man of the Mountain," had over his followers. When this chieftain had become powerful and terrible to the surrounding princes, he drew at last the attention of the Sulṭān Jalālu-d-daula, who sending an ambassador to require his submission, he thus received him: "When the ambassador appeared in his presence, he called before him some of his people; and giving the signal to a young man among them, said to him, 'Stab yourself,' and he did so; he ordered then another to precipitate himself from the castle, which he did, and was dashed to pieces. Then he said to the Sulṭān's ambassador, 'Of subjects such as these, seventy thousand are thus observant of me: let this be the answer.'" The words in the original are as follows: قَالَ لَهُ اُقْتُلْ نَفْسَكَ فَفَعَلَ ثُمَّ اَوْصَى اِلَى آخَرَ بِاَنْ يَرْمِيَ نَفْسَهُ مِنَ اَلْقَلْعَةِ فَفَعَلَ وَ تَقَطَّعَ.

a. In the Lowland Scotch dialect of the Anglo-Saxon I have frequently heard the expression "the sel' o't," *i.e.* "the self of it," instead of "itself," which last is probably a contraction of "its self." The expressions "himself" and "themselves" are apparently incorrect, for the amendment of which the late Dr. Gilchrist laboured unsuccessfully to substitute "his self" and "their selves," so as to conform with the Arabic idiom.

b. Pronouns are seldom used in the plural to express anything irrational; but the feminine singular is substituted in the place of it; thus, هَذِهِ ٱلْكُتُبُ is the proper expression for "these books," and not أُولَاءِ ٱلْكُتُبُ. This observation applies also to nouns, as will be more fully detailed in the Syntax.

SECTION III.

Of the Verb—اَلْفِعْلُ.

90. The theme of the Arabic verb is named أَصْلٌ "the root," which is the third person singular masculine of the Preterite tense, as of all the persons the simplest, consisting only of radical letters; the other inflexions being formed from it, by the prefixing, inserting, or adding one or more of the servile letters we have already mentioned § 48. The letters which compose the root are called أَصْلِيَّةٌ "radicals;" and the seven letters comprised in the word يَتَسَمَّنُوا ("they fatten"), are denominated زَوَائِدُ "serviles" or "letters of increase.".

a. It is customary with most writers on Arabic Grammar, when commencing their description of the verb, to perplex the learner with a long discussion on the formation and meaning of the various derivatives, or as they foolishly call them *conjugations*, which may emanate from the primitive verbal root. In this respect I differ from them *in toto*. I hold it to be by far the better plan, in the first place, to explain fully a single paradigm of a perfect primitive root; then the student will be enabled, with advantage, to comprehend the purport of the derivative formations.

91. The verbs are either Triliteral or Quadriliteral; the

first consisting of three radical letters, as فَعَلَ "he made;" the other of four, as دَحْرَجَ "he turned." They are also divided into Perfect, the root consisting of three strong consonants, as صَدَقَ "he spoke the truth;" قَرَّ "he was quiet." The only peculiarity of قَرَّ (for قَرَرَ) which is also called a Surd verb, consists merely in the fact that the third radical is the same letter as the second, (both coalescing on certain occasions, by *tashdīd* ـّ). The Perfect and Surd verbs are also called *firm* or *robust*. All other verbs which have one or more of the *infirm* letters ا, و, and ي for their radicals, are called *irregular*, *infirm*, or *imperfect*, as سَارَ "he went," قَالَ "he said," etc., which will be detailed in our next Section.

a. In triliterals the first letter is called the فَآء *fā* of the root, the second the عَيْن *'ain*, and the third the لَام *lām*, because the verb فَعَلَ ("he made"), as we have already stated, is usually taken as the paradigm of the regular triliteral verb. In quadriliteral roots, the model being فَعْلَلَ, the first letter is named *fā*, the second *'ain*, the third *lām the first*, and the fourth *lām the second.*

92. The Arabic Verb has only one Conjugation; and like the noun it has three numbers, the Singular, the Dual, and the Plural. They have also two genders, the Masculine and the Feminine. Their Persons, as in other languages, are three; but the third, being the root, precedes the second, and the second the first. The First Person has no Dual and both its singular and plural are of the common gender. All this

will appear sufficiently obvious from the paradigm given below under § 94, etc.

93. The Arabian grammarians arrange their moods and tenses differently from the Europeans, dividing their paradigm into five parts: 1st, the Preterite; 2nd, the Aorist; 3rd, the Imperative; 4th, the Participle; and 5th, the Infinitive. These, however, do not exactly correspond to our moods and tenses of those denominations; the Preterite in particular being frequently used to express the Present, while the Aorist represents both the Present and the Future, as well as the Conditional and other tenses, as will be explained more at large after the conjugation of the Perfect or Regular Verb.

94. We now proceed to exhibit a paradigm of a Perfect or Regular Arabic Verb, both active and passive, adopting as our model the root فَعَلَ "he made," "did," or "acted."

ACTIVE VOICE.

1st Part—The PRETERITE اَلْمَاضِي "he did" or "made."

PLURAL.		DUAL.		SINGULAR.		
FEM.	MASC.	FEM.	MASC.	FEM.	MASC.	PERSON.
فَعَلْنَ	فَعَلُوا	فَعَلَتَا	فَعَلَا	فَعَلَتْ	فَعَلَ	3rd
		COMM.				
فَعَلْتُنَّ	فَعَلْتُمْ	فَعَلْتُمَا		فَعَلْتِ	فَعَلْتَ	2nd
COMM.				COMM.		
فَعَلْنَا				فَعَلْتُ		1st

2nd Part—The AORIST اَلْمُضَارِعُ "he makes" or "will or may make."

PLURAL.		DUAL.		SINGULAR.		PERSON.
FEM.	MASC.	FEM.	MASC.	FEM.	MASC.	
يَفْعَلْنَ	يَفْعَلُونَ	تَفْعَلَانِ	يَفْعَلَانِ	تَفْعَلُ	يَفْعَلُ	3rd
		COMM.				
تَفْعَلْنَ	تَفْعَلُونَ	تَفْعَلَانِ		تَفْعَلِينَ	تَفْعَلُ	2nd
COMM.				COMM.		
نَفْعَلُ				أَفْعَلُ		1st

3rd Part—The IMPERATIVE اَلْأَمْرُ "make" or "do thou," etc.

اِفْعَلْنَ	اِفْعَلُوا	اِفْعَلَا	اِفْعَلِي	اِفْعَلْ	2nd

4th Part—The PARTICIPLE اَلْفَاعِلُ "the maker" or "he who makes."

PLURAL.		DUAL.		SINGULAR.	
FEM.	MASC.	FEM.	MASC.	FEM.	MASC.
فَوَاعِلُ or فَاعِلَاتٌ	فَاعِلُونَ	فَاعِلَتَانِ	فَاعِلَانِ	فَاعِلَةٌ	فَاعِلٌ

5th Part—The INFINITIVE or VERBAL NOUN اَلْفِعْلُ.

فَعْلٌ, فِعْلٌ, or فِعْلًا "the act of making" or "doing."

PASSIVE VOICE.

95. The Passive Voice has only three parts, viz., the Preterite, the Aorist, and the Participle. It wants the imperative and infinitive; but the want of the imperative may be supplied by a modification of the aorist with the particle لِ prefixed, as لِيُنْصَرْ "let him be assisted." The passive preterite differs from the active only in the vowels of the first and second radical letters; the first having always *ḍamma*, and the second *kasra*. In the Aorist the incremental or servile letters included in the technical word اتين, at the beginning always have *ḍamma* for their vowel, and

that of the second radical is always *fatḥa*, as may be seen in the following paradigm :

1st Part—The Preterite.

PLURAL. FEM.	PLURAL. MASC.	DUAL. FEM.	DUAL. MASC.	SINGULAR. FEM.	SINGULAR. MASC.	PERSON.
فُعِلْنَ	فُعِلُوا	فُعِلَتَا	فُعِلَا	فُعِلَتْ	فُعِلَ	3rd
فُعِلْتُنَّ	فُعِلْتُمْ	COMM. فُعِلْتُمَا		فُعِلْتِ	فُعِلْتَ	2nd
COMM. فُعِلْنَا				COMM. فُعِلْتُ		1st

2nd Part—The Aorist.

يُفْعَلْنَ	يُفْعَلُونَ	تُفْعَلَانِ	يُفْعَلَانِ	تُفْعَلُ	يُفْعَلُ	3rd
تُفْعَلْنَ	تُفْعَلُونَ	تُفْعَلَانِ		تُفْعَلِينَ	تُفْعَلُ	2nd
نُفْعَلُ				أُفْعَلُ		1st

3rd Part—The Participle.

مَفْعُولَاتٌ	مَفْعُولُونَ	مَفْعُولَتَانِ	مَفْعُولَانِ	مَفْعُولَةٌ	مَفْعُولٌ

96. Such is the Arabic verb "pur et simple," which the student is particularly requested to commit carefully to memory before he proceeds a step farther. In order to do this the more effectually he may write out as an exercise the two following verbs, viz., قَصَمَ "he broke;" and فَرَقَ "he separated." The first is precisely like فَعَلَ in every respect. The second differs in one single instance, viz., the vowel of the middle radical of the aorist active and consequently of the imperative throughout is *kasra*, not *fatḥa*; thus يَفْرِقُ,

etc., not يَفْرَق, as will be more fully explained hereafter. In the Passive Voice all verbs have precisely the same measure, as in فُعِلَ, thus نُصِحَ, فُرِقَ, etc.

Observations on the Tenses, of the Regular Triliteral Verb.

THE PRETERITE.

97. The reader may have observed that the persons of the Preterite Tense are formed by adding some sort of termination after the radicals. According to the Arabian grammarians these terminations are the personal pronouns in a more or less perfect state, either expressed or understood; and that is a good reason why the learner should have mastered the pronouns before coming to the verb. The middle radical of the preterite of several verbs takes *kasra*, and sometimes *ḍamma*, in place of *fatḥa*. Those that take *kasra* may be either transitive, as عَلِمَ "he knew," or intransitive, as فَرِحَ "he was glad," حَزِنَ "he was sad." Such verbs as take *ḍamma* for the middle radical of the preterite are always of an intransitive or neuter sense, as قَبُحَ "he was ugly," حَسُنَ "he was handsome."

a. There is this difference in meaning between neuters with *kasra* for the middle radical, and those that have *ḍamma*, viz., the former denotes an accidental state or condition, and the latter a state that is constant or natural; thus حَزِنَ "he was sad" from some accidental cause; قَبُحَ "he was deformed" naturally. In all verbs the vowels of the first and third radicals of the Preterite are always *fatḥa*.

b. There are some verbs that have two, or even all the three vowels, for the middle radical of the Preterite; but each with a shade of difference in the signification; thus, قَنَعَ "he begged humbly;" قَنِعَ "he was contented;" عَمَرَ "he built;" عَمِرَ "he lived long;" عَمُرَ "it was cultivated" or "inhabited."

c. When the third radical of the Preterite happens to be ت inert, and the appended termination begins with ت, the two similar letters naturally coalesce by *tashdīd*, thus ثَبَتْتَ in the 2nd person singular is written ثَبَتَّ and ثَبَتِّ, etc. In like manner when the third radical is ث it unites by *tashdīd* with the ت of the termination, but the ث does not alter its own form; لَبِثَ makes in the 2nd person singular لَبِثَّ. The same rule applies when the third radical is either د, ذ, ض, ط, or ظ, which have an affinity in sound to the letter ت; thus, عَبَدْتُ for عَبَدْتُ. If the third radical be ن it coalesces by *tashdīd* with the ن of the termination of 1st person plural and the 3rd person plural feminine, as أَمِنَّ for أَمِنْنَ, etc.

d. In De Sacy's "Grammaire Arabe," we are, at this stage of the work, treated with fifty or sixty pages 8vo. on the various idiomatic uses of the Preterite and Aorist Tenses. Such a discussion is altogether preposterous; as the subject evidently belongs to the Syntax, to which we accordingly postpone it.

THE AORIST.

98. The Aorist generally corresponds to our present tense and frequently to our future. It is formed, as may be observed in the paradigm, from the preterite by prefixing to the different persons, one or other of the letters ا, ت, ن or ي, and by adding one or more of the same as terminations.

The prefixed serviles have constantly *fatḥa*, excepting in the 1st, 2nd and 3rd of the derivative formations of the triliteral verb, and the primitive form of the quadriliterals, where they take *ḍamma*. If the second radical of the preterite has *ḍamma*, it remains also *ḍamma* in the Aorist; but if *kasra* it is changed to *fatḥa*, excepting نَعِمَ "it was pleasant," حَسِبَ "he thought," يَئِسَ "he despaired," يَبِسَ "it dried," فَضِلَ "he excelled," قَنِطَ "he despaired," and عَرِضَ "he appeared;" which may be pronounced either with *fatḥa* or *kasra* and even sometimes with *ḍamma*, as يَنْعَمُ, يَنْعِمُ, or يَنْعُمُ: so يَفْضَلُ, يَفْضِلُ, or يَفْضُلُ. But if the second radical takes *fatḥa* in the preterite it is changed in the Aorist to *ḍamma*, as كَتَبَ "he wrote," يَكْتُبُ: or to *kasra*, as ضَرَبَ "he struck," يَضْرِبُ; unless the second or third radical is a guttural letter, in which case, though it is frequently changed, it sometimes remains *fatḥa*, as نَبَحَ "he barked," يَنْبَحُ; دَخَلَ "he entered, يَدْخُلُ; شَغَلَ "he occupied," يَشْغَلُ; مَنَحَ "he presented," يَمْنَحُ; and in the same manner without a guttural رَكَنَ "he leant upon," يَرْكَنُ, and أَبَى "he refused," يَأْبَى—The last radical has *ḍamma*, but when followed by the serviles ا, ن, و, or ي, it is sometimes changed, and sometimes dropped. The Aorist, however, when preceded by certain particles, admits of several variations in the termination, which are classed under the grammatical heads of Apocope, Antithesis, and Paragoge.

a. The rules applicable to the middle vowel of the Aorist, and by consequence of the imperative, are neatly expressed in the following memorial couplet: فَتْحٌ كَسْرٍ۔فَتْحٌ ضَمٍّ۔فَتْحَتَانِ — كَسْرٌ فَتْحٍ۔كَسْرٌ كَسْرٍ۔ضَمَّتَانِ

which may be freely rendered "1. *Fatḥa* (on the medial of the preterite) may give *kasra* (as the medial of the aorist); 2. *Fatḥa* may give *ḍamma*; 3. They may be both *fatḥas*; 4. *Kasra* may give *fatḥa*; 5. *Kasra* may give *kasra*; and 6. *Ḍamma* gives *ḍamma*;" as in the six following examples:

	INFIN.	PART.	IMP.	AORIST.	PRET.	
"He struck."	ضَرْبًا	ضَارِبٌ	اِضْرِبْ	يَضْرِبُ	ضَرَبَ	1
"He assisted."	نَصْرًا	نَاصِرٌ	اُنْصُرْ	يَنْصُرُ	نَصَرَ	2
"He opened."	فَتْحًا	فَاتِحٌ	اِفْتَحْ	يَفْتَحُ	فَتَحَ	3
"He knew."	عِلْمًا	عَالِمٌ	اِعْلَمْ	يَعْلَمُ	عَلِمَ	4
"He counted."	حَسْبًا	حَاسِبٌ	اِحْسِبْ	يَحْسِبُ	حَسِبَ	5
"He was generous."	كَرَمًا	كَارِمٌ	اُكْرُمْ	يَكْرُمُ	كَرُمَ	6

99. Apocope, which, generally speaking, gives the Aorist a past signification, not only converts the *ḍamma* of the last radical into *jazm*, but cuts off the final ن everywhere, excepting in the feminine plural. The particles which occasion this apocope are لَمْ "not," لَمَّا "not yet, لا "no, not," and لِ when prefixed to the Aorist in an imperative sense: لَمْ يَنْصُرْ "he did not assist," may answer as a general example.

PLURAL. FEM.	PLURAL. MASC.	DUAL. FEM.	DUAL. MASC.	SINGULAR. FEM.	SINGULAR. MASC.	PER.
لَمْ يَنْصُرْنَ	لَمْ يَنْصُرُوا	لَمْ تَنْصُرَا	لَمْ يَنْصُرَا	لَمْ تَنْصُرْ	لَمْ يَنْصُرْ	3
لَمْ تَنْصُرْنَ	لَمْ تَنْصُرُوا	لَمْ تَنْصُرَا		لَمْ تَنْصُرِي	لَمْ تَنْصُرْ	2
لَمْ نَنْصُرْ				لَمْ أَنْصُرْ		1

a. To the above particles may be added the following: اِنْ "if;" مَنْ and اَيٌّ "whoever;" مَا "whatever;" along with its compounds كُلَّما "all that;" كُلَّمَا "every time that;" اَيْنَ , حَيْثُمَا , and اَيْنَمَا "wherever;" اَنَّي "howsoever;" كَيْفَمَا and كَيْفَ "however;" مَهْمَا "as often as;" اِذَامَا , مَتَي , and اَيَّانَ "when," "whenever;" and in poetry اِذَا "when;" provided, however, another verb in the retributive sense (as "whatever you will do, I will do") is subjoined in the same sentence. If both verbs are of a future signification, they conform to this rule; if only the first that does the same, but if the last alone is future, it follows either this, or the general rule; thus, مَا تَصْنَعْ اَصْنَعْ "whatever you will do, I will do;" مَا تَصْنَعْ صَنَعْتُ "whatever you will do, I did;" مَا صَنَعْتَ اَصْنَعْ or مَا صَنَعْتَ اَصْنَعُ "whatever you did, I will do." This rule holds good also when an imperative precedes, to which the future is responsive; thus, اُنْصُرْنِي اَنْصُرْكَ "assist me, I will assist thee."

100. Antithesis, by the influence of another set of particles, cuts off the final ن in the same manner, and changes the *ḍamma* of the third radical to *fatḥa*. These are لَنْ "by no means, not at all;" لِ , اَنْ , كَيْ , لِكَيْ , كَيْلَا , لِكَيْلَا "that, in order to, because;" لِئَلَّا , اَلَّا , "lest not, so as not;" اَوْ "or;" حَتَّي "until." Also فَ prefixed to a future, referring to a preceding word, اُنْصُرْنِي فَاَنْصُرَكَ "assist me, and I will assist you;" likewise وَ when it implies "and at the same time," as لَا تَأْكُلِ ٱلسَّمَكَ وَتَشْرَبَ ٱللَّبَنَ "do not eat fish, and at the same time drink milk;" and also اِذَنْ or اِذًا "well! do so! come

on!" etc.: لَنْ يَنْصُرَ "he will by no means assist," is here put for a general example.

PLURAL. FEM.	PLURAL. MASC.	DUAL. FEM.	DUAL. MASC.	SINGULAR. FEM.	SINGULAR. MASC.	PER.
لن ينصرن	لن ينصروا	لن تنصرا	لن ينصرا	لن تنصر	لن ينصر	3
لن تنصرن	لن تنصروا	لن تنصرا		لن تنصري	لن تنصر	2
لن ننصر				لن انصر		1

101. Paragoge adds to the Aorist ـَنَّ or ـَنْ (but this last is added only in the singular, and in the plural masculine and common) when it denotes "commanding," "wishing," "intreating," or "asking about futurity," in the manner following. For example, when preceded by the particle هَلْ, which has no equivalent in English, but corresponds to the Latin *an?* or *num?* it will be as follows: هَلْ يَنْصُرَنَّ "will he assist?"

EXAMPLE.

PLURAL. F.	PLURAL. M.	DUAL. F.	DUAL. M.	SINGULAR. FEM.	SINGULAR. MASC.
هل ينصرنانِّ	هل ينصرنّ	هل تنصرانِّ	هل ينصرانِّ	هل تنصرنّ	هل ينصرنّ
هل تنصرنانِّ	هل تنصرنّ	هل تنصرانِّ		هل تنصرِنّ	هل تنصرنّ
هل ننصرنّ				هل انصرنّ	

The particle لَيْتَ "would to God," etc., requires ـَنْ to be added to the singular of the Aorist and to the plural masculine and common; as لَيْتَ يَنْصُرَنْ "would to God he would assist," where the single نْ merely is added, and the *ḍamma* of the last radical changed into *fatḥa*.

EXAMPLE.

	SINGULAR. MASC.	SINGULAR. FEM.	PLURAL. MASC.
3	لَيْتَ يَنْصُرَنَّ	لَيْتَ تَنْصُرَنَّ	لَيْتَ يَنْصُرُنَّ
2	لَيْتَ تَنْصُرَنَّ	لَيْتَ تَنْصُرِنَّ	لَيْتَ تَنْصُرُنَّ
1	لَيْتَ أَنْصُرَنَّ		لَيْتَ نَنْصُرَنَّ

After this mode may be inflected لِيَنْصُرَنَّ and لِيَنْصُرَنْ "let him assist;" لَا تَنْصُرَنَّ and لَا تَنْصُرَنْ "do not assist;" or when preceded by an oath, as وَٱللّٰهِ يَنْصُرَنَّ "by God he will assist;" or فَوَٱللّٰهِ لَنَقْتُلَنَّ "then by God we will kill."

102. The Aorist is restricted to a future signification when preceded by the negative لن "not at all," together with the particles سَوْفَ, سَفْ, سَوْ, and سَ; which is also often the case with لَا, as فَنَحْنُ لَا نَرْحَمُ مَنْ شَكَا وَلَا نَرِقُّ لِمَنْ بَكَا "for we will not pity him who laments, nor be moved for him who weeps." This effect of لَا, however, takes place only when neither of the negative particles لَمْ, لَمَّا, or مَا, have occurred in the phrase before. When these rules do not operate, or when the indefinite is preceded by مَا, it becomes a present tense: مَنْ يَفْعَلْ ذَلِكَ عُدْوَانًا وَ ظُلْمًا فَسَوْفَ نُصْلِيهِ نَارًا "he who shall do that maliciously and unjustly, we will punish him by fire."

OF THE IMPERATIVE.

103. The Imperative, which is used only in the second person, corresponds with our Imperative in affirmative com-

mands and exhortations. Like the Aorist it sometimes adds the Paragogical *nūn* annexed, as أُنْصُرَنَّ "do thou assist," etc. This mood is formed by prefixing ا, called the *alif* of union, and written آ when another word precedes. When beginning a sentence it has always *kasra*, as اِعْلَمْ "know thou;" اِضْرِبْ "strike thou;" unless the vowel of the penult radical, which is always the same with that of the future, be *ḍamma*, when ا also takes *ḍamma*, as أُنْصُرْ "assist thou;" the first and last radicals being inert. The initial *alif* is sometimes dropped when فَ or وَ are prefixed. In the formation of the genders and numbers, the final serviles ا, ن, و, and ي are employed as in the Aorist. The Imperative being used, as we have stated, only in the second person, the other persons are supplied by the Aorist; لِ with a *kasra* being prefixed, as لِيَنْصُرْ "let him assist;" لِنَنْصُرْ "let us assist;" which is also sometimes the case with the second, as لِتَنْصُرْ "assist thou;" but the ل drops *kasra* and becomes inert when فَ or وَ is prefixed, as فَلْيَنْصُرْ "then let him assist;" لِ itself being even then sometimes omitted. The second person singular of the Imperative of the primitive verb is sometimes represented by an indeclinable word of the form فَعَالِ or فِعَالِ; thus نَزَالِ or نِزَالِ "alight thou."

OF THE PARTICIPLE ACTIVE OR NOUN OF AGENCY.

104. The participle of the primitive triliteral verb in the active voice is of the form فَاعِلٌ; and in the passive of the form مَفْعُولٌ. There are however many other forms; and particularly فَعِيلٌ and فَعُولٌ, which are both active and passive.

It has been objected to these participles that they are merely verbal adjectives, conveying no idea of time. It would seem, however, that they are rather of all times, according to the context, as in the following instance, وَٱللّٰهُ بَصِيرٌ بِمَا يَعْمَلُونَ "God is seeing (sees) what they do," where بَصِيرٌ evidently expresses present time.

OF THE INFINITIVE OR VERBAL NOUN.

105. The Infinitive, in Arabic, differs somewhat from the same part of the verb in most European languages; inasmuch as it is always a verbal noun, and generally declinable in the singular as a triptote. It is used often adverbially in the accusative case, and, by a peculiar idiom, is joined sometimes in construction with its own verb, to give a greater energy to the expression, thus ضَرَبَهُ ضَرْبًا literally, "he struck him striking," *i.e.*, "he struck him severely."

a. Mr. Richardson, in his Arabic Grammar, and of course his mere copyists, say "that the Infinitive (in Arabic) differs *greatly* from those of *all other* languages!" This is too sweeping an assertion, and besides, it contains *three bits* of nonsense—1st, it is ungrammatical or illogical; 2nd, it is untrue; and 3rd, it is absurd in any *one* man to speak in this style of "all other languages." In Greek, German, and Italian, the Infinitive is frequently employed as a verbal noun—just as it is in Arabic.

b. The Infinitives of the primitive transitive verbs are formed regularly, as فَعْلٌ, etc., in the paradigm; but those of the intransitives are irregular, and reducible to no rule, without innumerable exceptions. Grammarians make in all thirty-six different forms, as under:

نَصِرٌ	28	نُصْرَى	19	نَصْرَةٌ	10	نَصْرٌ	1
نَصِرَةٌ	29	نِصْرَى	20	نُصْرَةٌ	11	نُصْرٌ	2
نُصُورٌ	30	نَصَرَى	21	نِصْرَةٌ	12	نِصْرٌ	3
نَصُورَةٌ	31	نَصْرَانٌ	22	نَصَرَةٌ	13	نِصَرٌ	4
نُصُورَةٌ	32	نُصْرَانٌ	23	نَصِرَةٌ	14	نُصَرٌ	5
مَنْصَرٌ	33	نِصْرَانٌ	24	نَصَارَةٌ	15	نَصَرٌ	6
مَنْصَرَةٌ	34	نَصَرَانٌ	25	نُصَارَةٌ	16	نَصَارٌ	7
مَنْصِرٌ	35	نَصُورٌ	26	نِصَارَةٌ	17	نُصَارٌ	8
مَنْصِرَةٌ	36	نَصِيرٌ	27	نَصْرَى	18	نِصَارٌ	9

c. The Infinitives of the derivative intransitives are formed in a similar manner, by inserting the characteristic serviles, and observing the general rules, as in the other inflections. They are, however, subject to various irregularities, for attaining a knowledge of which, a dictionary is the simplest mode, and indeed the only proper guide.

OF THE DERIVATIVE FORMATIONS.

106. There are twelve distinct formations of verbs derived from the primitive triliteral. The last we have just detailed in full; and the derived forms, all of which bear some affinity more or less close to the primitive, are divided into three classes according as they are augmented by one, two, or three of the servile letters. The verb فَعَلَ "he made," is still re-

tained as a general paradigm. It is well adapted to serve as a model, as its three radical letters are so clearly perceptible to the eye.

107. The Derivative Formations are inflected precisely on the same principles as the primitive form; the persons having the same relation to the leading word in each tense, as those in the foregoing paradigms have to فَعَلَ يَفْعُلُ and فَعِلَ يَفْعَلُ etc. It will be only requisite, therefore, in place of swelling the grammar unnecessarily with a great number of whole length paradigms, to give the first word alone of every tense, leaving it to the learner, by way of exercise, to fill up the other persons, which he may find to be a considerable help to his memory, as tending to make a more lasting impression than several cursory readings. Of the Derivatives, the 3rd, 4th, 6th, 7th, and 9th formations in general appear to occur most frequently, and therefore ought to have the greatest attention bestowed upon them. Next to these are the 1st, 2nd, and 5th formations; whilst the other four, but more especially the two last, are more confined in their use. The 3rd, 6th, and the following formations which take servile ا in the beginning, drop that letter in the aorist and participle, as may be observed in the paradigms; and the 4th and 5th, where the initial is تَ, frequently omit the latter in those persons of the aorist whose characteristic is ت, as تَنَصَّرُ for تَتَنَصَّرُ. We have subjoined a table of all the formations of the Derivative Verbs, in which the student will see at one view the third person singular of the preterite and aorist of each; the second person singular of the imperative as well as the participles and infinitives.

PRIMITIVE FORM.

INFIN.	PART.	IMP.	AORIST.	PRET.
فِعل	فَاعِل	اِفعَل	يَفعَلُ	فَعَلَ

DERIVATIVE FORMATIONS.

Class	INFIN.	PART.	IMP.	AORIST.	PRET.	
Class First.	تَفعِيلٌ	مُفَعِّلٌ	فَعِّلْ	يُفَعِّلُ	فَعَّلَ	I.
	مُفَاعَلَةٌ	مُفَاعِلٌ	فَاعِلْ	يُفَاعِلُ	فَاعَلَ	II.
	اِفعَالٌ	مُفعِلٌ	اَفعِلْ	يُفعِلُ	اَفعَلَ	III.
Class Second.	تَفَعُّلٌ	مُتَفَعِّلٌ	تَفَعَّلْ	يَتَفَعَّلُ	تَفَعَّلَ	IV.
	تَفَاعُلٌ	مُتَفَاعِلٌ	تَفَاعَلْ	يَتَفَاعَلُ	تَفَاعَلَ	V.
	اِنْفِعَالٌ	مُنفَعِلٌ	اِنفَعِلْ	يَنفَعِلُ	اِنفَعَلَ	VI.
	اِفْتِعَالٌ	مُفتَعِلٌ	اِفتَعِلْ	يَفتَعِلُ	اِفتَعَلَ	VII.
	اِفْعِلَالٌ	مُفعَلٌّ	اِفعَلِلْ	يَفعَلُّ	اِفعَلَّ	VIII.
Class Third.	اِسْتِفعَالٌ	مُستَفعِلٌ	اِستَفعِلْ	يَستَفعِلُ	اِستَفعَلَ	IX.
	اِفْعِيلَالٌ	مُفعَالٌّ	اِفعَالِلْ	يَفعَالُّ	اِفعَالَّ	X.
	اِفْعِيعَالٌ	مُفعَوعِلٌ	اِفعَوعِلْ	يَفعَوعِلُ	اِفعَوعَلَ	XI.
	اِفْعِوَّالٌ	مُفعَوِّلٌ	اِفعَوِّلْ	يَفعَوِّلُ	اِفعَوَّلَ	XII.

General Significations of the Derivative Verb with reference to the Primitive.

108. It remains for us now to describe briefly the nature and peculiarities of the Derivative Formations of the Verb which may be deduced from the primitive triliteral root. These are generally reckoned to be twelve in number, or, according to some Grammarians, fourteen. They have all the same terminations or inflections as the primitive verb. Grammarians very improperly call them conjugations; but this term is apt to mislead the student, whose ideas of a conjugation are already formed according to the general usage of the Latin and French grammars, etc. Let not the student be alarmed, then, when he hears of the fifteen conjugations of the Arabic language, for there is in reality but one conjugation, according to our notions of the term. Instead of conjugations, then, I have here throughout made use of the term Formations.

a. Upon the various significations of the different derived formations of the verb, some grammarians have entered into long details; but, although well worth the notice of the curious investigator, these inquiries need not long occupy the attention of the student, especially at the present stage of his studies. The brief remarks here made will not be found without use, but it is only by reading and consulting the dictionary, that a knowledge can be gained of the true significations of the various formations. However minute might be the observations made upon the different meanings of the derivatives, we should still find many exceptions, which can only be learned by use; and the same must be said as to the particular formations, in which any given verb is to be found. Some roots are to be met with in only one formation, most are in several, none in all.

109. The source, or third person singular, of the preterite tense of the primary verb, consists, as we have before stated, of three consonants, the first and last of which have always *fatḥa* for their vowel; and the middle letter has *fatḥa*, as a general rule, when the verb is transitive or active; and either *kasra* or *ḍamma* when neuter or intransitive; thus, كَتَبَ "he wrote," حَزِنَ "he was sad," عَظُمَ "he was great."

110. The first derivative formation doubles the middle letter of the primitive root, and its vowels are always three *fatḥas*, as in the preceding table. If the primitive root is transitive, the first formation is *causal;* thus, كَتَبَ "he wrote," becomes in the first formation كَتَّبَ which means "he caused to write," or "taught writing." Again, when the root is a neuter or intransitive verb, the first formation is transitive; thus, حَزِنَ "he was sad," حَزَّنَ "he saddened," or "he vexed." A few verbs of this formation are derived from nouns, and signify to form or produce whatever the noun signifies; thus, from خُبْزٌ "bread," is formed خَبَّزَ "he made bread, or baked." Another peculiarity of this formation is the ascribing of the sense of the primitive root to a given object; thus, from كُفْرٌ "infidelity," comes the infinitive تَكْفِير, which signifies "calling one an infidel;" so from كِذْب "lying," comes تَكْذِيب "accusing one of falsehood," or "giving one the lie."

a. Verbs in the first formation are frequently, however, mere synonyms of the primitive, or only distinguished by being understood as a species of intensives; as كَسَرَ and كَسَّرَ "he broke," فَرَقَ and فَرَّقَ "he separated" or "dispersed," etc.

111. The second formation inserts *alif* after the first radical, and its vowels are always three *fatḥas*, as in the table. It is generally transitive, and often denotes a reciprocal action; thus, بُولُسُ ضَارَبَ بُطْرُسَ "Paul beat Peter," implying, at the same time, that "Peter beat Paul in return;" and, in an intransitive sense, as بُطْرُسُ قَاعَدَ بُولُسَ "Peter sat down with Paul;" كَاتَبَ "he wrote to" or "corresponded with" (another person).

a. The second formation has frequently the signification of the primitive, with this difference, however, that the indirect complement of the primitive triliteral root, which in the original form demanded the intervention of a preposition, becomes here a direct complement and meets the verb immediately; thus, كَتَبَ and رَسَلَ have in the original form the preposition إِلَي before the indirect complement of the preceding verb; as كَتَبْتُ إِلَي ٱلْمَلِكِ رِسَالَةً "I wrote a letter to the king." Now if we here employ the second formation, the person to whom we write becomes the direct complement, and dispenses with the preposition إِلَي; thus, كَاتَبْتُ ٱلْمَلِكَ and رَاسَلْتُ ٱلْوَزِيرَ "I wrote to the king," "I sent to the Vazīr." So with intransitive verbs also; as جَلَسَ "he sat down," in the third form signifies, to sit down with, or near one; as جَالَسَ ٱلسُّلْطَانَ "he sat down near the Sultan." In the first form this would be جَلَسَ عِنْدَ ٱلسُّلْطَانِ.

112. The third formation prefixes *alif*, and it has always for its vowels three *fatḥas*, as in the table. Like the first

formation, it gives a causal or active signification to the primitive; thus, اَكْتَبَ "he taught writing," or "he dictated," or "made another write;" so, from عَظُمَ "he was great," comes اَعْظَمَ "he deemed (another) to be great," that is, he honoured," or "he respected" (another). It will be observed, then, as a general rule, that the first and third formations are the causals of the primitive triliteral root.

113. The fourth formation, which prefixes the letter ت, with a *fatḥa*, to the first formation, is generally of the passive or submissive sense of the root; thus, عَلِمَ "he knew;" عَلَّمَ "he taught;" تَعَلَّمَ "he was taught," or "he learned." So, from اَدَبْ "manners," "morals," or "polite literature," comes the infinitive of the first formation تَأْدِيبْ "teaching manners," "chastisement;" and thence the infinitive of the fourth formation تَأَدُّبْ "submitting to be taught manners."

114. The fifth formation prefixes ت, with a *fatḥa*, to the second. It generally denotes reciprocity, co-partnership, or association; thus, مُضَارَبَةْ "beating each other;" مُقَاتَلَةْ "slaying each other;" مُحَارَبَةْ "fighting together," etc. So تَكَاتَبَ "he corresponded (by writing);" تَلَاعَبَ "he played with" (some one). Lastly, it may denote "pretending," the sense of the primitive; thus, تَمَارَضَ "he feigned sickness," or, as they say at sea, "he shammed Abram;" so from جَهْلْ "ignorance," comes تَجَاهُلْ "pretending ignorance."

115. The sixth formation prefixes the syllable اِنْ to the triliteral root, which is then pronounced with three *fatḥas*,

whatever it may have originally been. This formation is always of a passive signification; hence, strictly speaking, it is never used in the passive form; thus, كَسَرَ "he broke;" اِنْكَسَرَ "it was broken;" so the infinitives, اِنْقِلابٌ "being changed," اِنْكِسارٌ "being broken," are altogether passive in signification.

116. The seventh formation prefixes ا, and inserts ت (sometimes د or ط) between the first and second radical of the triliteral, as may be seen in the table. Generally speaking, it denotes the passive or reflexive sense of the primitive triliteral root; thus, فَرَقَ "he divided;" اِفْتَرَقَ "it went to pieces;" ضَرَبَ "he beat;" اِضْطَرَبَ "he beat himself" (in agitation, etc.); hence the infinitive اِضْطِرَابٌ "perplexity." Sometimes it denotes reciprocity, etc., like the fifth formation; thus, اِخْتِصَامٌ "mutual contention;" اِجْتِمَاعٌ "collecting together."

a. In this seventh formation the place of the servile ت is supplied by د whenever the first letter in the root is د, ذ, or ز; thus, for اِدْتَرَأَ "he was repelled," is written اِدَّرَأَ; for اِذْتَكَرَ "it was recorded" اِدَّكَرَ, where the radical ذ is changed into د, or اِذَّكَرَ, where the د becomes ذ, or اِذْدَكَرَ, where both remain. When the first letter of the root is one of these, ص, ض, ط, or ظ, the ت is changed into ط, as اِصْطَبَغَ "it was dyed," for اِصْتَبَغَ; اِطَّبَعَ "it was printed," for اِطْتَبَعَ; اِظَّلَمَ "he was unjustly treated," for اِظْطَلَمَ, in which instance the ط is also changed into ظ, and is joined to the first by *tashdīd.* Lastly, when the first radical is ث, و, or ي, it is changed into ت, and the two ت's unite by *tashdīd*, as اِتَّبَتَ for اِتْتَبَتَ, اِتَّجَرَ for اِوْتَجَرَ, اِتَّسَرَ for اِيْتَسَرَ.

117. The eighth and tenth formations designate *colours*, the tenth with more intensity; thus, اِصْفَرَّ "it was yellow;" اِصْفَارَّ "it was very yellow." These formations are also used for expressing deformity, as اِضْجَمَّ or اِضْجَامَّ "he was wry-faced," "he had a distorted face;" اِعْوَجَّ "it was crooked."

118. The ninth formation prefixes اِسْتَ to the primitive root, as shewn in the table. Its general property is, asking, wishing, or demanding, the state or action expressed by the primitive; thus, غَفَرَ "he pardoned;" اِسْتَغْفَرَ "he begged pardon." This formation agrees nearly with the Latin Desiderative Verbs, formed from the second supine by adding *rio*, such as *esurio*, "I desire to eat," from *esu;* so *cœnaturio*, "I wish I had my supper," from *cœnatu.* For a full account of the various shades of meaning peculiar to the derivative formations of the Verb, the reader may consult Dr. Lumsden's Persian and Arabic Grammar, as well as De Sacy's Grammaire Arabe, where the subject is absolutely exhausted.

119. The eleventh and twelfth formations, which occur but seldom, are only employed to heighten the energy of the primitive, as we do by adding "exceedingly," "very," or some such synonymous word; thus, from خَشُنَ "it was harsh," is formed اِخْشَوْشَنَ "it was very harsh;" from عَلَا "he adhered," comes اِعْلَوَّطَ "he adhered firmly" (to the neck of his camel): hence, figuratively, "he strenuously prosecuted his undertaking."

120. We now come to the Passive Voice of the Derivative Verbs, and for the sake of variety we will adopt as our model the verb نَصَرَ "he assisted." It cannot *now* lead to any mistake, after we have fully detailed the model فَعَلَ. The student has only to bear in mind that the three letters ن, ص, and ر, have taken the place of ف, ع, and ل respectively.

PASSIVE VOICE.

	PARTICIPLE.	AORIST.	PRETERITE.	FORMATION.
CLASS FIRST.	منصر	ينصر	نصر	I.
	مناصر	يناصر	نوصر	II.
	منصر	ينصر	أنصر	III.
CLASS SECOND.	متنصر	يتنصر	تنصر	IV.
	متناصر	يتناصر	تنوصر	V.
	منصر	ينصر	أنصر	VI.
	منتصر	ينتصر	أنتصر	VII.
CLASS THIRD.	مستنصر	يستنصر	أستنصر	IX.
	منصوصر	ينصوصر	أنصوصر	XI.
	منصور	ينصور	أنصور	XII.

a. The student may observe that we have in the above table omitted the VIII. and X. formations, which, from their nature, have no Passive Voice.

On Quadriliteral Verbs.

121. Of these there are only three different formations from the primitive which itself corresponds with the primitive of the triliterals; the first Quadriliteral formation agrees with the fourth triliteral; the second with the sixth; and the third with the eighth. They are formed as follows: primitive formation قَمْطَرَ; first derivative تَقَمْطَرَ; second اِقْمَنْطَرَ; and third اِقْمَطَرَّ. The primitive consists simply of the four radicals, as دَحْرَجَ "he turned, or revolved;" the first derived formation is augmented by one servile, as تَدَحْرَجَ "it was turned;" and the second and third by two, as اِحْرَنْجَمَ "it was tumultuous;" اِقْشَعَرَّ "he was horror-struck," "his hair stood on end."

a. This species of verbs, however, bears a very small proportion to the triliteral, occurring but seldom. There will be no occasion therefore to detain the learner longer upon the subject than just to present him with the leading words of each tense, as in the derivative triliterals; the other persons being inflected from these on the same principles, by the addition of the servile characteristics, already described.

Active Voice.

PRIMITIVE FORM.

INFINITIVE.	PARTICIPLE.	IMPERATIVE.	AORIST.	PRETERITE.
قِمْطَارًا	مُقَمْطِرٌ	قَمْطِرْ	يُقَمْطِرُ	قَمْطَرَ

DERIVATIVE FORMATIONS.

INFINITIVE.	PARTICIPLE.	IMPERATIVE.	AORIST.	PRET.	FORMATION.
تقمطرا	متقمطر	تقمطر	يتقمطر	تقمطر	I.
اقمنطارا	مقمنطر	اقمنطر	يقمنطر	اقمنطر	II.
اقمطرارا	مقمطر	اقمطرر	يقمطر	اقمطر	III.

Passive Voice.

PRIMITIVE FORM.

PARTICIPLE.	AORIST.	PRETERITE.
مقمطر	يقمطر	قمطر

DERIVATIVE FORMATIONS.

متقمطر	يتقمطر	تقمطر	I.
مقمنطر	يقمنطر	اقمنطر	II.
مقمطر	يقمطر	أقمطر	III.

b. The observation made, § 106, with regard to the initial characteristics ا and ت, in the derivative verbs, answers likewise to the 1st, 2nd, and 3rd of the above formations.

122. In concluding my description of the Perfect Arabic Verb, I must offer a few observations on those points in which I have differed from preceding writers. In the first place, I have deviated from them entirely in the arrangement and mode of treatment of the subject; secondly, I have discarded the term Future Tense from the paradigm, and instead thereof, have used the word Aorist as the more appropriate;

and lastly, I have dismissed from my work the term Conjugation, which, in the sense hitherto employed in Arabic grammars and lexicons, is a downright absurdity; and to be tolerated only because writers on the subject have not had the moral courage to substitute a more appropriate denomination. I shall most probably be told by gentlemen of the *red tape* that these innovations of mine will lead to confusion in perusing the best Arabic lexicons, such as Freytag's edition of Golius, etc. I can prove to them in a moment that their objection is utterly groundless. I am the very last person to adopt an innovation of any sort unless I feel convinced that it is a rational improvement. Let us for example take the following verbal root with such of its (so-called) conjugations as are in use, slightly abridged from Freytag's edition of Golius, and partly from Schalch's Vocabulary:

a. سَلَمَ (Fut. i.) "he constructed a bucket for drawing water;" سَلِمَ "he was safe, sound, or unblemished." II. conj. "he made secure;" "he saluted." III. conj. "he made peace or friendship with another." IV. conj. "he submitted or obeyed;" "he became a Muslim." V. conj. "he accepted or received;" "he was made a Muslim." VI. conj. (dual or plur.) "they made peace one with another." VIII. conj. "he touched with his hand or lips the sacred black stone in the temple of Mecca." X. conj. "he submitted himself to the power of another;" "he gave himself up."

b. Now if I were to compile or edit an Arabic lexicon, the preceding article would stand as follows: viz. سَلَمَ (Aor. i.) "he constructed a bucket," etc.; سَلِمَ "he was safe, sound," etc.—I. formation, سَلَّم "he made secure," "he saluted."—II. f. سَالَمَ "he made peace," etc.—III. f. أَسْلَمَ "he submitted or obeyed," etc.—IV. f. تَسَلَّمَ "he accepted," etc.—V. f. تَسَالَمَ (dual or plur.) "they mutually made peace or friendship."—VII. f. إِستَلَمَ "he touched," etc.—IX. f. إِستَسلَمَ "he surrendered himself into the power of another," etc. Here the reader will observe that what Freytag and others call the *Second Conjugation*, I call the *First Formation*—and so on with the rest. In short, if you drop a *unit* from Freytag's Roman Numerals denoting the *Conjugation*, you will have *my numeral* which denotes the *Derivative Formation;* and, *vice versâ*, if you add a unit to my numerals, you will have the good old conjugation, if you think it of any advantage to you.

c. I cannot help drawing the reader's attention to a very serious omission on the part of Freytag in his otherwise invaluable Lexicon. The work abounds in certain Latin abbreviations, such as *cca.* "construitur cum accusativo;" *ccga.* "construitur cum gemino accusativo," etc. etc.; together with some thirty or forty others. Now what I complain of is, that—at least in my copy of Freytag's Lexicon, in four quarto volumes—the learned Professor has nowhere condescended to give one scrap of information respecting the abbreviations aforesaid. Whether he has been more attentive to the learner's convenience in his abridged edition I am not able to say, as I have not got the work at hand.

Of the Surd Verb—الأَصَمّ, *also called* المُضَاعَف, i.e. "*doubled.*"

123. The term *Surd* is applied to such triliteral verbs as have the second and third radicals the same; thus, فَرَّ for فَرَرَ "he fled," and مَدَّ for مَدَدَ "he extended," are called *Surds*. In all the

Arabic grammars that I have yet seen (and I have seen several), this class of verbs is, I think, very improperly placed among the *irregulars.* Now the seeming irregularity is really *euphonic* and is reducible to a few simple rules, as follows. In all the inflections where, according to the conjugation of the perfect triliteral verb, the last radical is movable the penult radical coalesces with the last by *tashdīd,* and the vowel of the penult is then suppressed, unless the letter preceding it has *jazm,* for then the vowel of the penult radical is given to the latter, which would otherwise have *jazm.* In all the inflections where, on the contrary, the last radical has *jazm,* these verbs are conjugated regularly; thus in the third person singular and masculine of the preterite, حَبَبَ "he loved," becomes حَبَّ ; but the second person singular of the same tense is regular; as حَبَبْتَ or حَبَبْتِ "thou hast loved."

a. In the third person of the singular masculine of the aorist يَحْبُبُ is contracted into يَحُبُّ, the *ḍamma* of the second radical passing to the first, in place of its *jazm.* If the aorist follows a particle producing *jazm,* or an apocope, it becomes regularly يَحْبُبْ because the last radical having *jazm,* no contraction takes place. Under the influence of these particles, *fatḥa* or *kasra* may be given to the last radical in lieu of *jazm*; in this case the contraction returning يَفِرَّ , يَفِرِّ for يَفْرِرْ. In verbs of which the second radical in the indefinite tense bears *ḍamma,* the same vowel may also be given to the last; thus, instead of يَمْدُدْ we may write with the contraction يَمُدَّ, يَمُدِّ, or even يَمُدُّ.

b. The imperative preserves its regular form. According to the rule of the Surd Verb we should write اِفِرِّي , اِفِرَّا , and اِفِرُّوا , but the reason why the rule is not here followed, is, that the *alif* of union is always followed by a letter bearing *jazm*. Beside the regular form, the imperative has another, in which the insertion of the second radical in the third does take place, except in the plural feminine. *Alif* of the imperative is omitted here, according to the rule, by which it is never prefixed to a letter bearing a vowel.

PLURAL.		DUAL.	SINGULAR.		
FEM.	MASC.	COMM.	FEM.	MASC.	PERS.
اِفْرِرْنَ	فِرُّوا	فِرَّا	فِرِّي	فِرَّ or فِرِّ	2

c. Surd Verbs follow in the passive voice the same rules as in the active; thus, فُرَّ is for فُرِرَ, *kasra* being dropped, because the preceding letter already bears a vowel; in the aorist it is يُفَرُّ for يُفْرَرُ, *fatḥa* being given to the preceding letter which before had *jazm;* but in the third person plural feminine without contraction يُفْرَرْنَ. The derivative formations of Surd Verbs follow a similar rule of contractions in those forms which admit it. All the peculiarities above mentioned are fully illustrated in the following paradigm of مَدَّ "he extended," and فَرَّ "he fled."

Active Voice.

PRETERITE.

PLURAL.		DUAL.		SINGULAR.		
FEM.	MASC.	FEM.	MASC.	FEM.	MASC.	PERSON.
مَدَدْنَ	مَدُّوا	مَدَّتَا	مَدَّا	مَدَّتْ	مَدَّ	3rd
مَدَدْتُنَّ	مَدَدْتُمْ	مَدَدْتُمَا		مَدَدْتِ	مَدَدْتَ	2nd
مَدَدْنَا				مَدَدْتُ		1st

AORIST.

PLURAL. FEM.	PLURAL. MASC.	DUAL. FEM.	DUAL. MASC.	SINGULAR. FEM.	SINGULAR. MASC.	PERSON.
يَمْدُدْنَ	يَمُدُّونَ	تَمُدَّانِ	يَمُدَّانِ	تَمُدُّ	يَمُدُّ	3rd
تَمْدُدْنَ	تَمُدُّونَ	تَمُدَّانِ		تَمُدِّينَ	تَمُدُّ	2nd
نَمُدُّ				أَمُدُّ		1st

IMPERATIVE.

اُمْدُدْنَ	اُمْدُدُوا	اُمْدُدَا		اُمْدُدِي	اُمْدُدْ	2nd

PARTICIPLE.

مَادَّاتٌ	مَادُّونَ	مَادَّتَانِ	مَادَّانِ	مَادَّةٌ	مَادٌّ

INFINITIVE.

مَدًّا

d. The preterite of this class, with regard to the vowel points, follows the same rule with those of the perfect verbs whose middle radical is *ḍamma* or *kasra*, as مَسَّ "he touched," for مَسِسَ ; مَسِسْتَ "thou hast touched," etc. And the aorist corresponds with such as have *fatḥa* or *kasra* on the penult, as يَعَضُّ "he will bite," for يَعْضَضُ and يَفِرُّ "he will flee," for يَفْرِرُ. If preceded by the apocope-particles (see § 99) the last radical takes *jazm*, and the whole becomes regular, as لَمْ يَمْدُدْ "it does not extend;" or if the contraction do take place, *fatḥa* or *kasra* are substituted for *jazm*, as لَمْ يَعَضَّ or لَمْ يَعَضِّ "he will not bite;" and sometimes *ḍamma*, when the penult takes *ḍamma* also, as لَمْ يَمُدُّ "it does not extend."

Passive Voice.

PRETERITE.

مُدِدْنَ	مُدُّوا	مُدَّتَا	مُدَّا	مُدَّتْ	مُدَّ	3rd
مُدِدْتُنَّ	مُدِدْتُمْ	مُدِدْتُمَا		مُدِدْتِ	مُدِدْتَ	2nd
مُدِدْنَا				مُدِدْتُ		1st

AORIST.

PLURAL. FEM.	PLURAL. MASC.	DUAL. FEM.	DUAL. MASC.	SINGULAR. FEM.	SINGULAR. MASC.	PERSON.
يَمْدُدْنَ	يَمُدُّونَ	تَمُدَّانِ	يَمُدَّانِ	تَمُدُّ	يَمُدُّ	3rd
تَمْدُدْنَ	تَمُدُّونَ	تَمُدَّانِ		تَمُدِّينَ	تَمُدُّ	2nd
نَمُدُّ				أَمُدُّ		1st

PARTICIPLE.

مَمْدُودٌ مَمْدُودَةٌ | مَمْدُودَانِ مَمْدُودَتَانِ | مَمْدُودُونَ مَمْدُودَاتٌ

124. The imperative, it may be observed, is inflected regularly, though it is sometimes contracted, in which case the initial ا is dropped, because the following letter has a vowel (see § 36, *a.*) as,

مُدَّ مُدِّي مُدَّا مُدُّوا اُمْدُدْنَ

125. The derivative formations have the same affinity to the primitives as those of the perfect forms have to theirs; excepting, however, the 1st, 4th, and other derived formations, which, having already one characteristic *tashdīd*, cannot take another upon the same letter, and are conjugated therefore like the corresponding verbs of the regular system; thus, in the preterite active—أَمَدَّ for أَمْدَدَ; اِنْمَدَّ for اِنْمَدَدَ; اِسْتَمَدَّ for اِسْتَمْدَدَ. In like manner in the aorist active—يُمِدُّ for يُمْدِدُ; يَنْمَدُّ for يَنْمَدِدُ; يَسْتَمِدُّ for يَسْتَمْدِدُ.

PRET. OF 4TH FORMATION. SINGULAR. FEM.	MASC.	PRET. OF 1ST FORMATION. SINGULAR. FEM.	MASC.	PERSON.
تَمَدَّدَتْ	تَمَدَّدَ	مَدَّتْ	مَدَّ	3rd
تَمَدَّدْتِ	تَمَدَّدْتَ	مَدَدْتِ	مَدَدْتَ	2nd
تَمَدَّدْتُ		مَدَدْتُ		1st

And so on in the same manner with respect to the other formations, tenses, and persons.

a. The 8th and 10th formations of the perfect triliteral verbs, with the 3rd of the quadriliterals, which have their last radical doubled by *tashdīd*, it may be here remarked, are conjugated as this class of verbs ; for example: from the verb صَفَرَ we have,

AORIST.			PRETERITE.			FORMATION.
يَصْفَرُّ	for	يَصْفَرِرُ	اِصْفَرَّ	for	اِصْفَرَرَ	VIII.
يَصْفَارُّ		يَصْفَارِرُ	اِصْفَارَّ		اِصْفَارَرَ	X.
يَقْمَطِرُّ		يَقْمَطْرِرُ	اِقْمَطَرَّ		اِقْمَطْرَرَ	3rd Quad.

When the second letter of the *tashdīd* radicals requires *jazm*, they are then written separately, as اِقْمَطْرَرْتَ اِصْفَرَرْتَ.

126. The jazmated aorist and imperative may either be separated or contracted (the contraction taking *fatḥa* or *kasra*); as,

AORIST.

يَصْفَرِرْ	or	يَصْفَرَّ	or	يَصْفَرِّ
يَصْفَارِرْ		يَصْفَارَّ		يَصْفَارِّ
يَقْمَطْرِرْ		يَقْمَطِرَّ		يَقْمَطِرِّ

IMPERATIVE.

اِصْفَرِّ or اِصْفَرَّ or اِصْفَرِرْ

اِصْفَارِّ اِصْفَارَّ اِصْفَارِرْ

اِقْمَطِرِّ اِقْمَطِرَّ اِقْمَطْرِرْ

a. In further illustration of § 122 to 124 we subjoin two tables of the derived formations of the verb فَرَّ "he fled." We may also observe that in the derivative formations in Table I., as in the primitive, the contraction may be preserved in the aorist, and in the imperative, whenever the third radical ought by the influence of a particle preceding, to bear the symbol *jazm;* thus,

Derivative Formations bearing contraction.

IMPERATIVE.	AORIST.	PRETERITE.	FORMATION.
فَارِرْ	يُفَارُّ	فَارَّ for فَارَرَ	II.
أَفْرِرْ	يُفِرُّ	أَفَرَّ for أَفْرَرَ	III.
تَفَارَرْ	يَتَفَارُّ	تَفَارَّ for تَفَارَرَ	V.
اِنْفَرِرْ	يَنْفَرُّ	اِنْفَرَّ for اِنْفَرَرَ	VI.
اِفْتَرِرْ	يَفْتَرُّ	اِفْتَرَّ for اِفْتَرَرَ	VII.
اِسْتَفْرِرْ	يَسْتَفِرُّ	اِسْتَفَرَّ for اِسْتَفْرَرَ	IX.
اِفْرَوْرِرْ	يَفْرَوِرُّ	اِفْرَوَرَّ for اِفْرَوْرَرَ	XI.

b. The derivative formations to which *tashdīd* naturally belongs, or in which the 2nd and 3rd radicals are separated by servile letters, are not susceptible of contraction, as in those which follow.

Derivatives that do not contract.

IMPERATIVE.	AORIST.	PRETERITE.	FORMATION.
فْرِرْ	يَفِرُّ	فَرَّ	I.
تَفَرَّرْ	يَتَفَرَّرُ	تَفَرَّرَ	IV.
اِفْرِرْ	يَفْرِرُ	اِفَرَّ	VIII.
اِفْرَارِرْ	يَفْرَارُ	اِفْرَارَّ	X.
اِفْرَوِرْ	يَفْرَوِرُ	اِفْرَوَرَ	XII.

127. Verbs ending in ت or ن double these letters by *tashdīd* in those persons whose final characteristic serviles are respectively ت or ن, as زَيَّنَّا "we adorned," for زَيَّنْنَا; and سَكَتُّ "thou wert silent," for سَكَتْتُ. When the 3rd radical is ث, د, ذ, ض, ط, or ظ, although retained in writing, it coalesces in the same case with ت, which then takes *tashdīd*, as مَدَدتُّ: but neither these, nor the words beginning with ت or ن, when they coalesce with the initial characteristics of the 4th, 6th, and other derivative formations, are considered as irregulars; اِنَّقَب "it was dug through," for اِنْنَقَب; and اِتَّجَر "it was negociated," for اِتْتَجَر etc., being in every respect perfect verbs.

a. The penult of the aorist of the 8th and 10th formations takes also *kasra*, which drops in the contraction, because the antecedent letter has a vowel.

SECTION IV.

Of the Infirm or Imperfect Verbs, etc.

128. With regard to these, their irregularities arise entirely from the mutable nature of the infirm letters ا, و, and ي when used as radicals, which are either changed from one to another, dropped altogether, or deemed quiescent, when they remain; having, in general, no sound, according to Arabian grammarians, but what they derive from the vowel of the preceding letter. These deviations, however, are subject to certain rules and principles with which it is necessary for the learner to make himself acquainted. For the satisfaction, therefore, of those who may wish for a minute investigation of the causes of these interchangeable powers, the following observations are translated from Erpenius, with corrections from De Sacy, etc. This section the former of these grammarians not inaptly styles *vere aurea*; and it is every way deserving of the student's strictest attention.

a. The use of the term "quiescent," or "silent," in the above paragraph is *the true one*, meaning "not sounded;" and it shews at the same time the aptness of what I stated on the subject in § 26, *a.* In the Grammars by Richardson and Stewart the term *quiescent* is applied to an *inert* letter as well as to one *not sounded.*

General Rules on the Nature and Permutation of the Letters ا, و, *and* ي.

129. The letters ا, و, and ي, are often reciprocally substituted for one another, but never at the beginning of a word; nor in the middle or end, if preceded by *jazm*, in which case they always remain unchanged. When they are themselves destitute of vowels, preceded by a heterogeneous vowel (§ 30, *a.*), they are in that case rendered homogeneous to the preceding vowel; thus, ا is changed to و, as نُؤْيٌ for نَأْيٌ "a trench;" ا to ي, as بِئْرٌ for بِأْرٌ "a well;" و to ا, as نَارٌ for نَوَرٌ "fire;" و to ي, as مِيْعَادٌ for مِوْعَادٌ "said time or place;" ي to ا, as زَارٌ for زَيَرٌ "the roaring of a lion;" ي to و, as مُوقِنٌ for مُيْقِنٌ "rendering certain."

a. The letters و and ي sometimes remain after *fatḥa;* in this case, if inert, they form a diphthong with the preceding *fatḥa;* as in يَوْمٌ "a day," لَيْلٌ "a night;" but if they be not inert they are pronounced as a long *alif,* as رَمَيَهُ "he threw it," like رَمَاهُ ; غَزْوَةٌ "an assault."

b. The letters ا, و, and ي when quiescent, and followed by a jazmated letter are omitted, as يَخَفْ "let him dread," for يَخَافْ ; يَقُمْ "let him stand," for يَقُومْ ; يَسِرْ "let him go," for يَسِيرْ. The *alif* of union, however (see § 36), is not subjected to this rule, as فَٱنْصُرْ "therefore assist thou;" بِسْمِ for بِٱسْمِ "in the name of."

Rules peculiar to the Letter ا *Alif.*

130. The letter *alif,* in the middle of a word, when movable by *ḍamma* is changed into و; when by *kasra,* into ي, whether pre-

ceded by a vowel or jazmated letter; thus, أَوْبٌ for آاْبٌ "pastures;" سُئِلَ for سُالَ "he was asked." So after a long *alif* a similar rule holds, as قَائِلٌ for قَآءِلٌ "saying;" مَآؤُهُ for مَاءُهُ "his or its waters."

a. Alif, in the middle of a word, movable by *fatḥa*, if preceded by *ḍamma*, is changed into و; if by *kasra*, into ي, as دُوَبٌ for دُأَبٌ "studies;" فِيَةٌ for فِاَةٌ "a body of men." At the end of a word the letter *alif*, if preceded by *ḍamma*, is changed into و; if by *kasra*, into ي; thus, دَنُؤَ for دَنُأَ "it was vile;" خَطِيَ for خَطِاَ "he sinned or erred."

131. *Hamza* or *alif*, when inert, in the middle of a word, is changeable into ا, و, or ي inert, agreeably to the vowel preceding; the symbol of the *hamza* being wholly suppressed; thus, رَاسٌ for رَأْسٌ "the head;" so بُوسٌ for بُؤْسٌ "misfortune;" and ذِيبٌ for ذِئْبٌ "a wolf."

a. The symbol *hamza*, preceded by و or ي inert, acting as servile letters, is changeable after و into و, and after ي into ي, uniting with the preceding letter by *tashdīd*, and suppressing the *hamza* altogether; thus, مَقْرُوَّةٌ for مَقْرُوءَةٌ; خَطِيَّةٌ for خَطِيئَةٌ; and هَنِيٌّ for هَنِيءٌ.

b. In the middle of a word, if *hamza* should be preceded by an inert letter, other than و or ي, the *hamza* may be suppressed, and the vowel belonging to it transferred to the preceding letter, as مَسَلَةٌ for مَسْأَلَةٌ; مَسُولٌ for مَسْؤُولٌ; and تَسَلُ for تَسْأَلُ.

132. The letter أ, at the end of a word preceded by *fatḥa*,

when movable by *ḍamma*, is changed into و ; when by *kasra*, into ي , as تَقْتَؤُ for تَقْتَأُ "thou shalt desist;" سَنَيٍ for سَنَإٍ "of the leaves of senna." It is not incorrect, however, to write تَقْتَأُ or تَقْتَاءُ. *Alif-hamza*, at the end of a word, if preceded by *jazm*, is written as *hamza* only; but the vowel may be transferred to the jazmated letter, and *hamza* then becomes ا, و, or ي, according to the vowel preceding; thus, اَلْجَزُو for اَلْجَزْءُ ; اَلْجَزِي for اَلْجَزْءِ ; and اَلْجَزَا for اَلْجَزْءَ.

a. Should two *alif-hamzas* meet together in the same word, and the first be moved by a vowel, and the second be inert, the latter loses its *hamza*, and becomes merely an *alif* of prolongation changed, if need be, into و or ي ; thus, اٰامَنَ or آمَنَ for أَأْمَنَ "he believed." The *alif* of prolongation, preceded by another *alif* movable by *fatḥa*, is sometimes dropped; this is pointed out by the position of the *fatḥa*, which is then written perpendicularly, or by *madda*; thus, رَحْمٰنٌ for رَحْمَانٌ "merciful:" قِيٰمَةٌ for قِيَامَةٌ "the resurrection."

133. The inseparable particles بِ, فَ, لَ, لِ and وَ, which are used at the beginning of words, alter nothing in the nature of the *alif*, which is still considered to be the initial letter of the word, though those particles may be prefixed, as لِأَبٍ "to the father;" كَأُمٍّ "like the mother;" and not لِبٍ or كَوُمٍّ. Some particles, however, must be excepted, in which custom has established the change, as لِئَلَّا for لِأَنْ لَا "lest that;" and أَئِنْ for أَإِنْ "whether if."

134. When the interrogative particle أ (Lat. *an?* or *num?*) is followed by *alif-hamza*, if the second be moved by *fatḥa*, one of

them, with its vowel, is dropped, or a *hamza* is placed first, and then an *alif* with *madda*: thus, أَنتَ or آنتَ for أَأَنتَ; أَنذَرتَهُم or آنذرتهم for أَأَنذَرتَهُم; أَلآن or آلآن for أَأَلآن; أَلدّ or آلدّ for أَأَلدّ. If the second *hamza* have *ḍamma* for its vowel, the *alif* becomes و, or the second ا is suppressed and its *hamza* only retained: thus, أَونَبِّئُكُم or أُنَبِّئُكُم for أَأُنَبِّئُكُم. Finally, if the second *hamza* should have *kasra*, the *alif* is changed into ي; as أَيِن for أَإِن; أَيِذا for أَإِذا.

Rules peculiar to the letter و *Wāw.*

135. The letter *wāw* in the beginning of a word, when followed by another *wāw*, movable by a vowel, is changed into *alif-hamza*, to avoid the meeting of two *wāws*; thus, أَوَاصِل for وَوَاصِل pl. of وَاصِلَةٌ; أَوَاضِع for وَوَاضِع pl. of وَاضِحَةٌ; أَوَاقِي for وَوَاقِي pl. of وَاقِيَةٌ. If there be two *wāws* at the beginning of a word and the first be movable by *ḍamma*, it may be changed into *hamza*; thus, أُورِيَ for وُورِيَ.

a. The letter و in the middle of a word, movable by *fatḥa,* and preceded by *kasra,* is sometimes changed to ي, as ثِيَابٌ for ثِوَابٌ "clothes," "garments." When و in the middle of a word is followed by another و quiescent, the latter و is often thrown out, as طَاوُسٌ for طَاوُوسٌ "a peacock;" رُؤُسٌ for رُؤُوسٌ "heads," "chiefs."

136. The letter و when final, and preceded by *fatḥa,* rejecting its vowel, and throwing the nūnation, if there happens to be any, on the preceding *fatḥa,* is changed to ا inert if it be the third letter of the word, or to ي if it be the fourth,

etc.; as غَزَا for غَزَوَ "he assaulted;" عَصًا for عَصَوٌ "a staff;" يُغْزَى for يُغْزَوُ "he will be assaulted;" مُعْطًى for مُعْطَوٌ "given."

a. The letter و final, after *ḍamma*, takes neither *ḍamma* nor *kasra*, but throwing them away becomes quiescent, as رَدُو for رَدُوُ or رَدُوِ "perishing;" but if there is a nūnation, it is thrown upon the preceding letter, and و is dropped; as, أَدْلٍ for أَدْلُوٌ and أَدْلِوٌ "buckets." When و final is preceded by *kasra*, it is changed to ي; as, رَضِيَ from رَضِوَ "he was pleased or content."

137. The letter و when servile at the end of certain persons of the verb (see § 37, *b*), is followed by silent ا; as نَصَرُوا for نَصَرُو where the final ا is not sounded.

a. When in the middle of a word there are two *wāws*, the first movable by *ḍamma*, and the second inert, if the letter preceding the first is neither inert nor silent, and the first is not doubled by *tashdīd*, the first و is often changed into *hamza*, preserving the figure of و; thus, خُؤُولَةٌ for خُوُولَةٌ; نُؤُورَةٌ for نُوُورَةٌ. In this case it may be observed that one of the two *wāws* is sometimes dropped; this occurs particularly when the first و is preceded by a long *alif*: thus, دَاوُدُ for دَاوُودُ; طَاوُسٌ for طَاوُوسٌ. But if they meet only in consequence of a contraction, this rule is not observed.

Rules peculiar to ي *Yā.*

138. The letter ي in the middle of a word, movable by *fatḥa*, and preceded by *ḍamma*, is sometimes changed to و; as رُمُوَانٌ for رُمُيَانٌ "a throw," "a shot," "darting;" but, according to De Sacy, this change is of rare occurrence. The letter ي in the middle of a word, followed by another ي

inert, often expels the latter; as رَئْسٌ for رَئِيسٌ "a governor," "prefect," "chief;" but this takes place only when the first of the two ي *yās* has taken the place of a hamzated *alif.* In all other cases the two ي *yās* unite by *tashdīd.*

139. The letter ي final, preceded by *fatḥa*, cannot be made movable by any short vowel, but rejecting its own vowel, and throwing back the nūnation, if there is any, on *fatḥa*, it becomes quiescent like ا; as أُولَي for أُولَيُ "the first;" أُولَيِ "of the first;" أُولَي "the first;" فَتًى for فَتَيًا "a youth;" فَتَيٍ "of a youth;" فَتَيٌ "a youth." If another ي precedes, it is changed to ا; as هَدَايَا for هَدَايِيُ "gifts" (excepting a few proper names).

140. The letter ي final, preceded by *kasra*, takes neither *ḍamma* nor *kasra*, but throwing them away is silent; as حَافِي for حَافِيُ and حَافِيِ "barefoot;" and, in this instance, if there be a nūnation denoting the nominative or genitive case, it is thrown back on the preceding letter, and the ي is dropped; as رَامٍ for رَامِيٌ and رَامِيٍ "a shooter," "a darter."

141. The letter ي final, preceded by *ḍamma*, changes it to *kasra*, remaining itself unaltered; as تَمَنِّي for تَمَنُّيٌ "a wish;" أَيْدٍ for أَيْدُيٌ "hands;" and this rule holds also when و intervenes; as مَرْمِيٌّ for مَرْمُويٌ "thrown," "shot," or "hurled."

Rules peculiar to Wāw and Yā in common.

142. The letters و and ي, preceded by a short vowel, and being themselves movable, followed by و or ي inert, are en-

tirely dropped, rejecting the vowel, if *fatha* precedes (with which it forms a diphthong), or, if *damma* or *kasra*, throwing them back, in place of the vowel of the foregoing letter; as رَمَوْا for رَمَيُوا "they threw;" تُغْزَيْنَ for تُغْزَوِينَ "thou (*f.*) wilt be assaulted;" غَازُونَ for غَازِوُونَ "assailants;" يَرْمُونَ for يَرْمِيُونَ "they will throw." If, however, in this case, the vowel preceding be *damma* or *kasra*, it is suppressed, and replaced by the vowel belonging to the و or ي which has been dropped; as اُغْزِي for اُغْزُوِي "assail thou;" غَازُونَ for غَازِيُونَ "assailants."

a. The letters و and ي movable, preceded by *fatha*, and followed by a movable letter, are often changed into inert ا; thus, قَامَ for قَوَمَ "he stood;" سَارَ for سَيَرَ "he went," "set forth."

b. The same two letters meeting in such a manner that the first has no vowel, change و to ي, both coalescing by *tashdīd*; thus, أيّام for أيوام "days:" كَيٌّ for كَوْيٌ "a cautery."

143. The letters و and ي final, when preceded by a servile ا, are changed to *hamza*; as رِدَآءٌ or رِدَاءٌ for رِدَايٌ "a cloak;" سَمَآءٌ for سَمَاوٌ "heaven," "the sky."

a. When, in the foregoing rules, the letters ا, و, and ي are said to be preceded by any vowel, such vowel is supposed to be immediate, not in combination with a letter of prolongation, nor when *jazm* interposes, either expressed over an inert letter, or concealed under *tashdīd*; for a letter marked by *tashdīd* always contains a latent *jazm*; thus, مُدٌّ is the same as مُدْدٌ.

b. *Alif* is considered as medial when followed by the affixed pronouns; not so و or ي; as مَآءٌ, مَآؤُهُ not مَآءهُ "its water;" مَآءٍ, مَآئِهِ

not مَآءٌ "of its water;" رَمَي, رَمَيهُ not رَمَاهُ nor رَمَيَهُ "he threw or shot him;" غَزَا, غَزَاهُ not غَزَوَهُ "he assaulted him."

c. Where a letter is called *movable* in the foregoing rules, it denotes that it carries a short vowel, in opposition to *inert,* when it has none; where, in the language of grammar, it is said ي final after *fatḥa,* cannot be rendered movable, it implies simply that ي in that case cannot have a short vowel.

144. When the و and ي in the middle of a word bear a vowel, are preceded by *jazm,* and followed by a letter bearing a vowel also, they often transfer their own vowel to the letter having *jazm,* and become inert; thus, يَطُوْلُ for يَطْوُلُ "it will lengthen," so يَسِيرُ for يَسْيِرُ "he will set forth." In this case, if the vowel is *fatḥa,* the و or ي changes into ا; if *kasra,* the و changes into ي, according to the second general rule; thus, يَخَافُ for يَخْوَفُ "he will be afraid;" يَهَابُ for يَهْيَبُ "he will dread."

a. If after *alif* inert, a letter bearing *jazm* follow, the *alif* is dropped, and *ḍamma* or *kasra* substituted for the *fatḥa* preceding. *Ḍamma,* when the و whose place is taken by *alif,* would bear *ḍamma* or *fatḥa,* as طُلْتَ for طَالْتَ, of which the regular form would be طَوُلْتَ, and so قُمْتَ for قَامْتَ, regularly قَوَمْتَ. When the *alif* inert is in the place of ي or of و, moved by *kasra,* the *kasra* is used instead of *ḍamma;* as سِرْتَ for سَارْتَ, reg. سَيَرْتَ; خِفْتَ for خَافْتَ reg. خَوِفْتَ.

b. When و and ي in the middle of a word are moved by *kasra,* and preceded by *alif* inert, they are replaced by ئ with a *hamza;* thus,

قَآئِل for قَاوِل "a speaker," "one who says;" مَآئِل for مَايِل "inclined," etc.

Of the Hamzated Verb—مَهْمُوز.

145. This species of verb has *alif* or *hamza* as a radical, either at the beginning, as اَثَرَ "he chose or selected;" in the middle, as سَأَلَ "he asked;" or at the end, as هَنَأَ "he cooked" or "he seasoned (the food)." The irregularity rests simply in dropping ا in some persons, and substituting و and ي for it in others, agreeably to the principles laid down in the preceding rules. A paradigm of the leading persons is all that will be requisite in the conjugation of the *Hamzated* Verbs; thus, when the first radical is *hamza*, the *Active Voice* runs as follows: The Preterite, اَثَرَ is conjugated regularly; Aorist, يَأْثِرُ regular; Imperative, اِيثِرْ for اِأْثِرْ (according to § 131); Participle, اٰثِرٌ or آثِرٌ for ااْثِرٌ; Infinitive, اَثْرًا regular. In like manner in the *Passive Voice:* the Preterite, اُثِرَ is conjugated regularly; Aorist, يُوثَرُ for يُأْثَرُ by the preceding rules; Participle, مَأْثُورٌ regular.

a. When ا the characteristic of the imperative has *damma*, the *hamza* or radical *alif* is changed to و; as اُومُلْ "hope thou," for اُأْمُلْ: but اَخَذَ "he received;" اَكَلَ "he did eat;" اَمَرَ "he commanded," throw away not only *hamza*, but also the characteristical ا; as خُذْ, كُلْ, مُرْ; sometimes, however, though rarely, you will find اُوكُلْ and اُومُرْ; or with the copulatives وَ and فَ prefixed; as وَأْمُرْ and فَأْمُرْ; the imperative ا being dropped, and the radical *hamza* returning.

b. In the 1st derivative formation, both active and passive, Aorist يُوثِرُ or يُوثَرُ (for يُأْثِرُ and يُأْثَرُ); Part. مُوثِرٌ or مُوثَرٌ (for مُأْثِرٌ and مُأْثَرٌ). In the 2nd formation, Aorist يُوَاثِرُ or يُوَاثَرُ (for يُأَاثِرُ and يُأَاثَرُ); Part. مُوَاثِرٌ or مُوَاثَرٌ (for مُأَاثِرٌ and مُأَاثَرٌ); Infin. مُوَاثَرَةٌ (for مُأَاثَرَةٌ). In the 3rd formation Preterite آثَرَ or أُوثِرَ (for أَأْثَرَ and أُأْثِرَ); Aorist يُؤْثِرُ or يُؤْثَرُ (for يُأْثِرُ and يُأْثَرُ); Part. مُؤْثِرٌ or مُؤْثَرٌ (for مُأْثِرٌ and مُأْثَرٌ); Infin. إِيثَارًا (for إِأْثَارًا). And thus in the other formations, *hamza*, on account of *ḍamma*, *kasra*, or another *hamza*, being either changed or dropped entirely, agreeably to the rules mentioned above. The other tenses are all regular; as are also the rest of the derivative formations.

c. It is only necessary to apply the same rules to all the other derivative formations in order to find their root, when *hamza* is changed into وْ or يْ. Thus, أُسْتُوصِلَ is the passive voice of إِسْتَأْصَلَ. In the fifth formation it must be observed that the *hamza*, preceded by *fatḥa*, followed by *alif* inert, may be changed into و; thus, from the primitive verb, أَكَلَ may be written in the fifth formation تَوَاكَلَ or تَآكَلَ.

146. Those verbs whose middle or final radical is *hamza*, are inflected on the same principles; as سُئِلَ "he was asked," for سُأِلَ; سَائِلٌ "interrogating," for سَاأِلٌ; and هُنِيَ "it benefited," for هُنِئَ;" هَانِئٌ "benefiting," for هَانِأٌ. When *hamza* is the second radical, it is preserved or changed into وْ or ىْ, according to the vowel belonging to it, or im-

mediately preceding it; thus, in the preterite is written سَالَ, بَؤُسَ for بَأُسَ; صَئِبَ for صَأِبَ; in the aorist يَسْأَلُ, يَبْؤُسُ; يَصْأَبُ in the passive voice it is سُئِلَ.

a. Verbs having *hamza* for their medial radical are sometimes, though seldom, conjugated after the manner of the concave verbs, of which more anon, *hamza* being then quiescent; as سَالَ "he asked," for سَأَلَ; يَسَالُ "he will ask," for يَسْئَلُ; سَلْ "ask thou," for إِسْأَلْ; where both the *alifs* drop; the radical *hamza*, according to the preceding rules.

147. Bearing in mind the rules already laid down respecting ا *alif* (§ 130, etc.), the learner will meet with no serious difficulty in the derivative formations of a primitive whose medial letter is *hamza*: for example, let us take the verb لَأَمَ "he consolidated," whose second, third, seventh, and ninth derivative formations are as follows—

INFINITIVE.	PARTICIPLE.	IMPERATIVE.	AORIST.	PRETERITE.	FORMATION.
مُلَاءَمَةٌ	مُلَائِمٌ	لَائِمْ	يُلَائِمُ	لَاءَمَ	II.
إِلْآمٌ	مُلْئِمٌ	أَلْئِمْ	يُلْئِمُ	أَلْأَمَ	III.
إِلْتِئَامٌ	مُلْتَئِمٌ	إِلْتَئِمْ	يَلْتَئِمُ	إِلْتَأَمَ	VII.
إِسْتِلْآمٌ	مُسْتَلْئِمٌ	إِسْتَلْئِمْ	يَسْتَلْئِمُ	اِسْتَلْأَمَ	IX.

148. When *hamza* is the last radical, it is either retained or changed into و or ي according to the preceding rules

(§ 130, etc.); thus, بَرَأَ "he recovered from illness," has the 3rd person feminine of the preterite regularly بَرَأَتْ; also the 2nd person singular masculine and feminine بَرَأْتَ and بَرَأْتِ. Again, from هَنَأَ "he digested," the 3rd pers. sing. fem. of the preterite is هَنَئَتْ; and the 2nd persons sing. of the same, masc. and fem., are هَنِئْتَ and هَنِئْتِ. A similar rule obtains in the passive voice and derivative formations; thus, from جَشَأَ "the mind was excited," in the 1st formation the preterite is جُشِئَ, and the aorist يُجْشَأُ; so in the 4th formation تَجَشَّأَ and يَتَجَشَّأُ; and in the 11th formation اِسْتَخْذَأَ and يَسْتَخْذِئُ.

a. The quadriliteral verbs, such as دَأْدَأَ جَأْجَأَ, present no new difficulty; the rules are always the same: thus from طَمْأَنَ comes in the 3rd formation the preterite اِطْمَأَنَّ; in the aorist يَطْمَئِنُّ; and in the imperative اِطْمَأْنِنْ; or by contraction اِطْمَئِنَّ.

b. Verbs that have *hamza* for their second radical letter, are, as we have already stated, sometimes conjugated like concave verbs, in which *alif* is inert, as coming from و or ي radical. This is particularly observable in the verb سَأَلَ "he asked," which is often written سَالَ, aorist يَسَالُ or يَسَلُ. The imperative is سَلْ for اِسْأَلْ; where both the *alifs* are dropped, the radical *hamza* by the general rule, and the servile *alif* because the following letter bears a vowel. Verbs, of which the last radical is *hamza*, are often confounded also with verbs properly called defective, that is, such as have for their last radical و or ي.

Of the Simile Verb.

149. The imperfect or infirm verbs are divided into three classes, which are commonly called the Simile, the Concave, and the Defective. The Simile Verb has و or ي for the first radical, and is named by the Arabians مِثَالٌ, implying resemblance, because in the preterite it quite resembles a perfect verb; and it differs from the latter only by throwing away, in general, the quiescent radical و in the aorist active, and in the imperative of the primitive triliteral verb, and also in the infinitive, when of the form نَصْرَةٌ, as يَمِقُ "he will love," for يَوْمِقُ; مِقْ "love thou," for اِوْمِقْ; مِقَةٌ "to love," for وَمْقَةٌ. When ي quiescent is the radical, it is changed to و (when *jazmated* after *ḍamma*, agreeable to § 138); as أَيْسَرَ "he was rich," which has in the aorist يُوسِرُ for يُيْسِرُ, like يُنْصِرُ; and in the participle مُوسِرٌ for مُيْسِرٌ, like مُنْصِرٌ. In every other respect (with some very rare exceptions) both species of Simile Verbs, whether active or passive, together with their derivative formations, are regular, the 7th formation only substituting *tashdīd* in place of the initial infirm radicals, over its characteristic ت; as اِتَّعَدَ "he promised," for اِوْتَعَدَ; اِتَّسَرَ "he was enriched," for اِيْتَسَرَ. These however sometimes remain, become homogeneous, or take the sound of the preceding vowel; as اِيتَسَرَ; يَاتَسِرُ for يَيْتَسِرُ; مُوتَسِرٌ for مُيْتَسِرٌ; اِيتَعَدَ for اِوْتَعَدَ; مُوتَعِدٌ; اِيتِعَادًا for اِوْتِعَادًا.

a. When the second radical in the aorist does not bear *kasra*, that tense is regularly formed; as يَوْجَلُ from وَجِلَ, and يَوَدُّ from وَدَّ "he loved." When the aorist is regular, the imperative is so likewise; as أُوجَهْ, ٳيْجَلْ, ٳيدَدْ. In the last two examples, the ي is substituted for و radical, according to the rules of permutation; thus, ٳيْدَدْ imperative of وَدَّ, is for ٳوْدَدْ.

b. Several verbs lose و in the aorist though their second radical in that tense bears *fatha.* These verbs are وَطِيَ "he trod under foot," which is for وَطِأَ; وَسِعَ "it was large;" وَقَعَ "it fell or occurred;" وَدَعَ "he took leave;" وَهَبَ "he gave;" وَضَعَ "he placed;" which make in the aorist يَطَأُ, يَسَعُ, يَقَعُ, يَدَعُ, يَهَبُ, يَضَعُ. The verb وَذِرَ "he sowed or planted," is only used in the aorist and imperative; as يَذَرُ and ذَرْ.

c. The irregularity of all these verbs exists only in the active voice of the primitive form. In the passive voice of that form, and in all the derivative formations, they present no irregularity except indeed in the seventh formation, as will be observed immediately. Verbs having ي for first radical, are not, properly speaking, irregular; as يَبِسَ, "it was dry," يَيْبَسُ, يَسَرَ, يَيْسِرُ, يَسَّرَ, يُيَسِّرُ. It must only be observed that the radical ي is changed into و when it is quiescent after *damma*; thus, يَسَرَ makes in the aorist of the third formation يُوسِرُ, instead of يُيْسِرُ; the rule of permutation is merely to be observed.

150. Verbs whose first radical is و or ي have this in common, that in the seventh formation they change the first radical into ت, which then unites by *tashdīd* with the servile ت peculiar to that formation: hence from وَعَدَ "he promised,"

comes the Pret. اِتَّعَدَ for اِوْتَعَدَ; Aorist, يَتَّعِدُ for يَوْتَعِدُ; Imper. اِتَّعِدْ for اِوْتَعِدْ; Part. مُتَّعِدٌ for مُوْتَعِدٌ; Infin. اِتِّعَادٌ for اِوْتِعَادٌ. In like manner from يَسَرَ "he played dice," we have in the seventh formation: Pret. اِتَّسَرَ for اِيْتَسَرَ; Aorist, يَتَّسِرُ for يَيْتَسِرُ; Imper. اِتَّسِرْ for اِيْتَسِرْ; Part. مُتَّسِرٌ for مُيْتَسِرٌ; Infin. اِتِّسَارٌ for اِيْتِسَارٌ.

a. Sometimes the و and ي remain unchanged into ت and adapt themselves to the preceding vowel according to the rules already laid down; thus the two verbs just specified may be conjugated as follows, viz.: Pret. اِيْتَعَدَ for اِوْتَعَدَ; Aorist, يَاتَعِدُ for يَوْتَعِدُ; Imper. اِيْتَعِدْ for اِوْتَعِدْ; Part. مُوتَعِدٌ; Infin. اِيْتِعَادٌ for اِوْتِعَادٌ: so in like manner, Pret. اِيْتَسَرَ; Aorist, يَاتَسِرُ for يَيْتَسِرُ; Imper. اِيْتَسِرْ; Part. مُوتَسِرٌ for مُيْتَسِرٌ; Infin. اِيْتِسَارٌ.

Of Concave Verbs.

151. Such verbs as have و or ي for their middle radical are by Arabian grammarians called أَجْوَفُ *i.e.*, "Concave." Their irregularity consists chiefly in this, that in the primitive form, as also in the 3rd, 6th, 7th, and 9th derivative formations, those middle radicals are either dropped, become inert, or remain without a vowel assuming the sound of that which belongs to the preceding letter. They are also called ذُو ٱلثَّلَاثَةِ *i.e.* "having three (letters);" because one of their characteristics is, to have only three letters in the first person singular of the preterite, whereas the regular and defective verbs have four letters in the same person, as may be seen by comparing قُلْتُ "I said"

(concave verb), with فَعَلْتُ "I did." These verbs, and those of the next class, depart most widely from the regular forms; their number is very considerable, and it is therefore essential to be well acquainted with their conjugation.

a. In the third persons of the preterite (except the plural feminine), the letters و and ي are changed to ا inert after *fatḥa*; thus, instead of

PLURAL.	DUAL.		SINGULAR.		PERSON.
MASC.	FEM.	MASC.	FEM.	MASC.	
قَوَلُوا	قَوَلَتَا	قَوَلَا	قَوَلَتْ	قَوَلَ	3
سَيَرُوا	سَيَرَتَا	سَيَرَا	سَيَرَتْ	سَيَرَ	2

they write قَالَ and سَارَ, etc., as may be seen in the two following paradigms (§ 152).

b. In the other persons those radicals are dropped altogether, throwing back the vowel on the preceding letter (see paradigm next page); but if that vowel is *fatḥa,* as in قَوَلَ and سَيَرَ above, it is changed in the concave و to *ḍamma,* and in the concave ى to *kasra;* so that in those persons Concave Verbs in و have either *ḍamma* or *kasra* on the first radical, and those in ى always *kasra.*

152. The primitive forms of the verbs قَالَ for قَوَلَ "he said," and سَارَ for سَيَرَ "he went," are conjugated at full length in the two following paradigms. As verbs of this species are of frequent occurrence in the language, the student will do well to study their peculiarities very carefully.

CONJUGATION OF THE CONCAVE و WĀW.

Active Voice.

Preterite.

PLURAL. FEM.	PLURAL. MASC.	DUAL. FEM.	DUAL. MASC.	SINGULAR. FEM.	SINGULAR. MASC.	PERSON.
قُلْنَ	قَالُوا	قَالَتَا	قَالَا	قَالَتْ	قَالَ	3
قُلْتُنَّ	قُلْتُمْ		قُلْتُمَا	قُلْتِ	قُلْتَ	2
	قُلْنَا				قُلْتُ	1

Aorist.

PLURAL. FEM.	PLURAL. MASC.	DUAL. FEM.	DUAL. MASC.	SINGULAR. FEM.	SINGULAR. MASC.	PERSON.
يَقُلْنَ	يَقُولُونَ	تَقُولَانِ	يَقُولَانِ	تَقُولُ	يَقُولُ	3
تَقُلْنَ	تَقُولُونَ		تَقُولَانِ	تَقُولِينَ	تَقُولُ	2
	نَقُولُ				أَقُولُ	1

Imperative.

PLURAL. FEM.	PLURAL. MASC.	DUAL. FEM.	DUAL. MASC.	SINGULAR. FEM.	SINGULAR. MASC.	PERSON.
قُلْنَ	قُولُوا		قُولَا	قُولِي	قُلْ	2

Participle.

PLURAL. FEM.	PLURAL. MASC.	DUAL. FEM.	DUAL. MASC.	SINGULAR. FEM.	SINGULAR. MASC.	PERSON.
قَائِلَاتٌ	قَائِلُونَ	قَائِلَتَانِ	قَائِلَانِ	قَائِلَةٌ	قَائِلٌ	

Infinitive—قَوْلًا.

Passive Voice.

Preterite.

PLURAL. FEM.	PLURAL. MASC.	DUAL. FEM.	DUAL. MASC.	SINGULAR. FEM.	SINGULAR. MASC.	PERSON.
قِلْنَ	قِيلُوا	قِيلَتَا	قِيلَا	قِيلَتْ	قِيلَ	3
قِلْتُنَّ	قِلْتُمْ		قِلْتُمَا	قِلْتِ	قِلْتَ	2
	قِلْنَا				قِلْتُ	1

Aorist.

PLURAL. FEM.	PLURAL. MASC.	DUAL. FEM.	DUAL. MASC.	SINGULAR. FEM.	SINGULAR. MASC.	PERSON.
يُقَلْنَ	يُقَالُونَ	تُقَالَانِ	يُقَالَانِ	تُقَالُ	يُقَالُ	3
تُقَلْنَ	تُقَالُونَ		تُقَالَانِ	تُقَالِينَ	تُقَالُ	2
	نُقَالُ-				أُقَالُ	1

Participle.

PLURAL. FEM.	PLURAL. MASC.	DUAL. FEM.	DUAL. MASC.	SINGULAR. FEM.	SINGULAR. MASC.	PERSON.
مَقُولَاتٌ	مَقُولُونَ	مَقُولَتَانِ	مَقُولَانِ	مَقُولَةٌ	مَقُولٌ	

CONJUGATION OF THE CONCAVE ي *YĀ.*

Active Voice.

Preterite.

PLURAL. FEM.	PLURAL. MASC.	DUAL. FEM.	DUAL. MASC.	SINGULAR. FEM.	SINGULAR. MASC.	PERSON.
سِرْنَ	سَارُوا	سَارَتَا	سَارَا	سَارَتْ	سَارَ	3
سِرْتُنَّ	سِرْتُمْ	سِرْتُمَا		سِرْتِ	سِرْتَ	2
سِرْنَا				سِرْتُ		1

Aorist.

PLURAL. FEM.	PLURAL. MASC.	DUAL. FEM.	DUAL. MASC.	SINGULAR. FEM.	SINGULAR. MASC.	PERSON.
يَسِرْنَ	يَسِيرُونَ	تَسِيرَانِ	يَسِيرَانِ	تَسِيرُ	يَسِيرُ	3
تَسِرْنَ	تَسِيرُونَ	تَسِيرَانِ		تَسِيرِينَ	تَسِيرُ	2
نَسِيرُ				أَسِيرُ		1

Imperative.

PLURAL. FEM.	PLURAL. MASC.	DUAL. FEM.	DUAL. MASC.	SINGULAR. FEM.	SINGULAR. MASC.	PERSON.
سِرْنَ	سِيرُوا	سِيرَا		سِيرِي	سِرْ	2

Participle.

PLURAL. FEM.	PLURAL. MASC.	DUAL. FEM.	DUAL. MASC.	SINGULAR. FEM.	SINGULAR. MASC.
سَائِرَاتٌ	سَائِرُونَ	سَائِرَتَانِ	سَائِرَانِ	سَائِرَةٌ	سَائِرٌ

Infinitive—سَيْرًا.

Passive Voice.

Preterite.

PLURAL. FEM.	PLURAL. MASC.	DUAL. FEM.	DUAL. MASC.	SINGULAR. FEM.	SINGULAR. MASC.	PERSON.
سِرْنَ	سِيرُوا	سِيرَتَا	سِيرَا	سِيرَتْ	سِيرَ	3
سِرْتُنَّ	سِرْتُمْ	سِرْتُمَا		سِرْتِ	سِرْتَ	2
سِرْنَا				سِرْتُ		1

Aorist.

PLURAL. FEM.	PLURAL. MASC.	DUAL. FEM.	DUAL. MASC.	SINGULAR. FEM.	SINGULAR. MASC.	PERSON.
يُسَرْنَ	يُسَارُونَ	تُسَارَانِ	يُسَارَانِ	تُسَارُ	يُسَارُ	3
تُسَرْنَ	تُسَارُونَ	تُسَارَانِ		تُسَارِينَ	تُسَارُ	2
نُسَارُ				أُسَارُ		1

Participle.

PLURAL. FEM.	PLURAL. MASC.	DUAL. FEM.	DUAL. MASC.	SINGULAR. FEM.	SINGULAR. MASC.
مَسِيرَاتٌ	مَسِيرُونَ	مَسِيرَتَانِ	مَسِيرَانِ	مَسِيرَةٌ	مَسِيرٌ

General Remarks on the Concave Verbs.

153. In the active voice, if the penult vowel of the preterite is *fatḥa*, it is changed in the aorist into *ḍamma* before quiescent و, and to *kasra* before quiescent ي. If the penult is *kasra*, it becomes in the aorist *fatḥa*; and if *ḍamma*, it remains so; throwing back the vowel to the first radical in place of *jazm*; if that vowel happens to be *fatḥa*, the و and ي are changed to ا. In the feminine plural the letters و and ي are dropped on account of the subsequent *jazm*; and, when the last radical is ن it coalesces, by *tashdīd*, with the servile ن in the 3rd person feminine plural of the preterite, the 3rd and 2nd plural feminine of the aorist, and the feminine plural of the imperative. The و and ي are likewise thrown out every where, if an *apocope* takes place; as لم يَقُلْ "he says not" (for لَمْ يَقُولْ); لَمْ تَسِرْ "she walks not;" لَمْ نَخَفْ "we fear not," etc.; the last radical, as may be observed, being then always *jazmated.* The imperative has no *alif* of union, because the first radical bears a vowel, as in قُلْ and سِرْ; and *alif* of union can only come before a letter bearing *jazm*.

a. The concave radical letters are also dropped in the singular masculine and plural feminine of the imperative; the servile initial *alif* being also omitted in every person (see paradigms, pp. 126 and 127). But they return when the paragogical ن takes place; as قُولَنَّ "say thou;" سِيرَنَّ "go thou;" خَافَنَّ "fear thou."

b. The radical *alif* in the participle, following the characteristical inert *alif*, ought to have a vowel, as two inert letters cannot meet, but *hamza* or movable *alif* is substituted for it, which (by § 130, etc.) is changed to ئ; thus, قَائِلٌ for قَاإِلٌ, and that for قَاوِلٌ; so سَائِرٌ for سَاإِرٌ, and that again for سَايِرٌ.

c. Verbs having و for their second radical, take *damma* in the aorist, when the preterite is either of the form فَعَلَ or فَعُلَ; as يَقُولُ the aorist of قَالَ, which is for قَوَلَ; and يَطُولُ aorist of طَالَ, which is for طَوُلَ; but if the second radical have *kasra* for its vowel in the preterite, the aorist takes *fátha*, as يَخَافُ for يَخْوَفُ, aorist of خَافَ, which is for خَوِفَ. Verbs having ي for their second radical, generally take *kasra* in the aorist, because they are of the form فَعَلَ, aorist يَفْعِلُ; as يَسِيرُ, aorist of سَارَ, which is for سَيَرَ. There are some, however, of the form فَعِلَ, aorist يَفْعَلُ; these take *fatha* in the aorist, as يَهَابُ for يَهْيَبُ, aorist of هَابَ, which is for هَيِبَ.

154. In the preterite passive, the vowel *kasra*, of the middle radical, is thrown back to the first, whose own vowel is then lost; thus, قِيلَ is for قُوِلَ; and سِيرَ for سُيِرَ. The 1st and 2nd persons of the concave ي are the same in the passive as the active, and are only to be distinguished by the sense of the passage.

a. In the aorist passive, the *fatha* of the middle radical falling back upon the first, و and ي are changed to ا inert (according to § 142), يُقَالُ and يُسَارُ being for يُقْوَلُ and يُسْيَرُ. There is no difference in the preterite and aorist of the passive voice, between verbs whose second radical is و, or those having ي for the same.

b. In the passive participle, the *damma* of the second radical being removed to the first, the original و is thrown out; thus, مَقُول for مَقْوُول : but in concave ي *damma* is also changed to *kasra*; as مَسِير for مَسْيُور. In approved authors, however, particularly among the poets, many of these participles are regularly formed, as مَصْوُون "guarded;" but especially those of concave ي, as مَخْيُوط "sewn together;" مَكْيُول "measured," etc.

155. Concave verbs whose last radical is ت, incorporate the same by *tashdīd*, with the ت forming the second persons of the preterite, and the first person singular of the same tense; thus, from مَاتَ "he is dead," or "mated" (in chess), comes in the first person singular مُتُّ, and in the second persons مُتَّ, مُتِّ, مُتُّمَا. In concave verbs whose last radical is ن, a similar rule obtains, whenever this ن, being jazmated, is followed by ن forming the person. Thus from صَانَ (for صَوَنَ) "he carefully preserved," is made in the third person plural feminine of the preterite, and in the second person plural feminine of the imperative صُنَّ; in the first person plural of the preterite صُنَّا; and in the third person plural feminine of the aorist يَصُنَّ. These observations equally apply to the derivative verbs, and are of importance in finding the root by those who are reading Arabic works written without vowel-points or orthographical signs.

Derivative Formations from Concave Roots.

156. We have already observed that amongst derivatives from concave roots, the third, sixth, seventh, and ninth only are irregular. In these derivatives no difference exists between those whose second radical is و, and those where it is

ي. It will therefore quite suffice to give as a paradigm of these forms, the first word of each tense, as in the following paradigms :—

Active Voice.

INFINITIVE.	PARTICIPLE.	IMPERATIVE.	AORIST.	PRETERITE.	FORMATION.
إقالة	مقيل	أقل	يقيل	أقال	III.
إسارة	مسير	أسر	يسير	أسار	
إنقيالا	منقال	إنقل	ينقال	إنقال	VI.
إنسيارا	منسار	إنسر	ينسار	إنسار	
إقتيالا	مقتال	إقتل	يقتال	إقتال	VII.
إستيارا	مستار	إستر	يستار	إستار	
إستقالة	مستقيل	إستقل	يستقيل	إستقال	IX.
إستسارة	مستسير	إستسر	يستسير	إستسار	

a. The learner will perceive that in the above formations the concaves in و and ي are conjugated alike; and that the active participles of the 6th and 7th formations are exactly the same with the passives, the difference in sense being only discoverable from the tenor of the subject. In the infinitives of the 3rd and 9th formations, و and ي throwing their *fatha* back upon the preceding letter, which otherwise would be *jazmated*, are changed to *alif* inert; and the servile final *alif* (employed in forming the infinitives of the regular verbs إنصارا and إستنصارا) is dropped, ة being substituted in its room, إقالة and إستقالة being for إقوالا and إستقوالا. The middle radicals of the infinitives of the 6th and 7th formations, as may be observed in the paradigms, are regularly movable (*i.e.* have vowels); the concave و however being changed to ي.

Passive Voice.

PART.	AORIST.	PRET.	PART.	AORIST.	PRET.	FORMATION.
مُسَارٌ	يُسَارُ	أُسِيرَ	مُقَالٌ	يُقَالُ	أُقِيلَ	III.
مُنْسَارٌ	يُنْسَارُ	اُنْسِيرَ	مُنْقَالٌ	يُنْقَالُ	اُنْقِيلَ	VI.
مُسْتَارٌ	يُسْتَارُ	اُسْتِيرَ	مُقْتَالٌ	يُقْتَالُ	اُقْتِيلَ	VII.
مُسْتَسَارٌ	يُسْتَسَارُ	اُسْتُسِيرَ	مُسْتَقَالٌ	يُسْتَقَالُ	اُسْتُقِيلَ	IX.

The other derivative formations are inflected regularly; thus,

INFINITIVE.	PARTICIPLE.	IMPERATIVE.	AORIST.	PRETERITE.	FORMATION.
تَقْوِيلًا	مُقَوِّلٌ	قَوِّلْ	يُقَوِّلُ	قَوَّلَ	I.
مُقَاوَلَةً	مُقَاوِلٌ	قَاوِلْ	يُقَاوِلُ	قَاوَلَ	II.
تَسْيِيرًا	مُسَيِّرٌ	سَيِّرْ	يُسَيِّرُ	سَيَّرَ	I.
مُسَايَرَةً	مُسَايِرٌ	سَايِرْ	يُسَايِرُ	سَايَرَ	II.

Also تَقَوَّلَ, تَقَاوَلَ, إِسْوَدَّ, إِبْيَضَّ, etc., etc.

157. Some verbs of this species however in the primitive form are conjugated regularly; thus, عَوِرَ "he was one-eyed;" Aor. يَعْوَرُ; Imp. إِعْوَرْ; Part. عَاوِرٌ; so also صَيِدَ "he hunted;" Aor. يَصْيَدُ; Imp. أُصْيُدْ; Part. صَائِدٌ. In the derivative formations the 3rd, 6th, 7th, and 8th are أُعْوَرَ, إِنْعَوَرَ, إِعْتَوَرَ, إِسْتَعْوَرَ, and أُصْيَدَ, إِنْصَيَدَ, إِصْطَيَدَ, إِسْتَصْيَدَ respectively. A few verbs though imperfect in the primitive form are sometimes regular, sometimes irregular in the third formation; as رَاحَ "he

rested," which has أَرَاحَ and أَرْوَحَ; so غَامَ "it (the sky) was cloudy," which has أَغَامَ and أَغْيَمَ. The concave و in the 9th formation is likewise often perfect; as إِسْتَجَابَ and إِسْتَجْوَبَ "he heard," "he answered," إِسْتَصَابَ and إِسْتَصْوَبَ "he approved," etc.

a. The other derivatives are regular; it is to be observed, however, that in the passive voices of the second formation فَاعَلَ and of the fifth, تَفَاعَلَ of concave verbs, whose second radical is و, that the *alif* characteristic of these forms, and which is changed into و on account of the *ḍamma* preceding, does not unite by *tashdīd* with the radical و that follows it, thus from قَامَ (for قَوَمَ) "he stood," we have قُووِمَ and not قُوِّمَ. If the second radical is ي, the و and the ي must be kept distinct; thus from بَاعَ (for بَيَعَ) "he sold," we have in the second formation active بَايَعَ which in the passive voice makes بُويِعَ.

The Substantive Verb—كَانَ.

158. We here subjoin the Substantive Verb كَانَ (for كَوَنَ) "he was;" it is conjugated as قَالَ (for قَوَلَ) "he said," already described, with this difference only, that the last radical coalesces by *tashdīd* with ن servile, in those persons where that letter forms the final characteristic agreeably to § 97, *c.*

a. This verb, unless to avoid an ambiguity, is seldom used in the present tense, being then, as in the Latin, for the most part understood; as أَنَا ٱلطَّرِيقُ وَٱلْحَقُّ وَٱلْحَيٰوةُ *ego (sum) via, veritas et vita,* "I (am) the way, and the truth, and the life." The use and application of this verb will be further explained in the Syntax.

Active Voice.

Preterite.

PLURAL. FEM.	PLURAL. MASC.	DUAL. FEM.	DUAL. MASC.	SINGULAR. FEM.	SINGULAR. MASC.	PERSON.
كُنَّ	كَانُوا	كَانَتَا	كَانَا	كَانَتْ	كَانَ	3
كُنْتُنَّ	كُنْتُمْ	كُنْتُمَا		كُنْتِ	كُنْتَ	2
كُنَّا				كُنْتُ		1

Aorist.

PLURAL. FEM.	PLURAL. MASC.	DUAL. FEM.	DUAL. MASC.	SINGULAR. FEM.	SINGULAR. MASC.	PERSON.
يَكُنَّ	يَكُونُونَ	تَكُونَانِ	يَكُونَانِ	تَكُونُ	يَكُونُ	3
تَكُنَّ	تَكُونُونَ	تَكُونَانِ		تَكُونِينَ	تَكُونُ	2
نَكُونُ				أَكُونُ		1

Imperative.

PLURAL. FEM.	PLURAL. MASC.	DUAL. FEM.	DUAL. MASC.	SINGULAR. FEM.	SINGULAR. MASC.	PERSON.
كُنَّ	كُونُوا	كُونَا		كُونِي	كُنْ	2

Participle.

PLURAL. FEM.	PLURAL. MASC.	DUAL. FEM.	DUAL. MASC.	SINGULAR. FEM.	SINGULAR. MASC.
كَائِنَاتٌ	كَائِنُونَ	كَائِنَتَانِ	كَائِنَانِ	كَائِنَةٌ	كَائِنٌ

Infinitive—كَوْنًا.

Passive Voice.

Preterite.

PLURAL. FEM.	PLURAL. MASC.	DUAL. FEM.	DUAL. MASC.	SINGULAR. FEM.	SINGULAR. MASC.	PERSON.
كِنَّ	كِينُوا	كِينَتَا	كِينَا	كِينَتْ	كِينَ	3
كِنْتُنَّ	كِنْتُمْ	كِنْتُمَا		كِنْتِ	كِنْتَ	2
كِنَّا				كِنْتُ		1

Aorist.

PLURAL. FEM.	PLURAL. MASC.	DUAL. FEM.	DUAL. MASC.	SINGULAR. FEM.	SINGULAR. MASC.	PERSON.
تُكَنَّ	يُكَانُونَ	تُكَانَانِ	يُكَانَانِ	تُكَانُ	يُكَانُ	3
تُكَنَّ	تُكَانُونَ	تُكَانَانِ		تُكَانِينَ	تُكَانُ	2
نُكَانُ				أُكَانُ		1

Participle.

PLURAL. FEM.	PLURAL. MASC.	DUAL. FEM.	DUAL. MASC.	SINGULAR. FEM.	SINGULAR. MASC.
مَكُونَاتٌ	مَكُونُونَ	مَكُونَتَانِ	مَكُونَانِ	مَكُونَةٌ	مَكُونٌ

Of the Defective Verb—اَلنَّاقِصُ.

159. This class of imperfect verbs has و or ي for the last radical letter; as غَزَوَ "he assaulted;" رَمَيَ "he threw." They are also called ذُو آلْأَرْبَعَة or "possessed of four letters," because they have four letters in the 1st person singular of the preterite; as غَزَوْتُ wherein they differ from the concave verbs which have only three in the same person. The last radical undergoes changes resembling those to which the second radical is subject in concave verbs; sometimes it is changed into another letter, sometimes it disappears altogether, and sometimes its vowel passes to the preceding letter. The chief anomalies of these verbs are founded on the rules of permutation, as will be seen in the following paradigms:—

The Defective و—*Active Voice.*

PLURAL. FEM.	PLURAL. MASC.	DUAL. FEM.	DUAL. MASC.	SINGULAR. FEM.	SINGULAR. MASC.	PERSON.
			Preterite.			
غَزَوْنَ	غَزَوْا	غَزَتَا	غَزَوَا	غَزَتْ	غَزَا	3
غَزَوْتُنَّ	غَزَوْتُمْ	غَزَوْتُمَا		غَزَوْتِ	غَزَوْتَ	2
غَزَوْنَا				غَزَوْتُ		1
			Aorist.			
يَغْزُونَ	يَغْزُونَ	تَغْزُوَانِ	يَغْزُوَانِ	تَغْزُو	يَغْزُو	3
تَغْزُونَ	تَغْزُونَ	تَغْزُوَانِ		تَغْزِينَ	تَغْزُو	2
نَغْزُو				أَغْزُو		1
			Imperative.			
أُغْزُونَ	أُغْزُوا	أُغْزُوَا		أُغْزِي	أُغْزُ	2
			Participle.			
غَازِيَاتٌ	غَازُونَ	غَازِيَتَانِ	غَازِيَانِ	غَازِيَةٌ	غَازٍ	

Infinitive—غَزْوًا.

The Defective ي*—Active Voice.*

Preterite.

PLURAL. FEM.	PLURAL. MASC.	DUAL. FEM.	DUAL. MASC.	SINGULAR. FEM.	SINGULAR. MASC.	PERSON.
رَمَيْنَ	رَمَوْا	رَمَتَا	رَمَيَا	رَمَتْ	رَمَي	3
رَمَيْتُنَّ	رَمَيْتُمْ	رَمَيْتُمَا		رَمَيْتِ	رَمَيْتَ	2
رَمَيْنَا				رَمَيْتُ		1
Aorist.						
يَرْمِينَ	يَرْمُونَ	تَرْمِيَانِ	يَرْمِيَانِ	تَرْمِي	يَرْمِي	3
تَرْمِينَ	تَرْمُونَ	تَرْمِيَانِ		تَرْمِينَ	تَرْمِي	2
نَرْمِي				أَرْمِي		1
Imperative.						
إِرْمِينَ	إِرْمُوا	إِرْمِيَا		إِرْمِي	إِرْمِ	2
Participle.						
رَامِيَاتٌ	رَامُونَ	رَامِيَتَانِ	رَامِيَانِ	رَامِيَةٌ	رَامٍ	

Infinitive—رَمْيًا.

160. In the preterite the radical و is changed to inert ا. and رَمَي is put for رَمَيَ, the final ي remaining quiescent, Both و and ي with their vowels are dropped entirely in the 3rd person feminine singular and dual, and in the masculine plural; thus, غَزَتْ is substituted for غَزَوَتْ: and رَمَتْ for رَمَيَتْ, etc. In the 3rd person plural masculine, the last radical with its vowel disappear, and غَزَوْا and رَمَوْا are contractions for غَزَوُوا and رَمَيُوا, according to the rule of permutation. When the middle radical has *ḍamma*, و is not changed, but when it has *kasra*, و becomes ي; as رَضِيَ "he consented,"

for رَضِوَ ; or as رَضِيتَ ,رَضِيتِ for رَضِوْتَ ,رَضِوْتِ. Again in the 3rd person feminine singular and dual the radical letter remains; thus, from سَرُوَ "he was generous," we have سَرُوَتْ and سَرُوَتَا ; so رَضِيَتْ and رَضِيَتَا. The plurals masculine are سَرُوا and رَضُوا.

161. In the aorist the last radical throwing away *ḍamma* remains silent. If the penult of the preterite has *fatḥa*, it here (as in the concaves) becomes *ḍamma*, with quiescent و, and *kasra* with quiescent ي, unless the middle radical is a guttural letter, when *fatḥa* in that case remains, as in the perfect verbs; thus, رَعَي "he pastured" or "fed," يَرْعَي ; if *ḍamma* is the penult vowel of the preterite, it remains regular, as يَسْرُو "he travels by night;" but if *kasra*, it is changed to *fatḥa*, as يَرْضَي "he will approve;" where ي substituted for و is quiescent, and is inflected as follows:—

PLURAL. FEM.	PLURAL. MASC.	DUAL. FEM.	DUAL. MASC.	SINGULAR. FEM.	SINGULAR. MASC.	PERSON.
يَرْضَيْنَ	يَرْضَوْنَ	تَرْضَيَانِ	يَرْضَيَانِ	تَرْضَي	يَرْضَي	3
تَرْضَيْنَ	تَرْضَوْنَ	تَرْضَيَانِ		تَرْضَيْنَ	تَرْضَي	2
نَرْضَي				أَرْضَي		1

a. In the plural masc. and in the 2nd pers. fem. sing. a contraction is made of the و and ي, when the penult of the aorist has *ḍamma*, which removes all distinction between the masculine and feminine plural; as تَغْزُونَ and يَغْزُونَ, and also between the 2nd persons feminine singular and plural, when either *fatḥa* or *kasra* happen to be the penult vowels, as تَرْضَيْنَ the above example.

162. Where the apocope particles precede, the last radical

is dropped, and ن is regularly thrown away, except in the feminine plural, as

PLURAL.		DUAL.		SINGULAR.		
FEM.	MASC.	FEM.	MASC.	FEM.	MASC.	
تَغْزُونَ	يَغْزُوا	تَغْزُوَا	يَغْزُوَا	تَغْزُ	يَغْزُ	لَمْ
تَغْزُونَ	تَغْزُوا	تَغْزُوَا		تَغْزِي	تَغْزُ	
نَغْزُ				أَغْزُ		

And so with respect to لَمْ يَرْمِ and لَمْ يَرْضَ; sometimes, however, though rarely, these final letters remain. When the antithesis particles (§ 100) go before, these radicals take regularly *fatḥa*; as لَنْ يَغْزُوَ; لَنْ يَرْمِيَ, etc., unless the penult has *fatḥa* (when the ي forbids it), as لَنْ يَرْضَي, etc. و is also silent sometimes after *ḍamma*, but seldom.

163. The imperative, as in the regulars, is formed from the aorist jazmated, prefixing the characteristic *alif*; but when the paragogical nūn takes place the last radical, which was dropped in the singular masculine aorist, returns, as أُغْزُوَنَّ, إِرْمِيَنَّ, إِرْضَيَنَّ. In the singular feminine and plural masculine a contraction occurs similar to that in the aorist.

164. In the singular masculine of the participle, و final after *kasra* is changed to ي; غَازِيٌ being put for غَازِوٌ; and as ي final after *kasra* cannot take *ḍamma* it rejects it, and throwing the nūnation on the preceding letter, is dropped; as غَازٍ for غَازِيٌ: but if the nūnation is removed by the article, ي then returns; as اَلْغَازِي for اَلْغَازِيُ. The same rule holds in the defective ي; as رَامٍ for رَامِيٌ; اَلرَّامِي for اَلرَّامِيُ; and as

ي final after *kasra* refuses another *kasra*, غَازٍ and رَامٍ are used also in the genitive for غَازِيٍ and رَامِيٍ. The accusative is, however, regular; as غَازِيًا and رَامِيًا. In غَازِيَةٌ and رَامِيَةٌ the rejected ي returns, as not being final; and غَازُونَ makes a contraction, as in the aorist. The infinitive is always regular.

165. The passive voice follows the active on the same principle as in those verbs which we have already exemplified, regard being always had to the rules of permutation.

Defective ي.		*Defective* و.		
		Preterite.		
SINGULAR.		SINGULAR.		
FEM.	MASC.	FEM.	MASC.	PERSON.
رُمِيَتْ	رُمِيَ	غُزِيَتْ	غُزِيَ	3
etc. رُمِيتِ	رُمِيتَ	etc. غُزِيتِ	غُزِيتَ	2
رُمِيتُ		غُزِيتُ		1
		Aorist.		
تُرْمَي	يُرْمَي	تُغْزَي	يُغْزَي	3
etc. تُرْمَيْنَ	تُرْمَي	etc. تُغْزَيْنَ	تُغْزَي	2
أُرْمَي		أُغْزَي		1
		Participle.		
etc. مَرْمِيَّةٌ	مَرْمِيٌّ	etc. مَغْزُوَّةٌ	مَغْزُوٌّ	

a. غُزِيَ is used instead of غُزِوَ. In the aorist يُغْزَي, و is changed to ي quiescent, like *alif*; and يُرْمَي (by the rules already laid down) is put for يُرْمَيُ ; مَغْزُوٌّ stands by contraction for مَغْزُووٌ ; and مَرْمِيٌّ for مَرْمُويٌ by the same foresaid rules.

166. We now subjoin a paradigm of a defective verb whose middle radical has the vowel *kasra*, such as رَضِيَ (for رَضِوَ) "he was content."

Active Voice.

Preterite.

PLURAL. FEM.	PLURAL. MASC.	DUAL. FEM.	DUAL. MASC.	SINGULAR. FEM.	SINGULAR. MASC.	PERSON.
رَضِينَ	رَضُوا	رَضِيَتَا	رَضِيَا	رَضِيَتْ	رَضِيَ	3
رَضِيتُنَّ	رَضِيتُمْ	رَضِيتُمَا		رَضِيتِ	رَضِيتَ	2
رَضِينَا				رَضِيتُ		1

Aorist.

PLURAL. FEM.	PLURAL. MASC.	DUAL. FEM.	DUAL. MASC.	SINGULAR. FEM.	SINGULAR. MASC.	PERSON.
يَرْضَيْنَ	يَرْضَوْنَ	تَرْضَيَانِ	يَرْضَيَانِ	تَرْضَي	يَرْضَي	3
تَرْضَيْنَ	تَرْضَوْنَ	تَرْضَيَانِ		تَرْضَيْنَ	تَرْضَي	2
نَرْضَي				أَرْضَي		1

Aorist Antithetic.

PLURAL. FEM.	PLURAL. MASC.	DUAL. FEM.	DUAL. MASC.	SINGULAR. FEM.	SINGULAR. MASC.	PERSON.
يَرْضَيْنَ	يَرْضَوْا	يَرْضَيَا	يَرْضَيَا	تَرْضَي	يَرْضَي	3
تَرْضَيْنَ	تَرْضَوْا	تَرْضَيَا		تَرْضَي	تَرْضَي	2
نَرْضَي				أَرْضَي		1

Aorist Apocopate.

PLURAL. FEM.	PLURAL. MASC.	DUAL. FEM.	DUAL. MASC.	SINGULAR. FEM.	SINGULAR. MASC.	PERSON.
يَرْضَيْنَ	يَرْضَوْا	تَرْضَيَا	يَرْضَيَا	تَرْضَ	يَرْضَ	3
تَرْضَيْنَ	تَرْضَوْا	تَرْضَيَا		تَرْضَيْ	تَرْضَ	2
نَرْضَ				أَرْضَ		1

Aorist Paragogic.

PLURAL. FEM.	PLURAL. MASC.	DUAL. FEM.	DUAL. MASC.	SINGULAR. FEM.	SINGULAR. MASC.	PERSON.
يَرْضَيْنَانِّ	يَرْضَوُنَّ	تَرْضَيَانِّ	يَرْضَيَانِّ	تَرْضَيَنَّ	يَرْضَيَنَّ	3
تَرْضَيْنَانِّ	تَرْضَوُنَّ	تَرْضَيَانِّ		تَرْضَيِنَّ	تَرْضَيَنَّ	2
نَرْضَيَنَّ				أَرْضَيَنَّ		1

Imperative.

PLURAL. FEM.	PLURAL. MASC.	DUAL. FEM.	DUAL. MASC.	SINGULAR. FEM.	SINGULAR. MASC.	PERSON.
إِرْضَيْنَ	إِرْضَوْا	إِرْضَيَا		إِرْضَيْ	إِرْضَ	2

Participle.

PLURAL. FEM.	PLURAL. MASC.	DUAL. FEM.	DUAL. MASC.	SINGULAR. FEM.	SINGULAR. MASC.
رَاضِيَاتٌ	رَاضُونَ	رَاضِيَتَانِ	رَاضِيَانِ	رَاضِيَةٌ	رَاضٍ

Infinitive—رَضًى.

167. The derivative formations have likewise the same affinity to their primitives, observing only, that the ي, which, in the preterite of the defective و, is substituted for و, remains in the first and second persons, forming a diphthong with *fatha*; as أَغْزَيْتِ, أَغْزَيْتَ, أَغْزَيْ, quite otherways, as in the primitive, where و returns.

Defective Derivative Formations.

PASSIVE.		ACTIVE.		
AORIST.	PRETERITE.	AORIST.	PRETERITE.	FORMATION.
يُغْزَي	غُزِيَ	يَغْزِي	غَزَّي	I.
يُغَازَي	غُوزِيَ	يُغَازِي	غَازَي	II.
يُغْزَي	أُغْزِيَ	يُغْزِي	اَغْزَي	III.
يُتَغَزَّي	تُغُزِّيَ	يَتَغَزَّي	تَغَزَّي	IV.
يُغْتَزَي	أُغْتُزِيَ	يَغْتَزِي	إِغْتَزَي	VII.
يُسْتَغْزَي	أُسْتُغْزِيَ	يَسْتَغْزِي	إِسْتَغْزَي	IX.
يُرْمَّي	رُمِيَ	يَرْمِي	رَمَّي	I.
يُرَامَي	رُومِيَ	يُرَامِي	رَامَي	II.
يُرْمَي	أُرْمِيَ	يُرْمِي	اَرْمَي	III.
يُتَرَمَّي	تُرُمِّيَ	يَتَرَمَّي	تَرَمَّي	IV.
يُرْتَمَي	أُرْتُمِيَ	يَرْتَمِي	إِرْتَمَي	VII.
يُسْتَرْمَي	أُسْتُرْمِيَ	يَسْتَرْمِي	إِسْتَرْمَي	IX.

Of Verbs Doubly Imperfect.

168. Such verbs as have any two of the infirm letters ا, و, or ي for their radicals, are said to be doubly imperfect. They follow the mode of the simple imperfect, according to the position of those radicals, and are divided into two classes. The first class comprehends the hamzated and inert, of which there are four subdivisions :

1. The first radical hamzated, the second inert ; as آبَ (for أَوَبَ) "he returned," which is conjugated with a regard to the vowels of the first radical (here represented by *madda*) like أَثَرَ and with respect to the second, like قَالَ ; as

INFINITIVE.	PARTICIPLE.	IMPERATIVE.	AORIST.	PRETERITE.
أَوْبًا	آئِبٌ	أُبْ	يَؤُوبُ	آبَ

2. The last radical hamzated, the second inert, as سَاءَ (for سَاوَءَ) "he mourned ;" and جَاءَ (for جَيَأَ) "he came," of which the former partakes of the inflections of قَالَ and هَنَأَ ; the other of سَارَ and هَنَأَ ; thus,

INFINITIVE.	PARTICIPLE.	IMPERATIVE.	AORIST.	PRETERITE.
سَوَاءٌ	سَايِئٌ	سُوْ	يَسُوءُ	سَاءَ
مَجِيئًا and جِيئَةً	جَايِئٌ	جِيْ	يَجِيءُ	جَاءَ

3. The first hamzated, the last inert ; as أَتَي "he came," inflected like أَثَرَ and رَمَي ; thus,

INFINITIVE.	PARTICIPLE.	IMPERATIVE.	AORIST.	PRETERITE.
إِتْيًا	آتٍ	تِهْ and إِيْتِ	يَاتِي	أَتَي

4. The middle hamzated, the last inert; as نَأَي "he retired," which follows سَأَلَ and رَمَي; thus,

PARTICIPLE.	IMPERATIVE.	AORIST.	PRETERITE.
نَآءٍ	إِنْأَ	يَنْأَي	نَأَي

169. رَأَي "he saw" should be regularly conjugated; but, on account of its frequent occurence, the *hamzated alif* is dropped, and its vowel thrown upon the preceding letter, as often as the ر is *jazmated.* In the primitive form, therefore, the Aorist and Imperative are inflected as follow:

Active Voice.

Aorist.

PLURAL. FEM.	PLURAL. MASC.	DUAL. FEM.	DUAL. MASC.	SINGULAR. FEM.	SINGULAR. MASC.	PERSON.
يَرَيْنَ	يَرَوْنَ	تَرَيَانِ	يَرَيَانِ	تَرَي	يَرَي	3
تَرَيْنَ	تَرَوْنَ	تَرَيَانِ		تَرَيْنَ	تَرَي	2
نَرَي				أَرَي		1

for يَرْأَي, تَرْأَي, etc., which however, when the verse requires, are sometimes found in the poets.

Imperative.

رَيْنَ	رَوْا	رَيَا	رَيْ	رَ or رَهْ	2

or with the paragogical *nūn*,

رَيْنَانِّ	رَوُنَّ	رَيَانِّ	رِنَّ	رَيَنَّ	2

It is frequently also formed regularly, as إِرْأَ, إِرْأَي, etc.

a. In the 3rd formation of this verb *hamza* is everywhere thrown out; as

INFINITIVE.	PART.	IMPER.	AORIST.	PRET.
إِرَاءً or إِرَاءَةً or إِرَيَةً	مُرٍ	أَرِ	يُرِي	أَرَى

b. The other verbs of this species may also throw away *hamza* in the 4th formation, in the manner of أَرَى, making either أَنْأَى يُنْئِي مُنْئًا or أَنَى يُنِي مُنٍ. The imperative with the paragogical ن is أَرِيَنَّ.

c. When ر is not *jazmated* it is conjugated regularly, retaining *hamza*; as in the preterite رَأَى, in the participle رَآءٍ, in the infinitive رَأْيًا; and also in the participle passive it is مَرْئِيٌّ, although ر takes *jazm*.

170. The second class of the Double Imperfects, which are called Involutes, comprise such as have two of the letters و and ي for radicals, and are of two kinds, the Separate and the Conjunct. The Separate are those which have و or ي for the first and last radicals; as وَقَى "he guarded" or "took care;" وَجِيَ "he had a worn hoof" (speaking of a horse): the first being inflected like وَعَدَ and رَمَى, the other as وَجِلَ and رَضِيَ.

PARTICIPLE.	IMPERATIVE.	AORIST.	PRETERITE.
وَاقٍ	قِ or قِهْ	يَقِي	وَقَى
وَاجٍ	إِيجَ	يَوْجَى	وَجِيَ

The Imperative قِ in the other persons resumes ي; as

قِ قِي قِيَا قُوا قِينَ

and in the singular masculine with the paragogical *nūn* it is قِيَنَّ.

171. The Involute Conjunct has the middle and final radicals و or ي; as شَوَي "he roasted;" قَوِي "he was strong or powerful;" حَيِي "he lived;" which, with regard to the middle radical, are conjugated perfectly; and in the final imperfectly; شَوَي following the mode of رَمَي and the other two that of رَضِي; as

INFINITIVE.	PARTICIPLE.	IMPERATIVE.	AORIST.	PRETERITE.
شَيًّا	شَاوٍ	إِشْوِ	يَشْوِي	شَوَي
قُوَّةٌ	قَاوٍ	إِقْوَ	يَقْوَي	قَوِي
حَيَوةٌ	حَايٍ	إِحْيَ	يَحْيَا	حَيِي

a. The Infinitive شَيًّا is put for شَوْيًا, and قُوَّةٌ for قُوْوَةٌ; قَوِي stands here for قَوِوَ, the last و being changed to ي, avoiding thereby having the penult and last radicals the same, and becoming a surd or doubled verb; whilst, on the contrary, حَيِي converting و final to ي, makes both radicals similar, and is frequently contracted by *tashdīd*; as حَيِي or حَيَّ; and, in the Aorist, يَحْيَا or يَحَيُّ. Instead of the participle حَايٍ the adjective حَيٌّ is most generally used. The radical و in the infinitive, throwing away its vowel, is changed to quiescent *alif*, according to the rules respecting و and ي.

b. In the same manner are conjugated the Derivative verbs; only حَيِي rejects sometimes the first ي in the 9th formation, throwing its vowel back upon the preceding letter; as,

INFINITIVE.	PARTICIPLE.	IMPERATIVE.	AORIST.	PRETERITE.
إِسْتِحْيَاءٌ	مُسْتَحْيٍ	إِسْتَحْيِ	يَسْتَحْيِي	إِسْتَحْيَا
إِسْتِحَاءٌ	مُسْتَحٍ	إِسْتَحِ	يَسْتَحِي	إِسْتَحَي

Of Verbs Triply Imperfect.

172. A very few verbs are Triply Imperfect, and are divided into two classes. Class first consists of such as have *hamza* for the first radical, and the other two و and ي; as أَوَى "he betook himself to some place," etc., or the middle *hamzated* and the first and last و and ي, as وَأَى "he promised;" the first of which is inflected like أَثَرَ and شَوَى, the other as وَقَى and سَأَلَ; as,

INFINITIVE.	PARTICIPLE.	IMPERATIVE.	AORIST.	PRETERITE.
أُيًّا	آوٍ	إِئْوِ	يَأْوِي	أَوَى
وَأْيًا	وَاءٍ	إِهْ or إِ	يَئِي	وَأَى

There is no verb having all the radicals, or even the two first, consisting of و and ي.

Of the Negative Verb.

173. The Negative Defective Verb لَيْسَ, though conjugated only in the preterite, is quite unlimited in point of time, signifying "it is not," "it was not," or "it will not be," etc. It is apparently formed of the particle لَا "not," and أَيْسَ "is" or "exists;" and is inflected as follows:

PLURAL.		DUAL.		SINGULAR.		
FEM.	MASC.	FEM.	MASC.	FEM.	MASC.	PERSON.
لَسْنَ	لَيْسُوا	لَيْسَتَا	لَيْسَا	لَيْسَتْ	لَيْسَ	3
لَسْتُنَّ	لَسْتُمْ	لَسْتُمَا		لَسْتِ	لَسْتَ	2
لَسْنَا				لَسْتُ		1

a. Sometimes لَاتَ is employed instead of لَيْسَ, but without any inflection. Most Arabian grammarians consider لَاتَ as merely the negative particle لَا augmented by the letter ت.

Verbs of Praise and Censure.

174. These verbs, which the Arabian grammarians denominate اَفْعَالُ ٱلْمَدْحِ وَٱلذَّمِّ, or "verbs of praise and censure," admit only of very limited inflection. They are نِعْمَ, sometimes pronounced نِعِمَ, نَعِمَ, and نَعْمَ "it is good," and بِئْسَ "it is bad." They may be regarded as a species of interjections with something of a verbal inflection. They receive also a feminine termination; as نِعْمَتْ, بِئْسَتْ, when applied to feminine nouns. They are sometimes, but very rarely, written نِعْمَا in the dual; and نِعْمُوا in the plural. The word حَبَّذَا may be looked upon as a verb of this kind; it is compounded of حَبَّ and ذَا, and signifies "that is excellent," or "worthy of love." To these three verbs may also be added سَآءَ "it is bad;" and حُسْنَ for حَسُنَ "it is beautiful;" but these last, under other acceptations, are regularly conjugated.

Of Verbs of Admiration, or Surprise.

175. These are called أَفْعَالُ ٱلتَّعَجُّبِ "verbs of admiration." Like the preceding, they are rather a kind of interjectional formulæ than a particular species of verb. They are employed in two ways; the first مَا أَفْعَلَ, the form of the third person singular masculine of the preterite of the third derivative formation, preceded by the particle مَا, and followed by an accusative case. The second mode is to employ the second person singular masculine of the imperative of the third formation

اَفْعِلْ, followed by the object admired having the preposition بِ prefixed; as مَا اَفْضَلَ زَيْدًا or اَفْضِلْ بِزَيْدٍ "how excellent is Zaid!" or "Zaid is very excellent." This subject will be more fully examined in the Syntax.

176. As an appropriate Appendix to our two Sections on the Verb, we here subjoin a series of useful tables which we recommend to the student's careful and frequent perusal till he has committed them all to memory. Table I., page 149, exhibits at one view the Preterite Active of the eleven species of Verbs, which we have already explained § 90 to § 167. The upper line (No. 1) shews the Regular Verb قَتَلَ. No. 2 shews the inflection of a Surd Verb. Nos. 3, 4 and 5 exhibit the three species of *Hamzated* Verbs. Nos. 6 and 7 exhibit the Simile Verbs. Nos. 8 and 9, the Concave Verbs. Lastly, Nos. 10 and 11 are examples of the Defective or Irregular Verbs. In like manner Table II. exhibits the Aorist Active of each of the foregoing species of Verbs in the same order. Table III., the Imperative, the Participle Active, the Infinitive, and the Participle Passive, which is inserted here because there is more room than we could have in either of the next two tables which exhibit the Preterite and Aorist Passive on the same plan as Tables I. and II. respectively. It has not been deemed necessary to insert in the Tables those verbs which are called the Doubly and Triply Imperfect, described from § 168 to § 172, inclusive; as they are not very numerous, and their inflection is more irregular than that of the others.

TABLE I.

PRETERITE ACTIVE.

First Person.		*Second Person.*					*Third Person.*						
PLURAL.	SINGULAR.	PLURAL.		DUAL.	SINGULAR.		PLURAL.		DUAL.		SINGULAR.		
COMM.	COMM.	FEM.	MASC.	COMM.	FEM.	MASC.	FEM.	MASC.	FEM.	MASC.	FEM.	MASC.	NO.
قبلنا	قبلتُ	قبلتنّ	قبلتم	قبلتما	قبلتِ	قبلتَ	قبلن	قبلوا	قبلتا	قبلا	قبلتْ	قبل	1
رققنا	رققتُ	رققتنّ	رققتم	رققتما	رققتِ	رققتَ	رققن	رقّوا	رقّتا	رقّا	رقّتْ	رقّ	2
أكلنا	أكلتُ	أكلتنّ	أكلتم	أكلتما	أكلتِ	أكلتَ	أكلن	أكلوا	أكلتا	أكلا	أكلتْ	أكل	3
بأسنا	بأستُ	بأستنّ	بأستم	بأستما	بأستِ	بأستَ	بأسن	بأسوا	بأستا	بأسا	بأستْ	بأس	4
هنأنا	هنأتُ	هنأتنّ	هنأتم	هنأتما	هنأتِ	هنأتَ	هنأن	هنأوا	هنأتا	هنأا	هنأتْ	هنأ	5
ورثنا	ورثتُ	ورثتنّ	ورثتم	ورثتما	ورثتِ	ورثتَ	ورثن	ورثوا	ورثتا	ورثا	ورثتْ	ورث	6
يسرنا	يسرتُ	يسرتنّ	يسرتم	يسرتما	يسرتِ	يسرتَ	يسرن	يسروا	يسرتا	يسرا	يسرتْ	يسر	7
قلنا	قلتُ	قلتنّ	قلتم	قلتما	قلتِ	قلتَ	قلن	قالوا	قالتا	قالا	قالتْ	قال	8
سرنا	سرتُ	سرتنّ	سرتم	سرتما	سرتِ	سرتَ	سرن	ساروا	سارتا	سارا	سارتْ	سار	9
غزونا	غزوتُ	غزوتنّ	غزوتم	غزوتما	غزوتِ	غزوتَ	غزون	غزوا	غزتا	غزوا	غزتْ	غزا	10
رمينا	رميتُ	رميتنّ	رميتم	رميتما	رميتِ	رميتَ	رمين	رموا	رمتا	رميا	رمتْ	رمي	11

TABLE II.

AORIST ACTIVE.

First Person.		Second Person.					Third Person.						
PLURAL.	SINGULAR.	PLURAL.		DUAL.	SINGULAR.		PLURAL.		DUAL.		SINGULAR.		
COMM.	COMM.	FEM.	MASC.	COMM.	FEM.	MASC.	FEM.	MASC.	FEM.	MASC.	FEM.	MASC.	NO.
نقبل	اقبل	تقبلن	تقبلون	تقبلان	تقبلين	تقبل	يقبلن	يقبلون	تقبلان	يقبلان	تقبل	يقبل	1
نرق	أرق	ترقن	ترقون	ترقان	ترقين	ترق	يرقن	يرقون	ترقان	يرقان	ترق	يرق	2
نأكل	آكل	تأكلن	تأكلون	تأكلان	تأكلين	تأكل	يأكلن	يأكلون	تأكلان	يأكلان	تأكل	يأكل	3
نباس	اباس	تباسن	تباسون	تباسان	تباسين	تباس	يباسن	يباسون	تباسان	يباسان	تباس	يباس	4
نهنو	اهنو	تهنأن	تهنوون	تهناان	تهنئين	تهنو	يهنأن	يهنوون	تهناان	يهناان	تهنو	يهنو	5
نرث	أرث	ترثن	ترثون	ترثان	ترثين	ترث	يرثن	يرثون	ترثان	يرثان	ترث	يرث	6
نيسر	أيسر	تيسرن	تيسرون	تيسران	تيسرين	تيسر	ييسرن	ييسرون	تيسران	ييسران	تيسر	ييسر	7
نقول	اقول	تقلن	تقولون	تقولان	تقولين	تقول	يقلن	يقولون	تقولان	يقولان	تقول	يقول	8
نسير	اسير	تسرن	تسيرون	تسيران	تسيرين	تسير	يسرن	يسيرون	تسيران	يسيران	تسير	يسير	9
نغزو	اغزو	تغزون	تغزون	تغزوان	تغزين	تغزو	يغزون	يغزون	تغزوان	يغزوان	تغزو	يغزو	10
نرمي	ارمي	ترمين	ترمون	ترميان	ترمين	ترمي	يرمين	يرمون	ترميان	يرميان	ترمي	يرمي	11

TABLE III. IMPERATIVE AND PARTICIPLE ACTIVE, ETC.

Participle Passive.		Infinitive.	Participle Active.		Second Person.					
					PLURAL.		DUAL.	SINGULAR.		
FEM.	MASC.		FEM.	MASC.	FEM.	MASC.	COMM.	FEM.	MASC.	NO.
مَقْبُولَةٌ	مَقْبُولٌ	قَبْلٌ	قَابِلَةٌ	قَابِلٌ	اُقْبُلْنَ	اُقْبُلُوا	اُقْبُلَا	اُقْبُلِي	اُقْبُلْ	1
مَرْقُوقَةٌ	مَرْقُوقٌ	رَقٌّ	رَاقَّةٌ	رَاقٌّ	إِرْقُقْنَ	إِرْقُقُوا	إِرْقُقَا	إِرْقُقِي	إِرْقُقْ	2
					إِرْقُقْنَ	رِقُّوا	رِقَّا	رِقِّي	رِقِّ	
مَأْكُولَةٌ	مَأْكُولٌ	أَكْلٌ	آكِلَةٌ	آكِلٌ	كُلْنَ	كُلُوا	كُلَا	كُلِي	كُلْ	3
مَبْؤُوسَةٌ	مَبْؤُوسٌ	بَأْسٌ	بَائِسَةٌ	بَائِسٌ	إِبْأَسْنَ	إِبْأَسُوا	إِبْأَسَا	إِبْأَسِي	إِبْأَسْ	4
مَهْنُوءَةٌ	مَهْنُوءٌ	هَنْءَةٌ	هَانِئَةٌ	هَانِئٌ	إِهْنَأْنَ	إِهْنَئُوا	إِهْنَأَا	إِهْنَئِي	إِهْنَأْ	5
مَوْرُوثَةٌ	مَوْرُوثٌ	وَرْثٌ	وَارِثَةٌ	وَارِثٌ	رِثْنَ	رِثُوا	رِثَا	رِثِي	رِثْ	6
مَيْسُورَةٌ	مَيْسُورٌ	يَسْرٌ	يَاسِرَةٌ	يَاسِرٌ	إِيْسِرْنَ	إِيْسِرُوا	إِيْسِرَا	إِيْسِرِي	إِيْسِرْ	7
مَقُولَةٌ	مَقُولٌ	قَوْلٌ	قَائِلَةٌ	قَائِلٌ	قُلْنَ	قُولُوا	قُولَا	قُولِي	قُلْ	8
مَسِيرَةٌ	مَسِيرٌ	سَيْرٌ	سَائِرَةٌ	سَائِرٌ	سِرْنَ	سِيرُوا	سِيرَا	سِيرِي	سِرْ	9
مَغْزُوَّةٌ	مَغْزُوٌّ	غَزْوٌ	غَازِيَةٌ	غَازٍ	أُغْزُونَ	أُغْزُوا	أُغْزُوَا	أُغْزِي	أُغْزُ	10
مَرْمِيَّةٌ	مَرْمِيٌّ	رَمْيٌ	رَامِيَةٌ	رَامٍ	إِرْمِينَ	إِرْمُوا	إِرْمِيَا	إِرْمِي	إِرْمِ	11

Table IV. PRETERITE PASSIVE.

First Person.		Second Person.					Third Person.						
PLURAL.	SING.	PLURAL.		DUAL.	SINGULAR.		PLURAL.		DUAL.		SINGULAR.		
COMM.	COMM.	FEM.	MASC.	COMM.	FEM.	MASC.	FEM.	MASC.	FEM.	MASC.	FEM.	MASC.	NO.
قُبِلْنَا	قُبِلْتُ	قُبِلْتُنَّ	قُبِلْتُمْ	قُبِلْتُمَا	قُبِلْتِ	قُبِلْتَ	قُبِلْنَ	قُبِلُوا	قُبِلَتَا	قُبِلَا	قُبِلَتْ	قُبِلَ	1
رُقِقْنَا	رُقِقْتُ	رُقِقْتُنَّ	رُقِقْتُمْ	رُقِقْتُمَا	رُقِقْتِ	رُقِقْتَ	رُقِقْنَ	رُقُّوا	رُقَّتَا	رُقَّا	رُقَّتْ	رُقَّ	2
أُكِلْنَا	أُكِلْتُ	أُكِلْتُنَّ	أُكِلْتُمْ	أُكِلْتُمَا	أُكِلْتِ	أُكِلْتَ	أُكِلْنَ	أُكِلُوا	أُكِلَتَا	أُكِلَا	أُكِلَتْ	أُكِلَ	3
بُئِسْنَا	بُئِسْتُ	بُئِسْتُنَّ	بُئِسْتُمْ	بُئِسْتُمَا	بُئِسْتِ	بُئِسْتَ	بُئِسْنَ	بُئِسُوا	بُئِسَتَا	بُئِسَا	بُئِسَتْ	بُئِسَ	4
هُنِئْنَا	هُنِئْتُ	هُنِئْتُنَّ	هُنِئْتُمْ	هُنِئْتُمَا	هُنِئْتِ	هُنِئْتَ	هُنِئْنَ	هُنِئُوا	هُنِئَتَا	هُنِئَا	هُنِئَتْ	هُنِئَ	5
وُرِثْنَا	وُرِثْتُ	وُرِثْتُنَّ	وُرِثْتُمْ	وُرِثْتُمَا	وُرِثْتِ	وُرِثْتَ	وُرِثْنَ	وُرِثُوا	وُرِثَتَا	وُرِثَا	وُرِثَتْ	وُرِثَ	6
يُسِرْنَا	يُسِرْتُ	يُسِرْتُنَّ	يُسِرْتُمْ	يُسِرْتُمَا	يُسِرْتِ	يُسِرْتَ	يُسِرْنَ	يُسِرُوا	يُسِرَتَا	يُسِرَا	يُسِرَتْ	يُسِرَ	7
قِلْنَا	قِلْتُ	قِلْتُنَّ	قِلْتُمْ	قِلْتُمَا	قِلْتِ	قِلْتَ	قِلْنَ	قِيلُوا	قِيلَتَا	قِيلَا	قِيلَتْ	قِيلَ	8
سِرْنَا	سِرْتُ	سِرْتُنَّ	سِرْتُمْ	سِرْتُمَا	سِرْتِ	سِرْتَ	سِرْنَ	سِيرُوا	سِيرَتَا	سِيرَا	سِيرَتْ	سِيرَ	9
غُزِينَا	غُزِيتُ	غُزِيتُنَّ	غُزِيتُمْ	غُزِيتُمَا	غُزِيتِ	غُزِيتَ	غُزِينَ	غُزِيُوا	غُزِيَتَا	غُزِيَا	غُزِيَتْ	غُزِيَ	10
رُمِينَا	رُمِيتُ	رُمِيتُنَّ	رُمِيتُمْ	رُمِيتُمَا	رُمِيتِ	رُمِيتَ	رُمِينَ	رُمِيُوا	رُمِيَتَا	رُمِيَا	رُمِيَتْ	رُمِيَ	11

TABLE V.

AORIST PASSIVE.

First Person.		Second Person.					Third Person.						
PLURAL.	SINGULAR.	PLURAL.		DUAL.	SINGULAR.		PLURAL.		DUAL.		SINGULAR.		
COMM.	COMM.	FEM.	MASC.	COMM.	FEM.	MASC.	FEM.	MASC.	FEM.	MASC.	FEM.	MASC.	NO.
نقبل	اقبل	تقبلن	تقبلون	تقبلان	تقبلين	تقبل	يقبلن	يقبلون	تقبلان	يقبلان	تقبل	يقبل	1
نرق	أرق	ترققن	ترقون	ترقّان	ترقّين	ترق	يرققن	يرقون	ترقّان	يرقّان	ترق	يرق	2
نؤكل	أؤكل	تؤكلن	تؤكلون	تؤكلان	تؤكلين	تؤكل	يؤكلن	يؤكلون	تؤكلان	يؤكلان	تؤكل	يؤكل	3
نباس	أباس	تباسن	تباسون	تباسان	تباسين	تباس	يباسن	يباسون	تباسان	يباسان	تباس	يباس	4
نهنو	أهنو	تهنأن	تهنوون	تهناان	تهنيين	تهنو	يهنأن	يهنوون	تهنآن	يهناان	تهنو	يهنو	5
نورث	أورث	تورثن	تورثون	تورثان	تورثين	تورث	يورثن	يورثون	تورثان	يورثان	تورث	يورث	6
نوسر	أوسر	توسرن	توسرون	توسران	توسرين	توسر	يوسرن	يوسرون	توسران	يوسران	توسر	يوسر	7
نقال	أقال	تقلن	تقالون	تقالان	تقالين	تقال	يقلن	يقالون	تقالان	يقالان	تقال	يقال	8
نسار	أسار	تسرن	تسارون	تساران	تسارين	تسار	يسرن	يسارون	تساران	يساران	تسار	يسار	9
نغزي	أغزي	تغزين	تغزون	تغزوان	تغزين	تغزي	يغزين	يغزون	تغزوان	يغزوان	تغزي	يغزي	10
نرمي	أرمى	ترمين	ترمون	ترميان	ترمين	ترمي	يرمين	يرمون	ترميان	يرميان	ترمي	يرمي	11

SECTION V.

Of the Indeclinable Particles—اَلْحُرُوفُ (plural of حَرْفٌ).

177. Arabian grammarians designate those parts of speech which we call Prepositions, Adverbs, Conjunctions, and Interjections, under the general appellation of Particles, as we stated, § 44. In treating of these we shall commence with the Preposition, thus far differing from the arrangement usually observed in European grammars. The Prepositions, Adverbs, and Conjunctions are each divided into two classes, the Inseparable and the Separable; the first being always directly prefixed, and the other, though not joined, invariably preceding the word which they govern. One or other of them may occur in every line, and are of much consequence to a proper understanding of the language; the Inseparable Prepositions, Adverbs, and Conjunctions together with the servile letters, are very apt to perplex the beginner in various ways; but more especially by fatiguing his patience in turning over, to no purpose, the leaves of a dictionary, for vocables which he can never find, till he has learned to analyse and separate those letters or particles from the words to which they are prefixed. It will be requisite for him, therefore, to pay very great attention to

the observations upon them, which we are about to offer, in order that they may make a necessary impression on the memory.

a. Most of the Particles, as we shall immediately see, are either substantives, adjectives, or verbs slightly modified; hence it often happens that the same word may belong to more than one of the subdivisions of particles; just as in Latin the word *ante* is either a preposition or an adverb, according to its application.

Of Prepositions—حُرُوفُ ٱلْجَرِّ

178. Of these, five are inseparable, viz., بِ, تَ, كَ, لِ, and وَ, all of which govern the genitive case of the noun to which they are prefixed. The Preposition بِ has *kasra* for its vowel, and signifies generally "in," as بِٱلْمَسْجِدِ, "in the mosque;" so نَصَرَكُمُ ٱللّٰهُ بِبَدْرٍ "God aided you (when you were) in Badr." It also denotes "with," "along with," or "together with;" as أَكَلْتُ خُبْزًا بِتَمْرٍ "I ate bread with dates;" so, كَتَبْتُ بِقَلَمٍ "I wrote with a pen." When subjoined to verbs of "coming" and "going," it denotes "along with," and then the phrase conveys the signification of "bringing," or of "taking away;" as أَتَي بِٱلْكِتَابِ "he came with the book," *i.e.* "he brought the book;" ذَهَبَ بِٱلنُّورِ "he went away with the light," *i.e.* "he took away the light." It sometimes denotes "compensation" or "retribution," equivalent to our words "for," "on account of;" as follows: ٱلنَّفْسُ بِٱلنَّفْسِ وَٱلْعَيْنُ بِٱلْعَيْنِ "life for life, and an eye for an

eye;" اَللّٰهُ تَتَلَكَ بِرُجُوعِكَ عَنِ ٱلْإِسْلَامِ "may God destroy thee on account of thy relapse from Islam!" It is sometimes a particle of swearing; as يَحْلِفُونَ بِٱللّٰهِ "they swear by God." It is often put before the predicate of a negative, and becomes a species of expletive; as مَا ٱللّٰهُ بِغَافِلٍ "God does not neglect;" literally, "God is not in neglecting;" لَسْتُ بِعَالِمٍ "I do not know." After إِذَا "lo!" "behold!" بِ is prefixed to the name indicating the object of attention; as إِذَا بِرَجُلٍ "behold a man!" Lastly, it is used idiomatically along with many verbs; as حَسَّ بِٱلشَّيْءِ "he perceived the thing;" مَرَرْتُ بِرَجُلٍ نَائِمٍ "I passed near a man (who was) sleeping."

179. The Prepositions تَ and وَ are employed chiefly in a few phrases to express swearing; as تَٱللّٰهِ "by God!" تَرَبِّ ٱلْكَعْبَةِ "by the Lord of the Ka'ba!" In like manner the particle وَ is employed, (when it is a preposition), as وَٱللّٰهِ "by God!" We may observe, however, that وَ is generally used as a conjunction denoting "and." It sometimes signifies "with," or "along with," indicating a simultaneous event or action, and in that case it governs the accusative; as إِسْتَوَى ٱلْمَاءُ وَ ٱلْحَاشِيَةَ "the water is even with the bank;" جَاءَ ٱلْأَمِيرُ وَٱلْجَيْشَ "the Amīr came with the army."

180. The Preposition كَ denotes "resemblance," corresponding to our words "like," or "as," and governs the

genitive; as كَرَجُلٍ "like a man." It is prefixed also to the isolated pronouns; thus, كَأَنَا "like me;" كَأَنْتَ "like thee;" كَهُوَ "like him;" but it is very rarely used with the affixed, though De Sacy quotes a few instances; as كِي "like me," etc. The word كَذَا composed of كَ and of the demonstrative ذَا, is considered as a noun, and if governed by a preceding word, the antecedent loses the nūnation, as in the following example: فِي شَهْرِ كَذَا مِنْ سَنَةِ كَذَا "in such a month of such a year." Of this particle, and the relative pronoun مَا, is formed the word كَمَا, signifying "in the same manner as."

a. I consider كَ, which is generally called an adverb, to be as genuine a preposition as either بِ or لِ. My reasons are—1st, that it uniformly governs the genitive case like the two last particles; 2nd, that it is *virtually* a preposition in English, as in the phrases "like me," "like him," etc., where "like" governs the objective case, the same as any other preposition; 3rd, it is viewed as a preposition by De Sacy (Grammaire Arabe, p. 468). Lastly, it is invariably a preposition governing the dative or ablative case in the Gaelic language, whether Highland or Irish. Stewart in his Gaelic Grammar, Edinburgh, 1812, p. 126, gives *mar*, "like," as a preposition. So does O'Donovan in his Irish Grammar, 1845, p. 285.

181. The Preposition لِ, with the vowel *kasra*, denotes "to," the sign of the dative case as لِرَبٍّ "to a master," اَلْحَمْدُ لِلّٰهِ "praise be to God." With the affixed pronouns it bears the vowel *fatḥa*; as لَكَ "to thee;" لَنَا "to us,"

etc., with the exception of the affixed pronoun of the first person singular; as لِي "to me." It also signifies "for," "because," "on account of;" تأجَّجَ كَرْبِي لِمُصَابَةِ بِنَاظِرَيهِ "my grief was increased on account of what had happened to his two eyes." It sometimes expresses swearing with a mixture of surprise; as لِلّٰه "by God!" As a conjunction, when prefixed to a verb, it sometimes means "in order that," or "to the end that;" as اِلْتَمَسَ شَيْئًا لِيَأكُلَهُ "he sought something that he might eat it." When prefixed to the aorist it forms an imperative in the 1st and 3rd persons; as لِنَنْصُرْ "let us assist;" لِيُنْصَرْ "let him be assisted." It is elegantly prefixed with *fatha*, by way of pleonasm, before that part of the sentence which grammarians call the Predicate (or that which is affirmed of any person or thing), especially when إِنَّ is placed before the subject (or the person or thing of which somewhat is affirmed); as إِنَّ إِسْكَنْدَرَ لَقَدِيرٌ "for Alexander (is) powerful," or "the powerful." When prefixed with *fatha* it gives to the Preterite the sense of the Optative, as more fully explained in the Syntax. Sometimes it is used idiomatically as a species of interjection expressive of "a cry for assistance;" as يَالَزَيْدٍ "help, O Zaid!" When the particle لَ, with a *fatha*, comes before the article, the latter loses its *alif*; as وَ إِنَّهُ لَلْحَقُّ مِنْ رَبِّكَ "verily that is the truth coming from thy Lord." Here لَلْحَقُّ is for لَأَلْحَقُّ. In conditional prepositions it answers to the antecedent لَوْ "if;" or لَوْلَا "if not;" as لَوْ جِئْتَنِي لَأَكْرَمْتُكَ "if thou comest to me, I will certainly honour thee," or more correctly, "hadst thou come to me, I would certainly have honoured thee."

182. It is, I think, inaccurately asserted in most Arabic Grammars that عَ and مِ are also inseparable prepositions; whereas they are so only in appearance. They are merely the initial letters of the particles عَنْ and مِنْ denoting "from," "out of," etc.; but then the second letter of the particle generally follows, changed by the rules of euphony into مْ (see § 19); as عَمَّا "from that which," for عَنْ مَا; so عَمَّنْ for عَنْ مَنْ. In like manner مِمَّا "out of that which," is for مِنْ مَا; and I think it would puzzle the grammarians to persuade us, that in this last instance, مِ is the prefix, and مَّا the word to which it is prefixed, which would involve us in a serious absurdity. In some very rare instances, however, مِ is really employed instead of مِنْ when followed by the article اَلْ; as مِلْحَيَّيْنِ "from the two tribes," instead of مِنَ ٱلْحَيَّيْنِ.

183. The Separable Prepositions of the Arabic language are not very numerous. Like the Inseparable they all govern the genitive case. We here give them in their alphabetical order.

184. The preposition إِلَي indicates the terminus of an action, "to," "until;" as جَاءَ إِلَي ٱلْمَدِينَةِ "he came to the city;" إِلَي ٱلْآنِ "until the present time." It also denotes "accession" or "addition;" as زَادُوا حِكْمَةً إِلَي حِكْمَتِهِمْ "they added wisdom to (their) wisdom."

185. The prepositions حَاشَا, خَلَا, and عَدَا, denote "exception;" thus, قُتِلُوا جَمِيعُهُم عَدَا زَيدٍ "they were all slain except Zaid." These were originally verbs signifying "being beyond," or "being separated from."

186. The preposition حَتَّي denotes "the termination" or "extremity" of a portion of time or space, like the Latin *usque ad*, or our phrase "as far as;" thus, حَتَّي مَطْلَعِ ٱلْفَجْرِ "as far as the place of rising of the dawn." When it is applied to time it signifies "until;" as سَارُوا حَتَّي طَلَعَتِ ٱلشَّمْسُ "they travelled until the sun arose." It is equivalent to our words "yea" and "even;" as اكَلْتُ ٱلسَّمَكَةَ حَتَّي رَأْسَهَا "I have eaten the fish, even its head." Had the particle إِلَي been used here instead of حَتَّي it would have meant "I have eaten the fish up to, or as far as, its head." When preceding the aorist used as a future, it affects it with antithesis, and answers to the Latin *donec* followed by the subjunctive mood. إِمْشِ حَتَّي تُدْرِكَهُمْ "march until thou overtakest them."

187. The preposition عَلَي "on," "above," denotes superiority as regards space or time; as عَلَيهِ "upon him;" عَلَي عَهْدِهِ "in," or "in the course of his time" or "reign." It sometimes denotes "against;" thus, اَسَدٌ مَرَّةً خَرَجَ عَلَي ثَورَينِ "a lion once upon a time went forth against two bulls." It sometimes signifies "according to;" as عَلَي عَادَةٍ "according to custom." It is idiomatically employed to express "debt"

or "duty;" as عَلَيَّ أَلْفُ دِينَارٍ literally, "upon me a thousand dīnārs," *i.e.* "I owe a thousand dīnārs;" عَلَيْكَ أَنْ تَفْعَلَ هٰذَا "you ought to do this." In this latter sense عَلَيْكَ is used to signify خُذْ "take;" as عَلَيْكَ زَيْدًا "take Zaid," an ellipsis for عَلَيْكَ أَنْ تَأْخُذَ زَيْدًا "it is your duty to take Zaid."

a. It is a curious coincidence that the idiomatic use of the Arabic عَلَي expressive of debt is also very common in the Gaelic language; thus, *Tha lā faghairidh agad orm,* "I owe you a day in harvest," literally, "you have a day in harvest upon me."

188. The preposition عَنْ signifies "separation from," "distance" or "transition;" as رَمَيْتُ ٱلسَّهْمَ عَنِ ٱلْقَوْسِ "I shot the arrow from the bow." It is sometimes used in the sense of "without;" as إِنَّ ٱللّٰهَ غَنِيٌّ عَنِ ٱلْعَالَمِينَ "verily God is rich enough without men." It also denotes "passing by" or "leaving behind;" as مَاتَ عَنْ وَلَدٍ "he died leaving (behind him) a son."

189. The preposition فِي denotes "in;" with reference to time or place; as اَلْمَالُ فِي ٱلْكِيسِ "the money (is) in the purse." It is used idiomatically to express multiplication in arithmetic; as ثَلَاثَةٌ فِي خَمْسَةٍ "three multiplied by five." It sometimes answers to the preposition "with;" as follows: تَوَجَّهَ فِي خَمْسِينَ أَلْفًا "he departed with fifty thousand (men)."

190. The prepositions لَدْ, لَدُ, لَدَا, لُدْ, لَدُنْ, and لَدَي generally denote "to," "up to," "as far as," "nigh," etc. According

to De Sacy these are all modifications of a substantive rather than prepositions.

191. The prepositions مِذْ, مُذْ, or مِنْذُ, مُنْذُ, denote the commencement of an action with reference to time elapsed, or still passing, and are equivalent to "since;" as follows: مَا رَأَيْتُهُ مُنْذُ يَوْمِ ٱلْجُمْعَةِ "I have not seen him since Friday." When the period is not yet finished, مُذْ or مُنْذُ governs the genitive; as مَا كَلَّمْتُهُ مُذْ شَهْرِنَا هٰذَا "I have not spoken to him during this month."

192. The preposition مِنْ denotes "from," "of," "than;" as عِنْدَ خُرُوجِ ٱلْأَمِيرِ مِنَ ٱلدَّارِ "when the Amīr departed from the palace." Sometimes it is used to express composition; as الْإِنْسَانُ مُرَكَّبٌ مِنْ نَفْسٍ وَجَسَدٍ "man is made up of a soul and a body;" جَنَّةٌ مِنْ نَخِيلٍ وَأَعْنَابٍ "a garden (consisting) of palm-trees and vines." It is used in the sense of our word "than" to express the comparative degree (see § 81). In negative propositions, or interrogative propositions implying negation, it often happens that the subject, or object of the verb, instead of appearing in its proper case, is idiomatically expressed by the preposition مِنْ governing the genitive; as مَا جَاءَنِي مِنْ رَجُلٍ "no man came to me;" مَا لَكُمْ مِنْ إِلٰهٍ غَيْرُهُ "you have no God but him."

193. The rest of the prepositions are expressed by nouns substantive, employed in the accusative case, the

nūnation being rejected. The principal prepositions of this sort are the following, viz., اَمَامَ "before," "in front of;" بَعْدَ "after;" بَيْنَ "between," "among;" تَحْتَ "beneath," "under;" حَوْلَ "round," "around;" خَلْفَ "after;" دُونَ "beneath," "under," "below;" سِوًى, سِوَى, or سُوَى "besides," "except;" شَطْرَ "towards;" عَبْرَ "beyond;" عِنْدَ "in possession of," "near," "with" (Latin *penes*, *apud;* French *chez*); عِوَضَ, "instead of;" غَيْرَ "except;" فَوْقَ "above;" قَبْلَ "before" (in regard to time); قُدَّامَ "before" (in regard to place); مَعَ or مَعْ "with;" وَرَآءَ "beyond," "behind;" وَسَطَ "amidst," "among." All these are themselves liable to be used in the genitive case when they are preceded by a simple preposition, inseparable or separable; as مِنْ بَعْدِ "after," "in the sequel."

Adverbs.

194. The Adverbs of the Arabic language are so numerous, that it would be a useless labour to attempt detailing them in any Grammar. Every substantive, adjective, active participle, and infinitive in the language may be employed adverbially by being put in the accusative case absolutely; thus, دَاخِلًا "within;" خَارِجًا "without;" كَثِيرًا "much;" قَلِيلًا "little;" مَعًا "together with;" يَوْمًا "one day;" لَيْلًا "by night;" نَهَارًا "by day;" اِتِّفَاقًا "by chance;" يَمِينًا "on the right hand;" شِمَالًا "on the left hand;" سَرِيعًا "quickly;" رَغْبَةً "eagerly;" طَوْعًا "willingly;" كَرْهًا "with aversion;"

أَبَدًا "eternally," etc. These are all substantives, adjectives, or nouns of action, which being put in the accusative case become adverbs.

a. According to De Sacy, nouns thus put in the accusative case, are often found in elliptical expressions, where they depend upon a verb understood; as سَمْعًا وَ طَاعَةً "by hearing and obeying," meaning "I am ready to obey you;" سَقْيًا "by watering," meaning "may God water this land;" سُبْحَانَهُ "by his praise," *i.e.* "may he be praised." These are elliptical expressions for سَمِعْتُ سَمْعًا وَأَطَعْتُ إِطَاعَةً "I heard by hearing and obeyed with obedience;" سَقَاكَ ٱللّٰهُ سَقْيًا "may God water thee by watering!" أُسَبِّحُهُ سُبْحَانَهُ "I praise him with his due praise." These modes of speaking are very common in Arabic; as تَعْسًا لَكَ "may you perish!" مَرْحَبًا وَ سَهْلًا "you are welcome," literally, "at your ease and convenience;" حُبًّا وَ كَرَامَةً "all is at your service," literally, "with love and with respect;" or, negatively, لَا وَ لَا كَرَامَةً which is a double ellipsis for لَا حُبًّا وَلَا كَرَامَةً "no love and no respect," *i.e.* "expect nothing from me." See De Sacy's Grammaire Arabe, Tome 1, p. 502, where the phrase is rendered "une cruche et un couvercle."

195. The following list comprises the most common adverbs of the Arabic language, independent of those already referred to (§ 194). It is a translation partly from De Sacy, and partly from Rosenmüller, whose Grammar is a very useful abridgment of De Sacy's more extensive work.

أَ, this is an inseparable particle denoting interrogation, like the Latin *an? num?* or *numquid?* thus, أَمَاتَ "is he dead?"

أَجَلْ "yes," "even so," "assuredly," "verily." Rosenmüller says that it differs from نَعَمْ in this respect, أَجَلْ is a stronger affirmation than نَعَمْ "yes," if the sentence which precedes be not interrogative; thus, if we say to a person "go away," and if he say أَجَلْ "yes," the affirmation is stronger than if he had said نَعَمْ. Again, if we say, "will you go?" نَعَمْ expresses the more emphatic assent.

إِذْ, إِذَا, إِذْمَا, and إِذَامَا "when." إِذَا, إِذَامَا are conjunctive adverbs usually employed with a future sense. إِذْ is limited to the present, or rather it expresses the simultaneous occurrence of two events; it also signifies "seeing that," "provided that." إِذْ and إِذَا signify also, "then," "behold." إِذَّاكَ or إِذْ ذَاكَ "then," "at that time." إِذَنْ or إِذًا "well done!"

أَلَا or أَلَّا "verily," "rest assured;" thus, from the voyage of Sindbad, وَ لَوْلَا وُصُولُكَ إِلَيْنَا وَ أَلَّا هَلَكْتَ فِي هَذَا ٱلْمَكَانِ "and had it not been (for) thy arrival amongst us, rest assured that thou wouldst have perished in this place."

إِلَّا (from إِنْ and لَا) "if not," *nisi*, "si non," "except." لَا حَوْلَ وَ لَا قُوَّةَ إِلَّا بِٱللّٰهِ "there is no power and no strength except in God."

أَمْ "whether?" (Latin *num? an?*) This is properly a conjunction expressive of doubt, and then signifies "or else."

أَمَا (from أَ and مَا "not") "is it not?" *nonne?*

أَمْسِ, أَمْسَ, أَمْسُ, and بِالْأَمْسِ "yesterday."

إِنْ. When this particle is followed by إِلَّا it signifies "not;" as إِنِ ٱلْحُكْمُ إِلَّا لِلّٰهِ "there is no judgment but with God." Sometimes when the word إِلَّا does not follow, it still expresses negation; as وَإِنْ أَدْرِي لَعَلَّهُ فِتْنَةٌ لَكُمْ "and I know not whether this may be a trial to you."

إِنَّ "assuredly," "verily," "indeed," "even so." It governs the accusative case, being one of the مِائَتْ عَامِلٍ or "Hundred Governing Words;" thus, إِنَّ ٱللّٰهَ غَفُورٌ "assuredly God is forgiving."

إِنَّمَا "unless," "since," "only;" as إِنَّمَا أَجْرِي عَلَى ٱللّٰهِ "my reward is only with God," *i.e.* "I expect my reward from God, and from no one else."

أَنَّي "how?" "wherefore?" "whence?"

إِيْ "yes," "verily," "even so." It is nearly equivalent to نَعَمْ but used only when a form of oath follows; thus, إِيْ وَرَبِّي إِنَّهُ ٱلْحَقُّ "verily, by the Lord it is the truth." It is equivalent to the interjection O, used in calling.

أَيَّانَ and إِيَّانِ "when," "whensoever."

أَيْنَ "where?" مِنْ أَيْنَ "whence?" إِلَي أَيْنَ "whither?" أَيْنَمَا "wheresoever?"

إِيهِ, إِيهٍ, إِيهِ an adverb of admiration, "bravo!" "well done!" إِيهًا "enough," "stop."

أَيُّهَا or يَاأَيُّهَا an adverb expressive of calling equivalent to our interjection O. It is used before a noun that is defined by the article; as, أَيُّهَا ٱلنَّاسُ or يَا أَيُّهَا ٱلنَّاسُ "O ye people!"

بَعْدُ "after," "afterwards," "behind;" مِنْ بَعْدُ "hereafter." When this word is used as a preposition it ceases to be indeclinable, and appears either in the accusative بَعْدَ, or in the genitive, if preceded by the preposition مِنْ, as مِنْ بَعْدِ. The phrase أَمَّا بَعْدُ is commonly employed after the prefaces of books, or in letters, in order to announce the commencement of the main subject, after the author or writer has expressed the praises of God, and the eulogy of the Prophet, or the usual formula of politeness, in epistolary correspondence.

بَعْدُ "afterwards," "thereafter," "yet;" in this last sense it is employed with a negative, and signifies "not yet," *nondum.*

بُعَيْدُ the diminutive of the preceding, signifies "a little after."

بَلَي "yes," "certainly," "it is so," "in reality." This particle is used after an interrogative or negative proposition, and then it affirms the contrary of what may be asserted in such proposition.

بَيْنَ "between;" this is merely the noun بَيْنٌ "difference," "separation," in the accusative case.

بَيْنَا "whilst," "meanwhile;" it sometimes denotes "between," like the preceding.

بَيْنَمَا "whilst," "in the mean time," "during this."

تَحْتُ "below," "under," "during" (when applied to time)

as تَحْتَ لَيْلَه "by night" (literally "under the night"); مِنْ تَحْتُ "from below;" تُحَيْتُ "a little lower."

ثَمَّ "here," "in this place."

ثُمَّ and ثُمَّتَ "then," "afterwards;" generally viewed as a conjunction.

جَيْرَ, جَيْرِ, and جَيْرُ "yes," "certainly," "of a verity." جَيْرِ اَجَلْ "assuredly it is so."

حَاشَ, حَاشَا, and حَاشًا "may it not be." When this word appears with the nūnation, it becomes an adverb; we have already described its use as a preposition. حَاشَ لِلّهِ or حَاشَا لِلّهِ "may God forbid!" حَاشَا لَكَ "far be it from thee!"

حَيَّ or حَيَّ هَلَا "hallo!" "come!" "come hither!"

حَيْثُ "where," "wheresoever;" مِنْ حَيْثُ "whence;" اِلَي حَيْثُ "whither;" حَيْثُمَا "wheresoever;" it is also written حَيْثَ.

دُونَ as a preposition, "except," "under," "besides." As an adverb it is used idiomatically in the sense of "seize" or "stop;" as دُونَكَ زَيْدًا "seize upon Zaid!" دُونَكَ وَمَا تُرِيدُ "do what thou wishest."

The particle رُبَّ (also written رُبَ, رَبَّ, رَبَ, رُبُ, رُبْ, رُبَّتَ, رُبَتَ, رَبَتَ) signifies "many," "much," "often," "perhaps." It takes idiomatically an affixed pronoun; as رُبَّهُ رَجُلًا "many men."

رُبَّمَا "often," "sometimes." This is compounded of رُبَّ and مَا, and signifies "sometimes," "occasionally," "often."

رَيْثَ and رَيْثَمَا "until," *usque dum.*

سَ, سَوْفَ, سَوْ, سَيْ, سَفْ. These when preceding the aorist give it a positive future signification.

سِيَمَا, سِيَّمَا, لَا سِيَمَا, and لَا سِيَّمَا "above all," "principally."

عَلُ "over," "above;" مِنْ عَلُ or *poeticé* مِنْ عَلُو "from above;" مِنْ عَلَا is also used.

عَلَّ. لَعَلَّ "perhaps," "by chance." This adverb receives the affixed pronouns; as عَلِّي, لَعَلِّي, عَلَّنِي "perhaps I;" لَعَلَّكَ "perhaps thou;" لَعَلَّكُم "perhaps you."

عَوْضَ and عَوْضُ; also عُوَضُ, عَوَضُ, and عُوَضُ. This adverb is always accompanied by a negation; and is only employed with a verb having a future signification. It is equivalent to our word "never."

غَيْرَ "except," "besides." This is the accusative case of the noun غَيْرٌ "change" or "difference;" it is also used adverbially; thus, لَا غَيْرُ signifying "not otherwise;" and is then indeclinable, like بَعْدُ, تَحْتُ, etc.

فَضْلًا, فَضْلًا أَنْ, and فَضْلًا عَنْ "far from," "much less," etc.

فَقَطْ "only," "solely;" compounded of فَ and قَطْ (*q.v.*).

فَوْقُ and فَوْقَ "above." This word is liable to the same remarks as those we made respecting بَعْدُ (*q.v.*).

قَبْلُ and قَبْلَ "before," "prior to." This word, like the preceding, is subject to similar rules. قِبَلًا "before," "right in front of one's eyes." قُبَيْلُ diminutive of قَبْلُ "a little before."

قَدْ, لَقَدْ, فَقَدْ, "certainly," "sometimes." This word is usually prefixed to verbs. Before the aorist it indicates a present or future action or event; sometimes it is equivalent to رُبَّمَا (*q.v.*).

قَطّ, قُطّ, قَطِ, قَطْ, قُطُ, "at any time." This particle is used only in company with a negation, and with a verb in the preterite; as مَا رَأَيْتُهُ قَطّ literally "I saw him not at any time," *i.e.* "I never saw him." If a future time is spoken of, عَوْضُ or أَبَدًا must be used.

كَأَنَّ "as if" (comp. of كَ and أَنَّ). كَذَا "thus," "so" (from كَ and ذَا). كَمَا and كَأَنَّمَا "as if," "according to" (comp. of كَ and مَا or كَأَنَّ and مَا).

كَأَيِّنْ "how much?" (comp. of كَ and أَيٍّ.)

كَلَّا "assuredly not" (in reply to a question).

كُلَّمَا "every time that," "as often as," "how often soever."

كَمْ "how much?" "how many?"

كَيْفَ "wherefore?" "how?" كَيْفَمَا "any how."

لَ. This prefix, as an adverb, has been already described under the preposition لِ.

لَا "no," "not," "not at all," "is not." It is a negation applied to a future action or event. لَابُدَّ "necessarily;" لَاجَرَمَ "undoubtedly."

لَمْ "no," "not;" applied absolutely. It is prefixed to the aorist, to which it then gives the sense of the preterite tense. لِمَا and لِمَ "why?" (comp. of the prep. لِ and مَا.) لَمَّا (from لَمْ and مَا) "not yet." As a conjunction it denotes "when," "after," or "after that," *posteaquam.*

لَنْ "no," "not." It is always prefixed to the aorist, and restricts it to a future signification. It is a comp. of لَا and أَنْ, literally "it shall not be that."

لَوْلَا or لَوْمَا "unless." Both of these adverbs are compounded of the conjunction لَوْ "if," and the negative particles لَا and مَا.

لَيْتَ "I wish" (Latin *utinam*), "would to God that!" لَيْتَ مُحَمَّدًا حَاضِرٌ "I wish (or would to God) that Muhammad were present." This admits the affixed pronouns; as يَا لَيْتَنِي حُرٌّ "I wish (or would to God) I had been a free man."

مَا, as an adverb, denotes "no," "not;" as مَا أَدْرِي "I know not." It also denotes "whilst," "as long as;" thus, مَا دُمْتُ حَيًّا "as long as I remain alive." We have already explained its pronominal application.

مَتَي "when?" مَتَي مَا "whenever."

مَعَ or مَعًا "with," "together with," "along with."

مَهْمَا "as often as," "as long as."

نَعَمْ, نَعَمْ, نِعَمْ, or نَعِمَ "yes," "very well," "even so." It is used in confirming what another person has said, whether the statement be affirmative or negative. It also denotes "bravo!" "well done!" It is placed before the nominative case if the noun has the article prefixed, and before the accusative when it is not so restricted.

وَا a particle denoting admiration and approbation, "bravo!" "well done!" It is properly an interjection (*q.v.*).

وَحْدَ. This word always requires an affixed pronoun; thus, وَحْدَهُ "he alone;" وَحْدَهَا "she alone."

وَيْ and وَيْكَ. Adverbs of admiration or reproach.

هَا "behold!" "seize!" "catch!" This, with the affixed pronoun of the second person, has the signification of خُذْ "take." The affixed pronoun changes, however, then into *hamza*; as هَاءَ, هَاءِ, هَاؤُمَا, هَاؤُمْ, هَاؤُنَّ; according to the variation of gender and number, for هَاكَ "take thou" (masc.); هَاكِ "take thou" (fem.); هَاكُمَا "take, you two," etc. (See Rosenmüller.)

هَاأَنَذَا masc. "see here!" "behold!" هَاأَنَذِهِ fem. nearly equivalent to our expressions, "there he is," and "there she is;" or the Italian *eccolo* and *eccola*.

هَلْ "whether?" An interrogative adverb, *an? num?*

هَلَا and هَلَّا "whether?" "is it not?" "well done!"

هَلُمَّ and هَلُمَّ لَكَ; or هَلُمَّ لَكُمْ "come on!" "approach!"

هُنَا and هَنَا "here," "in this place." From this adverb other demonstrative adverbs are formed, in the same manner as demonstrative pronouns; as هُنَاكَ, هُنَالِكَ "there," in speaking of things at a distance; هَاهُنَا "here," in speaking of things at hand. مِنْ هُنَا "from this place;" مِنْ هُنَالِكَ "from that place."

هُوذا and هَا هُوذا "see there!" "behold!"

هَيَّا, هَيْتَ, هَيتِ, هَيتُ, and هِيْتَ; these adverbs are employed in invocation and speaking to; they are more properly interjections used when calling to a person; as "hallo!" "come hither!" "hark you!"

يَا. This particle is, strictly speaking, an interjection used to signify warning, encouraging or admiration. يَا أَيُّهَا and يَا أَيَّتُهَا are nearly of the same import. They are applied indifferently to what is remote or near; and are followed by the nominative case.

Conjunctions.

196. It is with conjunctions as with adverbs, they are to be best learned by the Dictionary; but a few of the most common may be here enumerated.

أَلَّا. This is compounded of the conjunction أَنْ "that," and the negative adverb لَا "not;" with the prefixed particle لِ; it is written thus, لِئَلَّا "that it may not."

إِلَّا "if not;" (Latin) *nisi*, (French) "si non."

أَمْ an interrogative particle *an? num? necne?* It is used in the second member of an interrogative sentence or proposition beginning with أَ; thus, أَقُلْتَ هٰذَا أَمْ لَا "hast thou said this, or not?"

أَمَّا a particle used at the commencement of a clause or sentence; "but," "however," "nevertheless," "notwithstanding."

إِمَّا "or," "or else;" فَأَمَّا "if," "but" (comp. of إِنْ and مَا). إِمَّا followed by وَإِمَّا are equivalent to our expressions "either," "or;" thus, جَاءَنِي إِمَّا زَيْدٌ وَإِمَّا عَمْرٌو "there came to me either Zaid or 'Amru," (I know not which).

أَنْ, أَنَّ "that," used both with the aorist and the preterite; as أُرِيدُ أَنْ أَكْتُبَ "I wish that I may write;" عَجِبْتُ أَنْ كَتَبْتَ "I wonder that thou hast written." أَنَّ is used when immediately followed by a noun. It is often written with the affixed pronoun هُ; the purpose of which addition is to remove the influence of the conjunction, which would otherwise require the accusative case after it as it is one of the hundred governing words.

إِنْ "if indeed," "if at any time."

إِنَّ, and by contraction إِنْ. This conjunction comes before the subject of a preposition, when that subject is placed before the verb, and adds energy to the expression. It is also written إِنَّهُ, as is done with أَنَّهُ, and for the same reason; from the inseparable particle فَ, joined to this conjunction, are formed the words فَإِنَّ and فَإِنَّهُ, signifying "and indeed."

فَ. This is one of the inseparable conjunctions. Generally speaking it corresponds to our conjunction "and;" but it may also be occasionally translated "now," "for," "so then," etc. It is often redundant, particularly at the beginning of sentences, as is very often the case in our version of the Holy Scriptures. It is also frequently prefixed to the imperative and in that instance it generally marks the passage with a peculiar emphasis.

أَوْ "or," "or else," "unless," "until;" thus, لَأَضْرِبَكَ أَوْ تَتُوبَ "verily, I will beat thee, unless thou wilt repent."

كَأَنَّ "as if," "even as," "just as."

كَيْ "in order that;" لِكَيْ is used in the same sense and with the negative adverb لا, it becomes كَيْلَا and لِكَيْلَا "lest," "so as not."

لَكِنْ and لَكِنَّ "but." The form لَكِنَّ is used only before nouns and pronouns.

لَوْ "if," "although;" لَوْلَا "if not," "unless," *nisi*, "si non." It occasionally signifies, especially in the Kur,ān, "why not?" The affixed pronouns may also be joined to it; as لَوْلَاكَ مَا خَلَقْتُ ٱلدُّنْيَا "were it not for thee the world had not been created."

وَ. This is also an inseparable conjunction, corresponding to our connective "and;" sometimes it means "but." It is closely akin to فَ and yet in no instance can the one be used instead of the other. The general distinction between them seems to be as follows: the conjunction وَ is employed to connect words; as بَرًّا وَ بَحْرًا "by land and by sea." It is used also in connecting the various clauses of a sentence provided each clause has reference to the same nominative case. If a new nominative appears فَ is used, as may be seen in the following short fable:

أَسْوَدُ فِي يَوْمٍ نَزَعَ ثِيَابَهُ ـ وَأَقْبَلَ يَأْخُذُ ٱلثَّلْجَ ـ وَيَعْرُكُ بِهِ جِسْمَهُ * فَقِيلَ لَهُ ـ مَاذَا تَعْرُكُ جِسْمَكَ بِٱلثَّلْجِ ؟ فَقَالَ لَعَلِّي أَبْيَضُ * فَأَتَى رَجُلٌ حَكِيمٌ وَ قَالَ لَهُ ـ يَا هٰذَا ! لَا تُتْعِبْ نَفْسَكَ ـ فَقَدْ يُمْكِنُ أَنَّ جِسْمَكَ يُسَوِّدُ ٱلثَّلْجَ ـ وَهُوَ لَا يَرْتَدُّ ٱلسَّوَادُ *

"A negro on a certain day took off his garments and (*wa*) began to take up snow, and (*wa*) to rub his body with it. And (*fa*) it was said to him, why do you rub your body with snow? And (*fa*) he said, peradventure I may become white. And (*fa*) there came by a certain man of sense, and (*wa*) he said to him, O such a one! torment not yourself; for (*fa*) truly it is possible that your body may blacken the snow; but (*wa*) it will not (thereby) lose its (own) blackness."

Interjections.

197. أَخْ and أَخٍّ, an interjection expressive of pain, etc., like our words "ah!" "oh!" "alas!" "pish!" "tush!"

أُفُّ, أُفِّ, أُفَّ, أُفٍّ, أُفًّا, and أُفَّتًا; all these words are expressive of aversion or disgust such as our "foh!" "fie!" "away!"

آهْ, أَوْهْ, also آهٍ, and آهِ or أَوِّهْ. All these are expressive of pain and sorrow, etc. (nearly the same as أَخْ), like our "ah!" "alas!" "woe unto me!"

وَا "ah!" "alas!" This exclamation may be followed by

the nominative case; or, omitting the nūnation it may take instead the syllable ـَاهْ, or simply ـَا, وَا زَيْدٌ, or وَا زَيْدَا, or وَا زَيْدَاهْ. When two nouns in construction follow, the syllable ـَاهْ is added to the last; as وَا غُلَامَ زَيْدَاهْ "alas the boy or slave of Zaid!"

وَيْلٌ "alas!" "woe!" This is sometimes used disjunctively; as وَيْلٌ لَهُ "woe to him!" or conjoined, وَيْلَكَ, "woe to thee!" يَا وَيْلَنِي "woe to me!"

هَيَّ, هَيَّكَ, "quick!" هَيْتَ or هِيْتَ "come on!" "this way!"

يَا corresponds to our interjection O used in calling or addressing. It is used before the nominative case of proper names and nouns without the article; thus, يَا زَيْدُ "O Zaid!" (§ 67.) يَا وَزِيرُ "O Wazīr!" Before nouns having the article prefixed يَا أَيُّهَا is employed; as يَا أَيُّهَا ٱلرَّجُلُ "O man!"

SECTION VI.

On the Derivation and Formation of Nouns.

198. In this Section I employ the term Noun in its more extensive signification comprehending Substantives, Adjectives, Infinitives, and Participles. A primitive noun, جَامِدٌ "solid," is that which is not derived from any other word, whether noun or verb, such as لَحْمٌ "flesh;" اَسَدٌ "a lion;" فَرَسٌ "a horse." A derivative noun (مُشْتَقٌّ) is that which is derived from another word (verb or noun), by means of one or more of the servile letters, such as مِفْتَاحٌ "a key," from فَتَحَ "he opened;" مَأْسَدَةٌ "a place abounding in lions," from اَسَدٌ; so فُرَيْسٌ "a little horse," from فَرَسٌ "a horse."

199. We have already stated (§ 48) that the servile letters are seven in number, viz., ا, ت (or ة), س, م, ن, و, and ي, all included in the technical word يَتَسَمَّنُوا. The servile *alif* in the formation of nouns is used at the beginning and likewise in the interior of a word; as in اَكْبَرُ "greater," from كَبُرَ "he was great;" إِغْفَالٌ "negligence," from غَفَلَ "he neglected." It is also used at the end of a word, and represented by *hamza* preceded by an *alif* of prolongation; as in كِبْرِيَآءُ "pride" or "grandeur," from كَبُرَ "he was great." The

servile ت is employed both at the beginning, in the interior, and at the end of a word (in this latter case it is represented by ة); thus, تَطْوِيل "prolongation," from طال (for طَوُل) "it lengthened;" إِعْتِرَاف "confession," from عَرَفَ "he knew or confessed," etc.; رَحْمَةٌ "mercy," from رَحِمَ "he took pity." The letter س never serves alone in the formation of a noun. It is peculiar only to verbal nouns and participles of the ninth derived formation; and always preceded by ا or م and followed by ت as in the words اِسْتِخْرَاج "extracting," and مُسْتَخْرِج "an extractor," both from root خَرَجَ "he went forth." The letter م is servile at the beginning of a word; as مَمْلُوك "a slave," "a Mameluke," from مَلَكَ "he possessed;" sometimes, but rarely, it is added at the end of a word; as اِبْنَمْ which is the same as إِبْن "a son." The servile ن is used as the second letter of a derived noun, the first being in that case either ا or م as in the verbal noun and participle of verbs of the sixth formation; thus, اِنْقِطَاع "severance," from قَطَعَ "he cut short;" it serves also at the end of a word, as in غُفْرَان "pardon," from غَفَرَ "he forgave." The letter و is employed only in the interior of a word; as قَبُول "acceptance," from قَبِلَ "he accepted." The letter ي is used both in the interior and at the end of a word, as in كُلَيْب "a little dog," from كَلْب "a dog;" شَمْسِيٌّ "solar," from شَمْس "the sun;" sometimes, but very rarely, it is employed at the beginning of a word; as يَنْبُوع "a fountain," from نَبَعَ "it gushed out."

NOUNS DERIVED FROM VERBAL ROOTS.

200. Of these, grammarians reckon eight classes, viz.: 1. The Abstract Verbal Noun or Infinitive. 2. The Noun of Agency or Present Participle Active. 3. The Noun expressive of the Patient, that is the Participle Passive. 4. The Noun of Time and Place. 5. Noun of Instrument. 6. Noun of Unity. 7. Noun of Specification. 8. Noun of Intensity. Of the first three classes we need not here take any further notice. We gave a table of the Infinitives of the triliteral verbal root in § 105 *b*; and the formation of the Participles, Active and Passive, is abundantly obvious from the various paradigms given in Sections III. and IV.

Noun of Time and Place—اِسْمُ آلزَّمانِ وَ آلْمَكانِ.

201. The noun expressive of the time and place of an action, is formed from the aorist of the primitive triliteral verb, by substituting مَ in place of the initial servile letters ا, ت, ن, and ي, which are severally prefixed to the persons of that tense. If the penult vowel of the aorist be *fatḥa*, or *kasra*, they remain unchanged in the noun of time and place, if *ḍamma* it is changed into *fatḥa*; thus, مَشْغَلْ "the time and place of labour," from يَشْغَلُ "he labours" or "will labour; مَضْرِبْ "time or place of beating," from يَضْرِبُ "he beats" or "will beat;" مَكْتَبْ "the place of writing," "a school;" we may further observe that these nouns of place take the final ة; as مَقْبَرَة "place of burial," "a cemetery;" مَشْرِقَة "the place of sun-rising;" مَغارَة "a deep place," "a cavern;" مَنارَة "a place proper for a light-house," "a tower;" hence,

"a minaret." In the quadriliteral or derivative formations the noun of time and place is exactly the same as the participle passive.

a. There are twelve nouns of place formed by converting the *ḍamma* of the aorist, not into *fatḥa*, but into *kasra*, viz., مَجْزِرٌ "the place where camels are slaughtered;" مِرْفَقٌ "a place on which the elbow rests;" مَسْجِدٌ "the place of adoration, a mosque;" مَسْقِطٌ "the place where a thing falls;" مَسْكِنٌ "the place of residence," "a habitation;" مَشْرِقٌ "the place of rising," "the east;" مَطْلِعٌ "the place of rising (of a heavenly body);" مَغْرِبٌ "the place of setting," "the west;" مَفْرِقٌ "the place on the head where the hair divides;" مَنْبِتٌ "the place where a plant grows;" مَنْخِرٌ "the place of breathing," "the nostril;" مَنْسِكٌ and مَنْحِرٌ "the place where a camel is sacrificed." Of these twelve, however, مَسْجِدٌ, مَسْكِنٌ, مَطْلِعٌ, مَفْرِقٌ, and مَنْسِكٌ may indifferently take *fatḥa* or *kasra* as the vowel of the second syllable; and مَنْخِرٌ may, irregularly, take *kasra* as the vowel of the initial م, thus مَنْخِرٌ or مِنْخِرٌ "the place of sacrifice."

b. Nouns of time and place derived from a simile verb, whose first radical is و, have always *kasra* for the second radical, and the و is preserved, even when dropped in the aorist; thus, مَوْعِدٌ "time and place of promise," from وَعَدَ "he promised;" of which the aorist is يَعِدُ; so from وَضَعَ "he deposited" (aorist يَضَعُ); مَوْضِعٌ "place and time of depositing."

c. The noun of time and place derived from concave verbs (§ 151), whose second radical in the aorist has either *fatḥa* or *ḍamma*, is formed by substituting an *alif* inert in place of the second radical, and by carrying to the first radical the *fatḥa* which had belonged to the second; thus, from قَامَ "he stood" (aorist يَقُومُ), is formed مَقَامٌ for مَقْوَمٌ. If the second radical of the aorist has *kasra* for its vowel, it undergoes a change; thus, سَارَ "he travelled" (aorist يَسِيرُ); مَسِيرٌ "the place where one travels."

d. Nouns of time and place sometimes assume the termination ـَةٌ; as مَقْبَرَةٌ "a cemetery;" مَشْرَقَةٌ "the east;" مَرْعَاةٌ "the time and place of pasturing." Occasionally the middle radical takes *ḍamma* instead of *fatḥa*; as مَشْرُقَةٌ, مَقْبُرَةٌ for مَشْرَقَةٌ, etc.

e. Nouns of time and place derived from quadriliteral roots, or from derivative formations, are formed from the aorist passive, by substituting م for the initial incremental letters of that tense, so that they differ in nothing from the name of the patient, or the participle passive; thus from دَحْرَجَ "it revolved," is formed مُدَحْرَجٌ "the place of revolution;" from يُلْتَقَي passive aorist of إِلْتَقَي "he met," is formed مُلْتَقَي "the place of meeting," "the confluence of two rivers;" from اِنْصَرَفَ "he returned," مُنْصَرَفٌ "place or time of returning;" so from صَلَّي "he prayed," مُصَلًّي "the time and place of prayer," "an oratory."

Noun of Instrument—اِسْمُ آلَةٍ.

202. Nouns expressive of the instrument employed in the performance of an action are of the forms مِفْعَلٌ, مِفْعَالٌ, or مِفْعَلَةٌ. They are formed like the nouns of time and place with this difference, that the noun of instrument has *kasra* for its initial servile م; thus, مِفْتَاحٌ "a key," from فَتَحَ "he opened;" مِيزَانٌ "a balance," from وَزَنَ "he weighed;" مِكْنَسَةٌ

"a broom," from كَسَحَ "he swept;" مِحْلَاجٌ "an iron instrument employed in cleaning cotton," from حَلَجَ "he extracted the seeds," etc.

a. There are a few nouns of this class of the forms مُفْعُلٌ and مُفْعُلَةٌ; as مُنْخُلٌ "a sieve," from نَخَلَ "he sifted;" مُدُقٌّ "an instrument with which flax or cotton is beaten," from دَقَّ "he has beaten, thumped, or pounded."

b. Some nouns of instrument are formed on the measure فِعَالٌ; as نِظَامٌ "the instrument or means of adorning," "a string of pearls;" خِيَاطٌ "a needle;" سِرَادٌ "a saddler's awl." There are several other forms of rare occurrence mentioned by Dr. Lumsden, p. 311.

Noun of Unity—إِسْمُ الْمَرَّةِ.

203. This species of noun denotes one solitary action or event, and it dispenses with the use of the adjective وَاحِدَةٌ, which might be otherwise requisite. It is formed from the infinitive of the primitive triliteral verb, and is always of the form فَعْلَةٌ; as نَصْرَةٌ "one single victory;" ضَرْبَةٌ "one single beating." In the derivative formations and quadriliterals the noun of unity is formed by simply adding ـَةٌ to the infinitive; as إِسْتِخْرَاجَةٌ "one extraction," and دَحْرَاجَةٌ "one revolution." In the case of verbs of the second derivative formation, whose infinitives already end in ـَةٌ, the infinitive itself accompanied by the numeral وَاحِدَةٌ forms the noun of unity; thus, رَحْمَةٌ وَاحِدَةٌ "one solitary act of mercy." The same rule applies to all such infinitives

as assume ـَةٌ for a termination; as إِقَامَةٌ وَاحِدَةٌ "one solitary act of raising up," from أَقَامَ, third formation of قَامَ "he stood up."

Noun of Specification—اِسْمُ ٱلنَّوْعِ.

204. This kind of noun serves to specify what is asserted of a person with regard to a particular act, as when we say, "he excels in writing;" هُوَ حَسَنٌ كِتْبَةً; so هُوَ حَسَنٌ نِصْرَةً "he excels in defending or conquering." It invariably is of the form فِعْلَةٌ; and in the derivative formations and in quadriliterals it differs in no wise from the noun of unity just described.

Noun of Intensity—إِسْمُ مُبَالَغَةٍ.

205. This species of noun is of the measure فَعَّالٌ. It is closely akin to the present participle, or noun of agency; but it gives intensity to the expression; thus, كَاذِبٌ denotes simply "one who utters a falsehood," but كَذَّابٌ means "an out-and-out liar." From its nature it may be used either as an adjective or substantive. As an adjective it is equivalent to the superlative degree; as حَسَّانٌ "very beautiful;" وَهَّابٌ "very liberal." As a substantive it serves to indicate a person who follows as a trade or profession, whatever action or condition is expressed by the primitive root; thus, خَبَّازٌ "a baker," from خَبَزَ "he baked;" in like manner, نَجَّارٌ "a carpenter;" خَيَّاطٌ "a tailor," etc.

NOUNS DERIVED FROM SUBSTANTIVES.

206. Nouns derived from substantives are not nearly so numerous in Arabic as those derived from verbs. They may be comprised under four classes, viz., 1. Noun of Abundance. 2. Noun of Singularity. 3. Noun of Capacity. 4. Diminutive Nouns.

Noun of Abundance—إِسْمُ ٱلْكَثْرَةِ.

207. Nouns indicating the place in which things abound, are nearly allied to nouns of time and place both in form and in signification. They are of the measures مَفْعَلَةٌ and مَفْعَلٌ. such as مَأْسَدَةٌ and مَسْبَعَةٌ "a place in which there are many lions," derived from أَسَدٌ and سَبُعٌ both of which signify "a lion;" مَقْثَأَةٌ "a field of cucumbers," from قِثَّاءٌ "a cucumber;" مَذْأَبَةٌ "a place where wolves abound," from ذِئْبٌ "a wolf;" مَنْصَرَةٌ "a place famed for many victories," from نَصْرٌ "victory."

Noun of Singularity—اسْمُ ٱلْوَحْدَةِ.

208. This species of noun is formed from a primitive substantive by suppressing the nūnation, and then adding the termination ـَةٌ. It denotes a single portion or a single individual out of a whole genus which consists of several such portions; thus from تِبْنٌ "straw," is formed تِبْنَةٌ "a single straw;" from ذَهَبٌ "gold," comes ذَهَبَةٌ "a grain or small bit of gold;" from حَمَامٌ "the genus pigeon," comes حَمَامَةٌ "one single pigeon." It is formed in an analogous manner to the noun of unity, as to its termination, but not necessarily on the same measure.

Noun of Capacity—إِسْمُ ٱلْوِعَاءِ.

209. I call this species "a Noun of Capacity," from want of a better term. It denotes the vessel, case, or sheath, etc., in which things are contained or collected; thus, مِحْلَبٌ "a milk-pail," from حَلَبٌ "milk;" مِئْبَرٌ "a needle case," from إِبْرَةٌ "a needle." It will be observed that this noun is of the same measure as the first form of the Noun of Instrument, § 202. They both differ from the Noun of Time and Place by having *kasra* as the vowel of the initial servile م, and *fatḥa* for the middle radical.

The Diminutive Noun—الإِسْمُ ٱلْمُصَغَّرُ.

210. From triliteral nouns the diminutive is formed, by putting *ḍamma* over the first radical and by inserting the diphthong ـَيْ between the second and third; thus from رَجُلٌ "a man," رُجَيْلٌ "a little man;" so from جَبَلٌ "a hill" or "mountain," جُبَيْلٌ "a hillock" or "small mountain." If the primitive noun be quadriliteral the diminutive is of the form فُعَيْلِلٌ; thus, عُقَيْرِبٌ "a little scorpion," from عَقْرَبٌ "a scorpion." If the primitive triliteral is of the feminine gender, the diminutive is of the form فُعَيْلَةٌ; thus, شَمْسٌ "the sun," شُمَيْسَةٌ "a little sun" or "a mock sun;" أَرْضٌ "earth" or "land," أُرَيْضَةٌ "a small tract of land."

Adjectives derived from Verbal Roots.

211. In addition to the Participles Active and Passive both of the primary verb, and of its derivative formations,

there are several other descriptions of verbal adjectives chiefly derived from neuter verbs, the principal of which are the following:—1. فَعْلٌ ; as صَعْبٌ "difficult," from صَعُبَ. 2. فَعَلٌ ; as حَسَنٌ "fair," from حَسُنَ. 3. فَعِلٌ ; as خَصِرٌ "cold," from خَصِرَ. These are chiefly derived from neuter verbs of the measure فَعِلَ (aorist يَفْعَلُ). 4. فَعَالٌ ; as حَرَامٌ "sacred," from حَرُمَ. 5. فَعُولٌ ; as غَفُورٌ "forgiving," from غَفَرَ. 6. فَعِيلٌ ; as شَهِيدٌ "a martyr," from شَهِدَ. 7. فُعَالٌ ; as شُجَاعٌ, "brave," from شَجُعَ. 8. أَفْعَلُ ; as أَعْوَجُ "crooked," from عَوِجَ. Adjectives expressive of colour are generally of this form; as أَحْمَرُ "red," from حَمُرَ. The form أَفْعَلُ is also employed to denote the comparative and superlative degrees, as we have already stated in § 81 and § 82. 9. فَعْلَانٌ and فَعْلَانُ ; as نَدْمَانٌ "regretful," from نَدِمَ ; غَفْلَانُ "careless," from غَفِلَ. 10. فُعْلَانٌ ; عُرْيَانٌ "naked," from عَرِيَ.

a. Many verbal adjectives, or as some call them participles, of the measures فَعُولٌ and فَعِيلٌ derived from active verbs may have either an active or a passive signification.

212. Adjectives of the following measures, viz., فُعَّالٌ, فِعِّيلٌ, فِعْلٌ, فُعَلَةٌ, فَاعِلَةٌ, فَعُولَةٌ, مِفْعَلٌ, مِفْعَالٌ, and مِفْعِيلٌ are sometimes of an energetic or intensive signification; thus, فِخِّيرٌ "very boastful," etc.

a. We stated, § 205, that the measure فَعَّالٌ represents both an intensive verbal adjective and a substantive indicating trade or profession, etc. As an adjective it sometimes suppresses the nūnation and adds the termination ـَةٌ, even when applied to masculine nouns; as عَلَّامَةٌ "profoundly learned." According to De Sacy this increment adds still further to the intensity of the adjective.

Adjectives derived from Substantives.

213. From nouns substantive are derived what we may in general terms call Relative Adjectives, expressive of "nation," "locality," "sect," "race," etc., by rejecting the nūnation or final vowel of the substantive and adding ـِيٌّ; thus, مِصْرِيٌّ "Egyptian," from مِصْرُ or مِصْرٌ "Egypt;" شِيرَازِيٌّ "of or relating to Shīrāz;" إِنْسَانِيٌّ "human," from إِنْسَانٌ "man," أَرْضِيٌّ "earthly," from أَرْضٌ "earth."

a. If the substantive ends in ـَةٌ or يَةٌ the relative adjective is formed by rejecting these terminations and substituting ـِيٌّ; thus from مَكَّةُ "the city of Mecca," is formed مَكِّيٌّ "of or relating to Mecca;" so from طَبِيعَةٌ "nature," comes طَبِيعِيٌّ "natural." If the primitive triliteral noun should have *kasra* as the vowel of its middle radical, the same is changed into *fatḥa* in the relative adjective; thus from كَبِدٌ "the liver," is formed كَبَدِيٌّ "pertaining to the liver," "hepatic." If the first and second radicals should each have *kasra* for their vowels, it is optional in the second radical to retain the *kasra*, or change the same into *fatḥa*; thus from إِبِلٌ "a camel," is formed إِبِلِيٌّ or إِبَلِيٌّ "relating to the camel." If the first radical should have *kasra*, and the second *fatḥa* for their vowels, the *fatḥa* may optionally remain, or be changed into *kasra*; thus from عِنَبٌ "the grape," are formed either عِنَبِيٌّ or عِنِبِيٌّ "of or belonging to the grape."

b. Relative adjectives formed from substantives of the measures فَعِيْلٌ and فَعِيلَةٌ change the *kasra* of the second radical into *fatḥa* and reject the ي that follows; thus from جَزِيرَةٌ "an island," comes جَزَرِيٌّ "insular;" if nouns of these measures however be formed from surd verbs, no such modification takes place; thus from حَقَّ "it was necessary," comes the substantive حَقِيقَةٌ "truth;" and thence حَقِيقِيٌّ "truthful." Relative adjectives formed from proper names of the measures فُعَيْلٌ and فُعَيلَةٌ reject the ي of the primitive word; thus from قُرَيْشٌ "name of an Arab tribe," comes قُرَشِيٌّ "a Ḳuraishite" or "a man of the Ḳuraish tribe;" so from هُذَيل "the name of the founder of a certain sect," comes هُذَلِيٌّ "a follower of Hudhail." In some words, however, this modification is optional, as in the case of قُرَيْشٌ which makes قُرَشِيٌّ or قُرَيْشِيٌّ.

c. Some relative adjectives are formed by adding the termination ـَانِيٌّ; as جِسْمَانِيٌّ "corporeal," from جِسْمٌ "the body;" so نُورَانِيٌّ "illumined (divinely)," from نُورٌ "light." Adjectives of this kind are said to be used only in a metaphorical, theological, or spiritual sense, for in the ordinary sense of the words جِسْمِيٌّ and نُورِيٌّ are employed. Finally, some relative adjectives are formed in a very irregular manner; thus from رَيّ "the capital of Persian Irāk," is formed رَازِيٌّ "a native of Rhai;" such was the celebrated physician known in mediæval Europe as Rhasis. From طَبَرِسْتَانُ "the name of a province in Persia," is formed the relative adjective طَبَرِيٌّ; so from هَرَاةٌ "the city and province of Herat," comes هَرَوِيٌّ "a man of Herat."

Formation of the Broken Plurals—جَمْعُ ٱلتَّكْسِيرِ.

214. We very cursorily alluded to this important part of

Arabic Grammar, in § 58 and § 59. We now proceed to fulfil our promise there given of entering into a more minute detail of the subject when we should have arrived at the proper place for so doing. It would have been utterly absurd to have embarrassed the student at an early period of his progress, with matters which he was no ways *then* qualified to understand. The following portion of this Section is chiefly translated from Rosenmüller, always subjected to additions and improvements from the more copious works of De Sacy and Lumsden.

215. *The First Measure,* فُعَلٌ, is formed from the singulars فُعْلَةٌ and فُعْلَى, which are the feminines of adjectives of the measure أَفْعَلُ; thus, تُحْفَةٌ "a present," pl. تُحَفٌ; كُبْرَى "very great," pl. كُبَرٌ; صُورَةٌ "a form or figure," pl. صُوَرٌ. Plurals of this species, though of rare occurrence, may also be formed from the measures فَعْلَةٌ and فِعْلَةٌ; as قَرْيَةٌ "a town or village," pl. قُرًى (for قُرَيٌ); لِحْيَةٌ "the beard," pl. لُحًى (for لُحَيٌ).

216. *The Second Measure,* فُعُلٌ, is formed 1. from singular nouns of the measures فِعَالٌ and فَعَالٌ, and whose triliteral root is neither surd nor defective. It also applies to such measures as فَعِيلٌ, فَعِيلَةٌ, فَعُولٌ, provided they do not come from defective roots, that is roots having و or ي for their last radical; thus, كِتَابٌ "a book," pl. كُتُبٌ; سَرِيرٌ "a throne," pl. سُرُرٌ; عَمُودٌ "a pillar," pl. عُمُدٌ; سَفِينَةٌ "a ship," pl. سُفُنٌ; صَحِيفَةٌ "a leaf of a book," pl. صُحُفٌ. 2. From nouns of the measures فِعْلٌ, فَعَلٌ,

and فَعْلَةٌ; as نَمِرٌ "a leopard," pl. نُمْرٌ; أَسَدٌ "a lion," pl. أُسْدٌ; بُسْرَةٌ "the fruit of the date tree," pl. بُسْرٌ. 3. From verbal adjectives of the measures فَعِيلٌ and فَعُولٌ, provided they have not a passive signification; as نَذِيرٌ "a monitor," pl. نُذُرٌ; صَبُورٌ "patient," pl. صُبُرٌ.

217. *The Third Measure,* فُعْلٌ, is applicable to masculine adjectives of the measure أَفْعَلُ and to their feminines فَعْلَاءُ, provided they be not of the comparative or superlative degree; as أَحْمَرُ and حَمْرَاءُ "red," pl. (masc. and fem.) حُمْرٌ.

218. *The Fourth Measure,* فِعَلٌ, applies to singular nouns of the measure فِعْلَةٌ; as سِكَّةٌ "a coin," pl. سِكَكٌ; بِيعَةٌ "a temple or church," pl. بِيَعٌ; حِكْمَةٌ "a maxim," pl. حِكَمٌ.

219. *The Fifth Measure,* فِعَالٌ, applies to singulars of the measures فَعْلٌ, فِعْلٌ, فُعْلٌ, فَعُلٌ, فَعْلَةٌ, and فُعْلَةٌ; as بَحْرٌ "the sea," pl. بِحَارٌ; قِدْحٌ "an arrow," pl. قِدَاحٌ; رُمْحٌ "a spear," pl. رِمَاحٌ; رَجُلٌ "a man," pl. رِجَالٌ; قَصْعَةٌ "a dish or saucer," pl. قِصَاعٌ; رُقْعَةٌ "a short letter," "a note," pl. رِقَاعٌ. 2. It applies to the measures فَعَلٌ and فَعَلَةٌ, provided they be not derived from a surd or defective root; thus, جَبَلٌ "a mountain," pl. جِبَالٌ; رَقَبَةٌ "the neck," pl. رِقَابٌ. 3. It applies to the adjectives of the measures فَعِيلٌ and فَعِيلَةٌ, provided they be not of a passive signification; thus, شَرِيفٌ, fem. شَرِيفَةٌ "noble," pl. شِرَافٌ. 4. It applies to such

adjectives, as have the measures فَعْلَانُ, fem. فَعْلَانَةٌ; or فُعْلَانُ, fem. فُعْلَانَةٌ; thus, نَدْمَانُ and نَدْمَانَةٌ "penitent," pl. نِدَامٌ; خُمْصَانُ and خُمْصَانَةٌ "lean (from starvation)," pl. خِمَاصٌ. 5. Finally, it applies to many nouns of agency or verbal adjectives of the measure فَاعِلٌ; thus, تَاجِرٌ "a merchant," pl. تِجَارٌ; نَاهِلٌ "thirsty" (applied only to a camel), pl. نِهَالٌ.

220. *The Sixth Measure,* فُعُولٌ, applies to substantives of the measures فَعْلٌ, فِعْلٌ, فُعْلٌ, فَعَلٌ, and فَعِلٌ; and sometimes, though rarely, to adjectives of the measure فَاعِلٌ; as بَحْرٌ "the sea," pl. بُحُورٌ; ضِرْسٌ "a molar tooth," pl. ضُرُوسٌ; جُنْدٌ "an army," pl. جُنُودٌ; أَسَدٌ "a lion," pl. أُسُودٌ; كَبِدٌ "the liver," pl. كُبُودٌ; شَاهِدٌ "a witness," pl. شُهُودٌ. To these we may add a few irregulars; thus from بَاكٍ "weeping," pl. بُكِيٌّ and بِكِيٌّ (for بَاكِيٌ); جَاثٍ "kneeling," pl. جُثِيٌّ and جِثِيٌّ for جُثُويٌ.

221. *The Seventh and Eighth Measures,* فُعَّلٌ and فُعَّالٌ, apply to verbal adjectives of the measures فَاعِلٌ and (fem.) فَاعِلَةٌ, provided they be not derived from imperfect roots; thus, حَاكِمٌ "a judge," pl. حُكَّمٌ and حُكَّامٌ; كَاتِبٌ "a writer," pl. كُتَّابٌ; غَازٍ (for غَازِيٌ) "a combatant," pl. غُزَّآءٌ for غُزَّاوٌ; غَائِبٌ "absent," pl. غُيَّبٌ; بَاهِلَةٌ "a female camel that is turned loose," pl. بُهَّلٌ. According to De Sacy, the measure فُعَّالٌ belongs exclusively to masculine nouns.

222. *The Ninth Measure,* فَعَلَةٌ, is applicable to such verbal

adjectives as have the measure فَاعِل, when applied to rational beings, and not coming from a defective root; as كَامِل "perfect," pl. كَمَلَة; قَائِم "standing erect," pl. قَوَمَة; بَارّ (for بَارِر) "innocent," pl. بَرَرَة. A few words derived from infirm roots are somewhat irregular; or more strictly speaking, they follow the rules of permutation; thus, بَائِع "one who sells," pl. بَاعَة for بَيَعَة.

223. *The Tenth Measure*, فُعَلَة, belongs almost exclusively to verbal adjectives when applicable to rational beings, and of the measure فَاعِل formed from a defective root; thus, غَازٍ "a warrior," pl. غُزَاة (for غُزَوَة); قَاضٍ "a Kadi or judge," pl. قُضَاة (for قُضَيَة).

224. *The Eleventh Measure*, فِعَلَة, is formed from substantives singular of the measure فُعْل, and also from a few having the measures فَعْل and فِعْل; as دُبّ "a bear," pl. دِبَبَة; كُوز "a jug," pl. كِوَزَة; زَوْج "a husband or wife," *conjux*, pl. زِوَجَة; قِرْد "an ape," pl. قِرَدَة.

225. *The Twelfth Measure*, فِعْلَة, applies to substantives of the measures فَعْل, فُعْل, فَعَل, فَعَال, فُعَال, and فَعِيل; thus, ثَوْر "a bull," pl. ثِيرَة; أَخ (for أَخَو) "a brother," pl. إِخْوَة; غُصْن "a branch," pl. غِصَنَة; غَزَال "a gazelle or antelope," pl. غِزْلَة; غُلَام "a boy," "a slave," pl. غِلْمَة; صَبِيّ (for صَبِيو) "a youth, boy, or lad," pl. صِبْيَة.

226. *The Thirteenth Measure*, أفعُل, applies to substantives of the measure فَعْل ; and sometimes to the measures فَعَل, فِعْل, and فُعْل, provided they come not from a root whose medial letter is و or ي ; thus, وَجْه "the face," pl. أَوْجُه ; دَلْو "a bucket," pl. أَدْلٍ (for أَدْلُو) ; جَبَل "a hill," pl. أَجْبُل ; عَصًا "a staff," pl. أَعْصٍ (for أَعْصُو) ; رِجْل "the foot," pl. أَرْجُل ; قُفْل "a bolt (of a door)," pl. أَقْفُل. It is also applicable to feminine substantives of four letters, not ending in ـَة, and of which the penult is an inert ا, و, or ي ; thus, ذِرَاع "the arm," pl. أَذْرُع ; يَمِين "an oath," pl. أَيْمُن. It is further applicable, by prescription, to several measures different from those above indicated, and even to singulars coming from concave roots ; as سَبُع "a lion," pl. أَسْبُع ; نَهَار "the day," pl. أَنْهُر ; عَيْن "the eye," pl. أَعْيُن ; دَار "a house," pl. أَدْوُر.

227. *The Fourteenth Measure*, أَفْعَال, is applicable, 1. To substantives of three letters and of all measures, though seldom to the measure فَعْل, unless its middle letter be ا, و, or ي ; thus, مَطَر "rain," pl. أَمْطَار ; كَتِف "the shoulder," pl. أَكْتَاف ; إِبِل "a camel," pl. آبَال (for أَأْبَال) ; عَيْن "the eye," pl. أَعْيَان ; رُطَب "a date," pl. أَرْطَاب. 2. It is applicable to the measure فِعْل, when its medial consonant is a long vowel or diphthong (as already indicated), or when its initial letter is و ; thus, فِيل "an elephant," pl. أَفْيَال ; سَيْف "a sword," pl. أَسْيَاف ; يَوْم "a day," pl. أَيَّام (for أَيْوَام) ; وَقْت "time," pl. أَوْقَات. 3. It is applied, though rarely, to the measure

فَاعِل; thus طَاهِر "pure," pl. اَطْهَار; also to verbal adjectives of the measure فَعِيل, provided they be not of a passive signification; as شَرِيف "noble," pl. اَشْرَاف.

228. *The Fifteenth Measure*, اَفْعِلَة, is applicable, 1. To nouns of four letters, the penult of which is ا, و, or ي inert; as قِلَاد "a necklace," pl. اَقْلِدَة; إِلٰه "God," which is an abbreviation of إِلَاه, and always so pronounced, pl. آلِهَة (for أَأْلِهَة); عَمُود "a pillar," pl. اَعْمِدَة; رَغِيف "a cake," "a cracknell," pl. اَرْغِفَة. 2. It is especially applicable to singular nouns whose measures are فَعَال and فِعَال, if derived from a surd or defective root; thus, إِمَام "a priest or Imām," pl. اَئِمَّة (for أَأْمِمَة); قَبَآء "a short tunic or vest," pl. اَقْبِيَة.

229. *The Sixteenth Measure*, فَوَاعِل, is applicable to nouns of the measures فَاعِل and فَاعَل; thus, سَاحِل "the sea shore," pl. سَوَاحِل; خَاتَم "a signet-ring," pl. خَوَاتِم. It is also applicable to substantives and adjectives feminine of the measures فَاعِلَة and فَاعِلَآء; thus, صَاعِقَة "lightning accompanied with thunder," pl. صَوَاعِق; صَاحِبَة "a female companion," pl. صَوَاحِب; نَافِقَآء "the hole of the jerboa," pl. نَوَافِق.

230. *The Seventeenth Measure*, فَعَآئِل, is applicable to substantives singular feminine, consisting of four consonants, of which the third is one of the letters of prolongation, viz., ا, و, or ي, inert, each preceded by its homogeneous short vowel (§ 30, *a.*); thus, شَمَال "the north wind," pl. شَمَآئِل;

عَجُوز "an old woman," pl. عَجَائِز; قَصِيدَة "a species of poem," pl. قَصَائِد. The same rule applies to feminine substantives of the same measure, but adding ـَة at the end; as سَحَابَة "a cloud," pl. سَحَائِب; عَجُوزَة "an old woman," pl. عَجَائِز; عَجِيبَة "a wonder or rarity," pl. عَجَائِب.

231. *The Eighteenth Measure*, فِعْلَان, belongs to substantives singular of the measures فُعَال, فَعَال, and فَعَل; likewise to some nouns of the measures فُعْل, فَعْل, and فَاعِل, when derived from concave roots; as غُلَام "a youth," "a slave," pl. غِلْمَان; غَزَال "a gazelle or antelope," pl. غِزْلَان; حُوت "a fish," pl. حِيتَان; تَاج "a crown," pl. تِيجَان. This plural is also applicable to a few singulars that admit of other measures; as أَخ (for أَخَو) "a brother," pl. إِخْوَان; صَبِيّ "a young boy," pl. صِبْيَان; أَمَة (for أَمَوَة) "a handmaid," pl. إِمْوَان; حَائِط "a wall," pl. حِيطَان.

232. *The Nineteenth Measure*, فُعْلَان, applies to substantives of the measures فَعْل, فَعَل, and فَعِيل; as سَقْف "a roof," pl. سُقْفَان; بَلَد "a region," "a province," pl. بُلْدَان; رَغِيف "a cake," pl. رُغْفَان. It also applies to a few words of the measure فَاعِل when used substantively, and not derived from a concave root; as فَارِس "a horseman," pl. فُرْسَان.

233. *The Twentieth Measure*, فُعَلَاءُ, is applied to adjectives masculine, of the measure فَعِيل, not having a passive sense;

and to a few of the measure فَاعِلٌ not derived from a concave or defective root, and significant of a rational being; thus, فَقِيرٌ "a poor man," pl. فُقَرَآءُ; أَمِيرٌ "a prince," pl. أُمَرَآءُ; شَاعِرٌ "a poet," pl. شُعَرَآءُ. The masculine word خَلِيفَةٌ "a successor," makes the plural خُلَفَآءُ. There are a few other singular nouns, some of them derived even from a defective root, which admit of this kind of plural.

234. *The Twenty-first Measure,* أَفْعِلَآءُ, applies to singulars of the measure فَعِيلٌ, but is principally peculiar to those whose root is a surd verb, or a concave, or a defective; thus, حَبِيبٌ "a friend," "one beloved," pl. أَحِبَّآءُ (contracted for أَحْبِبَاءُ); غَنِيٌّ "a rich man," pl. أَغْنِيَآءُ; وَلِيٌّ "a friend," pl. أَوْلِيَآءُ. It occasionally applies to nouns of this measure derived from perfect roots; thus, صَدِيقٌ "sincere," pl. أَصْدِقَآءُ.

235. *The Twenty-second Measure,* فَعْلَى, applies to adjectives of the measure فَعِيلٌ, and sometimes, though rarely, also to فَاعِلٌ, فَعِلٌ, and أَفْعَلُ, when they are expressive of "pain," "wounds," "injuries in general (of body or mind);" as جَرِيحٌ "wounded," pl. جَرْحَى; قَتِيلٌ "slain," pl. قَتْلَى; هَالِكٌ "perishing," pl. هَلْكَى. The same plural applies also to verbal adjectives of the measure فَعْلَانُ; thus, كَسْلَانُ "lazy," pl. كَسْلَى; غَضْبَانُ "angry," pl. غَضْبَى.

236. *The Twenty-third Measure,* فَعَالِي. This is applicable to substantives singular, of the measures فَعْلَآءُ, فَعْلَى, and فِعْلَى;

also to adjectives feminine of the measures فَعْلَاءُ and فُعْلَي; thus, صَحْرَآءُ "a plain," or "a desert," pl. صَحَارِي; عِذْرَآءُ "a virgin," pl. عَذَارِي; فَتْوَي "the decision of a judge," pl. فَتَاوِي; حُبْلَي "pregnant," pl. حَبَالِي.

237. *The Twenty-fourth Measure,* فَعَالَي, applies, in the first place, to the same class of substantives and adjectives as the preceding; thus, عَذْرَآءُ "a virgin," pl. عَذَارَي. 2nd. To adjectives of the measure فَعْلَانُ; as سَكْرَانُ "intoxicated," pl. سَكَارَي. In this case the first letter of the plural may take *damma* instead of *fatha*; thus, سَكَارَي and سُكَارَي are both right.—The adjective كَسْلَانُ may have in the plural كَسَالَي, كُسَالَي, or كِسَالَي. Lastly, it applies to feminines of the form فَعِيلَةٌ coming from a defective root; as هَدِيَّةٌ "a gift," pl. هَدَايَا; خَطِيَّةٌ "sin," pl. خَطَايَا.

238. *The Twenty-fifth Measure,* فَعِيلٌ, is applicable to a few singulars of the measures فَعْلٌ, فِعَالٌ, and فَاعِلٌ; thus, عَبْدٌ "a slave," pl. عَبِيدٌ; حِمَارٌ "an ass," pl. حَمِيرٌ; غَازٍ "a warrior," pl. غَزِيٌّ.

239. *The Twenty-sixth Measure,* فُعُولَةٌ, is of very rare occurrence, and belongs to a few singulars of the measure فَعْلٌ; thus, بَعْلٌ "a husband," pl. بُعُولَةٌ; عَمٌّ "a paternal uncle," pl. عُمُومَةٌ.

240. *The Twenty-seventh Measure,* فِعَالَةٌ, is applicable to a

few singulars of the measures فَعَلٌ and فَاعِلٌ; thus, حَجَرٌ "a stone," pl. حِجَارَةٌ ; صَاحِبٌ "a companion," pl. صِحَابَةٌ; also صَحَابَةٌ is to be met with.

241. *The Twenty-eighth Measure,* فُعَلٌ, applies to a few singulars of the measures فَعْلَةٌ, فُعْلَةٌ, and فَاعِلٌ; thus, حَلْقَةٌ "a ring," pl. حِلَقٌ ; بَكْرَةٌ "a pulley," pl. بَكَرٌ ; طَالِبٌ "one who seeks," pl. طَلَبٌ.

242. We now proceed to describe the broken plurals of words consisting of four or more consonants, which we cursorily mentioned in § 58, *c* and *d*. They are divided by grammarians into three classes of measures, which, when added to the preceding twenty-eight, furnish in all thirty-one species of broken plurals as formerly stated, § 58, *a*.

243. *The Twenty-ninth Measure,* فَعَالِلُ (أَفَاعِلُ, تَفَاعِلُ, and مَفَاعِلُ). The first plural of these measures applies to quadriliteral nouns, the consonants of which are all radical; of course the servile final ـَةٌ does not here count as a letter; thus, ضِفْدِعٌ "a frog," pl. ضَفَادِعُ ; قَنْطَرَةٌ "a bridge," pl. قَنَاطِرُ. The other three measures apply respectively to quadriliterals formed from triliteral roots (the termination ـَةٌ as before not counting), by prefixing ا, ت, or م ; thus إِصْبَعٌ "a finger," pl. أَصَابِعُ ; تَجْرِبَةٌ "experience," pl. تَجَارِبُ; مَعِيشَةٌ "means of living," "victuals," pl. مَعَايِشُ.

244. *The Thirtieth Measure,* فَعَالِيلُ (أَفَاعِيلُ, تَفَاعِيلُ, مَفَاعِيلُ,

يَفَاعِيل, and فَوَاعِيل). This measure applies to singular nouns consisting of five letters, of which the penult is a letter of prolongation; as, سُلْطَان "a sultan or emperor," pl. سَلَاطِين; دِينَار (for دِنَّار), "a dinar," *denarius*, pl. دَنَانِير; قِنْدِيل "a lamp," pl. قَنَادِيل; يَنْبُوع "a source or fountain head," pl. يَنَابِيع; جَامُوس "a buffalo," pl. جَوَامِيس; مِسْكِين "poor," pl. مَسَاكِين; تَصْوِير "a picture," pl. تَصَاوِير.

245. *The Thirty-first Measure*, فَعَالِلَة, أَفَاعِلَة, etc. (as above). This is a modification of the preceding measure, by suppressing the penult ي of prolongation, and by adding the termination ـَة; thus, أُسْتَاذ "a preceptor," pl. أَسَاتِيذ and أَسَاتِذَة; تِلْمِيذ "a disciple," pl. تَلَامِيذ and تَلَامِذَة; فَيْلَسُوف "a philosopher," pl. فَلَاسِفَة. This measure belongs also to nouns of four or more letters of which the penult is not a letter of prolongation; and it applies more especially to foreign words, whether substantives or relative adjectives; thus أُسْقُف "a bishop," pl. أَسَاقِف and أَسَاقِفَة; قَيْصَر "an Emperor, Cæsar, Kaiser, or Czar;" pl. قَيَاصِرَة; مَغْرِبِيّ "a Mauritanian," pl. مَغَارِبَة; جَرْكَسِيّ "Georgian or Circassian," pl. جَرَاكِسَة; صَقْلَبِيّ "a Sclavonian," pl. صَقَالِبَة; بَغْدَادِيّ "a native or inhabitant of Bagdad," pl. بَغَادِدَة.

a. For a more detailed account of this portion of Arabic Grammar the learner is recommended to peruse the works of Lumsden and De Sacy. My object has been to observe a middle course between the profuseness of these great masters, and the meagreness of Richardson and Stewart.

The Plural of the Plural—جَمْعُ ٱلْجَمْعِ.

246. An additional plural is sometimes formed from the broken plurals of triliterals, which is called "the pl. of the plural;" thus, كَلْبٌ "a dog," pl. أَكْلُبٌ, and thence the plural of the plural أَكَالِبُ; so from ظُفْرٌ "a finger nail," is formed the pl. أَظْفَارٌ; and from that, the pl. of the pl. أَظَافِيرُ; from يَدٌ (for يَدْيٌ) "the hand," comes the pl. أَيْدٍ (for أَيْدُيٌ), and thence أَيَادِي; from سِوَارٌ "a bracelet," pl. أَسْوِرَةٌ, and from that again the pl. of the pl., أَسَاوِرُ. It may be observed that the plurals of the plural agree in measure with those of quadriliteral and quinquiliteral nouns, §§ 243, 244, and 245.

a. Broken plurals sometimes form an additional regular plural in ـَاتٌ; thus, from رِسَالَةٌ "an epistle," is formed the broken plural رَسَائِلُ, and thence the plural feminine of the plural رَسَائِلَاتٌ, "a collection of letters;" so from بَيْتٌ "a house," pl. بُيُوتٌ, and thence the pl. of the plural بُيُوتَاتٌ "a cluster of houses." According to De Sacy, these plurals can be employed only when the number is undetermined, and above nine.

b. Sometimes a dual is formed from a broken plural; thus, أَصْلٌ "a principle," or "foundation" (of a science), pl. أُصُولٌ; and thence is formed (what we may call "the dual of the plural") أُصُولَانِ which signifies "the principles of the two sciences," viz., Theology and Jurisprudence.

247. We stated briefly, § 58, *b*, that many Arabic nouns have more than one species of plural; the student must not,

however, conclude that they are all used indiscriminately. In this case he must be guided entirely by prescription or custom. For example, on examining carefully the preceding thirty-one measures of broken plurals, he will find that no fewer than nine of them, viz., فِعَل, فُعُول, فِعَلَة, فِعْلَة, أَفْعُل, أَفْعَال, فُعْلَان, فَعِيل, and فُعُولَة, are applicable to singulars whose measure is فَعْل. We may here further state that "the plurals of paucity," viz., measures 12th, 13th, 14th, and 15th, alluded to in § 58, *b*, are applied only to a number of persons or things, ranging from three to ten, both inclusive.

a. We noticed in § 58, *e*, a few words that formed their plural irregularly. The fact is that several of these irregular plurals are derived from singulars no longer in use; thus, أُمّ "a mother," has for its plural أُمَّهَاتٌ, apparently from أُمَّهَةٌ; فَمٌ "the mouth," pl. أَفْوَاهٌ from فُوهٌ; مَآءٌ "water," pl. أَمْوَاهٌ and مِيَاهٌ, as if from مَاهٌ. The word إِمْرَأَةٌ "a woman," has for its plural نِسَآءٌ, نِسْوَةٌ, and نِسْوَانٌ all of which come from a different root. The word إِنْسَانٌ "a man" or "a human being in general," has the pl. أُنَاسٌ and contracted نَاسٌ.

SECTION VII.

SYNTAX OF THE ARTICLE, SUBSTANTIVES, ADJECTIVES, AND PRONOUNS.

Analysis of Sentences.

248. In the preceding Sections we have treated of the letters, syllables, and words of the Arabic language. We now come to the most important part of our work—the construction of sentences, or, in other words, the rules for speaking and writing the language correctly. We have all along taken for granted that the student is acquainted with the ordinary terms of grammar, and is able to distinguish the various parts of speech (common to all languages) from one another. It is probable, however, that he may not have turned his attention to the analysis of sentences, which ought to form a preliminary step to the Syntax of every foreign tongue. On this account, we request his attention to the following general, or rather universal principles of language, an acquaintance with which will enable him to comprehend more fully some of the rules which we are about to state.

a. A simple sentence consists of three parts, viz., a nominative or agent; a verb; and an attribute, predicate, or complement; thus, "Fire is hot;" "Fire consumes wood." In the first sentence, *fire* is the nominative, or subject of affirmation; *hot* is the attribute, or that which is affirmed of the subject, *fire*; and the verb *is* serves to express the affirmation. Again, in the sentence "Fire consumes wood," *fire* is the nominative, or agent, *consumes* is the verb, and *wood* is the *object* or *complement*. Frequently a simple sentence consists *in appearance* of only two words; as "winds blow;" "ships sail;" which expressions are equivalent to "winds are blowing," "ships are sailing." It appears, then, that the shortest sentence must consist of three words, expressed or understood; and it will be found that the longest is always reducible to three distinct parts and no more. For the sake of illustration let us take the following sentence from the Letters of Junius, viz., "An unmerited outrage offered to a great or good man | naturally excites | some emotions of resentment even in hearts that have the least esteem for virtue." In this sentence the verb is "naturally excites;" what precedes the verb, is the nominative; and what follows it, is the complement.

b. Although every simple sentence is reducible to three distinct parts, yet it is not easy to find a general term that will accurately apply to each individual part with the exception of the verb. When the sentence is expressed by means of the verb "to be," the three parts may be called the *nominative* or *subject*, the *verb*, and the *attribute*; thus, "Zaid is diligent." When the sentence is expressed by any other neuter *verb*, the parts may be called *nominative*, *verb*, and *complement*; as "Zaid went from Mecca to Isfahān." When the verb of the sentence is active or transitive, the parts are *agent*, *verb*, and *object*; as "Zaid purchased a horse." Lastly, when the sentence is expressed by means of a passive verb, the three parts are *nominative*, *verb*, and *agent*; as "a horse was purchased by Zaid."

c. A compound sentence, or period, consists of two or more simple sentences connected by a conjunction, expressed or understood; thus,

"Knowledge fills the mind with entertaining views; and administers to it a perpetual series of gratifications; it gives ease to solitude; fills a public station with suitable abilities; and, when it is mixed with complacency, it adds lustre to such as are possessed of it." It will be a useful exercise for the student to analyze, by himself, the above compound sentence; which consists of five simple sentences, in all of which, *knowledge*, or its substitute *it*, is the nominative. The last two clauses make but one simple sentence, for they amount merely to this: "Knowledge, mixed with complacency, adds lustre to such as are possessed of it."

249. The leading principles of Arabic Syntax do not differ upon the whole, from those that prevail in our own and other European languages. As a general rule the verb agrees with its nominative in number, gender, and person; the adjective agrees with its substantive in number, gender, and case; and the relative agrees in number and gender with its antecedent. There are, however, in the Arabic language, some exceptions to the preceding general principles, together with many idiomatic peculiarities which may startle the European student, whose notions of grammar are derived from the languages of ancient Greece and Rome.

Arrangement of the Words in a Sentence.

250. We have just shewn (§ 248, *a*) that a sentence consists of three distinct parts; and the attentive student will find on examination that there are six ways of arranging these parts. In Arabic prose compositions, the general rule is to put the verb first, then the nominative, and lastly the complement; thus, ضَرَبَ زَيْدٌ عَمْرًا "Zaid struck 'Amru."

So in the following sentences, viz., قَالَ لُقْمَانُ لِٱبْنِهِ "Lukmān said to his son." فِي ٱلْبِدَايَةِ خَلَقَ ٱللّٰهُ ٱلسَّمَاوَاتِ وَ ٱلْأَرضَ "In the beginning God created the heavens and the earth." جَآءَ زَيْدٌ مِنْ إِصْفَهَانَ إِلَي بَغْدَادَ "Zaid came from Iṣfahān to Baghdād." When one substantive governs another in the genitive case the governing word comes first; as حُبُّ ٱلدُّنْيَا "love of the world;" سِمَاعُ ٱلْحِكْمَةِ "listening unto wisdom." In like manner a substantive precedes the adjective which serves to qualify it; as كِتَابٌ عَظِيمٌ "a great book;" اَلصَّدِيقُ ٱلصَّدُوقُ "the sincere friend."

a. Languages abounding in case terminations, such as the Sanskrit, the Latin, and the Greek, admit of any of the six modes of arrangement above alluded to; thus the simple sentence, "Cæsar vanquished Pompey," which we cannot arrange with perspicuity, except in one way, may in Latin be expressed, "Cæsar vicit Pompeium," or "Cæsar Pompeium vicit;" "vicit Cæsar Pompeium," or "vicit Pompeium Cæsar;" lastly, "Pompeium Cæsar vicit," or "Pompeium vicit Cæsar." The Arabic is more restricted in its arrangement; and it is a curious coincidence that the Gaelic exactly agrees with it; for example, the first verse of Genesis (above quoted) runs thus in Gaelic: "Anns an toiseach chruthaich Dia na neamhan agus an talamh," which corresponds word for word with the Arabic. The reader is not to infer, however, that I consider the two languages to have the least affinity with one another. I merely point out occasionally certain striking resemblances between the two, as to arrangement and idiom, which I hold to be purely accidental.

SYNTAX OF THE ARTICLE.

251. The definite article اَلْ of the Arabic generally cor-

responds in its use and application with the ὁ, ἡ, το of the Greek. For example, when a substantive is restricted by the article, and at the same time qualified by an adjective, the adjective as well as the substantive takes the article; thus, اَلْكِتَابُ ٱلْعَظِيمُ "the great (or valuable) book," ἡ βιβλος ἡ ἀξια. In like manner when the substantive is a proper name (and consequently definite in its nature), its qualifying adjective (if any) takes the article; thus, إِبْرٰهِيمُ ٱلْأَمِينُ "Abraham the faithful," Ἀβραὰμ ὁ πιστος. The article is always prefixed to names of peoples and sects; thus, اَلْيَهُودُ "the Jews;" اَلنَّصَارَي "the Christians;" اَلْعَرَبُ "the Arabians;" اَلْفُرْسُ "the Persians." It is used also before singular nouns to express collectively a whole species; as in the following example: اَلْهَجِينُ خَيْرٌ مِنَ ٱلْجَمَلِ "The dromedary is preferable to the camel."

a. The article is sometimes employed, as in German and French, instead of an affixed possessive pronoun, when the possessor cannot be mistaken; thus, "By *thine* absence thou hast troubled me, and in *my* trouble *my* reason has departed," بِٱلنَّوَى زَلْزَلْتَنِي وَٱلْعَقْلُ فِي ٱلزِّلْزَالِ زَالَ, where we see العَقْلُ employed for عَقْلِي. The article is also used, as in other languages, *per antonomasiam,* as in the expressions اَلنَّبِيُّ "the prophet," ὁ προφητης, for Muḥammad; اَلْكِتَابُ "the book," ἡ βιβλος, for the Ḳur,ān. Finally, the article is used as in German and French before nouns denoting an abstract idea in general, in which instances we employ no article in English; thus, بِٱلْعَمَلِ يَحْصُلُ ٱلثَّوَابُ لَا بِٱلْكَسَلِ "by activity the reward is obtained, not by slothfulness;" it is also used before names of sciences, arts, regions, etc.; as اَلْحِكْمَةُ "wisdom;" اَلْحُكُومَةُ "government;" اَلْعِرَاقُ "'Irāk;" اَلشَّامُ "Syria," or "Damascus."

SYNTAX OF SUBSTANTIVES.

Of the Nominative Case.

252. The nominative case is often employed at the beginning of a sentence in an absolute sense, independently of any grammatical construction with what follows. For example, the sentence "To God belongs whatever is in the heavens and upon the earth," is thus expressed in Arabic, اَللّٰهُ لَهُ مَا فِي ٱلسَّمٰوَاتِ وَ عَلَي ٱلْأَرْضِ literally, "God, (or, as to God,) to him (is) whatever (is) in the heavens and upon the earth;" so, اَللّٰهُ رَسُولُهُ عِنْدَكُمْ "As to God, his prophet is among you," *i.e.* "the prophet of God is among you." This use of the nominative absolute is called the inchoative case, اَلْمُبْتَدَأْ; such a mode of construction is by no means rare in our modern Anglo-Saxon, both English and Scotch, as in the following couplet from the exquisite ballad of "Auld Robin Gray:"

> "My heart—it said nay, for I look'd for Jamie back;
> But the wind—it blew high, and the ship—it was a wrack."

a. We mentioned (158, *a*) that the verb "to be," is seldom used in the present tense except when its omission might occasion an ambiguity; thus, زَيْدٌ عَالِمٌ "Zaid is learned;" اَللّٰهُ كَرِيمٌ "God (is) bountiful;" أَنْتَ شَرِيفٌ "thou (art noble)." Here we see that the verb is entirely omitted, and both the subject and attribute put in the nominative case in the order described, § 250. In many instances it is optional to make the subject precede the attribute or *vice versa*; thus we may say اَللّٰهُ اَكْبَرُ or اَكْبَرُ اَللّٰهُ "God (is) very great;" مُحَمَّدٌ نَبِيُّنَا or نَبِيُّنَا مُحَمَّدٌ "Muhammad (is) our prophet."

Of the Genitive Case.

253. When in Arabic two substantives are so combined that the first, which is indefinite in its signification, is restricted by the second, such a construction is called إِضَافَةٌ, which we may translate "state of regimen." The first word is termed اَلْمُضَافُ "the regent;" and the second, which is always put in the genitive case, is called اَلْمُضَافُ إِلَيْهِ or "the governed;" as حِكْمَةُ ٱللّٰهِ "the wisdom of God;" كِتَابُ سُلَيْمَانَ "the book of Solomon." The governing word has very frequently the effect of an adjective; as كَثْرَةُ ٱلنَّوْمِ "abundance of sleep," *i.e.* "much sleep;" طُولُ ٱلتَّجَارِبِ "length of experiences," *i.e.* "long experience." Such is uniformly the construction of the noun كُلٌّ "the totality," which answers to our words "every" or "all," according as the word governed is singular or plural; thus, كُلُّ شَيْءٍ "everything;" كُلُّ ٱلنَّاسِ "all men."

a. Like كُلٌّ are also construed the interrogative pronoun أَيٌّ and its feminine أَيَّةٌ denoting "what?" "which?" أَيُّ ٱلنَّاسِ "what or which men?" أَيَّةُ ٱمْرَأَةٍ "what woman?" لِأَيَّةِ عِلَّةٍ "for what reason?" A similar rule applies to the word غَيْرٌ signifying "difference," hence "negation;" for example, غَيْرُ مَخْلُوقٍ "increate;" جَاؤُا ٱلْوُزَرَآءُ وَٱلْقُضَاةُ وَغَيْرُهُمْ "the Wazīrs and Ḳāḍīs and others besides them came."

b. The state of regimen frequently expresses superiority or excellence in a superlative sense; as خَيْرُ ٱلْبَرِيَّةِ "the best of created things." When the governing word is an adjective the latter is sometimes restricted in its signification by the word governed; as سَرِيعُ ٱلْحِسَابِ "quick at calculation," instead of ذُو سُرْعَةِ ٱلْحِسَابِ "possessed of readiness at calculation;" شَدِيدُ ٱلْعِقَابِ "violent in chastising," instead of ذُو شِدَّةِ ٱلْعِقَابِ.

Of the Accusative Case.

254. We stated (§ 194) that every noun in Arabic may be converted into an adverb by being put in the accusative case. The accusative case in this language is frequently used adverbially in instances where the Latin would employ the ablative, or the accusative with a preposition; thus, مَاتَ جُوعًا "he perished of hunger," *mortuus est fame*; صُومُوا أَيَّامًا مَعْدُودَةً "do ye fast during certain specified days," *per certum dierum spatium.* An adjective or participle with the accusative termination frequently corresponds with the Latin gerund in *do*; as جَآءَ رَاكِبًا "he came riding," *venit equitando*; يَأْكُلُ وَاقِفًا "he eats standing," أُدْخُلُوا ٱلْبَابَ سُجَّدًا "enter the gate in adoration." The accusative is sometimes equivalent to the Latin gerund in *dum*; as ضَرَبْتُهُ تَأْدِيبًا "I struck him for (the sake of) instruction," *ad erudiendum.* Finally, the accusative, *pur et simple*, expresses in Arabic the sense of the Latin *quoad*, "by reason of," "with respect to," or "as to;" thus, طَابَ إِسْحَاقُ نَفْسًا "Isaac is good, with respect to his mind, or disposition," *i.e.* "he

is well disposed;" اَللّٰهُ عَظِيمٌ قُدْرَةً "God is great (as to) power;" وَهِيَ كَالْحِجَارَةِ اَوْ اَشَدُّ قَسْوَةً "and these (hearts) are like stones, or more intense (than stones), as to hardness."

a. The predicate in the accusative is sometimes put before the subject; thus in the Kur,ān, vi. 42; وَالنَّخْلَ وَالزَّرْعَ مُخْتَلِفًا اُكُلُهُ [He it is who hath brought forth] "the palm-tree and the corn-crop of which there is a variety of food;" where مُخْتَلِفًا اُكُلُهُ is equivalent to اَلَّذِي اُكُلُهُ مُخْتَلِفٌ "the food (resulting) from which is various." So in xxi. 3: وَهُمْ يَلْعَبُونَ لَاهِيَةً قُلُوبُهُمْ [They listen not to the admonition of their Lord except that] "they may turn it unto sport, their hearts being taken up with delight;" where لَاهِيَةً قُلُوبُهُمْ is equivalent to وَقُلُوبُهُمْ لَاهِيَةٌ. N.B.—In connection with quotations from the Kur,ān, as above, the Roman numerals indicate the *sūrat* or chapter, and the Arabian figures, the *āyat* or verse.

b. The present participle put in the accusative has sometimes the effect of what in Latin is called the subjunctive mood, which in Arabic is expressed by the preterite preceded by the conjunction لَوْ "although," "even if," as in the following verse from the *Ḥamāsa*: سَاَغْسِلُ عَنِّي الْعَارَ جَالِبًا عَلَيَّ قَضَآءُ اللّٰهِ مَا كَانَ جَالِبًا "verily, I will wash away dishonour from me, even if the decree of God should draw upon me whatever it may draw;" where جَالِبًا (when it first occurs) is equivalent to وَلَوْ جَلَبَ. So in the following sentence: مَنْ هَوِيَ شَيْئًا مَالَ بِهِ هَوَاهُ نَحْوَهُ كَائِنًا مَا كَانَ قَبِيحًا اَوْ جَمِيلًا "whoso coveteth anything, his avarice leadeth him on to it, whatever it may be, foul or fair."

c. In Arabic the accusative is very frequently employed where we should use the nominative, as in the following verses from the Ḳur,ān, ii. 242: وَلِلْمُطَلَّقَاتِ مَتَاعٌ بِٱلْمَعْرُوفِ حَقًّا عَلَي ٱلْمُتَّقِينَ "and to the divorced (wives is due) a reasonable provision (according to the husband's means); this is incumbent on the pious;" where we see حَقًّا in the accusative. So also in iv. 15, we have the following: وَإِن كَانُوا أَكْثَرَ مِن ذٰلِكَ فَهُمْ شُرَكَآءُ فِي ٱلثُّلُثِ وَصِيَّةً مِنَ ٱللّٰهِ "and if there should be more (brothers or sisters) than these (two) they shall be (equal) sharers in the third part (of the estate); this is an ordinance from God;" where we see فَرِيضَةً مِنَ ٱللّٰهِ used for هٰذَا فَرِيضَةٌ مِنَ ٱللّٰهِ.

Substantives in Apposition.

255. When one substantive is subjoined to another by way of description or designation, the two are said to be in "apposition," and must agree in gender, number, and case, as in the Ḳur,ān, xiv. 19: وَيُسْقَي مِنْ مَاءٍ صَدِيدٍ "and there shall be drinking of water (which is) poison." So in xxiv. 35: يُوقَدُ مِن شَجَرَةٍ مُبَارَكَةٍ زَيْتُونَةٍ "it (the lamp) is lighted with the oil of a blessed tree, the olive." The same rule holds when the second substantive defines the manner, measure, or quantity, of the first: thus, أَكَلْتُ ٱلرَّغِيفَ نِصْفَهُ "I ate half the cake," literally, "I ate the cake, the half of it." The same rule also applies to certain words added by way of "confirmation" or "corroboration" (تَوكِيدٌ), such as نَفْسٌ "the soul" or "self," and عَيْنٌ "the eye" or "essence," having subjoined to them the affixed pronoun appropriate to the first substantive. They thus become equivalent to the Latin *ipse*, *ipsa*, and *ipsum*. They agree in gender, number,

and case with the leading substantives, the forms used for both dual and plural being أَنْفُسٌ and أَعْيُنٌ, as may be seen in the following examples: جَآءَ زَيْدٌ نَفْسُهُ "Zaid himself came;" رَأَيْتُ زَيْدًا نَفْسَهُ "I saw Zaid himself;" جَاءَتْ زَيْنَبُ نَفْسُهَا "Zainab herself came;" رَأَيْتُ ٱلْأَمِيرَيْنِ أَنْفُسَهُمَا "I saw the two princes themselves." The words نَفْسٌ and عَيْنٌ may also be put in apposition after the affixed pronouns; for example, رَأَيْتُكَ نَفْسَكَ "I saw thyself," which may also be expressed رَأَيْتُكَ أَنْتَ نَفْسَكَ or رَأَيْتُكَ إِيَّاكَ نَفْسَكَ.

a. In a manner similar to the foregoing are used the words كُلٌّ and جَمِيعٌ denoting "totality," or "universality," as also عَامَّةٌ "people in general;" as جَآءَ ٱلْجَيْشُ كُلُّهُ "the whole army came," literally, "the army came, the whole of it;" so جَآءَتِ ٱلْقَبِيلَةُ كُلُّهَا "the whole tribe came;" رأيت القوم كلهم "I saw the multitude, all of them;" مَرَرْتُ بِٱلنِّسَآءِ كُلِّهِنَّ "I passed by all the women;" جَآءَ ٱلْجَيْشُ عَامَّتُهُ "the whole army came." In order to express duality in such instances the words كِلَا, fem. كِلْتَا or كِلَتَا, "both," are employed; as in the following examples: جَآءَ زَيْدٌ وَعَمْرٌو كِلَاهُمَا "both Zaid and 'Amru came;" رَأَيْتُ عَمْرًا وَعُمَرَ كِلَيْهِمَا "I saw both 'Amru and 'Umar;" زَوَّجْتُهُ زَيْنَبَ وَفَاطِمَةَ كِلْتَيْهِمَا "I gave unto him as wives both Zainab and Fatima." When the words كِلَا and كِلْتَا precede the substantives which they qualify they become indeclinable; thus, رَأَيْتُ كِلَا أَخَوَيْكَ "I saw both thy brothers;" مَرَرْتُ بِكِلْتَا أُخْتَيْكَ "I passed by both thy sisters."

b. To the word كُلٌّ thus used in apposition, the words أَجْمَعُ fem.

جَمْعَآءُ, together with their plurals أَجْمَعُونَ fem. جُمَعُ may be subjoined, agreeing in gender, number, and case with the leading word; thus, فَسَجَدَ ٱلْمَلَائِكَةُ كُلُّهُمْ أَجْمَعُونَ "and all the angels did worship." The word أَجْمَعُ thus applied is not used in the dual, either masculine or feminine.

c. The word أَجْمَعُ applied as above may be accompanied by one or all of the following words, which are of the same signification, viz.: أَبْتَعُ, أَبْصَعُ, and أَكْتَعُ, whose feminines are respectively, بَتْعَآءُ, بَصْعَآءُ, and كَتْعَآءُ; and their plurals masc. أَبْتَعُونَ, and أَبْصَعُونَ, and أَكْتَعُونَ; fem. بُتَعُ, بُصَعُ, and كُتَعُ. Sometimes these three words are all used at the same time in addition to أَجْمَعُ in the order observed in the following example: جَآءَ ٱلْجَيْشُ كُلُّهُ أَجْمَعُ أَكْتَعُ أَبْصَعُ أَبْتَعُ "the whole of the army came;" which it is impossible to translate *verbatim.* The last three words are very rarely used either singly or in combination, except when preceded by كُلٌّ and أَجْمَعُ.

SYNTAX OF THE NUMERALS.

Of the Cardinal Numbers.

256. We have seen (§ 69) that the cardinal numbers from 3 to 10 inclusive have this anomaly, that when they refer to a masculine noun they assume the feminine termination ـَةٌ; whereas the feminine nouns require the same numerals to be of the masculine form; thus, بَنُونَ ثَلَاثَةٌ "three sons;" بَنَاتٌ خَمْسٌ "five daughters." As adjectives they are placed after the noun to which they belong, and agree with the same in gender and case. At the same time they may be used as substantives, and prefixed to their nouns, which they

then govern in the genitive case; thus, سِتَّةُ اَيَّامٍ "six days;" خَمْسَةُ اَشْهُرٍ "five months." As a general rule the noun thus governed by the numerals 3 to 10 must be a broken plural.

a. The number one, as we shewed, § 69, is expressed by the words اَحَدٌ and وَاحِدٌ for the masculine, and by اِحْدَي and وَاحِدَةٌ for the feminine. The first form of each is used as a substantive when the object numbered is not expressed; as مَا جَآءَنِي اَحَدٌ "no one (masc.) came unto me;" مَا كَانَتْ اِحْدَي "there was no one (fem.)." They may also govern a genitive case; thus, اَحَدُ ٱلرِّجَالِ "one of the men;" اِحْدَي ٱلنِّسَاءِ "one of the women;" اَحَدُهُمْ "one of them." The forms وَاحِدٌ and وَاحِدَةٌ are adjectives, and follow their substantives; thus, شَيْءٌ وَاحِدٌ "one object;" دَرَجَةٌ وَاحِدَةٌ "one degree." They may, however, be employed by themselves, still agreeing in gender with the nouns which they represent; كُلُّ وَاحِدٍ مِنْ هٰذِهِ ٱلْخُلْجَانِ "each one of these gulphs (or bays);" كُلُّ وَاحِدَةٍ مِنْ هٰذِهِ ٱلْمُدُنِ "each one of these cities." They are also used in the sense of "one" or "the one" in contrast with "the other;" thus اَلنِّصْفُ ٱلْوَاحِدُ "the one-half;" اَلنِّصْفُ ٱلْآخَرُ "the other half." When repeated and used adverbially, they imply a distribution of individuality; thus, ثُمَّ اِنَّ ٱلْوُزَرَاءَ جَآؤُا وَاحِدًا وَاحِدًا "then, with regard to the counsellors, they came one by one."

b. The number "two," is sufficiently represented by the mere dual terminations of the objects numbered; thus, رَجُلَانِ "two men;" دَرَجَتَانِ "two degrees." Sometimes the numeral "two," اِثْنَانِ, fem. اِثْنَتَانِ or ثِنْتَانِ are employed as adjectives after nouns in the dual. In such instances the numeral "two" appears to be redundant but perhaps it adds more emphasis to the expression; for example, خَلَقَ مِنْ كُلِّ شَيْءٍ زَوْجَيْنِ ٱثْنَيْنِ "He created a pair of each species," where the numeral إِثْنَيْنِ is apparently superfluous.

257. The numerals 11 to 99, both inclusive, govern the substantive to which they refer in the accusative singular; as أَحَدَ عَشَرَ كَوْكَبًا "eleven stars;" تِسْعٌ وَتِسْعُونَ نَعْجَةً "ninety-nine sheep." The numerals 100 and 1,000, together with their multiples, govern the nouns denoting the objects numbered, in the genitive singular; thus, مِايَةُ رَجُلٍ "a hundred men;" ثَلَاثُ مِايَةِ رَجُلٍ "three hundred men;" so أَلْفُ دِينَارٍ "a thousand dīnārs;" أَحَدَ عَشَرَ أَلْفَ دِينَارٍ "eleven thousand dīnārs." Numerals made up of decades and units, when they exceed 20, place the units first and then the tens; thus, ثَلَاثَةٌ وَثَمَانُونَ عَامًا "eighty-three years" (literally, three-and-eighty years); اثْنَانِ وَعِشْرُونَ دِينَارًا "two-and-twenty dīnārs." If a number is composed of several classes, the noun expressive of the objects numbered is put after the total number, and is governed by the concluding numeral, according to the rules already stated; thus, for example, بَيْنَ ٱلْهِجْرَةِ وَبَيْنَ ٱلطُّوفَانِ ثَلَاثَةُ آلَافٍ وَتِسْعمِايَةٍ وَاربع وسبعون سَنَةً "between the Hijra and the Deluge (there elapsed) 3,974 years." In instances of this kind, however, the substantive may be repeated after each class of the numerals; as follows, viz., الغربيّة مَحْصُولُهَا أَلْفَا أَلْفِ دِينَارٍ وَمِايَةُ أَلْفِ دِينَارٍ وَاربعة واربعون أَلْفَ دِينَارٍ وَثَمَانُونَ دِينَارًا جَيْشِيَّةً "The revenue of Gharbīya (a province of Egypt,) is reckoned at 2,144,080 military dīnārs."

a. In order to express any large number, consisting of millions (or upwards), together with hundreds, decades, and units of thousands, it is usual to repeat the word أَلْفٌ after each class of the numerals; thus, جُمْلَةُ ذٰلِكَ تِسْعَةُ آلَافِ أَلْفٍ وَخَمْسُمِائَةِ أَلْفٍ وَأَرْبَعَةٌ وَثَمَانُونَ أَلْفًا وَمِائَتَانِ وَأَرْبَعَةٌ وَسِتُّونَ دِينَارًا "the amount of it (is) this, 9,584,264 dīnārs," literally, "nine hundred thousand of thousands, and five hundred of thousands, and four-and-eighty thousand, and two hundred, and four-and-sixty dīnārs."

b. In expressing a number of thousands, ranging from three to ten, both inclusive, أَلْفٌ is used in the genitive plural آلَافٍ; and the objects numbered follow the same in the genitive singular; thus, ثَلَاثَةُ آلَافِ رَجُلٍ "three thousand men." When the thousands range from 11 to 99 (both inclusive) أَلْفٌ is used in the accusative singular, and the objects numbered in the genitive singular, as just stated; thus, عِشْرُونَ أَلْفَ رَطْلٍ "20,000 lbs.;" أَحَدَ عَشَرَةَ أَلْفَ دِينَارٍ "11,000 dīnārs." When the number of the thousands consists of a hundred or any multiple thereof أَلْفٌ is used in the genitive singular, and the objects numbered in the same case, as above; thus, ثَلَاثُ مِائَةِ أَلْفِ دِينَارٍ "300,000 dīnārs.

258. Not only the cardinal numbers from three to ten, inclusive (§ 256), but also those of a higher denomination may be employed in apposition to the nouns denoting the objects numbered, as may be seen in the following example: وَجَذَبَ ٱلشَّبَكَةَ إِلَي ٱلْأَرْضِ-إِذْ هِيَ مُمْتَلِيَةٌ حِيتَانًا كِبَارًا مِائَةً ثَلٰثَةً وَخَمْسِينَ "and he drew the net to the land; lo, it was full of large fishes, one hundred and three-and-fifty."

259. When a numeral is employed to denote a certain number out of a collection, or class, or whole genus, it is usual to express the relation between the numeral and the class by means of the preposition مِنَ "from" or "out of;" for example: تِسْعَةٌ مِنَ ٱلرَّهْطِ "nine (men) out of the family;" ثَلَاثَةٌ مِنَ ٱلطَّيْرِ "three birds" *i.e.* "three birds from among the genus bird." It is further to be observed that the numeral in such instances, agrees in gender with the objects numbered; thus, in the expression ثَلَاثَةٌ مِنَ ٱلْغَنَمِ "three sheep;" the numeral is masculine because غَنَمٌ as a genus, is masculine; so ثَلَاثٌ مِنَ ٱلْبَطِّ "three ducks;" where ثَلَاثٌ is feminine, because بَطٌّ is feminine. If an epithet indicating the gender is added immediately after the numeral, the latter agrees in gender with such epithet; thus, ثَلَاثٌ أَنَاثٍ مِنَ ٱلْغَنَمِ "three females of the genus sheep;" ثَلَاثَةٌ ذُكُورٍ مِنَ ٱلْبَطِّ "three males from among the ducks."

a. Numerals used abstractedly, as in the science of arithmetic, are always put in the masculine form; thus, ثَلَاثَةٌ نِصْفُ سِتَّةٍ "three is the half of six." When nouns of different sexes are included under one and the same numeral, the latter agrees in gender with the noun immediately following it, provided the numeral denotes a number extending from six to ten, both inclusive; as لِي ثَمَانِيَةُ أَعْبُدٍ وَ إِمَاءٍ "to me (belong) eight slaves and [eight] female servants." If we here reverse the objects numbered, the expression will be as follows: لِي ثَمَانِي إِمَاءٍ وَ أَعْبُدٍ "to me (belong) eight handmaids and [eight] slaves." If the objects numbered be under six, then the appropriate numeral must be added to each of the two species.

b. When the compound numerals above ten apply to rational beings, they always take the masculine form, as in the following examples: عِنْدِي خَمْسَةَ عَشَرَ عَبْدًا وَجَارِيَةً "to me belong fifteen male slaves and [fifteen] female slaves;" عِنْدِي خَمْسَةَ عَشَرَ جَارِيَةً وَعَبْدًا "to me belong fifteen female and [fifteen] male slaves." If the numerals apply to irrational beings they take the gender of the nearest substantive; thus, عِنْدِي خَمْسَةَ عَشَرَ جَمَلًا وَنَاقَةً "there are in my possession (chez moi,) fifteen male camels and [fifteen] she-camels;" or, by transposition, عِنْدِي خَمْسَ عَشْرَةَ نَاقَةً وَجَمَلًا "I have fifteen she-camels and [fifteen] he-camels. If, however, in the case of irrational objects a qualifying word such as مَا بَيْنَ, etc., interposes immediately after the numerals, the latter are of the feminine form; thus for example: عِنْدِي خَمْسَ عَشْرَةَ مَا بَيْنَ جَمَلٍ وَنَاقَةٍ "I possess fifteen camels, what between males and females," that is, "partly male and partly female;" and the same construction holds, as to the numerals if in this last expression we transpose the last two words and read نَاقَةٍ وَجَمَلٍ.

260. The numerals agree in gender with that of the singular number of the objects numbered; thus, سَبْعُ سِنِينَ "seven years;" because سَنَةٌ "a year," is feminine in the singular. So ثَلَاثَةُ حَمَّامَاتٍ "three baths," for the singular حَمَّامٌ is masculine; and this rule holds when the name of the objects numbered is suppressed; as in the following example: وَمِنْهُمْ مَا يَمْشِي عَلَى أَرْبَعٍ "and among them (are creatures) that walk on four (feet)," رِجْلٌ "a foot," being feminine. So also إِنِّي أَرَى سَبْعَ بَقَرَاتٍ سِمَانٍ يَأْكُلُهُنَّ سَبْعٌ عِجَافٌ "Verily, I beheld seven fat kine, which seven lean (ones)

devoured," where سَبْعٌ is feminine, the word "kine" being understood.

a. When the objects numbered are of a vague or general nature, such as may apply to either sex, the numeral agrees with the same according to the grammatical gender of such objects. For example, the words شَخْصٌ and عَيْنٌ denote "a person" or "individual," the former being masculine and the latter feminine; hence they say ثَلَاثَةُ اَشْخُصٍ "three persons," where ثَلَاثَةُ is used in the masculine form whether the objects be male or female. In like manner ثَلَاثُ اَعْيُنٍ "three persons" or "individuals," whether applicable to females or males. If, however, another noun or epithet be added to such phrases as the foregoing serving to indicate the real sex of the objects numbered, the numeral will agree in gender with the word or words annexed; thus, فَكَانَ مِجَنِّي دُونَ مَنْ اَتَّقِي ثَلَاثُ شُخُوصٍ كَاعِبَانِ وَمُعْصِرُ "and I had for a shield against those whom I feared two (young) maidens and a (marriageable) woman." Here we see that ثَلَاثُ fem. is used with شُخُوصٍ masc. because the latter word is qualified by the epithets كَاعِبَانِ and مُعْصِرُ each of which is applicable only to females. Sometimes, however, regard is had more to the signification of the objects numbered than to their strict grammatical gender; thus the word نَفْسٌ "soul," is feminine; but when applied to persons of the male sex the numeral agrees with it in the masculine gender; thus, ثَلَاثَةُ اَنْفُسٍ "three souls" (meaning males), because in this instance نَفْسٌ has the same signification as رَجُلٌ.

b. If the name of the objects numbered be suppressed and its place supplied by an epithet descriptive of its quality, the numeral agrees in gender with the noun understood; thus in the Ḳur,ān, vi. 160:

مَنْ جَآءَ بِٱلْحَسَنَةِ فَلَهُ عَشْرُ امثالها "he who hath done a good (deed) shall receive (as his reward) ten (times) the equivalent thereof." Here the numeral عَشْرُ is feminine, although أَمْثَالٌ is masculine; because the latter is considered as a mere epithet of حَسَنَاتٌ (plural of حَسَنَةٌ) understood.

261. The cardinal numbers may be restricted by the article according to the rules laid down, § 251. 1. When the numeral is used substantively in an abstract sense; thus, اَلثَّلَاثَةُ نِصْفُ ٱلسِّتَّةِ "the (number) three is half of the (number) six." 2. When the name of the objects numbered is understood, having been previously expressed, and hence well known; as فَرَجَعَ ٱلسَّبْعُونَ بِفَرَحٍ "and the seventy (disciples) returned with joy." 3. When the numeral is employed in apposition as an adjective after a definite noun; for example: اَلرِّجَالُ ٱلْخَمْسَةُ "the five men." 4. When the numerals from 3 to 10 (both inclusive) precede the objects numbered in a state of regimen, in which case the article is generally prefixed only to the latter; as ثَلَاثَةُ ٱلرِّجَالِ "the three men" or "the trio of men." Occasionally, however, the numeral takes the article as well as the name of the objects numbered; as اَلسَّبْعَةُ دَعَائِمِ ٱلنَّامُوسِيَّةِ "the seven fundamental precepts of the law."

a. When the numerals from 11 to 19 (both inclusive) precede the name of the objects numbered, and as we already remarked, § 257, govern the same in the accusative singular, the article may be prefixed to the first member only or to both; thus, الاحدَ عَشَرَ دِرهمًا or

الأَحَدَ العَشَرَ دِرْهَمًا "the eleven dirhams;" also الاِثْنَتَا عَشْرَةَ نَاقَةً or الاِثْنَتَا العَشْرَةَ نَاقَةً "the twelve she-camels." From 20 to 99 (both inclusive), when the numeral consists of a multiple of ten only, it takes the article; and if such multiple be combined with units they both take the article; thus, العِشْرُونَ نَعْجَةً "the twenty sheep;" so السَّبْعَةُ وَالسَّبْعُونَ جَمَلًا "the seventy-seven camels."

b. With regard to numerals consisting of a hundred or a thousand, together with their multiples and accessories, it is optional to prefix the article either to the entire numeral, or to the name of the objects numbered; for example: ثَلَاثُمِائَةِ الدِّينَارِ "the three hundred dīnars;" ثَلَاثَةُ آلَافِ الدِّرْهَمِ "the three thousand dirhams;" so المِائَتَا أَلْفِ دِرْهَمٍ "the two hundred thousand dirhams;" so also, هٰذِهِ الأَلْفُ أَلْفِ دِينَارٍ "this million (literally, thousand of thousands) of dīnārs." In such examples as the last, where the demonstrative pronoun is employed, the article is prefixed to the word immediately following.

Of the Ordinal Numbers.

262. The Ordinals are mere adjectives, and up to the nineteenth they agree in gender, number, and case with the substantives to which they relate. We stated, § 73, that "the twentieth," and all multiples of ten above that number, are expressed by the cardinals, so that they are considered to be of the common gender, as they are indeclinable. The ordinals may, or may not, be restricted by the article; as عَامٌ أَوَّلُ "the first year;" الإِقْلِيمُ الأَوَّلُ "the first climate." When, as in this last phrase, they take the article, they are

connected with the sequel of the sentence, not in a state of regimen, but by means of the preposition مِنْ or فِي; thus, اَلْحَاكِمُ بِأَمْرِ ٱللّٰهِ وُلِدَ لَيْلَةَ ٱلْخَمِيسِ ٱلثَّالِثَ وَٱلْعِشْرِينَ مِنْ شَهْرِ رَبِيعٍ ٱلْأَوَّلِ فِي ٱلسَّاعَةِ ٱلتَّاسِعَةِ "Al Ḥākim bi-Amr-Illāhī was born on the night of Thursday, the three-and-twentieth of the month Rabī'u-l-awwal, at the ninth hour." When not accompanied by the article, the ordinals are usually put in a state of regimen with a noun or pronoun following; thus for example: وَسُلِّمَ عَلَيْهِ بِٱلْخِلَافَةِ بَعْدَ ٱلظُّهْرِ مِنْ يَوْمِ ٱلثُّلَاثَا ثَامِنِ وَعِشْرِينَ شَهْرِ رَمَضَان "He was hailed Caliph after mid-day on Wednesday, the twenty-eighth of the month of Ramaḍān;" فِي ثَالِثِ عِشْرِينِهِ نُودِيَ بِٱلْقَاهِرَةِ "On the twenty-third (day) of it, (viz., month), proclamation was made in Cairo."

a. An ordinal number, from the second to the tenth (both inclusive) is often found in a state of regimen with its corresponding cardinal; thus, أَنْتَ ثَانِي ٱثْنَيْنِ "thou art a second of the two," that is, "thou art one of the two;" so عَاشِرُ عَشَرَةٍ or (fem.) عَاشِرَةُ عَشْرٍ "a tenth of the ten," *i.e.* "one of the ten." With regard to the compound numerals from 11 to 19 (both inclusive), the same rule holds, with this difference, that it is optional either to use the two component parts of the ordinal, or to suppress the second of them; in which case the remaining part becomes declinable, agreeing in gender with the noun to which reference is made; thus, أَنْتَ ثَانِيَ عَشَرَ ٱثْنَيْ عَشَرَ or (fem.) أَنْتِ ثَانِيَةَ عَشْرَةَ ٱثْنَتَيْ عَشْرَةَ "thou art one of the twelve." We may also say (omitting the decades), أَنْتَ ثَانِيَ ٱثْنَيْ عَشَرَ or (fem.) أَنْتِ ثَانِيَةُ ٱثْنَتَيْ عَشْرَةَ. Sometimes the mere ordinal, indeclinable, bears a similar construction to the preceding; as هُوَ ثَالِثَ عَشَرَ "he is a thirteenth," *i.e.* "one of the thirteen."

b. There is another mode of employing the ordinal in a state of regimen, not with its own cardinal, but with the one less than the latter by unity; thus, هُوَ ثَالِثُ ٱثْنَيْنِ "he (forms) a third to two." This rule holds with regard to the ordinals from the third to the ninth (both inclusive), which in fact are viewed by grammarians as the present participles of the active verbs ثَلَثَ "he made three (out of two);" رَبَعَ "he made four (out of three)," etc.; hence they may as nouns of agency govern the genitive as in the example above; or as active participles they may govern the accusative; thus, هُوَ رَابِعٌ ثَلَاثَةً "he makes three into four," literally, "he *fourths* three;" so in the feminine, هِيَ رَابِعَةٌ ثَلَاثًا "she makes three into four." When the compound ordinals from the eleventh to the nineteenth (both inclusive) are thus employed, the units only are declinable, but not the ten; thus, هُوَ ثَالِثُ عَشَرَ ٱثْنَيْ عَشَرَ "he adds a thirteenth to twelve;" so with the feminine, هِيَ ثَالِثَةُ ٱثْنَتَيْ عَشْرَةَ "she," etc. In a similar manner are employed the numerals composed of units and decades, only that the decades are usually suppressed; thus, هُوَ رَابِعُ ثَلَاثَةٍ وَعِشْرِينَ or هُوَ رَابِعُ ثَلَاثَةٍ وَعِشْرِينَ "he makes a four-and-twentieth." The multiples of ten, viz., 20, 30, etc., up to 90, are considered as modifications of quadriliteral verbs; thus, عِشْرِينَ is a modification of عَشْرَنَ, the participle active of which is مُعَشْرِنٌ, employed as above; hence, we may say, هُوَ مُعَشْرِنُ تِسْعَةَ عَشَرَ "he *twentifieth* nineteen," which in honest plain English signifies that he is "one out of twenty."

263. In expressing the year of an æra such as the Alex-

andrine, the Hijra, etc., the Arabs employ the cardinal numbers as we do. The word سَنَةٌ (fem.) "year" is put in a state of regimen with the following numerals, which agree with it in gender; but in this case سَنَةٌ does not take the article as with us. The numerals, as we stated, § 79, are arranged in the following order, viz., first the units, then the tens, etc., all connected by means of the conjunction وَ as in the following example: ثُمَّ دَخَلَتْ سَنَةُ سِتٍّ وَ تِسْعِينَ وَثَلَثِمِائَةٍ "then commenced the year (of the Hijra) 396" literally "six, and ninety, and three hundred." On the other hand, in expressing the year of the age or reign of an individual the ordinal numbers, with the article, are employed precisely as with us; thus, فِي ٱلسَّنَةِ ٱلسَّادِسَةِ مِنْ مُلْكِ ٱلْمَلِكِ ٱلأَشْرَفِ شَعْبَانَ "in the sixth year of the reign of Al Malik Al Ashraf Sha'bān." The following example exhibits at one view the application of both the ordinal and the cardinal numbers: فِي ٱلسَّنَةِ ٱلثَّالِثَةِ وَ ٱلأَرْبَعُونَ مِنْ مُلْكِهِ - وَهِيَ سَنَةُ تِسْعٍ وَثَلَثِمِايَةٍ مِنْ تَارِيخِ ٱلإِسْكَنْدَرِ "In the three-and-fortieth year of his reign, and that (corresponds with) the year three hundred and nine of the æra of Alexander."

264. In expressing the day of the month, the more recent Arabian writers, like ourselves, employ the ordinal numbers, counting regularly from the first to the last day of the month. As they reckon by lunar time, the civil day naturally commences at sunset, as is still the case with the Jews, and I believe, till lately, with the Venetians. The month commences on the evening when the new moon (الغُرَّةُ or الهِلَالُ) becomes visible

from the tops of minarets, etc.; hence the earlier Arabian writers reckoned, not by the day, but by the night. Thus, the first of the month Rajab, is expressed لِأَوَّلِ لَيْلَةٍ مِنْ رَجَبٍ or لِغُرَّةِ رَجَبٍ "on the first night of Rajab." The first day (viz., that immediately following the first night) is expressed thus, لِلَيْلَةٍ خَلَتْ مِنْ رَجَبٍ literally, "one night of Rajab having elapsed." In like manner, the second day is expressed, لِلَيْلَتَيْنِ خَلَتَا "two nights having elapsed;" then, the third day is لِثَلَاثٍ خَلَوْنَ "three nights having elapsed." In this last expression the word لَيَالِي (pl. of لَيْلَةٌ) is understood, which if supplied would be لِثَلَاثِ لَيَالٍ خَلَوْنَ مِنْ رَجَبٍ "three of the nights of Rajab having elapsed;" and this rule holds, up to the tenth, inclusive. From the eleventh to the fourteenth, both inclusive, the word لَيْلَةٌ in the singular, is understood; thus, "the eleventh day of Rajab" is expressed لِإِحْدَي عَشْرَةَ (لَيْلَةً) خَلَتْ مِنْ رَجَبٍ. The fifteenth day is called نِصْفٌ, مُنْتَصَفٌ, or إِنْتِصَافٌ, denoting "half" or "middle;" thus, "the fifteenth of Rajab" is expressed فِي ٱلنِّصْفِ مِنْ رَجَبٍ or فِي مُنْتَصَفِ رَجَبٍ. After the fifteenth of the month the rule is to reckon, not the number of nights that have elapsed, but of those that still remain; hence the "sixteenth day" is expressed لِأَرْبَعَ عَشْرَةَ (لَيْلَةً) بَقِيَتْ مِنْ رَجَبٍ, literally, "fourteen nights of Rajab still remaining;" and this rule holds, up to the nineteenth, inclusive. From the twentieth to the twenty-seventh, both inclusive, the pl. لَيَالِي is understood; thus the twentieth day is expressed, لِعَشْرٍ (لِعَشْرِ لَيَالٍ) بَقِينَ مِنْ رَجَبٍ

"ten nights of Rajab still remaining." The twenty-eighth is expressed لِلَيْلَتَيْنِ بَقِيَتَا مِنْ رَجَبٍ "two nights of Rajab still left;" the twenty-ninth is لِلَيْلَةٍ بَقِيَتْ مِنْ رَجَبٍ "one night of Rajab remaining." Finally, the thirtieth is thus expressed, لِسَلْخِ رَجَبٍ or لِآخِرِ لَيْلَةٍ مِنْ رَجَبٍ "on the last night of Rajab;" and if the last night is elapsed the day following may be expressed لِسَلْخِ رَجَبٍ or لِإِنْسِلَاخِ رَجَبٍ or finally, لِآخِرِ يَوْمٍ مِنْ رَجَبٍ "on the last day (*i.e.* the last twelve hours of sunlight) of Rajab."

a. The Muhammadan or lunar months are so arranged as to consist of thirty and twenty-nine days alternately, as in the following table; but in a period of thirty years, it is found necessary to intercalate the twelfth month eleven times so as to be reckoned thirty days instead of twenty-nine. The months retain their Arabian names in all Muḥammadan countries, merely omitting the nūnation, or the final short vowel.

TABLE OF THE ARABIAN MONTHS.

1.	اَلْمُحَرَّمُ	has 30 days.		7.	رَجَبٌ	has 30 days.	
2.	صَفَرٌ	29	,,	8.	شَعْبَانُ	29	,,
3.	رَبِيعُ الأَوَّلُ	30	,,	9.	رَمَضَانُ	30	,,
4.	رَبِيعُ الآخِرُ	29	,,	10.	شَوَّالٌ	29	,,
5.	جُمَادِيُ ٱلْأُولَي	30	,,	11.	ذُو الْقَعْدَةِ	30	,,
6.	جُمَادِيُ ٱلْآخِرَي	29	,,	12.	ذُو ٱلْحِجَّةِ	29	,,

b. It is needless to add that in such months as consist of twenty-nine days, the nights and days *remaining* in the second half are less by unity than those we detailed respecting Rajab. For example, the 16th of Sha'bān is expressed as follows: لِثَلَاثَ عَشْرَةَ بَقِيَتْ مِنْ شَعْبَانَ "thirteen nights of Sha'bān still remaining;" and the same rule holds with every other month that consists only of twenty-nine days, except the last, which, as we above stated, is liable to intercalation eleven times in thirty years.

SYNTAX OF NOUNS WITH ADJECTIVES.

Concord of Adjectives with their Substantives.

265. We have already stated, §§ 250 and 251, that, as a general rule, the substantive always precedes the adjective or epithet which is employed to qualify it; as, كِتَابٌ عَظِيمٌ "an "estimable book." If, however, the substantive be restricted in its signification by being in a state of regimen, or by having the article prefixed or a pronoun affixed, the adjective or epithet will also take the article; thus, كِتَابُ مُوسَى ٱلْعَظِيمُ "the estimable book of Moses;" اَلْكِتَابُ ٱلْعَظِيمُ "the great (or estimable) book;" كِتَابُهُ ٱلْعَظِيمُ "his estimable book." The same rule holds with regard to proper names, which, of course, are definite in their own nature; thus, إِبْرٰهِيمُ ٱلْأَمِينُ "Abraham the faithful." We may further observe that when the substantive is not restricted in its signification, as above, the epithet does not take the article; thus, قَرَأْتُ فِي كِتَابٍ عَتِيقٍ "I have read in (some) ancient book."

266. The adjective or epithet agrees in case with its sub-

stantive; as, مَرَرْتُ بِزَيْدٍ ٱلْعَاقِلِ ٱلْكَرِيمِ ٱلْفَاضِلِ "I passed by Zaid, the prudent, the generous, the excellent." This agreement, however, is not a matter of necessity when the substantive is a proper name, consequently definite, and followed by several epithets, as in the preceding example; for in such instances the epithets may be put in the nominative singular, the word هُوَ "who is," or "which is," being understood; thus we may say, مَرَرْتُ بِزَيْدٍ ٱلْعَاقِلُ ٱلْكَرِيمُ ٱلْفَاضِلُ; or finally we may employ the epithets in the accusative case, the word أَعْنِي "I mean," or "I signify" being understood. If the substantive is indeterminate, as a general rule the nearest epithet agrees with it in case, and the rest may be put either in the nominative or in the accusative.

267. An adjective agrees in gender and number with its substantive if the latter be in the singular or dual number, whether it be masculine or feminine. If, however, the substantive be a broken plural and masculine, or a regular plural feminine, the qualifying adjective is usually put in the feminine singular, as in the following examples: أَوْلَادٌ كَثِيرَةٌ "many sons," *i.e.* "a numerous offspring;" ٱلْعَوَاصِلُ ٱلْوَاصِلَةُ "the provisions arriving (in abundance);" thus in the Ḳur,ān, iii. 12: زُيِّنَ لِلنَّاسِ حُبُّ ٱلشَّهَوَاتِ مِنَ ٱلنِّسَآءِ وَٱلْبَنِينَ وَٱلْفِضَّةِ وَٱلْخَيْلِ ٱلْمُسَوَّمَةِ "Men are gratified with the love of pleasures arising from women, and children, and silver, and horses of great value." In this last sentence the word خَيْلٌ, though singular, is employed in a collective sense, and is consequently equivalent to an irregular or broken plural. This mode of construction,

however, is applicable chiefly to irrational animals, and to things without life in general; for when the substantive denotes a rational being, the adjective agrees with it according to the general rule. A substantive plural masculine, not denoting rational beings, may also have the adjective in the feminine plural; thus, أُسُودٌ ضَارِبَاتٌ "destructive lions;" جِبَالٌ رَاسِيَاتٌ "mountains firmly fixed;" سُيُوفٌ مُرْهَفَاتٌ "sharpened swords;" أَيَّامٌ مَعْدُودَاتٌ "days enumerated."

a. The irregular concord of adjectives with their substantives, which we have just detailed, is the more usual; but the regular mode is by no means rare. A substantive plural not unfrequently takes the adjective in the plural, whether regular or broken; thus, Ḳur,an, lxvi. 11: مَلَآئِكَةٌ غِلَاظٌ شِدَادٌ "angels fierce and stern." There is this restriction, however, that the regular plural of adjectives is employed only with substantives denoting rational beings.

b. A collective noun in the singular usually takes the adjective in the plural; thus, Ḳur,ān, iii. 141: أُنْصُرْنَا عَلَي ٱلْقَوْمِ ٱلْكَافِرِينَ "Aid thou us against the unbelieving tribe." In like manner the adjective كَثِيرٌ "much" or "many," though under a singular form, is often employed with a plural substantive, as in the following examples from the Ḳur,ān, iii. 146: كَأَيِّنْ مِنْ نَبِيٍّ قُتِلَ مَعَهُ رِبِّيُّونَ كَثِيرٌ "how many of the prophets have been slain, and along with them many myriads (of men)?" Also iv. 1: وَبَثَّ مِنْهُمَا رِجَالًا كَثِيرًا وَنِسَآءً "and from these two (viz. Adam and Eve) he hath disseminated many men and women." We may, however, in these expressions consider كَثِيرٌ as employed in apposition, § 255, with the preceding substantives.

268. If a substantive in the dual or plural, that is, a substantive expressive of more individuals than one, be followed by adjectives, each of which has reference only to one of the individuals, each adjective must agree in gender and case with the noun to which it refers; but it must be in the singular number; thus, كَانَ لِي صَاحِبَانِ عَاقِلٌ وَجَاهِلٌ "I had two companions, a wise, and a foolish;" كَانَ لِبَعْضِ ٱلْمُلُوكِ ثَلَاثَةُ وُزَرَآءَ كَرِيمٌ وَبَخِيلٌ وَمُسْرِفٌ "a certain king had three wazīrs, (one) liberal, (one) stingy, and (one) extravagant." This, however, is merely an elliptical mode of expression; for instance, the first of the above sentences, if expressed in full, would be as follows: كَانَ لِي صَاحِبَانِ أَحَدُهُمْ عَاقِلٌ وَٱلْآخَرُ جَاهِلٌ "I had two companions, one of them wise, the other foolish;" or it might read كَانَ لِي صَاحِبَانِ صَاحِبٌ عَاقِلٌ وَصَاحِبٌ جَاهِلٌ "I had two companions, a wise companion, and a foolish companion."

269. If the same adjective or attribute refers to two or more singular nouns, all of which are in the same case and of the same gender, the attribute will be put in the dual or plural, according to the number of persons referred to; and it must agree with the latter in gender and case; thus, كَلَّمْتُ عَمْرًا وَكَاتَبْتُ زَيْدًا ٱلشَّاعِرَيْنِ "I have accosted 'Amru and I have written to Zaid, the two poets." If, however, the substantives be not in the same case, the predicate will agree with them only in gender; and it is optionally put either in the nominative or accusative, dual or plural, according to circumstances; thus we may say, كَلَّمْتُ عَمْرًا وَكَتَبْتُ إِلَي زَيْدٍ ٱلشَّاعِرَانِ

or we may say, كَلَّمْتُ عَمْرًا وَكَتَبْتُ إِلَي زَيْدٍ ٱلشَّاعِرَيْنِ. In the first of these last expressions the pronoun هُمَا "they both," is understood, and the sense is, "they are the two poets;" in the second, the verb أَعْنِي "I mean" or "I signify," is understood.

270. The verbal adjectives of the measures فَعُولٌ, فَعِيلٌ, مِفْعَالٌ, مِفْعَلٌ and مِفْعِيلٌ, are of the common gender, and sometimes assume the termination ـَةٌ, which gives them a more intensive signification; hence they apply alike to masculine or feminine nouns; thus, رَجُلٌ مَلُولَةٌ "a most wearied man;" إِمْرَءَةٌ مَلُولَةٌ "a most wearied woman;" so, رَجُلٌ مِقْدَامَةٌ "a very brave man;" رَجُلٌ دَاهِيَةٌ "a very cunning man." A few of these adjectives, however, assume the usual generic terminations; thus, ظَرِيفٌ "elegant," fem. ظَرِيفَةٌ; مِيقَانٌ "credulous," fem. مِيقَانَةٌ; مِسْكِينٌ "poor," fem. مِسْكِينَةٌ; عَدُوٌّ "hostile," fem. عَدُوَّةٌ; رَحِيمٌ "merciful," fem. رَحِيمَةٌ. Adjectives of the measure فَعُولٌ, when of a passive signification, follow a similar rule; otherwise, they are under the masculine form, common to both genders, thus, Ḳur,ān, ii. 66: إِنَّهَا بَقَرَةٌ لَا ذَلُولٌ تُثِيرُ ٱلْأَرْضَ "for she is a cow not accustomed to the yoke, nor to till the ground;" also lxvi. 8: تُوبُوا إِلَي ٱللّٰهِ تَوْبَةً نَصُوحًا "turn yourselves unto God with sincere repentance." Adjectives of the measure فَعِيلٌ, when of a passive or neuter signification, agree alike with nouns masculine or feminine; thus, رَأَيْتُ ٱمْرَءَةً قَتِيلًا "I saw a woman (that had been) slain;" مَرَرْتُ بِجَارِيَةٍ جَرِيحٍ "I passed by a wounded maiden." If, however, the substantive be

feminine, and not expressed but understood, an adjective of the foregoing measure assumes the feminine termination; thus, Ḳur,ān, v. 4: حُرِّمَتْ عَلَيْكُمُ ٱلْمَيْتَةُ وَٱلدَّمُ وَٱلنَّطِيحَةُ وَأَكِيلَةُ ٱلسَّبُعِ "it is forbidden to you (to eat an animal) that has died of itself, also blood, also (an animal) that has been gored to death, or (one that) has been (partially) devoured by wild beasts;" in which sentence the substantive بَهِيمَةٌ "a beast," is evidently understood. If an adjective of this measure be of an active signification, it generally agrees alike in the masculine form with nouns of either gender; thus, in the Ḳur,ān, li. 41: أَرْسَلْنَا عَلَيْهِمُ ٱلرِّيحَ ٱلْعَقِيمَ "we have sent against them a most devastating wind." In a few instances, however, the feminine termination is added to the adjective; thus, خَصْلَةٌ حَمِيدَةٌ "a praiseworthy quality," or خَصْلَةٌ ذَمِيمَةٌ "a quality deserving of censure."

271. In Arabic the substantive is frequently omitted, and then the adjective, if it refers to a living creature, is used in the masculine form; and in the feminine, if it refers to an inanimate object; thus, سَيِّآتُكُمْ "your evils," meaning "evil deeds;" عَجَائِبُ "wonders" or "wonderful things;" الصَّالِحَاتُ "the good (works)" or "virtues." Occasionally a masculine adjective is applied to a lifeless thing; as in the Ḳur,ān, ii. 59: وَ عَمِلَ صَالِحًا "and he (who) hath done a good deed." Frequently, when the substantive is thus omitted, the adjective, or its equivalent, remains in a state of concord with the former; thus, Ḳur,ān, lv. 56: فِيهِنَّ قَاصِرَاتُ ٱلطَّرْفِ "in these (gardens) there will be (damsels) of modest mien;" where

جَوَارِي is understood. So, يَرْمِي بِكَفَّيْ كَانَ مِنْ أَرْمَي ٱلْبَشَرِ, "he shoots (arrows) by the two hands (of one who is) the most expert archer of men;" where the word رَجُلٍ is understood as the complement of بِكَفَّيْ "by the two hands."

272. A substantive instead of an adjective is not unfrequently used as an epithet; for example, عَدْلٌ "justice," for عَادِلٌ "just;" in which case the qualifying noun remains always in the singular, agreeing with its substantive in case, and retaining its own gender; as رَجُلٌ عَدْلٌ "a just man;" رَجُلَانِ عَدْلٌ "two just men;" so in the plural, رِجَالٌ عَدْلٌ "just men." The epithet may also be a verb or clause of a sentence when the substantive is otherwise indeterminate; thus, مَرَرْتُ بِرَجُلٍ يَنُومُ "I have passed by a man (who) is asleep," where يَنُومُ is equivalent to نَائِمٌ "sleeping." So قَوْلٌ مَعْرُوفٌ وَمَغْفِرَةٌ خَيْرٌ مِنْ صَدَقَةٍ يَتْبَعُهَا أَذًى "a speech familiar and conciliating is better than alms which offence accompanieth." Again, Ḳur,ān, iii. 181, we have another example: إِنْ كَذَّبُوكَ فَقَدْ كُذِّبَ رُسُلٌ مِنْ قَبْلِكَ جَآءُوا بِٱلْبَيِّنَاتِ "If they have accused thee of falsehood; verily the apostles before thee have been falsely accused, (men who) came with proofs (of their divine mission)." So in the following expression: أَوَّلُ بَيْتٍ وُضِعَ لِلنَّاسِ "the first temple (that) hath been built for men."

a. In Arabic the relative pronoun is never used as with us in such sentences as the foregoing; for example, where the noun is indeterminate, it would be quite wrong to say مَرَرْتُ بِرَجُلٍ ٱلَّذِي يَنُومُ

because ٱلَّذِي يَنُومُ is equivalent to اَلنَّائِمُ. On the other hand, when the substantive has the article we then employ the relative; thus, for example: ٱلْمَلِكُ ٱلَّذِي يَعْدِلُ "the king who is just;" equivalent to اَلْمَلِكُ ٱلْعَادِلُ, § 251. When the qualifying verb or participle has a nominative of its own, the same must be accompanied by the affixed pronoun applicable to the noun qualified; thus, مَرَرْتُ بِرَجُلٍ ابُوهُ نَائِمٌ "I have passed by a man whose father is asleep" (*lit.* "is sleeping"); زَوَّجْتُ ٱبْنِي بِٱمْرَأَةٍ كَانَ عَمْرُو يُحِبُّهَا "I married my son to a woman with whom 'Amru was in love." This affixed pronoun, however, is optionally suppressed when the meaning of the sentence is quite evident from the context; thus—

فَمَا أَدْرِي أَغَيَّرَهُمْ تَنَآءٍ ـ وَطُولُ ٱلْعَهْدِ أَمْ مَالٌ أَصَابُوا

"And I know not whether it be distance and length of time (that) have estranged them; or the wealth (which) they have received." Here the last word أَصَابُوا "they have received" (for أَصَابُوهُ) omits the pronoun هُ, referring to مَالٌ, because the omission leads to no ambiguity or obscurity.

273. When an adjective is restricted in its signification by means of a substantive that follows it, as in the phrases "a man learned in the law," "a youth fair of countenance," etc.; the Arabs have three modes of expressing the same. In the first place, the adjective (when it has not the article) retains its *nūnation*, and the restrictive noun or complement is put in the nominative case; as جَآءَنِي رَجُلٌ حَسَنٌ ٱلْأَبُ "there came to me a man the father of whom is handsome;" in which expression we may also say حَسَنٌ أَبُوهُ. Again, مَرَرْتُ بِرَجُلٍ قَبِيحٍ ٱلْوَجْهُ "I passed by a man of ugly visage;"

where we might also say قَبِيحٍ وَجْهُهُ. Secondly, the adjective may be put in a state of regimen with the complement, as follows, جَآءَنِي رَجُلٌ حَسَنُ ٱلْوَجْهِ "there came to me a man fair of countenance;" where we may also say حَسَنُ وَجْهِهِ. So مَرَرْتُ بِرَجُلٍ حَسَنِ ٱلْوَجْهِ "I passed by a man of fair countenance;" where we may also say حَسَنِ وَجْهِهِ. Thirdly, the adjective (in the absence of the article) retains its *nūnation*, and the complement is put in the accusative case; thus, جَآءَنِي رَجُلٌ حَسَنٌ وَجْهًا "there came to me a man fair as to countenance;" or with the article حَسَنٌ ٱلْوَجْهَ. So in the following example: مَرَرْتُ بِرَجُلٍ حَسَنٍ وَجْهًا "I passed by a man fair as to countenance;" or with the article حَسَنٍ ٱلْوَجْهَ In this third mode of expression the classical scholar will not fail to recognise a well-known Greek construction, which the Latin poets have, not unfrequently, imitated; thus,—"Os humerosque deo similis;" "miles fractus membra," etc. Of course the reader would consider a translation of these phrases as an affront.

274. In the three kinds of construction just described, the adjective may or may not have the article, according as its preceding substantive is definite or indefinite. The complement may also be definite or indefinite. It is rendered definite, 1—by means of the article اَلْ; 2—by an additional complement having that article; 3—by an affixed pronoun; and 4—by an additional complement having an affixed pronoun. It follows as a consequence that we have a variety of different constructions, examples of which we here subjoin

from De Sacy, Tome II. p. 199, differing from that writer only in our arrangement of the subject, by presenting to the reader in the first place the correct and classical modes of expression such as are to be met with in the writings of the more esteemed Arabian authors.

1st—Classical constructions employed by the best authors.

رَجُلٌ حَسَنٌ ٱلْوَجْهُ
رَجُلٌ حَسَنٌ وَجْهُهُ
رَجُلٌ حَسَنٌ وَجْهًا
رَجُلٌ حَسَنُ ٱلْوَجْهِ
رَجُلٌ حَسَنُ وَجْهٍ

} A man of fair countenance.

رَجُلٌ حَسَنٌ وَجْهُ ٱلْأَبِ
رَجُلٌ حَسَنٌ وَجْهُ أَبِيهِ
رَجُلٌ حَسَنٌ وَجْهُ أَبٍ
رَجُلٌ حَسَنُ وَجْهِ ٱلْأَبِ
رَجُلٌ حَسَنُ وَجْهِ أَبٍ

} A man whose father is fair of countenance.

زَيْدٌ ٱلْحَسَنُ ٱلْوَجْهُ
زَيْدٌ ٱلْحَسَنُ وَجْهُهُ
زَيْدٌ ٱلْحَسَنُ ٱلْوَجْهَ
زَيْدٌ ٱلْحَسَنُ وَجْهَهُ
زَيْدٌ ٱلْحَسَنُ وَجْهًا
زَيْدٌ ٱلْحَسَنُ ٱلْوَجْهِ

} Zaid who is the fair of countenance.

زيد الحسن وجه الاب
زيد الحسن وجه ابيه
زيد الحسن وجه الاب
زيد الحسن وجه ابيه
زيد الحسن وجه اب
زيد الحسن وجه الاب

} Zaid whose father is fair of countenance.

2nd—Constructions not to be approved of, but which, nevertheless, are to be met with.

رجل حسن وجه — A man fair of countenance.

زيد الحسن وجه — Zaid fair of countenance.

رجل حسن وجه أب — A man whose father is fair of countenance.

زيد الحسن وجه أب — Zaid whose father is fair of countenance.

3rd—Constructions barely admissible, and not of frequent occurrence.

رجل حسن الوجه
رجل حسن وجهه
رجل حسن وجهه

} A man of fair countenance.

رجل حسن وجه الاب
رجل حسن وجه أبيه
رجل حسن وجه أبيه

} A man whose father is of fair countenance.

4th—Constructions to be altogether eschewed.

زيد الحسن وجهِهِ زيد الحسن وجهٍ	Zaid the fair of countenance.
زيد الحسن وجهِ أبِيهِ زيد الحسن وجهِ أبٍ	Zaid whose father is fair of countenance.

a. The adjective even when it has the article prefixed to it may also receive an affixed pronoun; as, اَلْقَبِيحُ ٱلْمَنْظَرِ ٱلشَّدِيدُ ٱلرَّأْسِ وَٱلصَّغِيرُهُ "the ugly of visage, the strong of head, and the small of it," *i.e.* "the small of head." In this form of construction, the adjective must obey the general rule respecting the use of the article, see § 251; for example: رَجُلٌ حَسَنُ ٱلْوَجْهِ "a man fair of countenance;" زَيْدٌ ٱلْحَسَنُ ٱلْوَجْهِ "Zaid the handsome of countenance."

b. If the adjective has a substantive following, which it governs in the genitive case it must itself agree with the preceding substantive in gender, number, and case; thus, مَرَرْتُ بِرَجُلٍ حَسَنِ ٱلْوَجْهِ "I passed by a man fair of countenance;" رَأَيْتُ ٱمْرَأَةً حَسَنَةَ ٱلْوَجْهِ "I saw a woman fair of countenance;" جَآءَنِي رَجُلَانِ حَسَنَا ٱلْوَجْهِ "there came to me two men fair of countenance." This concord of the adjective with the preceding substantive, equally holds, though the restrictive substantive may be in the accusative case; as in the following example: مَرَرْتُ بِرَجُلٍ حَسَنٍ وَجْهًا "I passed by a man handsome of countenance." If, however, the complement be put in the nominative, the adjective then agrees with the preceding substantive in case, but with the complement in gender and number; as for example: مَرَرْتُ بِرَجُلٍ حَسَنٍ وَجْهُهُ "I passed by a man whose face is handsome;" مَرَرْتُ بِٱمْرَأَةٍ حَسَنٍ وَجْهُهَا "I passed by a woman whose face is handsome." If the following substantive be a broken plural, the adjective is usually put in the feminine singular; as in the following examples: مَرَرْتُ بِرِجَالٍ حَسَنَةٍ وُجُوهُهُمْ "I passed by men whose faces are handsome;" فَوَيْلٌ لِلْقَاسِيَةِ قُلُوبُهُمْ "but woe be unto them whose hearts are hard!"

c. Before a substantive masculine in the plural number, the adjective is usually put in the masculine singular; as in the following example; رَأَيْتُ رَجُلاً مَرِيضًا غِلْمَانُهُ "I saw a man whose slave-boys are sick." The adjective may, however, be put in the plural, either broken or regular; as رَأَيْتُ رَجُلاً مَرْضَى غِلْمَانُهُ, or مَرِيضِينَ غِلْمَانُهُ.

Concord of the Attribute with the Subject.

275. When an adjective is employed as the attribute of a simple sentence (§ 248, *b.*), the general rule is to place the subject first and the attribute after it, the verb "to be," when in the present tense, being entirely omitted, as we observed in § 158, *a.*; thus, اَلسُّلْطَانُ مَرِيضٌ "the Sultān is sick;" أَبِي مَرِيضٌ "my father is sick;" يُوسُفُ مَرِيضٌ "Joseph is sick." The subject, as we have just seen, may be restricted by the article, by an affixed pronoun, or by its own nature as being a proper name; whereas the attribute is not necessarily so restricted, as is the case with a mere adjective, § 251. When it so happens that the attribute has the article, the third personal pronouns هُوَ, etc. (equivalent to "he is," etc.) come in between the subject and attribute in order to avoid an ambiguity; for otherwise the phrase might be mistaken

for a mere concord of an adjective with its substantive; thus, اَللّٰهُ هُوَ ٱلْحَيُّ ٱلْقَيُّومُ "God, he is the living, the eternal." The attribute agrees in gender and number with the subject; thus, كَانَ أَبَوَاهُ مُؤْمِنَيْنِ "his parents were true believers." If the subject be a broken plural masculine the attribute may be put in the feminine singular; thus, تَعْمَى ٱلْقُلُوبُ وَٱلعُيُونُ نَاظِرَةٌ "(their) hearts are blind although (their) eyes do see." So, Ḳur,ān, lxxix. 8: قُلُوبٌ يَوْمَئِذٍ وَاجِفَةٌ - أَبْصَارُهَا خَاشِعَةٌ "on that day (men's) hearts shall be perturbed;—their looks (shall be) cast down."

a. When the attribute precedes the subject (which takes place in interrogative and negative propositions), then if the subject be dual or plural, the attribute is to be placed in the singular; as follows: أَ دَاخِلٌ ٱلرَّجُلَانِ "do the two men enter?" مَا خَارِجٌ ٱلرِّجَالُ "the men do not go out." When the subject is a collective noun the attribute may be put in the plural; thus, كُلٌّ لَهُ قَانِتُونَ "all are obedient unto him."

b. When the subject consists of two nouns in a state of regimen, the attribute, which ought grammatically to agree with the governing noun, sometimes agrees in gender with the noun governed; thus, كُلُّ نَفْسٍ ذَائِقَةُ ٱلْمَوْتِ "every living (creature shall) taste of death;" so أَتْيُ ٱلْفَوَاحِشِ عِنْدَهُمْ مَعْرُوفَةٌ - وَلَدَيْهِمْ تَرْكُ ٱلْجَمِيلِ جَمَالٌ "the committal of crimes is with them meritorious, and among them the avoidance of decorum is a virtue." In this last sentence, the feminine singular مَعْرُوفَةٌ agrees with the word governed ٱلْفَوَاحِشِ, a broken plural as we have just stated above.

Of the Degrees of Comparison.

276. In § 211 we enumerated the more usual measures of verbal adjectives. The comparative and superlative degrees of all such are, as we observed in § 81, of the measure أَفْعَلُ for the masculine, and فُعْلَى for the feminine. These may be prefixed to a noun in a state of regimen; or used in an absolute sense, having the article اَلْ before it. When in a state of regimen with an indefinite noun, the adjective always remains in the singular number and masculine gender; thus, هِيَ أَفْضَلُ امْرَأَةٍ "she is a very excellent woman;" هُوَ أَفْضَلُ رَجُلٍ "he is a most excellent man;" هُمْ أَعْظَمُ رِجَالٍ "they are very great men." When the noun governed by the comparative adjective is definite, that is, when it has the article or an affixed pronoun, the comparative generally remains in the measure of the masculine singular, whatever may be the gender and number of the noun following; as هِيَ أَفْضَلُ ٱلنِّسَآءِ "she is the most excellent of women;" أَنْتُمَا أَصْدَقُ ٱلصَّادِقِينَ "you two are the most truthful of the truthful." So in Ḳur,ān, ii. 90: لَتَجِدَنَّهُمْ أَحْرَصَ ٱلنَّاسِ "verily thou wilt find them the most greedy of men." It not unfrequently occurs, however, that the comparative adjective is put in accordance with the following noun both in gender and in number; as in the following examples: هِيَ فُضْلَى ٱلنِّسَآءِ "she is a most excellent woman;" هُمَا أَفْضَلَا ٱلْقَوْمِ "they both are the most excellent (men) of the tribe."

277. When the comparative, having the article prefixed,

is placed absolutely, it agrees in gender and number with the noun or pronoun to which it refers; thus, هُمَا ٱلْأَعْدَلَانِ "they two are most upright men;" هُمَا ٱلصُّغْرَيَانِ "they two are very diminutive (women)." So from the Kur,ān, ix. 40: جَعَلَ كَلِمَةَ ٱلَّذِينَ كَفَرُوا ٱلسُّفْلَى وَكَلِمَةُ ٱللَّهِ هِيَ ٱلْعُلْيَا "He has caused the word (viz. the power) of those who have been unbelievers to become most insignificant; but the word of God is supreme." Again, هُمُ ٱلْأَفْضَلُونَ بَيْنَ ٱلنَّاسِ "they are the most excellent among men." The plural masculine of the adjective, as in this last example, may be either of the regular form أَفْضَلُونَ, or of the irregular or broken form أَفَاضِلُ; and in like manner, the feminine may be of the regular measure فُعْلَيَاتٌ, or irregular, as فُعَلٌ, see § 215. When the comparative adjective is neither accompanied by the article, nor in a state of regimen with the following noun, it is always employed in the form of the masculine singular; and when a comparison is made, the adjective is followed by the particle مِنْ which is equivalent to our "than;" for example: اَلْفِتْنَةُ أَشَدُّ مِنَ ٱلْقَتْلِ "sedition is worse than murder;" نَحْنُ أَحَقُّ بِٱلْمُلْكِ مِنْهُ "we are more worthy of the kingdom than he;" أَحْمَدُ أَصْدَقُ مِنْكَ "Ahmad is more truthful than thou;" مَا شَيْءٌ أَفْسَدُ لِطِبَاعِ ٱلنَّاسِ مِنْ هٰذِهِ ٱلشَّجَرَةِ ٱلْخَبِيثَةِ "there is nothing more hurtful to the constitution of men than this vile plant." When the comparative adjective governs another word, or is accompanied by the article, it then expresses the superlative degree; thus, اَللّٰهُ أَرْحَمُ ٱلرَّاحِمِينَ "God is the most merciful of the merciful;" اَللّٰهُ هُوَ ٱلْأَكْبَرُ "God is most great."

278. When the comparative adjective is followed by an indefinite complement, as in the expression هُوَ أَفْضَلُ رَجُلٍ or هُوَ أَفْضَلُ رَجُلًا "he is most excellent as a man," the complement must be of the same gender and number as the noun or pronoun which constitutes the subject of the proposition; thus, هُمَا أَفْضَلُ رَجُلَيْنِ "they two are most excellent as men." When the substantive governed by the adjective of comparison is followed by a complement, the same is put in the accusative case; thus, هُوَ أَفْضَلُ ٱلنَّاسِ رَجُلًا "he is the most excellent of men, *quoad* man." In an interrogative sentence, the order of the words being a little inverted, the preposition مِنْ does not follow the comparative adjective, but is prefixed to the object of comparison; as مِنْ أَيِّهِمْ أَنْتَ أَفْضَلُ "than which of the two art thou more excellent?" زَوَّدَتْ جَنَي ٱلنَّخْلِ بَلْ مَا زَوَّدَتْ مِنْهُ أَطْيَبُ "she presented (to us) the fruit of the date tree; nay, what she presented (was) better than that."

279. Between the adjective of comparison and the object compared a restrictive or complementary word may intervene; as زَيْدٌ أَكْثَرُ مَالًا مِنْ عَمْرٍو "Zaid is more abundant *in wealth* than 'Amru;" أَنْتَ أَحْظَي عِنْدِي مِنْ غَيْرِكَ "thou art more agreeable *in my view* than any besides thee." In these expressions the adjectives of comparison are in reality, أَكْثَرُ مَالًا and أَحْظَي عِنْدِي, and not simply أَكْثَرُ and أَحْظَي. If the noun which con-

stitutes the subject of comparison be in the nominative case, it must precede the comparative adjective; as in the following example: مَرَرْتُ بِرَجُلٍ أَبُوهُ أَحْسَنُ مِنْهُ "I passed by a man whose father (is) handsomer than he;" but on no account ought we to say مَرَرْتُ بِرَجُلٍ أَحْسَنَ مِنْهُ أَبُوهُ, though it is quite correct to say, as we formerly stated, مَرَرْتُ بِرَجُلٍ حَسَنٍ أَبُوهُ "I passed by a man whose father is handsome." Neither would it be correct to say مَرَرْتُ بِرَجُلٍ يَحْسُنُ مِنْهُ أَبُوهُ "I passed by a man whose father is fairer than he." When, as in this last sentence, the verb is made use of, the construction will run thus: مَرَرْتُ بِرَجُلٍ يَحْسُنُ أَبُوهُ أَكْثَرَ مِنْهُ "I passed by a man whose father is fair, more (or to a greater degree) than he is." When the preposition involving the comparative adjective is affirmative, but preceded by a negative preposition, the above arrangement will differ; as in the following example: مَا رَأَيْتُ رَجُلًا أَحْسَنَ فِي عَيْنِهِ ٱلْكُحْلُ مِنْهُ فِي عَيْنِ زَيْدٍ "I have not seen (any) man in whose eye the collyrium is more beautiful than in that of Zaid;" and if in this last sentence we employ the verb حَسُنَ instead of the adjective أَحْسَنُ, we may for the preposition مِنْ, substitute the particle كَ "like;" as follows: مَا رَأَيْتُ رَجُلًا يَحْسُنُ فِي عَيْنِهِ ٱلْكُحْلُ كَحُسْنِهِ فِي عَيْنِ زَيْدٍ, literally, "I have not seen (any) man in whose eye the collyrium is beautiful like the beauty of it in the eye of Zaid."

280. Verbal adjectives in the comparative state, even when derived from transitive verbs, never have the noun which they directly govern put in the accusative case. Such of them as are derived from verbs expressive of love or of aversion, are

combined with the complement, denoting the object of the sentence, by means of the preposition لِ; and to that denoting the subject, by إلي; thus, اَلْمُؤْمِنُ أَحَبُّ لِلّٰهِ مِنْ نَفْسِهِ "the true believer loveth God more than himself;" اَلْمُؤْمِنُ أَحَبُّ إلي اَللّٰهِ مِنْ غَيْرِهِ "the true believer is more beloved of God than (any) besides him." A comparative adjective derived from a verb signifying "to know," or "to recognise," is combined with its complement by means of the preposition بِ; thus, أَنَا أَعْرَفُ بِٱلْحَقِّ مِنْكُمْ "I am more conversant with the truth than you." When derived from a verb with any other signification, it is connected with its object by means of the preposition لِ; as may be seen in the following example: هُو أَطْلَبُ لِلْعِلْمِ مِنْكُمْ "he is more studious (*lit.* searchful) of knowledge than you." Comparative adjectives derived from intransitive verbs follow the construction of their roots; thus, هُو أَزْهَدُ فِي ٱلدُّنْيَا وَأَسْرَعُ إلي ٱلْخَيْرِ وَأَبْعَدُ مِنَ ٱلْإِثْمِ وَأَحْرَصُ عَلي ٱلْحَمْدِ "he is very abstinent in (affairs of) the world, and very swift (to follow) the good, and very far removed from crime, and most emulous of praise."

281. We may further observe, that in the employment of comparative adjectives, the construction may be somewhat elliptical; thus, هُوَ أَحْوَجُ إليَّ مِنِّي إلَيْهِ "he is more needful of me than I (am) of him;" where مِنِّي is for مِنْ إحْتِيَاجِي "than my necessity;" وَهُو بِٱلْجَامُوسِ أَشْبَهُ مِنْهُ بِٱلْفَرَسِ "and it is more similar to the buffalo than to the horse;" where

مِنْهُ is for مِنْ تَشَبُّهِهِ "than its resemblance." The ellipsis may extend still farther, as in the example already given: مَا رَأَيْتُ رَجُلًا أَحْسَنَ فِي عَيْنِهِ ٱلْكُحْلُ مِنْهُ فِي عَيْنِ زَيْدٍ "I have not seen any man in whose eye the collyrium appears more beautiful than in the eye of Zaid;" in which sentence مِنْهُ is ellipticaly used for مِنْ حُسْنِهِ "than the beauty of it (viz., the collyrium) in the eye of Zaid." We may even say here مِنْ عَيْنِ زَيْدٍ, or even مِنْ زَيْدٍ.

Government of Nouns.

282. When in Arabic one noun governs another in the genitive case, the governing word, as we stated, § 250, is put first, and is subject to the following modifications. In the first place, it loses its nūnation, retaining merely the simple vowels; thus, كِتَابٌ, كِتَابٍ, or كِتَابًا "a book," when governing another word, becomes كِتَابُ, كِتَابِ, and كِتَابَ respectively, as كِتَابُ زَيْدٍ "Zaid's book;" فِي كِتَابِ زَيْدٍ "in Zaid's book," etc. Secondly, if it be a dual, or a regular plural masculine, it drops its final syllable نِ or نَ (§ 68); as كِتَابَا زَيْدٍ "Zaid's two books," etc. Thirdly, if the governing word be a diptote (singular or broken plural), it then becomes a triptote, as we observed, § 68, *a*, with respect to the influence of the article. Lastly, when the word governed is an affixed pronoun, then the governing word undergoes some farther modifications, which we shall notice hereafter when we come to treat of the personal pronouns.

a. An adjective, or a participle used adjectively, when accompanied by a complement, is put in a state of construction similar to the preceding examples; as رَجُلٌ حَسَنُ ٱلْوَجْهِ "a man fair of face;" ضَارِبُ زَيدٍ "(a man) striking Zaid," (*lit.* "striking or striker of Zaid)." The adjective thus employed remains indefinite though its complement be definite; thus, Ḳur,an, v. 96: هَدْيٌ بَالِغُ ٱلْكَعْبَةِ "a gift (or victim) arriving at the Ka'ba." If the antecedent or subject is to be made definite, it of course takes the article; thus, ٱلْمُقِيمُوا ٱلصَّلَاةِ "those who are stedfast in prayer;" ٱلضَّارِبُ رَأْسِ ٱلْجَانِي "he who smites the head of the sinner;" مُحَمَّدٌ ٱلْحَسَنُ ٱلْوَجْهِ "Muḥammad who is fair of countenance."

b. The adjective or noun used adjectively is not unfrequently prefixed in a state of regimen to the substantive which it serves to qualify; thus, أَحَبُّ شَيْءٍ إِلَي ٱلنَّاسِ مَا مُنِعَ "the thing which pleases mankind the most (is) what is forbidden;" لَا تَكُنْ أَوَّلَ كَافِرٍ بِهِ "do not be the first unbeliever in him;" أَنْتُمْ خَيْرُ أُمَّةٍ أُخْرِجَتْ لِلنَّاسِ "you are the best nation that has appeared among mankind;" so likewise, إِنَّ أَوَّلَ بَيْتٍ وُضِعَ لِلنَّاسِ لَلَّذِي بِمَكَّةَ "verily, the first edifice built for mankind (wherein to worship God) is that (which is) at Mecca."

283. We have already stated that when two substantives signify the same thing they agree in case, and are put in a state of apposition. When, however, we meet with instances where they are put in a state of regimen, we are to consider the construction as elliptical; thus, زَيْدُ كُرْزٍ "Zaid of the sack (or wallet)," means زَيْدٌ ٱلْمُسَمَّي بِكُرْزٍ "Zaid nicknamed the sack;" so يَوْمُ ٱلْخَمِيسِ "the day of Thursday," is for ٱلْيَوْمُ ٱلْمُسَمَّي بِٱلْخَمِيسِ "the day called Thursday;" صَلَاةُ ٱلْأُولَي

"the first prayer," means صَلَاةُ ٱلسَّاعَةِ ٱلأُولَى "the prayer of the first hour;" بَيْتُ ٱلْمَقْدِسِ "the holy house (or temple)," is an elliptical expression for بَيْتُ ٱلْمُسَمَّى بِٱلْمُقَدَّسِ "the house called by (the epithet) holy;" which expression is by some improperly written in a state of concord; as بَيْتُ ٱلْمُقَدَّسُ.

a. When a noun which ought logically to be in the dual number is in a state of construction with a complement which is in the dual, the noun is generally put in the plural, but it may, less elegantly, be put in the dual or singular; thus from the Ḳur,ān, lxvi. 4: إِنْ تَتُوبَا إِلَى ٱللّٰهِ فَقَدْ صَغَتْ قُلُوبُكُمَا "if you both (wives of the prophet) turn unto God (penitently), for verily your hearts have swerved." The words كِلَا and (fem.) كِلْتَا "both," form an exception to this rule, for they can be prefixed only to nouns and pronouns of the dual number. See hereafter, § 285, *c*.

284. There are many words used only in a state of regimen, the word governed being either expressed or understood. It is always expressed after ذُو "possessor;" أُولُو "possessors;" مِثْلُ "likeness;" سِوَى "exception." There are others after which the word governed may be omitted; in which case the governing word takes the *nūnation* or the article; such are كُلٌّ "the totality;" بَعْضٌ "part" or "some;" and أَيٌّ "who," etc. (see § 88), as will be seen in the following sentences from the Ḳur,ān, thus, xxxvi. 40: لَا ٱلشَّمْسُ يَنْبَغِي لَهَا أَنْ تُدْرِكَ ٱلْقَمَرَ وَلَا ٱللَّيْلُ سَابِقُ ٱلنَّهَارِ وَكُلٌّ فِي فَلَكٍ يَسْبَحُونَ "it is not expedient that the sun should overtake the moon, neither doth the night outstrip the day; but each (of these

luminaries) moveth in a (peculiar) orbit;" where كُلٌّ is for كُلُّهُمَا, literally, "the totality of these two." Again, ii. 254: تِلْكَ ٱلرُّسُلُ فَضَّلْنَا بَعْضَهُمْ عَلَي بَعْضٍ "as to these apostles, we have distinguished a portion of them above a portion;" where عَلَي بَعْضٍ is for عَلَي بَعْضِهِمْ. So again in xvii. 109: أَيًّا مَا تَدْعُوا فَلَهُ ٱلْأَسْمَآءُ ٱلْحُسْنَي "by whichever (name) you invoke Him, (God, or the Merciful,) verily, He has most excellent names;" where أَيًّا مَا is for أَيَّ ٱسْمٍ مَا. Words which are thus used only in a state of regimen remain indefinite even when their complement is definite; thus—

يَا رُبَّ غَيْرِكِ فِي ٱلنِّسَآءِ غَرِيرَةٍ ـ بَيْضَآءَ قَدْ مَتَّعْتُهَا بِٱلطَّلَاقِ

"Ah, many besides thee among women (have been) deluded (by me), fair ones whom I have dismissed with a divorce," where the word غَيْرِ though accompanied by the affixed pronoun كِ remains indefinite.

285. Words expressive of time or portions of time, such as وَقْتٌ and حِينٌ "time;" يَوْمٌ "a day;" سَاعَةٌ "an hour," etc., when employed in a vague and indefinite sense are put in a state of regimen with a verbal proposition or sentence that follows; in which case they reject the *nūnation* and retain the single vowels; thus, from the Kur,ān, vi. 119: هٰذَا يَوْمُ يَنْفَعُ ٱلصَّادِقِينَ صِدْقُهُمْ "this (is) the day (on which) their veracity shall benefit the righteous;" حِينَ أَتَتْ مَنْزِلَهَا "at the time (when) she will arrive at her abode;" vi. 73: لَهُ ٱلْمُلْكُ يَوْمَ يُنْفَخُ فِي ٱلصُّورِ "to him (shall be) the kingdom (on

that) day (when) the trumpet shall be sounded." When words of time such as the foregoing refer to a past event they may be put in a state of regimen with a nominal proposition; thus, Ḳur,ān, xl. 16: يَوْمَ هُمْ بَارِزُونَ "on the day when they came forth;" so also زَمَنَ ٱلْحَجَّاجُ أَمِيرٌ "at the time when Ḥajjāj (was) governor." This rule does not apply to words of time employed in a specific sense; such as نَهَارٌ "a day," as the apposite of لَيْلَةٌ or لَيْلٌ "a night," etc.

a. The words يَوْمٌ, حِينٌ, and وَقْتٌ, and such like, may also be employed as indeclinable, in which case they have always a *fatḥa* for their final vowel; thus instead of هٰذَا يَوْمُ يَنْفَعُ (as above), we may say هٰذا يومَ يَنْفَعُ; in the phrase مِنْ يومِ حَادَثَنِي "from the day (when) he conversed with me," we may also say مِنْ يومَ حَادَثَنِي.

b. There are many indeclinable words whose final vowel is *ḍamma*, after which the word governed is generally suppressed. Such are قَبْلُ "before;" بَعْدُ "after;" حَسْبُ "sufficient;" غَيْرُ "other;" دُونُ "without" (*sine*); أَوَّلُ "first;" عَلُ "on high;" فَوْقُ "above;" وَرَآءُ "behind;" خَلْفُ "after;" أَمَامُ "before" (in presence of); يَمِينُ "to the right;" شِمَالُ "to the left," and such like, which are generally viewed as adverbs. When they are employed absolutely, they follow the ordinary rules of syntax; thus, عِنْدِي رَجُلٌ لَا غَيْرُ "I have one man, not any other;" قَبَضتُ عَشَرَةً فَحَسْبُ "I took ten, and (they are) sufficient." Sometimes such words as the foregoing may be viewed in the same phrase either as declinable or as indeclinable; thus, Kur,an, xxx. 4: لِلّٰهِ ٱلْأَمْرُ مِنْ قَبْلُ وَمِنْ بَعْدُ "To God belongs the command (both) before and after (the present time);" which sentence, according to some grammarians, we might read مِنْ قَبْلِ وَمِنْ بَعْدِ.

c. The words كِلَا and (fem.) كِلْتَا "both," or "twain," have this peculiarity, that the word which they govern must be a dual, and restricted either by the article or by an affixed pronoun, or be definite from its own nature, for instance, a proper name; thus, كِلَا ٱلرَّجُلَيْنِ وَكِلْتَا ٱلْإِمْرَأَتَيْنِ "both of these men and both of these women;" كِلَانَا فَعَلْنَا ذٰلِكَ "We both did that;" إِنَّ لِلْخَيْرِ وَلِلشَّرِّ مَدًى ـ وَكِلَا ذٰلِكَ وَجْهٌ وَقَبَلْ "Verily to the good and to the evil there is a limit, and both of these (have) an aspect and a power." When two nouns are expressed separately, the words كِلَا and كِلْتَا cannot govern the two together as with us; thus we are not allowed to say in Arabic, كِلَا زَيْدٍ وَعَمْرٍو "both Zaid and 'Amru;" but we must alter the expression and say, زَيْدٌ وَعَمْرٌو كِلَاهُمَا "Zaid and 'Amru, both of them." Sometimes, however, this rule is set aside by a poetical license, as in the following verse:

كِلَا أَخِي وَخَلِيلِي وَاجِدِي عَضُدًا ـ فِي ٱلنَّائِبَاتِ وَإِلْمَامِ ٱلْمُلِمَّاتِ

"Both my brother and my friend find in me a support in their misfortunes and adversities."

286. The governing word may be followed by more than one word governed; thus, عَالِمُ ٱلْغَيْبِ وَٱلشَّهَادَةِ "the knower of what is hidden and (of what is) manifest;" خَلْقُ ٱلسَّمٰوَاتِ وَٱلْأَرْضِ "the creation of the heavens and of the earth." Sometimes the governing word is omitted, when the sense is obvious without it, as in the following verse:

أَكُلَّ ٱمْرِئٍ تَحْسَبِينَ ٱمْرَأً ـ وَنَارٍ تُوقَدُ فِي ٱللَّيْلِ نَارًا

"Dost thou consider every man a man? and (every) fire (shining) in the night a fire (of hospitality)?" where we find, in the second line, the word كُلّ omitted before نَارٍ. The following sentence contains an ellipsis of a similar kind: لَمَّا كَانَتِ ٱلْأَيَّامُ ٱلنَّاصِرِيَّةُ مُحَمَّدِ بْنِ قَلَاوُنَ "when the Nāṣirī days of Muḥammad the son of Ḳalāwun arrived," which sentence, if expressed at full length, would have run as follows: لَمَّا كَانَتِ ٱلْأَيَّامُ ٱلنَّاصِرِيَّةُ أَعْنِي أَيَّامَ ٱلْمَلِكِ ٱلنَّاصِرِ مُحَمَّدِ بْنِ قَلَاوُنَ "when the Nāṣirī days arrived, I mean the days of Malik Alnāṣir Muḥammad the son of Ḳalāwun."

a. The fire alluded to in the last sentence but one is thus explained by De Sacy, viz.: "The hospitable Arabs were in the habit of lighting fires by night on elevated spots near their encampments, so that the wearied wanderer of the desert might know where to seek for shelter and hospitality."

287. As a general rule, the two nouns in a state of construction must not be separated by any intervening word. An exception may be made, however, in the case of interjectional phrases; thus, إِنَّ ٱلشَّاةَ تَسْمَعُ صَوْتَ وَٱللّٰهِ رَبِّهَا "verily, the sheep heareth the voice, by God, of her own master;" so in next sentence, كَأَنَّ بِرْذَوْنَ أَبَا عَاصِمٍ زَيْدٍ حِمَارٌ دُقَّ بِٱللِّجَامِ "one might say that the mule, O Abū 'Āṣim, of Zaid had been a worn out ass with a bridle." Sometimes, either by an abuse of language or by poetic licence, other words besides such as the foregoing are inserted between the nouns in a state of regimen; thus, كَمَا خُطَّ ٱلْكِتَابُ بِكَفِّ يَوْمًا يَهُودِيٍّ "as if the book was written by

the hand, *one day*, of a Jew;" هُمَا أَخَوَا فِي ٱلْحَرْبِ مَنْ لَا أَخَا لَهُ "they both are the brothers, *in war*, of him who has no brother."

SYNTAX OF THE PRONOUNS.

Personal Pronouns.

288. In a simple sentence the isolated personal pronouns (§ 83) placed between the subject and the attribute, supply the use of the verb "to be;" thus, اَللّٰهُ هُوَ ٱلْحَيُّ ٱلْقَيُّومُ "God, He (is) the Living, the Eternal;" أُولَئِكَ هُمْ وَقُودُ ٱلنَّارِ "as to those, they (are) the fuel of the fire;" اَلْغِنَي هُوَ ٱلْقُنُوعُ "opulence, it (is) contentment." The third personal pronouns supply the place of the verb "to be," even when the subject is a pronoun of the first or second person; as أَنَا هُوَ ٱلرَّبُّ إِلٰهُكَ "I am the Lord thy God;" أَنَا هُوَ نُورُ ٱلْعَالَمِ "I am the light of the world." When the proposition begins with the particle إِنَّ "verily," etc., the subject is then expressed by an affixed pronoun (§ 84) in the accusative case, followed by its own isolated pronoun, which last compensates for the verb "to be;" thus, إِنَّكَ أَنْتَ ٱلْوَهَّابُ "verily thou (art) the munificent," *lit.* "verily as to thee, thou (art) the munificent;" so إِنِّي أَنَا رَبُّكَ "verily, I am thy lord." When the affixed pronoun is thus employed in the genitive or accusative case (governed by a verb or particle) it is frequently accompanied, for the sake of emphasis, by its corresponding affixed pronoun in the nominative case, which, however, cannot be so trans-

lated in our idiom; thus, إِنْ تَرَنِي أَنَا أَقَلَّ مِنْكَ مَالًا وَوَلَدًا "if thou beholdest me, *me* (I say) less than thee as to wealth and offspring;" مَا مَنَعَكُمَا أَنْتُمَا مِنْ ذٰلِكَ ؟ "what hath prevented you two, *you two*, (I say,) from that?" لِمَنْ هٰذَا ٱلْكِتَابُ ؟ لَنَا نَحْنُ "to whom (belongs) this book? to us, *us*, (I say);" تُجَهِّزُهُ هُوَ وَأَتْبَاعَهُ "thou shalt equip him, *him*, (I say,) and his attendants;" ٱلْوَيْلُ لِي أَنَا ٱلْمِسْكِينِ "woe unto me, *me*, (I say,) the miserable."

a. The isolated personal pronouns denoting the nominative case are seldom used as such, but they are sometimes added to the verb to render the expression more emphatic; thus, إِنْ جِئْتَ جِئْتُ أَنَا "if thou wilt come, I will come, I, (even)." In such instances as these, however, the pronouns must be of the same person, number, and gender as the verb; a plural verb, however, may have several pronouns singular for its subject, and even of different persons; thus, جِئْنَا أَنَا وَأَنْتَ وَأَخَذْنَا حَاجَتَنَا مِنْهُ "we will come, I and thou, and we will take what is needful for us from him."

b. There is one instance where the verb is employed in the third person singular, although the subject of it be of the first or second person singular, dual or plural; this takes place when the proposition begins with the particle إِنَّمَا "only;" thus, إِنَّمَا قَامَ أَنَا "I only stood up;" أَنَا ٱلْحَامِي ٱلذِّمَامِ وَإِنَّمَا يُدَافِعُ عَنْ أَحْسَابِهِمْ أَنَا أَوْ مِثْلِي "I am the defender of (their) rights; only I, or the like of me, can repel the attacks made upon their reputation."

289. We slightly alluded (§§ 84 and 282) to the modifications undergone by words to which the affixed pronouns are

attached, as well as to those undergone by the affixes themselves. We have now arrived at that stage of our progress where we deem it most proper to treat of the subject at full length; and we cannot do better than to lay before the student De Sacy's rules to that effect (Gr. Ar. Tom. 1er. 457). In the first place, on receiving an affixed pronoun the *nūnation* of all the triptotes disappears and the simple vowels only remain, as we stated, § 282, with respect to the government of nouns. 2nd. The affixed pronoun of the first person ـِي displaces both the *nūnation* and the simple vowel (§ 84, *a*); hence, in this instance, the distinction of the three case terminations of the noun is entirely lost, and the cases must be inferred from the context, as we do in our own language. 3rd. Nouns ending in ة, change it into ت, on receiving the affixed pronoun; as نِعْمَةٌ "a benefit;" نِعْمَتُهُ "his benefit." 4th. The final نِ of the duals, and the final نَ of masculine plurals ending ـُونَ disappear; thus, nom. dual كِتَابَانِ gen. كِتَابَيْنِ "two books," with the affixed pronoun كُمْ, become كِتَابَاكُمْ and كِتَابَيْكُمْ "your two books;" so, nom. pl. بَنُونَ "sons," gen. and accus. بَنِينَ, with the affixed pronoun كَ, become respectively بَنُوكَ and بَنِيكَ "thy sons." 5th. Nouns ending in *hamza* change the same into و, if its vowel be *ḍamma*; and into ي, if it be *kasra*; thus, نِسَآءٌ "women;" نِسَآؤُهُ "his women;" لِنِسَآئِهِ "to his women." 6th. In the third person masc. pl. of verbs, the quiescent *alif* after و disappears; as نَصَرُوا "they assisted;" نَصَرُونِي "they assisted me;" رَمَوْا "they threw" or "shot;" رَمَوْهُمْ "they threw against them." 7th. After the verbal termination تُمْ, of the second person pl. masc. of the preterite, the م is made moveable by *ḍamma*, followed by و inert; as رَأَيْتُمْ "you saw;" رَأَيْتُمُوهُمْ "you saw them." 8th. In those persons of the aorist, which end in ـُونَ; as يَكْتُبُونَ "they write;" the final نَ is sometimes dropped before the affixed pronouns نِي and نَا; as تَأْمُرُونِي for تَأْمُرُونَنِي "you order me;" so تَقْلُونَا "you hate us," for تَقْلُونَنَا. In the third person sing. masc. of the preterite of such verbs as have نَ for the final radical, on receiving the affixed pronoun نِي the final نَ of the verb may coalesce, by *tashdīd*, with the ن of the affix; thus, مَكَّنِّي "he has rendered me powerful;" for مَكَّنَنِي (Ḳur. xviii. 94). 9th. The ي quiescent after *fatḥa*, may, in nouns as well as in verbs, either be retained or changed into *alif*; as فَتَي "a boy;" فَتَاهُ or فَتَيهُ "his boy;" رَمَي "he threw;" رَمَاهُ or رَمَيهُ "he threw him." 10th. In particles terminating in ي quiescent after *fatḥa*, the ي takes *jazm* when followed by the affixed pronouns; as عَلَي "upon;" عَلَيْنَا "upon us;" إِلَي "towards;" إِلَيْكَ "towards thee."

290. The principal modifications to which the affixes themselves are liable, are the following:—1. The affixed pronoun ـِي of the first person singular takes the vowel *fatḥa* instead of *kasra* when united with any word ending in ا, و, or ي inert; thus, خَطَايَا "sins," خَطَايَايَ "my sins;" غُلَامَانِ "two slaves," modified according to § 289 into غُلَامَا, (by dropping the final نِ), hence غُلَامَايَ "my two slaves." When the word to which the affix ـِي is to be joined ends in ي inert or quiescent, this last is united by *tashdīd* with the affix; as, فِي "in," فِيَّ "in me;"

عَلَي "upon," عَلَيَّ "upon me;" so, غُلَامَيْنِ (modified غُلَامَيْ) "of two slaves," غُلَامَيَّ "of my two slaves;" مُسْلِمِينَ (modified مُسْلِمِي) "of the Muslims," مُسْلِمِيَّ "of my Muslims." When the word to which the affix ي is attached ends in و preceded by *damma*—that is, in long *ū*,—the و is changed into ي, and the same unites by *tashdīd* with the affix, as in the case of the final ي inert or quiescent; thus, مُسْلِمُونَ (nom. pl.) "the Muslims," (modified مُسْلِمُو), becomes مُسْلِمِيَّ "my Muslims." 2. This same affix ـِي of the first person singular is sometimes entirely suppressed, its *kasra* only remaining. This often takes place when the noun is employed in a vocative sense; and almost always, when the word to which the affix is united ends in *hamza*, which last then becomes ي; as, أَحِبَّآئِي "my friends," for أَحِبَّآئِي; so آبَآئِي "my fathers," for آبَآئِي, from أَحِبَّآءُ and آبَآءُ. 3. نِي in place of ي, is used when joined to active verbs, and also to particles ending in ن; such as مِنْ, عَنْ, إِنَّ, أَنَّ, and also to لَكِنَّ and كَأَنَّ. The affixed pronoun here always represents an accusative case. The words إِنَّ and أَنَّ when taking this affix of the first person singular, are written إِنِّي and أَنِّي for إِنَّنِي and أَنَّنِي. The same rule holds with the first pers. pl., as إِنَّا and أَنَّا for إِنَّنَا and أَنَّنَا. In like manner لَكِنَّ makes لَكِنِّي and لَكِنَّا. 4. The affixed pronouns of the third person هُ, هُمَا, هُمْ, and هُنَّ, change their *damma* into *kasra* when the word to which they are united ends in *kasra* or in ي inert or quiescent; thus, دَارُهُ "his house;" فِي دَارِهِ "in his house;" فِي دَارِهِمَا "in the house of them two;" فِيهِ "in him" or "in it;" يَرْمِيهِ "he may throw (or shoot) him;" عَلَيْهِ "on him;" عَلَيْهِمْ "on them," etc.

a. The affix ﻩُ sometimes loses its own vowel and takes *jazm*; this, however, occurs only in poetry or in measured prose, such as the Kur,ān or the Maķāmāt of Ḥarīrī; thus, نُؤْتِهْ for نُؤْتِهِ "we shall give unto him." The affixes كُمْ and هُمْ when followed by *waṣla*, § 36, change the final *jazma* into *ḍamma*; but when, by a rule just stated, the affix هُمْ becomes هِمْ then the final م takes *kasra* before the *waṣla*; thus, عَلَيْكُمُ ٱلسَّلَامُ "on you be peace;" عَلَيْهِمِ ٱلسَّلَامُ "on them be peace." In this last instance, however, some grammarians hold that we may say عَلَيْهِمُ, and even عَلَيْهُمُ.

b. A transitive verb or a verbal noun, may have attached to it two different affixes, viz., an accusative and a genitive or dative, provided they be not of the same person; as أَعْطَانِيهِ "he gave it to me" (*lit.* "he gave to me it"); so يَكْفِيكَهُمْ "it will suffice thee (against) them." The two affixes, however, may be of the third person provided they be not identical, in other words they must differ in gender or in number; as أَطْعَمْتُهُمُوهُنَّ "I gave them to them to eat;" أَسْقَيْتُهُمَاهَا "I gave it to them two to drink." In such instances, it is a rule, that the affix of the first person precedes that of the second; and that of the second person precedes that of the third. The same rule holds with regard to verbal nouns or infinitives; as حُبِّيهِ "my affection for him." When the first of the affixes is كُمْ "you" or "to you;" the مْ of the كُمْ is made moveable by *ḍamma* and the letter و is inserted between it and the following affix; thus, يُرِيكُمُوهُمْ "he will shew them unto you," as in the case of the termination تُمْ, § 289.

c. We have already stated, § 84, *f*. that instead of employing two affixes, that which denotes the accusative is in many instances used separately, having the particle إِيَّا prefixed. This mode of construction serves to avoid all ambiguity in instances like the preceding, where it may not, at first sight, be obvious which is the accusative and which the secondary case; hence we must not say أَعْطَيْتُهُكَ "I gave thee to him," but أَعْطَيْتُهُ إِيَّاكَ. In like manner we must not say أَقْبَضْتُكَنِي "I caused thee to seize me;" but أَقْبَضْتُكَ إِيَّايَ. It is equally incorrect to say ظَنَنْتُكَكَ "I thought thee *thee*" (*i.e.* "thought thou wert thyself") but ظَنَنْتُكَ إِيَّاكَ. So for ظَنَنْتَنِينِي we must say ظَنَنْتَنِي إِيَّايَ "thou thoughtest me (to be) myself." Lastly, for ظَنَنْتُهَاهَا "I thought she was *she*" (*lit.* I thought her *her*"); we must say ظَنَنْتُهَا إِيَّاهَا.

d. We remarked in § 84, *d*. that the affix نِي of the first person singular is added to verbs only, to denote either the accusative or dative; it is often added, however, to participles and verbal adjectives; for example; هَلْ أَنْتُمْ صَادِقُونِي "are you acting truly towards me?" لَيْسَ ٱلْمُوَافِينِي لِيُرْفَدَ خَائِبًا "he who comes to me (that he may receive aught) shall never go away disappointed;" غَيْرُ ٱلدَّجَّالِ أَخْوَفُنِي عَلَيْكُمْ "another than the Antichrist inspires me with more fear for you."

e. With verbal adjectives the affixed pronoun which serves as a complement, or the first of the affixes when there are two, may be considered as either a genitive or accusative case. With a noun of action the affixed pronoun, or the first of them if there be two, ought always to be considered as a genitive, whether it be expressive of the subject of the verb, or the complement of a verb active, or the first complement of a verb doubly transitive. When there are two affixed pronouns as complements of the same verbal adjective, or of the same noun of action, the second of them ought always to be considered as an accusative case. We have shewn, § 84, *f.* that when two affixes are joined to a transitive verb that which denotes the accusative may be separated in combination with the particle إِيَّا; with the simple verb, however, it is more elegant to add the two suffixes, provided of course there occur no ambiguity. With infinitives and participles it is more correct to separate the last of the affixes or that denoting the accusative.

Demonstrative Pronouns.

291. As a general rule the demonstrative pronouns agree in gender and number with the nouns to which they refer, whether expressed or understood. There is, however, one notable exception, viz., a broken plural masculine or a regular feminine plural, usually takes for its demonstrative pronoun the feminine singular of the latter; for example: تِلْكَ ٱلْعَسَاكِرُ "those armies;" هٰذِهِ الايام "these days;" هٰذِهِ ٱلْخَيْلُ "these horses;" هٰذِهِ الالف الف دِينَارٍ "this million (*lit.* thousand of thousands) of dīnārs."

a. The demonstrative pronouns, being in their nature definite words, must have the noun which they specify also definite as is often the case in Greek in such phrases as *τουτο το ρημα* "this saying," etc. In a proposition, however, in which the noun is the attribute, the latter may remain indefinite; as قَالُوا هٰذَا سِحْرٌ "they say this is delusion." Sometimes the attribute is expressed by an entire phrase; thus, فَهٰذَا مَا عَلَي جَانِبِ بَحْرِ القُلْزُمِ "and this (is) what (is found) on the shore of the sea of Ḳulzum (*i.e.* the Red Sea)." In interrogative phrases the subject is put after the attribute; thus مَنْ هُوَ ذَاكَ "who is that?" ما هٰذَا "what is this?"

292. The remote demonstrative pronoun which is formed from the preceding by adding the affixes كِ, كَ, etc., of the second person, not only agrees in gender and number with the noun it qualifies, but the affixes themselves agree in gender and number with the person or persons addressed. For example, "that book," if you are speaking to one man, is expressed ذَلِكَ ٱلْكِتَابُ; and if to one woman ذَلِكِ ٱلْكِتَابُ; if you are addressing two men or two women you will say ذَلِكُمَا ٱلْكِتَابُ; if there be more than two men ذَلِكُمْ ٱلْكِتَابُ; and if more than two women, the expression is ذَلِكُنَّ ٱلْكِتَابُ. Practically speaking, however, the affix كَ alone is generally used, as ذَلِكَ and تِلْكَ without any respect to the gender and number of the persons addressed.

Of the Relative Pronouns.

293. The relative pronouns ٱلَّذِي and ٱلَّتِي being compounded of the article اَلْ and the demonstrative ذَا (modified into لَذِي) must have the word to which it relates in itself definite, either by means of the article اَلْ or of an affixed pronoun, or by being in a state of regimen, or being a proper name; thus, Ḳur. iv. 21: أُمَّهَاتُكُمْ ٱللَّاتِي أَرْضَعْنَكُمْ "your mothers who have suckled you;" also iv. 14: ٱللَّاتِي يَأْتِينَ ٱلْفَاحِشَةَ مِنْ نِسَائِكُمْ "those among your women who have come to disgrace." A broken plural or a regular feminine plural take the relative in

the feminine singular; as تَوَكَّلُوا عَلَي ٱللّٰهِ فِي ٱلشَّدائِدِ ٱلَّتِي تُصِيبُكُمْ "rely upon God in the afflictions which may befal you;" also بِآيَاتِ ٱللّٰهِ ٱلَّتِي أَنْزَلَهَا عَلَي نَبِيِّهِ "believe in the verses of God (viz., those of the Ḳur,ān), which he sent down upon his prophet."

294. The relatives اَلَّذِي and اَللَّتِي, as we stated in § 86, are never employed in the oblique cases singular, and rarely in those of the dual and plural; but the omission is supplied by means of an affixed pronoun that follows; for example: ٱلطَّبِيبُ ٱلَّذِي ٱبْنُهُ عِنْدِي "the physician whose son is with me;" ٱلسَّارِقُ ٱلَّذِي قَتَلَهُ ٱبْنِي "the robber whom my son slew;" ٱلتَّاجِرُ ٱلَّذِي تُوجَدُ عِنْدَهُ هٰذِهِ ٱلْجَارِيَةُ "the merchant with whom this maiden is found." The personal affix expressive of the accusative case is sometimes omitted when governed by a verb or participle active; as may be seen in the following example: ٱلْمَالُ ٱلَّذِي تَشْتَهِي أَنْفُسُنَا "the wealth for which our souls are longing;" where تَشْتَهِي is used elliptically for تَشْتَهِيهِ. So in the sentence ٱلرِّزْقُ ٱلَّذِي مُولِيكَ ٱللّٰهُ فَضْلٌ "the sustenance which God bestoweth on thee is a blessing;" where مُولِيكَ is for مُولِيكَهُ. The same affix may also be omitted when governed by a preposition; and both affix and preposition may be omitted when the relative itself is governed by the same preposition; as مَرَرْتُ بِٱلَّذِي مَرَّ سُلَيْمَانُ "I passed by him whom Sulaimān passed by;" where after مَرَّ the complement بِهِ is omitted. This last rule, however, does not hold when there are two distinct verbs in the

sentence; as زَهَدْتُ فِي ٱلَّذِي رَغَبْتَ فِيهِ "I abstained from that from which thou desiredst me;" where we cannot say زَهَدْتُ فِي ٱلَّذِي رَغَبْتَ by omitting the last word فِيهِ. Such construction may, however, be occasionally met with, which we are to regard as a poetic licence.

295. The relative اَلَّذِي like مَنْ and مَا of which more anon, sometimes includes the notion of an antecedent, as follows: اَلَّذِي ٱزْدَرَيْتُ فِيهِ هُوَ خَلَّصَنِي وَٱلَّذِي رَجَوْتُهُ أَهْلَكَنِي "that which I despised (would have) saved me, and that in which I confided has destroyed me." This kind of construction is adopted when the writer wishes to give an emphasis to certain words in the sentence; which will be better understood by a few examples. For instance, let us take the sentence, "The two poets sent a letter to the wazīrs." If the emphasis be on "the two poets," then the sentence will run as follows: اَللَّذَانِ بَلَّغَا ٱلْوُزَرَآءَ رِسَالَةً ٱلشَّاعِرَانِ literally, "those two who sent to the wazīrs a letter, are *the two poets*." If the emphasis be on "the wazīrs," the construction will be as follows: اَلَّذِينَ بَلَّغَهُمُ ٱلشَّاعِرَانِ رِسَالَةً ٱلْوُزَرَآءُ "they to whom the two poets sent a letter, (the same) are the wazīrs." Lastly, if the emphasis be on the word "letter," then the sentence will run thus, اَلَّتِي بَلَّغَهَا ٱلشَّاعِرَانِ ٱلْوُزَرَآءَ رِسَالَةٌ. In each of these three modes of expression it will be observed, that the relative begins the sentence, and that the noun on which the emphasis is to be placed, and with which the relative agrees in gender, number, and case, is placed at the end, and in the nominative case.

a. When, in a simple proposition, we wish to express emphatically a word having a reference to time or place, such as, "I fasted on Friday" صُمْتُ يَوْمَ ٱلْجُمُعَةِ; if we intend to lay an emphasis on the word Friday, we must employ the preposition فِي with the affixed pronoun, and put the word denoting Friday last, in the nominative case; thus, ٱلَّذِي صُمْتُ فِيهِ يَوْمُ ٱلْجُمُعَةِ "that day on which I fasted (was) Friday."

b. When a proposition includes a word expressive of "cause," "desire," or "purpose," and it is intended to render the same emphatic, the preposition لِ with the affixed pronoun is employed in a manner similar to the preceding; thus, جِئْتُ رُغْبَةً فِيكَ "I came with the desire of seeing thee;" if expressed emphatically will be, ٱلَّذِي جِئْتُ لَهُ رُغْبَةٌ فِيكَ, *i.e.*, "that for which I came, was the desire of seeing thee." We may observe, however, that in a construction of this kind, if the noun is feminine, as in last example, the pronouns, both relative and affix, may be masculine. The reason is that the true antecedent is the word الشَّيْءُ "the thing" or "object," which is of the masculine gender.

296. In a simple proposition consisting only of a subject and an attribute (the verb being understood), such as, زَيْدٌ أَبُوكَ "Zaid (is) thy father;" عَمْرٌو قَائِمٌ "'Amru is standing;" the emphasis, when required, is indicated by employing the relative ٱلَّذِي together with the appropriate personal pronoun. If it be meant to place the emphasis on the attribute, the preceding phrases will run thus, ٱلَّذِي هُوَ أَبُوكَ زَيْدٌ "he who (is) thy father is Zaid;" ٱلَّذِي هُوَ قَائِمٌ عَمْرٌو "he who (is) standing is 'Amru." If the emphasis is to be laid on the subject, we must say, ٱلَّذِي هُوَ زَيْدٌ أَبُوكَ "he who (is called) Zaid (is) thy

father;" اَلَّذِي هُوَ عَمْرٌو قَائِمٌ "he who (is called) 'Amru (is) standing." In each of these examples, the personal pronoun هُوَ is employed (§ 288) along with the relative, the real antecedent to both being اَلرَّجُلُ "the man," understood.

297. The article أَلْ sometimes supplies the place of the relative اَلَّذِي, especially in those instances where it is followed by a verb or a preposition, as in the following examples; viz., مَا أَنْتَ بِٱلْحَكَمِ ٱلْ تُرْضَي حُكُومَتُهُ "thou art not a judge whose judgment is satisfactory;" مَنْ لَا يَزَالُ شَاكِرًا عَلَي ٱلْمَعَهُ "he who ceaseth not to evince gratitude to those who are with him." In both of these examples أَلْ is evidently used for اَلَّذِي. So, in the following phrases, viz.: مِنَ ٱلْقَوْمِ ٱلرَّسُولُ ٱللّٰهِ مِنْهُمْ "from the tribe, out of which (sprung) the apostle of God." Kur,ān, lvii. 7: إِنَّ ٱلْمُصَدِّقِينَ وَٱلْمُصَدِّقَاتِ وَأَقْرَضُوا ٱللّٰهَ قَرْضًا حَسَنًا يُضَاعَفُ لَهُمْ "verily to those almsgiving men and women, and to those who have lent unto God an acceptable loan, it shall be doubled unto them." Here, again, the article أَلْ prefixed to the words مُصَدِّقِينَ and مُصَدِّقَاتِ is a substitute for the relative pronoun اَلَّذِي.

a. The article أَلْ may further be employed instead of the relative, in combination with a participle, active or passive, when used emphatically as a substitute for a verb. For example, let us take the sentence يَقِي ٱللّٰهُ ٱلْبَطَلَ "God protects the brave (man);" instead of which we may say emphatically, اَلْوَاقِي ٱلْبَطَلَ ٱللّٰهُ "he who protects the brave man (is) God;" or اَلْوَاقِيهِ ٱللّٰهُ ٱلْبَطَلُ "he whom God protects (is) the brave man;" in which last phrase the personal pronoun may be omitted. For further illustration, let us examine the following examples; thus, the sentence بَلَّغْتُ مِنَ ٱلزَّيْدَيْنِ إِلَي ٱلْمُسْلِمِينَ رِسَالَةً "I conveyed a letter from the two Zaids to the Muslims," may be expressed emphatically in four different ways, as follows, viz.: ٱلْمُبَلِّغُ مِنَ ٱلزَّيْدَيْنِ إِلَي ٱلْمُسْلِمِينَ رِسَالَةً أَنَا "the conveyer of a letter from the two Zaids to the Muslims was I," where the personal pronoun هُوَ is omitted after ٱلْمُبَلِّغُ. In the three following modes of emphatic construction, however, the affixed pronoun of the third person must be expressed, viz.: ٱلْمُبَلِّغُ أَنَا مِنْهُمَا إِلَي ٱلْمُسْلِمِينَ رِسَالَةً ٱلزَّيْدَانِ "the two (persons) from whom I conveyed a letter to the Muslims (are) the two Zaids;" ٱلْمُبَلِّغُ أَنَا مِنَ ٱلزَّيْدَيْنِ إِلَيْهِمْ رِسَالَةً ٱلْمُسْلِمُونَ "those to whom I conveyed a letter from the two Zaids (are) the Muslims;" ٱلْمُبَلِّغُهَا أَنَا مِنَ ٱلزَّيْدَيْنِ إِلَي ٱلْمُسْلِمِينَ رِسَالَةٌ "that which I conveyed from the two Zaids to the Muslims (was) a letter."

298. The pronouns مَنْ "he or she who," and مَا "that which," when employed as relatives, are indeclinable. They differ from ٱلَّذِي in this, that they include, absolutely, in themselves the force both of antecedent and relative; thus, مَنْ كَفَرَ "he who hath disbelieved;" مَا سَارَ "that which has passed." As a general rule مَنْ refers to rational beings, and مَا to whatever is irrational or lifeless. To this rule, however, there are occasional exceptions; for instance, مَنْ may be applied to irrational or lifeless beings when the latter are personified; or when in one and the same sentence both rational and irrational beings are included; thus, for example: لِلّٰهِ يَسْجُدُ مَنْ فِي ٱلسَّمٰوَاتِ وَٱلْأَرْضِ "unto God those who are in the heavens and (on the earth) make adoration;" or we might

say, لِلّٰهِ يَسْجُدُ مَا فِي ٱلسَّمٰوَاتِ وَمَا فِي ٱلأَرْضِ "unto God that which is in the heavens and that which is (on the earth) make adoration." Again, the relative مَا may be applied to rational beings when we indicate a class of such beings, distinguished from others as to quality or quantity; thus, Ḳur,ān, iv. 3: فَانْكِحُوا مَا طَابَ لَكُمْ مِنَ ٱلنِّسَآءِ مَثْنَي وَثُلَاثَ وَرُبَاعَ "and espouse ye whatsoever (for whomsoever) is agreeable unto you from among the women (to the number of) two, three, or four (each)."

299. The word أَيٌّ (fem. أَيَّةٌ) "who or whatsoever," has sometimes the effect of a relative. When so employed, it is declined in the singular as a triptote, but not in the dual or plural; thus, أَقْتُلُ أَيًّا حَارَبَنِي "I will slay (any one) whomsoever that makes war upon me;" جِئْنِي بِأَيٍّ عَصَوْا عَلَيَّ "bring unto me (lit., come unto me with) those who have rebelled against me;" إِعْرِفْنِي بِأَيٍّ قَالَتْ هٰذَا "inform me what (female) hath said that." We may here observe, that in such phrases as this last, it is not essential to employ the feminine بِأَيَّةٍ, though that would be quite correct. In certain situations أَيٌّ becomes indeclinable; viz., when it is in a state of construction with an affixed pronoun, or any other complement which is expressed, not merely understood, and followed by a nominal proposition, the subject of which is the personal pronoun which belongs to أَيٌّ, but which is merely understood, not expressed; thus, ثُمَّ لَنَنْزِعَنَّ عَنْ كُلِّ شِيعَةٍ أَيُّهُمْ أَشَدُّ عَلَي ٱلرَّحْمٰنِ عُتِيًّا "then we shall withdraw from the whole army whomsoever of them have been most violent in their rebellion against the

Merciful;" إذا ما لَقِيتَ بَنِي مَالِكٍ فَسَلِّمْ عَلَي أَيُّهُمْ أَفْضَلُ "if thou shouldst meet with the children of Mālik, salute whichever of them is most virtuous." In the first of the two preceding sentences, if the personal pronoun had been expressed, or had the affix of أَيٌّ been omitted, we should have to assume the regular declension of the word أَيٌّ; thus, أَيُّهُمْ هُوَ أَشَدُّ. So in the second sentence we should, under similar circumstances, have said, عَلَي أَيِّهِمْ هُوَ أَفْضَلُ.

a. The words أَيٌّ and أَيَّةٌ sometimes take after them the affix هَا, and become respectively أَيُّهَا and أَيَّتُهَا. They are thus employed in order to specify or particularise the noun following from others of the same kind; and the noun so specified is put in the accusative case; for example: أَنَا أَفْعَلُ كَذَا أَيُّهَا الرَّجُلَ "I will thus act, I for my part;" نَحْنُ نَفْعَلُ كَذَا أَيُّهَا الْقَوْمَ "we will thus act, we on our part;" اَللّٰهُمَّ اغْفِرْ لَنَا أَيَّتُهَا الْعِصَابَةَ "O God! pardon us, us who are a special band." If, however, the word following أَيُّهَا and أَيَّتُهَا be an adjective or a noun in apposition, the latter is to be put in the nominative case as the attribute of the subject هُوَ understood.

b. The words أَيُّهَا and أَيَّتُهَا may be omitted in such phrases as the preceding, if the noun specified be restricted by the article أَلْ, or if it be in a state of regimen with a substantive which is so restricted; thus, نَحْنُ الْعَرَبَ أَقْرَي النَّاسِ لِلضَّيْفِ "we Arabs are the most prompt of men for hospitality." This mode of expression is used only after a pronoun of the first person singular or plural.

Of the Interrogative Pronouns.

300. We have just shewn the use and application of مَنْ,

مَا, and أَيٌّ as relative pronouns; we shall now briefly notice the manner in which they are employed interrogatively. In asking a question مَنْ generally applies to rational beings, and مَا to irrational beings and lifeless things. If the noun to which they refer accompanies them, they are not subject to any variation on account of gender, number, or case. If, however, the noun be not expressed, then مَنْ is regularly declined as we shewed in § 87, *a*. For example, A says to B, جَآءنِي رَجُلٌ "a man came to me;" then should B ask "who?" without any additional word, the expression would be مَنُو; but if he asked, "who came?" it would be مَنْ جآء. In like manner, if A says قَتَلْتُ رَجُلاً "I killed a man," and B should ask "whom?" the expression is مَنَا in the accusative case. If, however, B asks "whom hast thou killed?" or "whom, O youth?" مَنْ alone is used; as مَنْ قَتَلْتَ or مَنْ يَا فَتَي. There are, however, some instances in which مَنْ is declined under such circumstances; as in the following example: أَتَوْا نَارِي فَقُلْتُ مَنُونَ أَنْتُمْ قَالُوا ٱلْجِنُّ "they came to my fire (of hospitality) and I said who are you? they said, the Jinns," in which sentence we see the regular nominative plural مَنُونَ used instead of مَنْ.

301. The application of أَيٌّ and أَيَّةٌ as interrogatives, differs from that of مَنْ inasmuch as if followed by the word to which they refer, the latter is put in the genitive case, as we stated in § 88. They are also subject to all the variations of number and case when used alone; as رَأَيْتُ رَجُلَيْنِ "I saw two men;" and if the speaker be asked "whom?" the expression will be أَيَّيْنِ يَا صَاحِبِي "what two, my friend?"

a. The interrogative أَيٌّ is also employed with an indefinite noun in a state of regimen, to express admiration; thus, جِئْتَنِي بِرَجُلٍ أَيِّ رَجُلٍ "thou camest unto me with (a certain) man, what a man!" If, however, a definite noun precedes, the word أَيّ is to be put adverbially in the accusative case; as, جَآءَنِي زَيْدٌ أَيَّ رَجُلٍ "Zaid came unto me, what a man!" The noun respecting which admiration is thus expressed by means of أَيٌّ may be itself understood, or virtually comprised in a verb; and أَيٌّ is then to be put in the same case as that in which the suppressed noun would have been were it expressed. For example, in the following phrase, أُنْتُكُوا أَيَّ نِكَايَةٍ "they were grievously vexed, what a vexation!" أَيٌّ is put in the accusative case, because the sentence, if stated in full, would have run thus, أُنْتُكُوا نِكَايَةً أَيَّ نِكَايَةٍ.

SECTION VIII.

SYNTAX OF VERBS AND PARTICLES.

Use and Application of the Preterite Tense.

302. The Arabic preterite corresponds with what we call the indefinite past, and also with our preterperfect. It has the former meaning in simple narration when preceded by the adverbs مَرَّةً "once on a time;" and others of the kind expressive of indefinite past time; as in the following example: أَسَدٌ مَرَّةً خَرَجَ عَلَي ثَوْرَيْنِ فَٱجْتَمَعَا جَمِيعًا "a lion once upon a time went forth against two bulls, now they (both) united together," etc. In the following sentences it corresponds with our preterperfect tense, قَدْ ذَكَرْنَا وِزَارَةَ جَدِّهِمْ وَنَذْكُرُ هَاهُنَا وِزَارَةَ ٱلْبَاقِينَ "verily we have described the administration of their ancestor, now we will narrate the vizīrate of those remaining;" أُذْكُرُوا نِعْمَتِيَ ٱلَّتِي أَنْعَمْتُ عَلَيْكُمْ وَأَنِّي فَضَّلْتُكُمْ عَلَي ٱلْعَالَمِينَ "remember my benefits that I have conferred upon you, and (remember) that I have rendered you superior to (the rest of) mankind." We may here observe, that when the preterite is preceded by the particle قَدْ "now," "verily," etc., it always signifies a past time, which is by no means the case in many other respects, as we shall see immediately. The same rule holds

with respect to لَمَّا and حِينَ "when," and other words synonymous with them.

303. The preterite is frequently employed to express, with greater energy, present or future time, especially in correlative propositions of a general application, or proverbial sentences, such as the following: مَنْ كَتَمَ سِرَّهُ بَلَغَ مُرَادَهُ "he who conceals his secret attains his (wished for) object," literally, "he who hath concealed," etc.; so مَنْ نَقَلَ إِلَيْكَ نَقَلَ عَنْكَ "he who reporteth unto thee (another's secret), will report from thee (thy secret to another);" literally, "he who hath brought thee hath carried from thee." When correlative propositions of this kind—the first of which begins with مَنْ or أَيٌّ "whosoever," مَا "whatsoever," كُلَّمَا "as often as," حَيْثُمَا "whithersoever," and such like—express only a particular not a general truth, the preterites in both clauses are to be translated by our future; thus, Ḳur,ān iv. 59: كُلَّمَا نَضِجَتْ جُلُودُهُمْ بَدَّلْنَاهُمْ جُلُودًا غَيْرَهَا "as often as their skins shall have been burnt out, we shall substitute for them other skins."

304. The pluperfect tense is formed in Arabic by employing the preterite of the verb كَانَ (§ 158), together with the preterite of the verb to be put in the pluperfect tense; thus, كَانَ كَتَبَ "he had written;" كَانَتْ كَتَبَتْ "she had written;" and so on, bearing in mind that the two verbs must strictly agree in gender, number, and person throughout. When several pluperfects are to be expressed, instead of repeating كَانَ with each, the particle قَدْ is inserted between the latter

and the preterite immediately following, which serves to throw the succeeding preterites also into the pluperfect; thus, وَمَاتَ ٱلرَّشِيدُ بِطُوسَ - وكَانَ خَرَجَ إِلَي خُرَاسَانِ لِمُحَارَبَةِ رَافِعِ بْنِ ٱللَّيْثِ - وَكَانَ هٰذَا ٱلرَّافِعُ قَدْ خَرَجَ وَخَلَعَ ٱلطَّاعَةَ وَتَغَلَّبَ عَلَي سَمَرْقَنْدَ - فَخَرَجَ ٱلرَّشِيدُ بِنَفْسِهِ إِلَيْهِ فَمَاتَ بِطُوسَ "and Rashīd died at Ṭūs; and he had gone into Khurāsān in order to fight Rāfi', the son of Laith; and this Rāfi', indeed, had (previously) revolted, and had shaken off his obedience, and had conquered Samarḳand; and Rashīd in person went forth against him, and died at Ṭūs." Here we see that in consequence of the particle قَدْ, the verb كَانَ, when it occurs for the second time in the preceding extract, throws the three following preterites خَرَجَ, خَلَعَ, and تَغَلَّبَ into the pluperfect tense.

a. The particle لَمَّا, when placed after كَانَ, has a similar effect to that of قَدْ on the preterites that follow in the same sentence; that is, it throws them all into the pluperfect tense; thus, for example: كَانَ لَمَّا بَلَغَ صَلٰحَ ٱلدِّينِ خَبَرُ ٱلْعَدُوِّ قَصْدِهِ عَكَّا جَمَعَ ٱلْأُمَرَاءَ "and when the news of the march of the enemy towards 'Akka had reached Ṣalāḥu-d-Dīn (Saladin), he had assembled the Amīrs." In such instances as these, however, the reader must be mainly guided by the purport of the context.

305. When the particle لَوْ "if," expressive of a supposition, is followed by two correlative sentences, each having its verb in the preterite tense, the first of such preterites is to be rendered by the pluperfect of the indicative, and the second, to which is prefixed the particle لَ, by the preterite of the subjunctive; as, لَوْ عَلِمْتُ هٰذَا لَنَصَحْتُكَ "if I had known this, assuredly

I should have admonished thee;" لَوْ هَدَانَا ٱللّٰهُ لَهَدَيْنَاكُمْ "if God had directed us, assuredly we should have directed you." If, however, the second member of the sentence be negative, the aorist is used with the particle لَمْ "not," which, as we explained in § 99, gives to the aorist the power of the preterite; thus, لَوْ كُنْتَ هَاهُنَا لَمْ يَمُتْ أَخِي "if thou hadst been here, my brother had not died."

a. If after لَوْ the verb of the first member of the proposition is in the aorist tense, and that of the second in the preterite, they take a future signification, and the first may be translated by the past subjunctive, and the second by the future conditional; thus, لَوْ يَمَسُّ ٱلْبَخِيلُ رَاحَةَ يَحْيَى لَسَخَتْ نَفْسُهُ بِبَذْلِ ٱلنَّوَالِ "if the miser touched the palm of Yaḥya, his soul would have become generous in bestowing gifts." After the compound particle لَوْلَا "if not," the verb of the first of the correlative propositions is frequently understood, but the construction of the second clause is not thereby affected; thus, لَوْلَا عَلِيٌّ لَهَلَكَ عُمَرُ "had it not been 'Alī (*i.e.* for 'Alī), verily 'Umar would have perished."

306. In a correlative proposition the negative particle لَا "not," gives to the preterite of the first clause a future signification, especially when the second clause has a subjunctive or conditional sense; as in the following example: لَا تَلَمَّظْتُ بِقِرَاكُمْ أَوْ تَضْمَنُوا لِي أَنْ لَا تَتَّخِذُونِي كَلًّا "I will not taste of your food, unless you will promise me that you will not inconvenience yourselves on my account." The peculiar effect of لَا is further observable in phrases expressive of a declaration on oath; as may be seen in the following sentence, viz.:

آلَيْتُ لا خَامَرَتْنِي ٱلْخَمْرُ مَا عَلِقَتْ ـ رُوحِي بِجِسْمِي وَ ٱلْفَاظِي بِإِفْصَاحِي
"I have sworn (I swear) that wine shall not disturb me, while my soul is in my body, and my words in my power of speaking."

a. When the negative particle لا has been preceded by another negative proposition in which the particles مَا and لَمْ have been employed, the لا loses all temporal influence on the following preterites; thus, بَلَوْتُ مِنَ ٱلْعَجَائِبِ مَا لَمْ يَرَهُ ٱلرَّاؤُونَ وَلَا رَوَاهُ ٱلرَّاوُونَ "I have experienced in (things) marvellous, what no spectators have ever seen, and (what) no narrators have related." The compound particles أَلَا, لَوَلَا, and هَلَّا (§ 195), in which لَا is the last member, have no influence on the tenses that immediately follow.

307. When the conditional particle إِنْ "if" precedes the preterite, the latter then acquires the force of the future or subjunctive; as, كُتِبَ عَلَيْكُمْ إِذَا حَضَرَ أَحَدَكُمُ ٱلْمَوْتُ إِنْ تَرَكَ خَيْرًا ٱلْوَصِيَّةُ "it hath been written to you, that when death hath approached unto one of you, if he (shall or should) leave property (let there be) a will." If the verb كَانَ should come between إِنْ and a verb in the preterite, the latter expresses a past signification; thus, إِنْ كُنْتُ أَجْرَمْتُ أَوْ جَنَيْتُ "if I have committed a crime or been guilty of a fault." When, after إِنْ, a present tense is to be expressed, the preterite of كَانَ and the aorist of the verb required are employed; thus, for example: أُشْكُرُوا لِلّٰهِ إِنْ كُنْتُمْ إِيَّاهُ تَعْبُدُونَ "give thanks to God, if it be him you serve."

a. When the particle إِنْ comes before two correlative propositions, of which the first is conditional and the second dependent on the first, the verbs, if in the preterite, may be rendered, the first by the present subjunctive, and the second by the simple future indicative; thus, إِنْ فَعَلْتُ ذَلِكَ ضَيَّعْتُ مَالِي "if I do that, I shall lose my property;" إِنْ قُلْتُمْ لِي قُلْتُ لَكُمْ "if you tell me, I will tell unto you." The same rule holds after the particle إِلَّا (for إِنْ لَا) "if not;" as, أَمَّا أَنْ تَخْرُجَ مِنْ حَلَبَ وَإِلَّا سَلَّمْتُ ٱلْقَلْعَةَ لِصَالِحٍ "but (it is essential) that thou shouldst depart from Ḥalab (Aleppo), and if not, I will hand over the citadel to Ṣāliḥ." The same rule holds if each clause be negative; as, إِنْ مَا قُلْتُمْ لِي لَمْ أَقُلْ لَكُمْ "if you tell not unto me, I will not tell unto you." Should the second clause not have a preterite tense, the first may be expressed either by our present indicative or present subjunctive; as, إِنْ كُنْتَ ٱبْنَ ٱللّٰهِ فَقُلْ "if thou art the son of God, then say so," etc.

308. The particle إِذَا "when" gives to the preterite a future signification; thus, إِذَا جَآءَ وَعْدُ ٱلْآخِرَةِ جِئْنَا بِكُمْ لَفِيفًا "when the promise of the future state shall have come (to be realized), we will assemble you together." If إِذَا be followed by two correlative clauses expressive of a general statement by means of two successive preterites, the latter, in both clauses, are to be translated by our present indicative; thus, for example: إِذَا رَاضَ يَحْيَى ٱلْأَمْرَ ذَلَّتْ صِعَابُهُ "when Yaḥya undertakes the affair, the difficulty becomes easy." It is needless to add, however, that in the narration of past events (as may be known by the context), the Arabic preterite, even when preceded by إِذَا, must necessarily be rendered into English by

our simple past tense; thus, إِذَا رَأَوْا تِجَارَةً أَوْ لَهْوًا ٱنْفَضُّوا إِلَيْهَا "when they saw (a chance of) doing business, or of gambling, they dispersed themselves for that purpose."

309. In Arabic the preterite is employed in an optative, benedictive, or maledictive sense. For example, when an Arab mentions the name of God, he adds, هُوَ تَعَالَى "may He be exalted." After naming the prophet Muḥammad, he adds, صَلَّى ٱللّٰهُ عَلَيْهِ وَسَلَّمَ "may God be propitious unto him, and may he have granted unto him peace;" so, رَضِيَ ٱللّٰهُ عَنْهُ "may God have been pleased with him." This last formula is used when speaking of holy men deceased, as is also نَوَّرَ ٱللّٰهُ قَبْرَهُ "may God illumine his tomb." When allusion is made to a reigning sovereign, the formula is, دَامَ مُلْكُهُ "may his reign be prolonged;" when speaking of a minister or commander-in-chief, the phrase is, عَزَّ نَصْرُهُ "may his victory be glorious." When people speak of ٱلشَّيْطَانُ "Satan," or of any other very evil spirit, they generally add, لَعَنَهُ ٱللّٰهُ "may the Lord curse him;" or some such pithy expression.

On the Use and Application of the Aorist.

310. This tense is improperly called "the future" in most grammars and dictionaries, in imitation of the Hebrew grammarians. I consider the term Aorist (as used by De Sacy) the more appropriate, inasmuch as this tense is employed to express not only futurity, but also time past or present, according to circumstances.

a. The aorist, as a general rule, expresses our present of the indicative, definite, or indefinite, except in such instances as we pointed out in § 99, etc. This is especially the case when it is preceded by the negative particle مَا "not;" as, مَا يُزَكِّي ٱلْإِنْسَانُ بِشَهَادَةِ أَهْلِ بَيْتِهِ "a man is not deemed just by the testimony of the people of his own house." In the following passage the aorist is to be translated partly by our present indicative and partly by our future of the indicative: إِنَّ ٱلَّذِينَ يَكْتُمُونَ مَا أَنْزَلَ ٱللَّهُ مِنَ ٱلْكِتَابِ و يَشْتَرُونَ بِهِ ثَمَنًا قَلِيلًا أُولَٰئِكَ مَا يَأْكُلُونَ فِي بُطُونِهِمْ إِلَّا ٱلنَّارَ وَلَا يُكَلِّمُهُمُ ٱللَّهُ يَوْمَ ٱلْقِيَامَةِ وَلَا يُزَكِّيهِمْ "verily they who conceal the book which God has sent down (from heaven), and who buy with (the price of) it a thing of small value, eat nothing but fire; and God on the day of judgment will not speak to them, neither will He justify them."

311. The aorist corresponds with our future simple or compound. 1. When preceded by the particle لَنْ "not at all," سَوْفَ, or one of its abridged forms سَوْ, سَفْ, سَ, all of which indicate futurity. 2. When preceded by the negative لَا "not," provided, however, that none of the other negative particles مَا, لَمْ, or لَمَّا has occurred in the phrase immediately before, as we cursorily observed § 102. 3. When, as is often the case, there is a plain indication of a future sense; as may be seen in the following sentences, Ḳur,ān, iv. 34: وَمَنْ يَفْعَلْ ذَٰلِكَ عُدْوَانًا وَظُلْمًا فَسَوْفَ نُصْلِيهِ نَارًا "whosoever shall do that malevolently and iniquitously, we shall cast him into (hell) fire;" سَتَجِدُ مَطْلَعِي عَلَيْكَ أَسْرَعَ مِنِ ٱرْتِدَادِ طَرْفِكَ إِلَيْكَ "thou shalt find my return unto thee more speedy than the twinkling of thine eye." The following sentence shews the

influence of the particle لَا, thus in Kur,ān, ii. 45, we have: إِتَّقُوا يَوْمًا لَا تَجْزِي نَفْسٌ عَنْ نَفْسٍ شَيْئًا وَلَا تُقْبَلُ مِنْهَا شَفَاعَةٌ "fear ye a day when (one) soul shall not in the least make satisfaction for another soul, neither shall any be accepted from them."

312. The aorist is frequently employed after the preterite of another verb, to which it then serves as a complement, without the intervention of any conjunction, in which case it may be translated by our infinitive, or by our subjunctive preceded by "that," "to the end that," etc.; thus, جَعَلَا يَتَشَاجَرَانِ "they two began to dispute with each other;" so, likewise: جَآءَ إِلَى عَيْنِ مَآءٍ يَشْرَبُ "he came to a fountain of water that he might drink." Sometimes the aorist thus employed may be translated by our present participle; as, وَوَقَعَ يُقَبِّلُ ٱلْأَرْضَ وَيَبْكِي "and he fell down kissing the ground and weeping;" وَهُوَ وَاقِفٌ فِي ٱلْمَآءِ يَسْتَحِمُّ "and he stood in the water bathing himself;" ظَعَنَ يَقْتَادُ ٱلْقَلْبَ بِأَزِمَّتِهِ "he departed, leading my heart (as it were) by a bridle;" فَلَبِثْنَا نَرْقُبُهُ رِقْبَةَ أَهِلَّةِ ٱلْأَعْيَادِ "we continued to watch his return, like the watching for the new moon of the festivities."

313. We have shewn, § 304, that the preterite of the substantive verb كَانَ, when combined with that of any other verb, gives the latter the sense of a pluperfect tense. When كَانَ is combined with the aorist of another verb, the two together have the effect of the Latin imperfect indicative; thus, كَانَ يَكْتُبُ "he was writing." Should the proposition, however, be negative, and the adverb لَمْ be employed, the

aorist يَكُنْ (of كَانَ) put before any other aorist, gives to the latter a similar meaning. When one or more verbs in the preterite have gone before, they communicate that sense to the following aorist, without the intervention of كَانَ, as may be seen by the following examples: كَانَا يَنْتَطِحَانِ بِقُرُونِهِمَا "they (the two bulls) were striking (or pushing) each other with their horns;" لَمْ تَكُنْ تَسْتَقِرُّ "it (the tortoise) never rested," etc.; كَانَ أَصْحَابُهُ مِنَ ٱلْوُحُوشِ يَأْتِي إِلَيْهِ وَيَعُودُهُ "his companions from among the wild beasts came unto him and visited him;" رَكِبَ جَعْفَرٌ إِلَي ٱلصَّيْدِ و جَعَلَ يَشْرَبُ تَارَةً و يَلْهُو أُخْرَي و تُحَفُ ٱلرَّشِيدِ و هَدَايَاهُ تَأْتِيهِ و عِنْدَهُ بَخْتِيشُوعُ ٱلطَّبِيبُ و أَبُو زَكَّارٍ ٱلأَعْمَي يُغَنِّيهِ "Ja'far rode to the chase; and he sometimes drank, and at other times amused himself; and presents and gifts came to him from Rashīd; and Bakhtishū'a the physician was with him, and Abū Zakkār the blind sang to him."

a. Sometimes the aorist bears the signification of the past indefinite, without being preceded by either the preterite or the aorist of the verb كَانَ; thus, قُلْ فَلِمَ تَقْتُلُونَ أَنْبِيَآءَ ٱللّٰهِ مِنْ قَبْلُ "Say (to them) why did you kill the prophets of God, before (now)?" In this sentence it is evident that the attending circumstances are quite sufficient to determine the sense in which تَقْتُلُونَ must be translated. When the particle لَوْ "if," precedes the combined aorists, the proposition will have the sense of the Latin imperfect subjunctive; as in the following expression: لَوْ كُنْتَ تَعْرِفُهُ لَكُنْتَ تُحِبُّهُ "if thou wert to know him, thou wouldst love him."

314. In addition to the pluperfect and imperfect, which the Arabs express by prefixing the preterite of the verb كَانَ

to the preterite and aorist of other verbs, they form another tense, which in our grammars is called the future perfect, by prefixing the aorist of كَانَ to a preterite, sometimes inserting the particle قَدْ between the two verbs; for example: يَقُولُونَ مَتَي هَذَا ٱلْوَعْدُ إِنْ كُنْتُمْ صَادِقِينَ قُلْ عَسَي أَنْ يَكُونَ رَدِفَ لَكُمْ بَعْضُ مَا تَسْتَعْجِلُونَ "they say, when will this menace (take effect) if you be trustworthy? Say thou perhaps somewhat of that which you wish to hasten, will have (already) mounted behind you." أَغِيرُوا عَلَي نَعَمِهِمْ فَلِنَأْخُذْهُ فَنَكُونُ قَدْ أَخَذْنَا عِوَضًا مِمَّا صُنِعَ بِنَا "Rush upon their camels, and let us seize them, and then we shall have taken retaliation for what has been done to us."

315. We have already pointed out the three modifications to which the aorist is subject in consequence of certain particles which may precede it. The aorist apocopated, which drops the vowel of the final radical, etc., § 99, is employed in conditional, hypothetic, or retributive propositions; thus, مَنْ يُحْسِنْ إِلَيكَ أَحْسِنْ إِلَيْهِ "he who may have benefited thee, do thou (in return) benefit him;" أَيْنَمَا تَكُونُوا يُدْرِكْكُمُ ٱلْمَوْتُ "wherever you may be, death will overtake you;" حَيْثُمَا تَذْهَبْ أَذْهَبْ "wherever thou mayest go, I (also) will go;" إِنْ تَخْرُجْ أَخْرُجْ مَعَكَ "if thou shouldst go out, I will go out with thee." In propositions of this kind, if each of the verbs indicates futurity, both of them are put in the apocopated form; but if the last of them only denotes future time, the same may optionally be of the apocopated or common form, see § 99, *a*. When the imperative is accompanied by a verb expressive of a con-

ditional future, the latter is put in the apocopated form; thus, أُنْصُرْنِي أَنْصُرْكَ "assist me, (and) I will assist thee."

a. When the particle لِ is prefixed to the apocopated aorist, the latter expresses command, and the لِ loses its vowel after the conjunctions فَ and وَ. When لَا comes before, it denotes prohibition; thus, فَمَنْ شَهِدَ مِنْكُمُ ٱلشَّهْرَ فَلْيَصُمْهُ "and whosoever among you shall see the month, let him fast (during) it." لَا تَقْرَبَا هٰذِهِ ٱلشَّجَرَةَ "approach not you (two) this tree."

b. The aorist apocopated preceded by the particle لَمْ "not," and لَمَّا "not yet," always bears a past signification; thus, for example: اِلْتَمَسَ شَيْئًا لِيَأْكُلَهُ فَلَمْ يَجِدْ "he sought for something that he might eat it, but found (it) not;" so, لَمَّا رَامَ عَلَي ٱلطُّلُوعِ لَمْ يَقْدِرْ "when he attempted to ascend, he was not able."

316. The aorist antithetic, whose peculiarity is to change the *ḍamma* of the third radical into *fatḥa*, and to reject the final ن of the terminations (except in the feminine plural)—corresponds to the Latin present subjunctive. In § 100 we have given a list of such particles as require this form of the aorist after them, on the more important of which we shall now add a few observations. Their general signification denotes "scope," "end," "aim," or "purpose," like our conjunctions "that," "in order that," "to the end that," etc.; thus, أُحِبُّ أَنْ تَنْصُرَ "I desire that thou mayest assist;" أَشْتَهِي أَنْ تَأْكُلَ عِنْدِي فِي هٰذِهِ ٱللَّيْلَةِ خُبْزًا "I wish that thou mayest eat bread with me (*chez moi*) this night."

a. When the particle أَنْ is followed by لَا "not," as in أَلَّا (for أَنْ+لَا),

it still retains its governing power, and requires the aorist antithetic after it. If the verb following أَنْ is intended to express simple, present, or future time, the regular form of the aorist is employed; as, أَعْلَمُ أَنْ يَنُومُ "I know that he sleeps;" أَعْلَمُ أَنْ يَنْصُرُ "I know that he will assist." After verbs expressive of "doubt," "opinion," "thinking," "considering," etc., such as ظَنَّ, حَسَبَ, زَعَمَ, etc., the regular form of the aorist is generally employed, but the antithetic form is sometimes to be met with."

b. It sometimes happens that the particle أَنْ corresponds with our words "that not," "lest" (Lat. *ne*). We are not to conclude, however, that أَنْ of itself bears a negative sense, but there may occur some word in the proposition which may imply a negation or prohibition; thus, in the Ḳur,ān ix. 46, we have the following example: لَا يَسْتَأْذِنُكَ ٱلَّذِينَ يُؤْمِنُونَ بِاللّٰهِ وَالْيَوْمِ الْآخِرِ أَنْ يُجَاهِدُوا بِأَمْوَالِهِمْ وَأَنْفُسِهِمْ "they who believe in God and the last day will not ask leave of thee that they may not fight, (for the true faith), with their substance and their persons;" so, xviii. 58: إِنَّا جَعَلْنَا عَلَي قُلُوبِهِمْ أَكِنَّةً أَنْ يَفْقَهُوهُ "verily we have cast veils over their hearts lest they should understand it (the Ḳur,ān)."

c. The particles كَيْ and لِ, denoting "that," "to the end that," "in order that," invariably require the aorist antithetic; as, جَاءَ كَيْ يَضْرِبَكَ "he came that he might beat thee," or "in order to beat thee." The same rule applies to the compounds كَيلَا and لِكَيلَا "lest, as also to the conjunction لِ; thus, اِلْتَمَسَ شَيْأً لِيَأْكُلَهُ "he sought for something that he might eat it." The particle حَتَّي "that," "in order that," "until," requires the antithetic form in like manner; thus, أَعْلِمْنِي حَتَّي اَطِيرَ عَنْكَ

"inform me that I may fly away from thee;" أَسِيرُ حَتَّي تَغِيبَ ٱلشَّمْسُ "I will march on till the sun sets."

d. The particle أَوْ (which properly signifies "or," or "else"), when denoting our conjunctions "that," "until," "unless," requires the antithetic aorist; thus, لَأَلْزَمَنَّكَ أَوْ تَعْطِيَنِي حَقِّي "verily I will persecute thee, or thou shalt give me my due," *i.e.*, "until thou wilt give me my due;" so, لَأَقْتُلَنَّ ٱلْكَافِرَ أَوْ يُسْلِمَ "verily I will slay the unbeliever, or he shall become a Muslim;" أَنْتَظِرُهُ أَوْ يَخْرُجَ "I will wait for him until he come out." Sometimes أَوْ, when repeated, has the signification of our words "whether," "or" (Latin *sive*); thus, for example: لَيْسَ لَكَ مِنَ ٱلْأَمْرِ شَيْءٌ أَوْ يَتُوبَ عَلَيْهِمْ أَوْ يُعَذِّبَهُمْ "it is no affair of thine whether (God) be gracious unto them, or chastise them."

e. The particles إِذَنْ and إِذاً "good!" "well!" when employed in a conditional sense depending on a preceding proposition, require the antithetic aorist, which then bears a future signification. This will be best understood by the following examples, viz.: أَلْتَجِي إِلَيْكَ "I will come for protection to thee;" when the reply may be, إِذَنْ أَنْصُرَكَ "good! I will assist thee;" or إِذَنْ وَٱللّٰهِ أَنْصُرَكَ "good! by the Lord I will assist thee;" إِذَنْ يَا حَبِيبِي أَنْصُرَكَ "good, O my friend! I will aid thee;" or إِذَنْ لَا أَنْصُرَكَ "well! I will not assist thee." In these examples we see that the particle إِذَنْ may be used alone before the verb, or may be accompanied by a word expressive of an oath; by a vocative case; or lastly, by a negative particle. If, however, any word different from the above intervenes, the common form of the aorist is used; thus, إِذَنْ أَنَا أَنْصُرُكَ "good! I will assist thee." When the pronoun أَنَا intervenes, the emphatic negative لَنْ "not at all," always requires the aorist apocopated, and gives it a future signification; thus, Ḳur,ān ii. 74: لَنْ تَمَسَّنَا ٱلنَّارُ إِلَّا أَيَّامًا مَعْدُودَةً "the fire (of Gehenna) shall by no means touch us, except for certain limited days."

f. When the conjunctions فَ and وَ join two propositions, indicating, in the second, an immediate dependence on the first, of which it is a consequence, they require to be followed by the aorist antithetic; as, لَاتَدْخُلُوا بَيْتًا غَيْرَ بُيُوتِكُمْ حَتَّي تَسْتَأْنِسُوا وَ تُسَلِّمُوا عَلَي أَهْلِهِ "do not enter any house, except your own houses, until you ask permission, and salute its inhabitants;" مَنَعَ دُخُولَ ٱمْرَأَةٍ إِلَي دَارِ ٱلْخِلَافَةِ حَتَّي يَعْرِفَ مَنْ هِيَ "he forbade any woman entering the palace of the Caliphate until he knew who she was;" اِغْفِرْلِي يَا رَبِّي فَأَدْخُلَ ٱلْجَنَّةَ "pardon me, O Lord! that I may enter paradise;" هَلْ زَيْدٌ فِي ٱلدَّارِ فَأَمْضِيَ إِلَيْهِ "is Zaid in his house, that I may go to him?" The particle فَ, when followed by a negative imperative, corresponds with the Latin "ne," and the English "lest;" as, لَا تُوَاخِذْنِي فَأَهْلِكَ "punish me not, lest I perish." The chief difference between فَ and وَ is that the former expresses the order of things, which the latter does not. When either of them is a mere connective of sentences not dependent on each other, it has no influence on the verb that follows.

317. The paragogic aorist is used always with a future signification; and is formed by affixing نَّ or simply نْ to the aorist antithetic, as may be seen in § 101. It is employed in commanding, urging, forbidding, wishing, asking, or strongly asserting; as may be seen in the Ḳur,ān, cii. 6: لَتَرَوُنَّ ٱلْجَحِيمَ ثُمَّ لَتَرَوُنَّهَا عَيْنَ ٱلْيَقِينِ ثُمَّ لَتُسْئَلُنَّ يَوْمَئِذٍ عَنِ ٱلنَّعِيمِ "verily ye shall see hell, again (I say) ye shall surely see it with

the eye of certainty; then shall ye be examined on that day concerning the pleasures (in which ye had indulged during life)." It is also employed after the particle إِمَّا (compounded of إِنْ and مَا); thus, Kur. vii. 33: يَا بَنِي آدَمَ إِمَّا يَأْتِيَنَّكُمْ رُسُلٌ مِنْكُمْ "O children of Adam, verily apostles from among yourselves shall come unto you." It is also used when preceded by the particle لَ, or by any expression denoting an oath; thus, وَٱللّٰهِ يَنْصُرَنْ "by God he will assist;" قَالَ فَبِعِزَّتِكَ لَأُغْوِيَنَّهُمْ أَجْمَعِينَ "he (the devil) said, verily (I swear) by thine eminence that I will deceive them all."

318. The imperative is used only in the second persons singular, dual, and plural of the active voice, as may be seen in the paradigm § 94 and in § 103. The first and third persons of the active voice are made imperative by means of the aorist as we have just shewn. In its use and application the imperative has no peculiarity beyond what we have already mentioned in § 103.

Use and Application of the Infinitive.

319. The infinitive or verbal noun, as we stated in § 105, is frequently combined in a sentence with its own verb in an adverbial sense, with a view to give additional energy to the expression; thus, كَلَّمَ ٱللّٰهُ مُوسَى تَكْلِيمًا "God spake unto Moses saying;" so in this passage from the Kur. lii. 9: يَوْمَ تَمُورُ ٱلسَّمَآءُ مَوْرًا وَتَسِيرُ ٱلْجِبَالُ سَيْرًا "the day on which the heavens shall be shaken with commotion, and the mountains shall utterly move away" (*lit.* "move away by moving"). It is also used adverbially to express "purpose," "intention,"

or "design," etc., like the Latin gerund in dum; as follows: قَامَ زَيْدٌ إِجْلَالًا لِعَمْرٍو "Zaid stood up for (the purpose of) doing honour to 'Amru."

320. When the subject of a sentence alone is expressed, or the complement alone, they may be governed in the genitive by the infinitive of a transitive verb; thus, Ḳur,ān ix. 115: وَكَانَ إِسْتِغْفَارُ إِبْرٰهِيمَ لِأَبِيهِ "and there was a prayer for pardon (on the part) of Abraham for his father;" where we see that Abraham, the subject, is governed in the genitive by the infinitive إِسْتِغْفَارُ, the object of the sentence being ٱللّٰهُ "God," understood, which will be more manifest if we express the sentence by means of the finite verb; thus, إِسْتَغْفَرَ إِبْرٰهِيمُ ٱللّٰهَ لِأَبِيهِ "Abraham begged pardon of God for his father." Again, in the Ḳur. xli. 49: لَا يَسْأَمُ ٱلْإِنْسَانُ مِنْ دُعَاءِ ٱلْخَيْرِ "man is not wearied in asking for what is good" (or "for happiness").

321. The noun denoting the object, may be put in the accusative, if any word intervenes between the infinitive and the object so as to prevent their being in a state of regimen; thus, Ḳur. xc. 14: إِطْعَامٌ فِي يَوْمٍ ذِي ٱلْمَسْغَبَةِ يَتِيمًا "(the act of) feeding the orphan in a day of famine;" where we see يَتِيمًا the object of the sentence put in the accusative case. If the infinitive should be preceded by the article أَلْ, its object in the accusative case may immediately follow it; thus, ضَعِيفُ ٱلنِّكَايَةِ أَعْدَاءَهُ "feeble in hurting his enemies;" لَمْ أَنْكُلْ عَنِ ٱلضَّرْبِ مِسْمَعًا "I do not timidly abstain from smiting

the ear." When both the subject and object connected with the infinitive are expressed, the subject is usually put in the genitive, and the object in the accusative; thus, for example: كَانَ قَتْلُ ٱلْخَلِيفَةِ جَعْفَرًا فِي هٰذِهِ ٱلسَّنَةِ "it was in this year that the Caliph put Ja'far to death," literally, "the slaying Ja'far (on the part) of the Caliph took place in this year;" so, likewise ذِكْرُ رَحْمَةِ رَبِّي عَبْدَهُ "a memorial of the mercy of my lord towards his slave." The preceding is the most common mode of construction, but the following is by no means unusual; that is to say, the object is put in the genitive and the subject in the nominative. This is more especially the rule when the object is a pronoun and the subject a noun; for example: مَنَعَ ٱلنَّاسَ كَافَّةً مِنْ مُخَاطَبَتِهِ أَحَدٌ وَمُكَاتَبَتِهِ بِسَيِّدِنَا وَمَوْلَانَا "he forbade unto all people whatsoever to style him our lord and our master whether in speaking to him, or in writing to him;" حَجُّ ٱلْبَيْتِ مَنِ ٱسْتَطَاعَ إِلَيْهِ سَبِيلًا "a pilgrimage to the (holy) house by whomsoever it is practicable."

322. Infinitives of intransitive verbs govern the subject (there being no object) in the genitive case; for example: وُقُوعُ زَيْدٍ إِلَى ٱلْأَرْضِ كَانَ كَذٰلِكَ "the falling of Zaid to the earth took place in this manner." As a general rule the infinitives of intransitive verbs follow the construction of such verbs with regard to the use of the prepositions; as in the following examples: مَا لِي قُدْرَةٌ عَلَى ذٰلِكَ "I have not the power over that," *i.e.* "I cannot do that;" إِخْرَاجُ أَهْلِهِ مِنْهُ "the expulsion of its inhabitants from it." The infinitives of abstract or substantive verbs have their subject in the genitive and their at-

tribute in the accusative; thus, كَوْنُ ٱلْإِنْسَانِ مَخْلُوقًا هُوَ مِنْ أُصُولِ ٱلدِّينِ "that man must have been created is one of the foundations of religion." Sometimes an infinitive derived from a transitive verb is employed in a vague and indeterminate manner, without a complement; as صَدٌّ عَنْ سَبِيلِ ٱللّٰهِ وَكُفْرٌ بِهِ أَكْبَرُ عِنْدَ ٱللّٰهِ "deviation from the way of God, and disbelief in him, is a most heinous sin in the sight of God."

Use and Application of the Participles.

323. Present participles follow the construction of those verbs from which they are derived; thus, عَمْرٌو ٱلْقَاتِلُ أَبُوهُ مَحْمُودًا "'Amru whose father slew Maḥmūd;" which is the same as if we said عَمْرٌو ٱلَّذِي قَدْ قَتَلَ أَبُوهُ مَحْمُودًا. So زَيْدٌ نَاكِحٌ ٱبْنُهُ غَدًا زُبَيْدَةَ "Zaid whose son is to wed Zubaida to-morrow;" which comes to the same thing as زَيْدٌ ٱلَّذِي يَنْكِحُ ٱبْنُهُ غَدًا زُبَيْدَةَ, by employing the aorist of the verb نَكَحَ instead of the present particle.

324. The present participle or noun of agency of a transitive verb admits of two modes of construction. 1. It may govern the object in the accusative case, like the verb from which it has been derived; as ٱلْكَاظِمُونَ ٱلْغَيْظَ "those who control (their) anger;" مَا أَنْتَ بِتَابِعٍ قِبْلَتَهُمْ "thou shalt not follow (with thy face) their Ḳibla. 2. It may govern the object in the genitive case; as رَبَّنَا إِنَّكَ جَامِعُ ٱلنَّاسِ "O our Lord, verily thou shalt assemble mankind;" كُلُّ نَفْسٍ ذَائِقَةُ ٱلْمَوْتِ "every (creature) living shall taste of death." In this last mode the noun of agency may take the article أَلْ, provided

the object or complement be also definite; thus, ٱلضَّارِبُ ٱلْعَبْدِ "the striker of the slave;" ٱلضَّارِبُ رَأْسِ ٱلْعَبْدِ "the striker of the head of the slave." It would be incorrect, however, here to say ٱلضَّارِبُ عَبْدٍ; neither ought we to say ٱلضَّارِبُ زَيْدٍ, nor ٱلضَّارِبُ عَبْدِهِ, nor ٱلضَّارِبُ عَبْدِ زَيْدٍ.

a. When the noun of agency governs its complement in the genitive and this complement is accompanied by another noun which ought to agree with it in case, such other noun may be put in the genitive agreeably to the grammatical concord, or it may be put in the accusative as the object; thus, مُبْتَغِي جَاهٍ وَمَالاً مَنْ نَهَضَ "whoever rises up (to labour) is a seeker of rank or of wealth." So, Kur,an vi. 96: إِنَّ ٱللّٰهَ فَالِقُ ٱلْحَبِّ وَٱلنَّوَى۔يُخْرِجُ ٱلْحَيَّ مِنَ ٱلْمَيِّتِ۔فَالِقُ ٱلْإِصْبَاحِ وَجَاعِلُ ٱللَّيْلِ سَكَنًا وَٱلشَّمْسَ وَٱلْقَمَرَ حُسْبَانًا "verily, it is God who causeth the grain and the date stone to put forth; he bringeth forth the living from the dead, and he bringeth forth the dead from the living. It is he who causeth the morning to appear; and he hath ordained the night for rest, and the sun and the moon for the computing (of time)."

b. When the noun of agency governs the accusative case it retains its nūnation in the singular as well as the final نِ and نَ of the dual and plural as we see in the first quoted expressions of the last paragraph. Sometimes, however, both the nūnation and final ن are rejected, as if the two words were in a state of regimen, (vide § 282); thus, ٱلضَّارِبَا زَيْدًا "the two (men) striking Zaid;" ٱلضَّارِبُوا زَيْدًا "the (three or more men) striking Zaid." If, however, the object thus put in the accusative be a pronoun, it may be either affixed directly to the participle, or the particle إِيَّا (§ 290 *c*), may intervene between them. When the pronoun is affixed directly, the participle loses its nūnation in the singular; but may optionally retain or reject the final ن of the dual and plural; hence we may say either اَلضَّارِبَانِهِ or اَلضَّارِبَاهُ "the two strikers of him." So in the plural we may say اَلضَّارِبُونَكَ or اَلضَّارِبُوكَ "the (three or more) strikers of thee."

325. The noun of agency of a verb doubly transitive, *i.e.* a verb governing two accusatives, may follow the rule of the verb from which it is derived, by putting the two objects in the accusative; or it may govern the first of its complements in the genitive and the second in the accusative. Hence we may say either أَنَا كَاسٍ زَيْدًا ثَوْبًا مُفْتَخَرًا, or أَنَا كَاسِي زَيْدٍ ثَوْبًا مُفْتَخَرًا "I have clothed Zaid with a precious garment." So we may say either هَلْ أَنْتَ ظَانٌّ عَمْرًا عَاقِلًا or هَلْ أَنْتَ ظَانُّ عَمْرٍو عَاقِلًا "dost thou consider 'Amru a wise man?" We may further observe that when the participle, thus doubly transitive, governs its first complement in the genitive and its second in the accusative, the latter may be placed between the participle and the word governed in the genitive; thus, مَانِعُ فَضْلَهُ ٱلْمُحْتَاجِ "refusing his bounty to him who is destitute." So, in Ḳur,ān xiv. 48: فَلَا تَحْسِبَنَّ ٱللّٰهَ مُخْلِفَ وَعْدَهُ رُسُلِهِ "do not imagine that God will act contrary to his promise (made) to his own apostles."

326. When the present participle expresses a quality inherent in the subject, and independent of any reference to time, it may govern its subject in the genitive; thus we may say زَيْدٌ ٱلْقَائِمُ ٱلْأَبِ "Zaid, whose father is standing." This mode of construction seldom takes place, except when the

participle is derived from a neuter verb. It is sometimes found, however, with participles that come from transitive verbs, when such participles are used as mere adjectives; thus, اَلرَّاحِمُ ٱلْقَلْبِ "the merciful of heart." The noun of agency accompanied by the article أَلْ is equivalent to the relative pronoun and a verb; thus, هٰذَا ٱلْقَاتِلُ أَبُوهُ عَمْرًا is equivalent to هٰذَا ٱلَّذِي قَتَلَ أَبُوهُ عَمْرًا "this is he whose father killed 'Amru."

a. The present participles of intransitive verbs are applied, with regard to the use of the prepositions, in the same manner as the verbs from which they came; thus, كُلٌّ لَهُ قَانِتُونَ "all are obedient unto him;" وَمَا ٱللّٰهُ بِغَافِلٍ عَمَّا تَعْمَلُونَ "God is not heedless of what ye are doing."

327. The subject to which the passive participle is attached is generally put in the nominative case; as in the following sentence: زَيْدٌ مَقْتُولٌ حَالاً أَبُوهُ "Zaid, whose father is now slain." It may, however, be put in the genitive, being then governed by the participle, or it may be employed adverbially in the accusative case; hence we may say either زَيْدٌ مَقْتُولُ ٱلْأَبِ or ٱلْمَقْتُولُ أَبًا. If the passive participle belongs to a verb doubly transitive, it preserves in the accusative the second of its complements; thus, زَيْدٌ مُعْطًى عَبْدُهُ دِرْهَمًا "the slave of Zaid has been presented with a dirham."

328. The construction of the passive participle, and of verbal adjectives derived from the passive voice, may be more clearly explained as follows:—1. By substituting, for

the participle or adjective, the verb itself, either in the preterite or the aorist of the passive voice. 2. In restoring, if necessary, the subject or nominative which may have been understood. 3. Lastly, in substituting, for the article أَلْ, the relative pronoun ٱلَّذِي, or if there be no article the relatives مَنْ or مَا ; as may be seen in the following examples, viz., Ḳur. ii. 233 : ٱلْوَالِدَاتُ يُرْضِعْنَ أَوْلَادَهُنَّ حَوْلَيْنِ كَامِلَيْنِ وَعَلَي مَوْلُودِ لَهُ رِزْقُهُنَّ "the mothers shall give suck unto their children for two years entire, and it is incumbent upon the father (to contribute to) their (the mothers') subsistence;" where عَلَي مَوْلُودِ لَهُ is equivalent to عَلَي ٱلرَّجُلِ ٱلَّذِي وُلِدَ لَهُ وَلَدٌ "upon the man to whom a child is born." So, 234 : لَا تُضَارُّ وَالِدَةٌ بِوَلَدِهَا وَلَا مَوْلُودٌ لَهُ بِوَلَدِهِ "a mother shall not be compelled (to do what is unreasonable) on account of her child, nor shall a father be compelled on account of his child;" where مَوْلُودٌ لَهُ is equivalent to مَنْ وُلِدَ لَهُ وَلَدٌ "he to whom a child has been born." So Ḳur. i. 6 and 7 : إِهْدِنَا ٱلصِّرَاطَ ٱلْمُسْتَقِيمَ صِرَاطَ ٱلَّذِينَ أَنْعَمْتَ عَلَيْهِمْ غَيْرِ ٱلْمَغْضُوبِ عَلَيْهِمْ "direct us in the straight way, the way of those to whom thou hast been gracious, and who have not been subject unto thine anger." In this passage the three last words, viz., غَيْرِ ٱلْمَغْضُوبِ عَلَيْهِمْ are equivalent to ٱلَّذِينَ لَمْ يُغْضَبْ عَلَيْهِمْ "against whom there has been no inveighing wrathfully;" or more exactly in Latin, *contra quos non est invectum cum iracundia.*

Concord of a Verb with its Nominative.

329. We have already mentioned in § 250 that, as a general rule (liable, however, to numerous exceptions), the

verb, in a simple sentence or proposition comes first, then the nominative or subject, and lastly the object. When the verb thus precedes the subject, if the latter be singular and masculine, the verb always agrees with it in gender and number; thus, أَنْسَاهُ ٱلشَّيْطَانُ ذِكْرَ رَبِّهِ "Satan made him forget the naming of his Lord." If, however, the subject be a feminine singular, the verb must agree with it in number, but not necessarily in gender. If the subject be really of the female sex, and if it immediately follow the verb, the verb must then be in the feminine; thus, قَالَتِ ٱمْرَأَةُ ٱلْعَزِيزِ "the wife of 'Azīz said." But if, however, any word intervenes between the verb and its feminine nominative that follows it, the verb may be used in the masculine; thus, إِنَّ ٱمْرَءً غَرَّهُ مِنْكُنَّ وَاحِدَةٌ "verily a man whom one of you hath led astray." In such instances, however, grammarians consider it to be the more correct mode to put the verb in the feminine.

330. If the subject be merely a grammatical feminine, the verb may be of either gender, whether it precede its subject immediately or not; thus in the following example; اللَّبَنُ ٱلصَّرِيحُ هُوَ الَّذِي قَدْ ذَهَبَ رَغْوَتُهُ وَإِذَا ذَهَبَتِ ٱلرَّغْوَةُ فَاللَّبَنُ عُرْيَانٌ "the pure milk is that from which the scum is gone, but when the scum is gone the milk is bare." When any word intervenes, the verb should rather be in the masculine; thus, لِئَلَّا يَكُونَ لِلنَّاسِ عَلَيْكُمْ حُجَّةٌ "in order that men may have no pretence against you." If the verb is separated from the nominative feminine by the particle إِلَّا "unless," or "except," it is put in the masculine; as مَا زَكَي إِلَّا فَتَاةُ ٱبْنِ ٱلْعَلَا

"there is no one innocent except the handmaid of Ibnu-l-'Ulā." The verb may, however, here agree with the noun in gender; the word فَتَاةٌ would then be understood directly after the verb زَكَتْ; thus, مَا زَكَتْ إِلَّا فَتَاةٌ. The verbs of praise نِعْمَ and بِئْسَ, § 174, when the subject is feminine may be employed either in the masculine or feminine, but the masculine is preferable; thus, it is better to say نِعْمَ ٱلْٱمْرَءَةُ زَيْنَبُ "excellent is the woman Zainab," than by putting the verb in the feminine; as نِعْمَتِ ٱلْٱمْرَءَةُ زَيْنَبُ.

331. When the subject is a masculine plural, the verb preceding it may be in the singular; thus, Kur,ān ii. 58: فَبَدَّلَ ٱلَّذِينَ ظَلَمُوا قَوْلًا "those who were impious altered their opinions;" أَنُؤْمِنُ كَمَا آمَنَ ٱلسُّفَهَآءُ "do we believe as fools have believed?" When the subject is the broken plural of either a masculine or feminine singular, the verb preceding it may be optionally put in the masculine or feminine singular; thus, Kur,ān ii. 69: ثُمَّ قَسَتْ قُلُوبُهُمْ مِنْ بَعْدِ ذَلِكَ "then their hearts became hardened after that;" again in vi. 34: لَقَدْ كُذِّبَتْ رُسُلٌ مِنْ قَبْلِكَ "verily apostles (sent) before thee were treated as liars."

332. When the subject is a regular plural masculine, the verb must not be put in the feminine, but it may be so with بَنُونَ plural of إِبْنٌ "a son," and with such like words; which, though having the termination of regular masculine plurals, do not preserve the forms of their singulars, for these plurals are in fact broken ones; as قَالَتْ بَنُوا إِسْرَآئِيلَ "the children of Israel said." The verb may also be put in the feminine, and

even in the plural feminine, when the noun following is a collective one; as قَوْمٌ "a tribe" or "nation;" or when it is the name of a whole species; as غَنَمٌ "sheep;" طَيْرٌ "bird," etc.; as تَأْكُلُ ٱلطَّيْرُ مِنْهُ "the birds eat thereof;" so, Kur. ii. 107; قَالَتِ ٱلْيَهُودُ لَيْسَتِ ٱلنَّصَارَي عَلَي شَيْءٍ وَقَالَتِ ٱلنَّصَارَي لَيْسَتِ ٱلْيَهُودُ عَلَي شَيْءٍ "the Jews have said (that) the Christians are (grounded) on nothing; and the Christians say the Jews are grounded on nothing," *i.e.* "the one sect accuses the other of not possessing the true religion." If the subject be a mere grammatical or conventional feminine, or a feminine broken plural, the verb preceding it may be put in the singular feminine, or even in the singular masculine; thus, قَالَ نِسْوَةٌ فِي ٱلْمَدِينَةِ "women in the city said;" فَأَصَابَهُمْ سَيِّآتُ مَا كَسَبُوا "and the evils which they have earned assail them." Occasionally, though rarely, a regular feminine plural may have the preceding verb in the singular masculine; thus, Kur,ān lx. 10: إِذَا جَاءَكُمُ ٱلْمُؤْمِنَاتُ مُهَاجِرَاتٍ فَٱمْتَحِنُوهُنَّ "when believing women come unto you seeking refuge then plight ye faith with them."

333. The names of Arab tribes are generally of the feminine gender, but as collectives they are not unfrequently found with their preceding verb in the masculine plural; thus, فَجَمَّعَتْ عَامِرُ بْنُ صَعْصَعَةَ عُقَيْلٌ وَقُشَيْرٌ وَتَشَاكَوْا مَا يَلْحَقُهُمْ مِنْ سَيْفِ ٱلدَّوْلَةِ "and there congregated together (the tribe of) 'Āmir son of Ṣa'ṣa', of 'Ukail, and of Kushair, and they complained one after another, of what befel them from (the conduct of) Saifu-d-Daula."

334. The dual follows the same rules of concord as the plural; thus, دَخَلَ ٱلسِّجْنَ مَعَهُ فَتَيَانِ "there entered the prison with him two youths;" قَالَتِ ٱلرَّجُلَانِ "the two men said." Although, as we have just seen, it is usual when the verb precedes the subject to put the verb in the singular, with a dual or plural subject, yet the verb may agree regularly in number and in gender with such subject; thus, رَأَيْنَ ٱلْغَوَانِي ٱلشَّيْبَ لَاحَ بِعَارِضِي "the young damsels have seen the grey hairs glisten upon my face (or cheek)."

335. When the noun which is the subject of the proposition is put in the inchoative case, § 252, and consequently precedes the verb, the latter must agree in gender and number with the noun; thus, ٱللّٰهُ يَبْدِيُ ٱلْخَلْقَ ثُمَّ يُعِيدُهُ "God produces creatures, then he gives them life;" هٰذِهِ بِضَاعَتُنَا رُدَّتْ إِلَيْنَا "this money of ours that has been returned unto us;" هَلِ ٱلْمُؤْمِنَاتُ رَجَعْنَ "have the true believing women come back?" The same rule holds when the subject, having been previously expressed, is evidently understood; for example: فَلَمَّا فَرَغَ ٱلشَّيْخُ مِنْ دُعَائِهِ أَجَالَ خَمْسَهُ فِي وِعَائِهِ فَأَبْرَزَ مِنْهُ رِقَاعًا قَدْ كُتِبْنَ بِأَلْوَانِ ٱلْأَصْبَاغِ فِي أَوَانِ ٱلْفَرَاغِ "and when the Shaikh had ceased from his prayer, he put his hand into his wallet, and he took out thence sundry papers which had been written in various colours at the time of his leisure." Here we see that the verbs أَجَالَ and أَبْرَزَ are in the singular masculine, the subject being the pronoun هُوَ referring to الشَّيْخ understood. Again,

كُتِبْنَ is the plural feminine, the pronoun هُنَّ being understood, referring to رِقَاعًا "the papers."

a. It must be observed, however, that if the subject be a broken plural, whether it come from a masculine or a feminine noun, or if it be a regular plural feminine, the verb may be, and usually is, employed in the feminine singular; as may be seen in the following example: أَلَا يَا حَمَامَاتِ ٱلْأَرَاكِ تَحَمَّلِي ـ رِسَالَةَ صَبٍّ لَا يُفِيقُ مِنَ ٱلسُّكْرِ "O doves who rest on the branches of the Arak! bear the message of a lover, who cannot recover from his intoxication."

b. If the broken plural be that of rational beings of the masculine gender, the verb may be put in the masculine plural; for example: لِلّٰهِ مَلَآئِكَةٌ يَتَعَاقَبُونَ فِيكُمْ مَلَآئِكَةٌ بِٱللَّيْلِ وَ مَلَآئِكَةٌ بِٱلنَّهَارِ "God has angels who by turns watch over you; angels in the night and angels in the day;" إِنَّ ٱلْمُلُوكَ إِذَا دَخَلُوا قَرْيَةً أَفْسَدُوهَا "when kings enter a town they lay it waste."

c. In such compound tenses as are expressed by the union of the verb كَانَ and the preterite or aorist of another verb, if the subject is put between the two verbs, the verb كَانَ follows the rules of concord of the verb which precedes its subject, and the second verb follows those of the verb placed after its subject. When the subject is a collective noun, and precedes the verb, the latter is commonly placed in the plural; thus, وَلٰكِنَّ أَكْثَرَ ٱلنَّاسِ لَا يَشْكُرُونَ "but the generality of men are not grateful;" فَرِيقٌ مِنْهُمْ يَخْشَوْنَ ٱلنَّاسَ "some of them are afraid of men."

336. The rules which we have hitherto laid down respecting the concord of verbs with their nominatives apply only to

the third persons singular, dual or plural. The verbs of the first and second persons must always agree in gender and number with the noun or pronoun which constitutes the subject of the proposition, unless the verb be separated from the subject by the particle إِلَّا "except," "besides;" as follows: مَاجَآءَ إِلَّا أَنْتِ "no one came except thee;" where أَحَدٌ "any one," is the real nominative to the verb جَآءَ.

337. When the subject consists of several nouns or pronouns singular, the verb may precede them in the plural; as جِئْنَا أَنَا وَأَنْتَ "I and thou came," literally, "we came, I and thou;" or the verb may be put in the singular and agree with the next nominative; thus, تَكَلَّمَتْ مَرْيَمُ وَهَرُونُ فِي مُوسَى "Maryam and Harūn spoke against Moses." When the subject consists of two nouns or pronouns, and precedes the verb, the latter requires the dual number; as in the following example: سُلَحْفَاةٌ وَأَرْنَبٌ مَرَّةً تَسَابَقَا وَجَعَلَا ٱلْحَدَّ بَيْنَهُمَا ٱلْجَبَلَ "a tortoise and a hare once upon a time contended one with the other (in running) and made the mountain the goal between them." If the subject consists of more than two nouns or pronouns and precedes the verb, the latter is put in the plural; thus, ٱلْبَطْنُ وَٱلرِّجْلَانِ تَخَاصَمُوا "the belly and the two feet (once) had a dispute."

338. When the subject consists of two or more nouns of different genders, and is placed before the verb, the latter is usually employed in the dual or plural, as the case may be; thus, ٱلْكَسَلُ وَكِثْرَةُ ٱلنَّوْمِ يُبْعِدَانِ مِنَ ٱللّٰهِ وَيُورِثَانِ ٱلْفَقْرَ "idleness and

too much sleep withdraw (men) from God and bequeath (as an inheritance) poverty." If the subject consists of a noun in the singular and another in the plural, provided it be a broken plural, the verb is put in the dual, as in the following sentence: فَإِذَا نُفِخَ فِي ٱلصُّورِ نَفْخَةٌ وَاحِدَةٌ وَحُمِلَتِ ٱلْأَرْضُ وَٱلْجِبَالُ فَدُكَّتَا دَكَّةً "and when there is sounded on the trumpet a single blast, and the earth and the mountains shall be carried away and shall be broken to pieces."

339. When the subject consists of two nouns in a state of regimen, the verb not unfrequently agrees with the word governed, instead of the governing word, which is the general rule; thus, Ḳur,ān iii. 28: يَوْمَ تَجِدُ كُلُّ نَفْسٍ مَا عَمِلَتْ مِنْ خَيْرٍ "on the day when every soul shall find whatever it has done of good;" كُنْتُمْ خَيْرَ أُمَّةٍ أُخْرِجَتْ لِلنَّاسِ "you are the best nation that has been produced from among mankind."

340. The verb must always agree with its nominative in person, whether such nominative be expressed or understood, which rule also holds when there are several nominatives of the same person. If, however, the same verb has several subjects of different persons, the verb agrees in person with the nearest subject; and in such case, the first person takes precedence of the other two, and the second of the third; thus, جِئْنَا أَنَا وَأَنْتَ وَأَخَذْنَا حَاجَتَنَا مِنْهُ "we have come, I and thou, and we have taken from him what may be necessary for us," where we see the verb put in the first person plural, because its nearest nominative is of that person. Again, in

the example, أَنْتَ وَجُمُوعُكَ ٱحْضُرُوا بَيْنَ يَدَيِ ٱللّٰهِ مَعَ هٰرُونَ "thou and thy multitude shall present yourselves before God (*lit.* between the hands of God) along with Aaron," where the nearest nominative is of the second person and the next to it of the third; hence the verb is put in the second person plural.

Government of Verbs.

341. A transitive verb generally governs its complement or object in the accusative case, without the intervention of any particle; as in the sentences ضَرَبَ زَيْدٌ عَمْرًا "Zaid struck 'Amru;" لَمْ يَشْرَبْ خَمْرًا قَطُّ "he does not drink wine at all." When, however, by an inversion, the object of the transitive verb precedes it, the object has the preposition لِ prefixed to it; as إِنْ كُنْتُمْ لِلرُّؤيَا تَعْبُرُونَ "if you will interpret the vision."

342. Verbs doubly transitive govern two accusatives of different persons, or of different things, or of a person and thing both; as سَقَي ٱلسُّلْطَانُ وَزِيرَهُ مَآءً مَسْمُومًا "the Sultan gave his wazīr poisoned water to drink;" أُطْعَمْتُ ٱبْنَكَ لَحْمًا "I gave thy son flesh to eat;" أَعْطَي زَيْدٌ عَمْرًا ثَوْبًا مُفْتَخَرًا "Zaid presented 'Amru with a splendid garment." Verbs expressive of "knowing," "believing," "thinking," "doubting," "considering," and such like, govern two accusatives, viz., that of a direct object and that of an attribute; thus, ظَنَنْتُ زَيْدًا عَاقِلًا "I believed Zaid (to be) intelligent;" لَا تَحْسِبَنَّ ٱلَّذِينَ قُتِلُوا فِي سَبِيلِ ٱللّٰهِ أَمْوَاتًا "do not consider those (as) dead who have been slain in the way of God" (*i.e.* in de-

fending the cause of God and the true faith); أَخَذُوا ٱلدِّينَ لَعِبًا "they received the (true) faith as a (matter for) jesting." There are, however, other modes of construction applicable to this class of verbs, as may be seen by the following examples: زَيْدٌ ظَنَنْتُ عَاقِلٌ زَيْدٌ عَاقِلٌ ظَنَنْتُ "Zaid is intelligent, I think;" or "Zaid, I am thinking, is intelligent;" or lastly ظَنَنْتُ لَزَيْدٌ عَاقِلٌ "I think, verily, Zaid is intelligent."

343. When transitive verbs are employed in the passive voice they of course lose their objects or accusative cases, which then become the subject. Verbs doubly transitive, in like manner, lose the first of their objects, which then becomes the subject, while the second object still remains in its preceding form; thus, in the active voice, سَقَى ٱلسُّلْطَانُ وَزِيرَهُ مَآءً مَسْمُومًا "the Sultan gave his wazir poisoned water to drink," becomes, in the passive voice, سُقِيَ ٱلْوَزِيرُ مَآءً مَسْمُومًا "the wazir received poisoned water to drink." In a similar manner, أَعْطَى زَيْدٌ عَمْرًا ثَوْبًا مُفْتَخَرًا "Zaid gave 'Amru a splendid garment," in the passive voice becomes, أُعْطِيَ عَمْرٌو ثَوْبًا مُفْتَخَرًا "'Amru has been presented with a splendid garment;" أُطْعِمَ ٱبْنُكَ لَحْمًا "thy son has been given flesh to eat." So in the Ḳur,ān, ii. 95: ٱلَّذِينَ أُوتُوا ٱلْكِتَابَ "those to whom has been brought the book;" *i.e.*, the Ḳur,ān.

344. It sometimes happens that the same noun may be the subject of one proposition and the object of another that follows it. If the verb which governs the noun as its object comes first, and then the verb to which that noun is the subject, the objective case is left to be understood, and the noun

appears only in the nominative; as, ضَرَبْتُ وَ ضَرَبَنِي زَيْدٌ "I struck (Zaid), and Zaid struck me;" مَرَرْتُ وَ مَرَّ بِي عَمْرٌو "I passed (by 'Amru), and 'Amru passed by me." It is permitted, however, according to some grammarians, to give an affixed pronoun as its object to the first verb; thus, ضَرَبْتُهُ وَ ضَرَبَنِي زَيْدٌ. If the verb to which the noun is the subject comes first, and then that which governs the object, the latter is in like manner suppressed, and the usual rules are observed in the agreement of the first verb with the subject; thus, ضَرَبَنِي وَ ضَرَبْتُ زَيْدَانِ "the two Zaids struck me, and I struck (them)."

345. The noun may also be put in the accusative case, the first verb having the termination that indicates its agreement with the understood pronoun, which represents that noun in the nominative case; as, ضَرَبُونِي وَ ضَرَبْتُ ٱلزَّيْدِينَ for ٱلزَّيْدُونَ ضَرَبُونِي وَ ضَرَبْتُ ٱلزَّيْدِينَ "the Zaids struck me and I struck them." If such a verb be employed as requires a subject and an attribute, like كَانَ and صَارَ "he" or "it was," or "became;" and if that attribute be common to two propositions, such as "I was ill, and Zaid was ill," the attribute may be given only once, or may be represented by a separate pronoun; as, كُنْتُ وَ كَانَ زَيْدٌ مَرِيضًا "I was (ill,) and Zaid was, ill," or, كُنْتُ إِيَّاهُ وَ كَانَ زَيْدٌ مَرِيضًا "I was so, and Zaid was ill," or كُنْتُ وَ كَانَ زَيْدٌ مَرِيضًا إِيَّاهُ "I was, and Zaid was, ill;" that is, "I was ill, and so was Zaid." The first of these three methods is the one most in use; but all of them require that the two subjects should be of the same gender and number, otherwise the attribute must be repeated.

346. The same rule takes place with such verbs as ظَنَّ "he believed, or deemed;" حَسِبَ "he supposed," when governing a complete proposition, formed by means of a subject and attribute both in the accusative case; as, ظَنَنْتُ زَيْدًا عَالِمًا "I believed Zaid (to be) learned." The attribute may be common to two propositions, and, of course, to two different subjects; and the noun, which in one of the propositions is the subject of the verb "to believe," may, in the other, be the subject of the proposition which is governed by that verb; thus, "Zaid has believed me learned, and I have believed Zaid learned." ظَنَّنِي وَ ظَنَنْتُ زَيْدًا عَالِمًا "he has believed me, and I have believed Zaid learned;" or ظَنَّنِي إِيَّاهُ وَ ظَنَنْتُ زَيْدًا عَالِمًا "he has believed me so, and I have believed Zaid learned;" or ظَنَّنِي وَظَنَنْتُ زَيْدًا عَالِمًا إِيَّاهُ "he has believed me, and I have believed Zaid learned;" that is, "I have believed Zaid to be learned, and he has believed me to be so." The first is the method most approved of by grammarians. If the subject be of different genders and numbers, the attribute must be repeated; thus, أَظُنُّ وَيَظُنَّانِي أَخًا زَيْدًا وَ عَمْرًا أَخَوَيْنِ "I regard Zaid and 'Amru as (my) two brothers, and they (two) regard me as a brother."

a. For a more detailed account of such peculiarities of Arabic Grammar as have been treated of in the four preceding paragraphs, the reader is referred to De Sacy's Grammaire Arabe, Tome ii. p. 246 to p. 252. From that excellent work the four paragraphs here alluded to have been abridged.

Of Abstract or Substantive Verbs.

347. The verb كَانَ "he (or it) was," expressing the existence of the subject of a proposition, and its relation to the attribute, takes the subject in the nominative case, and its attribute in the accusative; as ٱللّٰهُ كَانَ رَحِيمًا "God is merciful;" لَا يَكُونُ ٱلْحَكِيمُ حَكِيمًا حَتَّي يَغْلِبَ جَمِيعَ شَهَوَاتِهِ "the sage will not be a (true) sage until he shall have subdued all his passions;" مَنْ كَانَ ٱلطَّمَعُ لَهُ مَرْكَبًا كَانَ ٱلْفَقْرُ لَهُ صَاحِبًا "he who has greediness for his steed will have poverty for his companion;" لَا عِلْمَ إِلَّا مَا كَانَ مَكْتُومًا فِي ٱلصَّدْرِ "there is no (real) science except what is concealed in the breast;" كُونُوا حِجَارَةً أَوْ حَدِيدًا "be ye (either) stones or iron." The same rule holds when the attribute precedes كَانَ; thus, كَبِيرًا كَانَ أَوْ صَغِيرًا "be it great or small."

348. There are in Arabic several verbs denoting existence, called by grammarians أَخَوَاتُ كَانَ "the sisters of *kāna*," which are construed like the latter, such are صَارَ and آضَ "it became," or "came to pass;" عَادَ "it returned," etc.; أَمْسَي "it was" or "happened at eve;" أَصْبَحَ "it was or came to pass on the morning," etc. To these we might add many more which are best acquired by practice. All of them, however, like كَانَ, require their attributes to be put in the accusative; thus, زَيْدٌ صَارَ غَنِيًّا "Zaid has become rich;" أَصْبَحْتُمْ بِنِعْمَةِ ٱللّٰهِ إِخْوَانًا "ye are by the favour of God become brethren;" لَقَدْ أَمْسَيْتُ أَخَا عَيْلَةٍ "I have become the brother of poverty;" صَارَ وَجْهُهُ مُسْوَدًّا "his

face became black;" أَضْحَي ٱلْحَرُّ مُحْرِقًا "the heat became scorching;" مَا زَالَتْ ٱلْفَضِيلَةُ مَمْدُوحَةً "virtue never ceases to be worthy of praise;" سِيرُوا مَا دَامَ ٱلنَّهَارُ مَوْجُودًا "march ye whilst daylight continues."

349. The verb كَانَ is employed along with the preposition لِ to denote possession, in a manner similar to the Latin rule, *est pro habeo;* the Arabic language not possessing any word that corresponds exactly with our verb "to have," or with the Latin *habere.* This mode of construction will be obvious from the following examples, viz., مَلِكٌ كَانَ لَهُ وَزِيرٌ "a king had a minister," literally, "a king, there was to him a minister;" again, أَبِي كَانَ لَهُ جَمَلٌ "my father had a camel;" وَمِنْ أَمْثَالِ ذَلِكَ أَنَّهُ كَانَ تَاجِرٌ وَكَانَ لَهُ وَلَدٌ "and among the examples of this (is), that there was (once on a time) a merchant and he had a son."

350. The preterite of the verb كَانَ is often employed in a general sense denoting mere existence, without any reference to time, and serving as a copula or connective between a subject and an attribute; thus, أُولَئِكَ مَا كَانَ لَهُمْ أَنْ يَدْخُلُوهَا إِلَّا خَآئِفِينَ "those (people), it is not for them that they should enter it unless with fear." In a similar manner the negative verb لَيْسَ "he or it is not," (§ 173) requires its attribute to be put in the accusative. Sometimes, however, for the sake of emphasis, the attribute is combined with the subject by means of the preposition بِ; as لَيْسَ ٱللّٰهُ بِظَالِمٍ "God is not (assuredly) unjust." When the exceptive particle إِلَّا "unless," "except,"

intervenes between the subject and the attribute, the latter is put in the nominative; thus, لَيسَ ٱلْحَيٰوةُ إِلَّا خَيَالٌ زَائِلٌ "the (present) life is nothing but a transitory pageant." Sometimes لَيسَ is employed, without any variation, in the third person singular masculine with the affixed pronouns; thus, لَيسَهُ "it is not he;" لَيسَهَا "it is not she;" لَيسَهُمْ "it is not they," etc.

Verbs of Praise and Censure.

351. Verbs of praise and censure are very restricted in their inflection, being principally employed in the third person singular masculine of the preterite, and occasionally in the third person singular feminine of that tense. They are very rarely used in the dual or plural. The principal verbs of this kind are, as we stated, § 174, نِعْمَ (sometimes نِعِمَ, or نَعِمَ, or نَعْمَ) "he or it is good;" بِئْسَ "he or it is bad;" to which we may add حَبَّذَا (made up of حَبَّ + ذَا) "this is delightful." When the noun that is the object of praise or censure is accompanied by the article أَلْ it is put in the nominative case; as نِعْمَ ٱلنَّصِيرُ "he is an excellent assistant;" بِئْسَ ٱلْمِهَادُ "it is a bad dwelling." When the same noun is without the article it is put in the accusative; thus, نِعْمَ رَجُلًا زَيْدٌ "an excellent man is Zaid;" بِئْسَ عَبْدًا عَبْدُكَ "a bad servant thy servant is." Akin to بِئْسَ is سَآءَ "it is bad," which is construed in the same manner; thus, سَآءَ ٱلرَّجُلُ زَيْدٌ "wicked is the man Zaid;" or without the article, سَآءَ رَجُلًا زَيْدٌ "a bad man is Zaid."

Verbs of Admiration and Surprise.

352. Any primitive triliteral verb may be converted into a verb of admiration in two ways, as we stated in § 173, viz., مَا أَفْعَلَ and أَفْعِلْ. When the former expression is used, the name of the person or thing admired is added to it in the accusative case, without the intervention of any other word; thus, مَا أَحْسَنَ زَيْدًا "how very handsome is Zaid!" When the object of admiration is a pronoun the affixed pronoun is employed; thus, مَا أَكْيَسَ نَفْسَهُ وَأَظْهَرَ دَلَائِلَ ٱلْفَضْلِ عَلَيْهِ "how very acute is his genius, and how conspicuous are the proofs of excellence in him!" When the second form of the verb of admiration, viz., أَفْعِلْ, is employed, the object admired, follows it in the genitive case governed by the preposition بِ; thus, أَكْرِمْ بِخُلْقِ نَبِيٍّ "how very noble is the disposition of a prophet!"

a. Sometimes the noun or pronoun which is the object of admiration is omitted; but this very rarely happens, and only in such instances as lead to no obscurity in the sense. Between the verb of admiration and the object admired, it is allowed to admit words expressive of time or place, an adverb or a word in the vocative case; for example: مَا أَحْسَنَ فِي ٱلْهَيْجَاءِ لِقَاءَهَا "how beautiful is her rushing on in the battle-field!"

Inchoative and Approximate Verbs.

353. The peculiarity of these verbs is, that of themselves they convey merely a vague sense, and require another verb after them in the aorist, as a complement, with or without the

conjunction أَن "that." Among the inchoatives are أَخَذَ, إِبْتَدَأَ, أَقْبَلَ, أَنْشَأَ, جَعَلَ, شَرَعَ, عَلِقَ, طَفِقَ, and طَبِقَ. All of these denote *beginning* the action or state expressed by the following aorist, which will be best illustrated by a few examples; thus, جَعَلَا يَتَشَاجَرَانِ "they two began to dispute one with the other;" أَقْبَلَ يَلْحَسُهُ بِلِسَانِهِ "he began to lick it with his tongue;" جَعَلَ قَارُونُ يَقُولُ يَا مُوسَي أَرْحِمْنِي وَ مُوسَي يَقُولُ يَا أَرْضُ خُذِيهِمْ "Kārūn (Korah) began to say, O Moses pity me! and Moses (began) to say, O earth! receive them!"

354. Among the approximate verbs are عَسَي "it nearly happened that;" كَادَ, أَوْشَكَ, and قَرُبَ "little was wanting that" (Lat. *parum abfuit quin*). The verbs عَسَي and قَرُبَ are used only in the preterite, in which case they assume the meaning of our adverbs "perhaps," "it may be." A few examples will shew the use of these better than a long description; thus, عَسَي زَيْدٌ أَنْ يَخْرُجَ "perhaps Zaid may go out;" عَسَي يَرَي نَارَكَ مَنْ يَمُرُّ "perhaps the wayfarer may see thy fire (of hospitality);" يَكَادُ ٱلْبَرْقُ يَخْطَفُ أَبْصَارَهُمْ "the lightning very nearly took away their sight;" كَادَتِ ٱلنَّفْسُ تَزْهَقُ "the spirit was nearly departing." All of these rarely require the interposition of أَنْ; the verb عَسَي, however, when expressive of apprehension of any thing, and which may then be considered as an impersonal verb, requires the conjunction أَنْ; thus, عَسَي أَنْ تَكْرَهُوا شَيْأً وَ هُوَ خَيْرٌ لَكُمْ "it may happen that you dislike a thing, and (nevertheless) it may be good for you."

355. There are several other verbs whose mode of con-

struction is similar to the preceding. Such are—1. Verbs expressive of *entering* or *tending towards* a place; such as دَخَلَ "he entered;" مَضَي "he went or preceded;" thus, دَخَلَ إِلَي بَعْضِ ٱلْمَغَائِرِ يَتَظَلَّلُ بِهَا "he entered into a certain cave that he might enjoy the shade in it;" فَمَضَوْا إِلَي ٱلثَّعَالِبِ يَسُومُونَ مِنْهُمُ ٱلْحِلْفَ "then they went to the foxes that they might enter into a league with them." 2. Verbs expressive of "continuing," "persisting," "remaining," or "persevering;" such as بَقِيَ and أَقَامَ "he continued" or "persevered;" as بَقِيَ زَيْدٌ يُرَاسِلُ ٱبْنَ بُوَيْهِ "Zaid continued sending to Ibn Buwaih." The same rule applies to the verb رَسَا "he was firm" or "unmoved;" عَادَ "he was accustomed;" ظَلَّ "he continued," "he ceased not (during the day);" بَاتَ "he remained or put up (during the night)." So the verbs negative, مَا زَالَ "he ceased not;" مَا بَرِحَ, مَا فَتَرَ, and مَا ٱنْفَكَّ "he failed not," *i.e.* "he persevered (until the end of the period indicated in the proposition)."

a. When a negation is employed in such propositions as the foregoing, the same must be put before the first verb; thus, لَا يَكَادُ يُبَيِّنُ "he is hardly able to speak plainly;" مَا عَسَيْتُمْ أَنْ تَفْعَلُوا "perhaps you will not do (it)."

Syntax of Indeclinable Particles.

356. In Section V. we treated of most of the indeclinable particles of the Arabic language; and in the present section we have occasionally noticed the mode in which some of them influence the tenses of the verb, more especially the aorist.

We shall now conclude with a few additional remarks on the same subject, observing the order adopted in Section V. abovementioned.

357. All prepositions, whether separable or inseparable (§ 178, etc.), govern the genitive case; thus, بِٱللّٰهِ "in God;" لِلّٰهِ "to God;" تَحْتَ ٱلسَّمَاءِ "under the heavens;" فِي ٱلدَّارِ "in the house;" مِنْ جِهَةِ ٱلْجَنُوبِ إِلَي جِهَةِ ٱلشَّمَالِ "from the quarter of the south to the quarter of the north."

a. We have already stated, § 341, that, as a general rule, transitive verbs govern the accusative case direct, without the aid or intervention of any particle. This rule, however, is liable to some exceptions; for instance, the phrase رَمَي حَجَرًا "he threw a stone," may also be expressed رَمَي بِحَجَرٍ "he threw (or shot) with a stone;" so عَلِمَهُ and عَلِمَ بِهِ "he knew it." The latter phrase, however, may be rendered "he was conversant with it."

358. Intransitive or neuter verbs are naturally connected with their complements by means of a preposition; thus, جَاءَ إِلَي عَيْنِ مَاءٍ "he came to a fountain of water." When, however, an intransitive verb governs a complete proposition, either verbal or nominal, beginning with the conjunction أَنْ or أَنَّ, the preposition which ought to connect the verb with its complementary proposition is frequently omitted; thus, لَمْ يَقْدِرْ أَنْ يَفْعَلَ ذٰلِكَ, instead of لَمْ يَقْدِرْ عَلَي أَنْ يَفْعَلَ ذٰلِكَ "he could not do that;" so, عَجِبْتُ أَنْ يَخْرُجَ عَلَيَّ "I wonder that he revolts against me," instead of عَجِبْتُ مِنْ أَنْ; so likewise,

تَقَدَّمَ إِلَيْهِ أَلَّا يَأْذَنَ لِأَحَدٍ "he ordered him that he should not grant permission to any one," instead of بِأَلَّا يَأْذَنَ; the last example is particularly remarkable, as it is only by means of the preposition بِ that تَقَدَّمَ signifies "he ordered."

a. It is to be observed, however, that the preposition must never be omitted, if a doubtful meaning should be the result; we must not say for example, رَغِبْتُ أَنْ تَفْعَلَ ذٰلِكَ instead of رَغِبْتُ فِي أَنْ تَفْعَلَ ذٰلِكَ "I desire that thou wouldst do that:" for if the preposition فِي had been omitted we should have been left to supply its place by some other preposition, such as عَنْ for instance, in which case the sense would be رَغِبْتُ عَنْ أَنْ تَفْعَلَ ذٰلِكَ "I am averse from thy doing that."

359. After the negative adverb لَا the noun forming the subject of negation is generally put in the accusative case, but without the *nūnation*, provided no word intervenes between the negative and its subject; thus, لَا إِلٰهَ إِلَّا ٱللّٰهُ "there is no god but Allāh;" ذٰلِكَ ٱلْكِتَابُ لَا رَيْبَ فِيهِ "there is no doubt in this book;" لَا إِنْسَانَ فِي ٱلدَّارِ "there is no man in the house." In this last sentence we may also say, لَا فِي ٱلدَّارِ إِنْسَانٌ in which case the word إِنْسَانٌ is now in the nominative, because the words فِي ٱلدَّارِ intervene between it and the negative لَا. When, after لَا, two nouns follow, coupled by a conjunction, the second of them is optionally put in the nominative or the accusative; hence we may either say, لَا رَجُلَ وَٱمْرَأَةَ فِي ٱلدَّارِ "there is no man and (no) woman in the house," or we may say, لَا رَجُلَ وَٱمْرَأَةٌ. If the negative لَا,

however, be repeated before each noun, it may influence each of the nouns in the accusative case, or it may influence only one of them, no matter whether the first or last, or, finally, it may influence neither, both nouns being used in the nominative case; thus, we may say, لَا رَجُلَ وَلَا ٱمْرَأَةَ or لَا رَجُلَ وَلَا ٱمْرَأَةٌ or لَا رَجُلٌ وَلَا ٱمْرَأَةَ or finally, لَا رَجُلٌ وَلَا ٱمْرَأَةٌ فِي ٱلدَّارِ "there is no man and (there is) no woman in the house." So in the formula of exclamation frequently used by good Musalmans when anything surprising or extraordinary occurs to them; viz., لَا حَوْلَ وَلَا قُوَّةَ إِلَّا بِٱللّٰهِ, or لَا حَوْلَ وَلَا قُوَّةٌ إِلَّا بِٱللّٰهِ, or لَا حَوْلٌ وَلَا قُوَّةَ إِلَّا بِٱللّٰهِ, or lastly, لَا حَوْلٌ وَلَا قُوَّةٌ إِلَّا بِٱللّٰهِ "there is no power and no strength but in God."

a. If the subject of negation be qualified by an adjective the expression admits of three varieties; thus we may say لَا رَجُلَ نَائِمَ فِي ٱلدَّارِ, or لَا رَجُلَ نَائِمًا, or لَا رَجُلَ نَائِمٌ "there is no man sleeping in the house."

360. The negative particles لَا and مَا, when prefixed to a simple proposition, whose verb is كَانَ understood, require the attribute to be put in the accusative; thus, لَا رَجُلٌ حَاضِرًا "there is no man present;" مَا زَيْدٌ قَائِمًا "Zaid is not standing." In order that this rule may hold, however, it is necessary, 1st, that the attribute should follow the subject; 2nd, that between the subject and attribute the particle إِلَّا "except," may not intervene; 3rd, that the particle مَا may not have the particle إِنْ (in a negative sense) combined with it; and

lastly, when لَا is used, the subject, if an appellative noun, must be indefinite. Should any of these four conditions be wanting, the particle لَا and مَا lose their influence on the attribute which is then used in the nominative case; thus, مَا قَائِمٌ زَيْدٌ "Zaid is not standing;" مَا زَيْدٌ إِلَّا كَاذِبٌ "Zaid is nothing but a liar;" مَا إِنْ مُحَمَّدٌ نَائِمٌ "Muḥammad is not asleep;" لَا ٱللّٰهُ كَاذِبٌ "God is not a liar;" لَا مُسْتَوْدَعُ ٱلسِّرِّ ذَائِعٌ لَدَيْهِمْ "the secret trusted to them is not betrayed;" لَا زَيْدٌ مَرِيضٌ "Zaid is not ill." With an indefinite noun we should say لَا إِنْسَانٌ بَاقِيًا "there is no man immortal."

361. The interrogative particles كَمْ and كَأَيِّنْ or كَأَيٍّ "how much?" "how many?" govern the accusative; for example: كَمْ دِرْهَمًا "how many dirhams?" كَأَيِّنْ رَجُلًا "how many men?" If a preposition be prefixed to these particles they govern the genitive; thus, بِكَمْ دِرْهَمٍ "by" or "for how many dirhams (hast thou bought this)?" They also govern the genitive when not used interrogatively but merely as part of a narrative; thus, لَا أَدْرِي كَمْ رِجَالٍ قَتَلْتَ "I know not how many men thou mayest have killed."

362. The exceptive conjunction إِلَّا (إِنْ + لَا) "except," "besides," etc., governs the person or thing excepted in the accusative, when the proposition is affirmative; for example: جَآءَنِي ٱلنَّاسُ إِلَّا زَيْدًا "the men came to me except Zaid." When the proposition is negative, and the person or thing excepted is expressed, the latter may be put either in the accusative case, or it may agree with the subject from which

the exception is made; thus, مَا كَلَّمَنِي أَحَدٌ إِلَّا زَيْدًا "no one has accosted me except Zaid;" in which sentence we may optionally substitute إِلَّا زَيْدٌ; so also مَا أَتَيْتُ بِالْكُتُبِ إِلَّا ٱلتَّوْرَيَةَ "I have not brought the books, except the Pentateuch;" where instead of ٱلتَّوْرَيَةَ we may substitute ٱلتَّوْرَيةِ in the same case as كُتُبِ.

363. If the person or thing from which the exception is made, be not expressed, but understood, the object excepted must be in the same case in which would have been the unexpressed subject; thus, مَا يَعْلَمُ تَأْوِيلَهُ إِلَّا ٱللّٰهُ "no one knows the interpretation of it except God," where أَحَدٌ is understood; so مَا رَأَيْتُ إِلَّا زَيْدًا "I saw no one except Zaid," where أَحَدًا is understood; lastly, مَا مَرَرْتُ إِلَّا بِجَعْفَرٍ "I passed not (by any one) except by Ja'far," where we have بِأَحَدٍ understood. When the word which precedes إِلَّا is the subject, and that which follows it the attribute of a proposition, the two words must be in the nominative; as مَا جَعْفَرٌ إِلَّا كَاذِبٌ "Ja'far is not but a liar," *i.e.* "Ja'far is but a liar;" إِنَّ ٱلْكَافِرُونَ إِلَّا مَلْعُونُونَ "verily the unbelievers are but accursed." If the person or thing excepted be not of the nature of that comprised in the general subject, the noun following إِلَّا must be in the accusative case; thus, مَا جَاءَنِي أَحَدٌ إِلَّا فَرَسًا "no one (creature) came to me except a horse."

a. When the particle إِلَّا is repeated, forming fresh exceptions, and not merely used for the purpose of greater energy, the general subject being understood, and not expressed, the name of the first thing excepted is put in the nominative case, and the others in the accusative; thus, مَا قَامَ إِلَّا جَعْفَرٌ إِلَّا سَعِيدًا إِلَّا مُحَمَّدًا "no one stood up except Ja'far, except Sa'īd, except Muḥammad. If the general idea be expressed, and the proposition should be affirmative, all the exceptions are put in the accusative case; thus, قُتِلَ ٱلْقَوْمُ إِلَّا زَيْدًا إِلَّا عُمَرَ إِلَّا عَمْرًا "the people were slain except Zaid, except 'Umar, except 'Amru." If the general idea be expressed, and the proposition negative, and if there should be an inversion, the same rule holds; thus, مَا نَجَا إِلَّا جَعْفَرًا إِلَّا أَحْمَدَ أَحَدٌ "no one has escaped except Ja'far, except Aḥmad." If there be not an inversion, one of the nouns will be in the case in which would have been the noun following إِلَّا, if there be but one exception, and all the others will be in the accusative; thus, لَمْ يَنْجُ أَحَدٌ إِلَّا زَيْدٌ إِلَّا عَمْرًا إِلَّا جَعْفَرًا "no one has been saved except Zaid, except 'Amru, except Ja'far."

364. The exceptive particles حَاشَا, خَلَا, and عَدَا, § 185, may take after them, indifferently, the accusative, the genitive, or even the nominative, according to the light in which we view them. If we consider them as active verbs, then they naturally govern the accusative; thus, مَاتُوا حَاشَا زَيْدًا "they are dead except Zaid." If we view them as prepositions, then they of course govern the genitive; as مَاتُوا حَاشَا زَيْدٍ; and lastly, as mere adverbs, they may be followed by the nominative; as مَاتُوا حَاشَا زَيْدٌ. When, however, the expressions مَا خَلَا "that which is free from," and مَا عَدَا "what goes beyond," are employed, the object excepted must be put in the accusative case; thus, فَأَنْزَلُوهُمْ مَا خَلَا عَبَّاسًا "and they made them alight excepting 'Abbās."

365. The exceptive particles غَيْرٌ, بَيْدَ, سِوَي, سُوَي, and سِوَآءٌ, all of which are, in reality, substantives, signifying "difference," govern the person or thing excepted in the genitive; and are themselves always put in the same case in which the person or thing excepted would be, if the particle إِلَّا had been used; thus, مَا كَلَّمَنِي أَحَدٌ غَيْرُ زَيْدٍ or غَيْرَ زَيْدٍ "no one has spoken to me except Zaid;" مَا أَتَيْتُ بِالْكُتُبِ غَيْرَ ٱلتَّوْرَيةِ or غَيْرِ ٱلتَّوْرَيةِ "I have not brought the books except the Pentateuch;" جَاءَنِي ٱلنَّاسُ غَيْرَ زَيْدٍ "the men came to me except Zaid;" مَا جَاءَنِي غَيْرُ جَعْفَرٍ "no one came to me except Ja'far;" مَا مَرَرْتُ بِغَيْرِ جَعْفَرٍ "I have passed by no one except Ja'far;" لَمْ أَضْرِبْ غَيْرَ جَعْفَرٍ "I have struck no one except Ja'far;" مَا جَاءَنِي أَحَدٌ غَيْرَ فَرَسٍ "no one (creature) came to me except a horse." It is to be observed, however, that the particles سِوَي and سُوَي being indeclinable, or rather having their three cases alike, follow the preceding rule, only virtually, though not apparently.

366. The exceptive compound particle لَوْلَا "if not," "unless" (*nisi* or *si non*), has no influence on the subject of the sentence to which it is prefixed; and the verb of the hypothetic proposition that follows takes the particle لَ before it; thus, لَوْلَا زَيْدٌ لَزُرْتُكَ "if it were not Zaid, I should have visited thee," *i.e.* "if Zaid had not existed," or "had not prevented." So in Kur. ii. 252: لَوْلَا دَفْعُ ٱللّٰهِ ٱلنَّاسَ بَعْضَهُمْ بِبَعْضٍ لَفَسَدَتِ ٱلْأَرْضُ "and if God had not prevented men, the one (party) by the other, verily the earth would have been corrupted." Some-

times the affirmative part of a hypothetic sentence of this kind is omitted, when it may be easily inferred from the context; thus, Kur. xxiv. 10: لَوْلَا فَضْلُ ٱللّٰهِ عَلَيْهِمْ وَرَحْمَتُهُ وَإِنَّ ٱللّٰهَ تَوَّابٌ حَكِيمٌ "had not the clemency of God (been) upon them, and also his mercy [verily he would have punished the perjurers], for verily God is gracious (and) wise."

a. When the subject of the proposition following the particle لولا is a pronoun it is generally used in the affixed form; as in the following example: لَوْلَاهُ لَمْ تَخْرُجِ ٱلدُّنْيَا مِنَ ٱلْعَدَمِ "if it had not been for him the world would not have come out of nothing." Sometimes, however, the isolated pronoun is employed; thus, from the Kurān xxxiv. 30: لَوْلَا أَنْتُمْ لَكُنَّا مُؤْمِنِينَ "had it not been for you, verily we should have been (true) believers."

367. The particles إِنْ or إِنَّ "verily," "indeed;" أَنْ or أَنَّ "that," "with regard to," "anent;" كَأَنَّ "like as;" لٰكِنَّ "but;" لَيْتَ "I wish," "would it were!" (*utinam*) عَلَّ and لَعَلَّ "perhaps," "peradventure" (§ 66, *b*), have this peculiarity, that they require the noun that follows them to be put in the accusative case; thus, إِنَّ ٱللّٰهَ غَفُورٌ رَحِيمٌ "verily God is forgiving (and) merciful;" تَوَدُّ لَوْ أَنَّ بَيْنَهَا وَبَيْنَهُ أَمَدًا بَعِيدًا "she desires that between herself and him there should be a wide space;" زَيْدٌ قَائِمٌ لٰكِنَّ مُحَمَّدًا جَالِسٌ "Zaid is standing, but Muḥammad is sitting;" كَأَنَّ زَيْدًا أَسَدٌ "as if Zaid were a lion;" لَيْتَ مُحَمَّدًا حَاضِرٌ "would that Muḥammad were present!" لَعَلَّ مُحَمَّدًا رَاجِعٌ ٱلْيَوْمَ "perhaps Muḥammad is returning to-

day." That these particles, however, may retain their governing power, it is necessary that no other word should intervene between the particle and the noun, with the exception, perhaps, of a preposition with the noun it governs; as إِنَّ فِي ذَلِكَ آيَةً "verily in this (consists) a sign." When the preceding particles are combined with another particle, so as to form one word, their governing power ceases, as in the sentence إِنَّمَا ٱلْعِلْمُ عِنْدَ ٱللّٰهِ "verily knowledge is with God."

368. In § 197 we noticed the more ordinary interjections. Of these the most frequent of occurrence is يَا, corresponding to our "O," used in addressing or calling a person; and it takes after it the nominative case, and occasionally the accusative, there being no distinct form of a vocative case in the Arabic language. An exclamation is sometimes made use of elliptically, as in our own language; thus, ٱلْأَسَدَ ٱلْأَسَدَ "the lion! the lion!" that is, "beware of the lion!" so ٱلْعَدُوَّ "the enemy!" For a more detailed account of the vocative case, or rather of its substitutes, the student is referred to § 67.

SECTION IX.

Prosody—عِلْمُ ٱلْعَرُوضِ 'Ilmu-l-'Arūḍ.

369. The prosody of the Arabs, from which is derived that of the Persians, the Turks, and the Musalmāns of India, is founded on the following simple principles. In the first place, every word in the language begins with a consonant, which consonant is moveable by one or other of the three primitive vowels (§ 22). Secondly, a syllable consisting of merely one consonant, moveable by a primitive vowel, is naturally short; but if such syllable be followed by an inert consonant, the primitive vowel becomes long by position. For the sake of simplicity and perspicuity, we intend in this Section to make a free use of the Roman character; and in so doing let it be observed that the three vowels *a*, *i*, and *u*, when unaccented, represent the *fatḥa* ـَ, *kasra* ـِ, and *ḍamma* ـُ respectively. These vowels are, as we have just said, naturally short when followed, in the next syllable, by a single moveable consonant, and they become long by position when followed by an inert letter; hence it will not be necessary for us to perplex the student with a superfluity of long and short marks, very ridiculously applied, as they are, in

every work on Eastern Prosody which we have yet seen. The accented vowels *ā*, *ī*, and *ū*, are always understood to be long, as they are the representatives of the three letters of prolongation ا *alif*, ي *yā*, and و *wāw*, respectively.

a. In the present Section, with a view to "make assurance doubly sure," the short vowels are marked in those few instances where one foot happens to have the same vowels as another foot, but of different quantities; thus, in the Anapæstus فَعِلُن *Fădilun*, the first vowel is made to bear the short mark, to distinguish it from the Amphimacer فَاعِلُن *Fāḍilun*. In the tables representing the sixteen metres, pp. 328 and 329, we have also marked the short vowels as well as the long, except when two consonants follow the former, or a single consonant at the end of a hemistich.

Of the Metrical Feet—جُزْءٌ (plur. أَجْزَآءٌ).

370. We mentioned, § 50, that the Arabian Grammarians adopted the verbal root فعل with its various modifications, as a mere formula for representing the various *forms* and *measures* of nouns and verbs. This is not all, however: they have applied the same root together with its formations, as models for exemplifying the أَجْزَآءٌ or metrical feet in prosody. Thus, instead of saying that the word جَلَالٌ, for example, is an *Iambus*, they simply say that it is of the measure فَعُولٌ, and a similar rule applies to all the other feet. The Arabian method, then, of exhibiting the various poetic feet is exceedingly clear and simple, as it appeals at once to the *ear* and to the *eye*. The only objection to the employment of the root فعل, is, as we formerly stated, that it is altogether unsuitable

to European students, however satisfactory it may prove to the Arabs. We here, therefore, select as our *formula* the root فتل, which bears a close resemblance in form to فعل, with the important advantage of its having for its middle consonant a letter whose sound a European ear can easily realize.

a. The structure of the Arabic language differs most widely from that of the ancient tongues of Greece and Rome in one particular, viz., in Arabic we never meet with a concourse of two or more vowels such as we have in Πηληϊάδεω Ἀχιλῆος. Hence our classical rule that, "a vowel before another vowel is short," can have no place here. All the three languages, however, have the following rule in common, viz., "a vowel naturally short, if followed by two consonants becomes long by position." The last syllable of every foot ending with a consonant is always long in Arabic verse. The reason is, that the foot following *must* begin with a consonant (§ 369). This rule does not hold in Latin and Greek, for an equally obvious reason, viz., the foot following *may*, and often *does*, begin with a vowel. Finally, another classical rule, viz., "Ultima cujusque est communis syllaba versûs," does not apply in Arabic: for in the latter tongue, the last syllable of a verse *must be* either absolutely long, by position, or if naturally short, it is artificially prolonged.

371. The Perfect or Standard feet سَالِمَاتٌ *sālimāt* in Arabic are eight in number. Of these, two are quinqueliteral, each consisting of three syllables; four are septiliteral, each consisting of four syllables; and the remaining two are also septiliteral, but consisting each of five syllables.

All of these, with their measures, and their corresponding Latin names, may be seen in the subjoined Table of

STANDARD FEET.

NO.	MEASURE.		LATIN NAME.	QUANTITY.
1.	فَضُولُنْ	Faḍūlun	Bacchius	⏑ — —
2.	فَاضِلُنْ	Fāḍilun	Amphimacer	— ⏑ —
3.	مَفَاضِيلُنْ	Mafāḍīlun	Epitritus primus	⏑ — — —
4.	فَاضِلَاتُنْ	Fāḍilātun	„ secundus	— ⏑ — —
5.	مُسْتَفْضِلُنْ	Mustafḍilun	„ tertius	— — ⏑ —
6.	مَفْضُولَاتُ	Mafḍūlātu	„ quartus	— — — ⏑
7.	مَفَاضِلَتُنْ	Mafāḍilatun	Iambo-Anapæstus	⏑ — ⏑ ⏑ —
8.	مُتَفَاضِلُنْ	Mutafāḍilun	Anapæsto-Iambus	⏑ ⏑ — ⏑ —

372. The eight foregoing *Perfect* feet admit, each, of several modifications, either by the addition or abstraction of one or more letters or syllables. This result is called زِحَافْ *siḥāf* or عِلَّةْ *'illat*, i.e., "deviation," or "infirmity," which gives rise to some thirty or more additional feet, called *ghair sālimāt*, i.e., *Imperfect*. This distinction, however, appears to be of little practical utility, for in most poetic compositions the so-called Imperfect feet occur, intermingled with the Perfect. The student, therefore, had better make himself acquainted with all the feet simply as established facts, without troubling his head about the circumstance of their being Perfect or Imperfect. For example, the regular *Bacchius* فَضُولُنْ may give rise to a *Spondeus* by becoming فَضْلُنْ; but then, the regular feet فَاضِلُنْ and فَاضِلَاتُنْ, together with some others, may also become فَضْلُنْ,

according to certain rules which our restricted limits here do not permit us to enter upon. The Imperfect Feet of ordinary occurrence may be reckoned at about nineteen in number; but to these the native grammarians add several more; which, however, being matters rather of curiosity than of practical utility, are here passed over.

TABLE OF IMPERFECT FEET.

NO.	MEASURE.	LATIN NAME.	QUANTITY.
1.	فَضْ or فَاضْ Faḍ or Fāḍ	Cæsura	—
2.	فَضَ Faḍa	Pyrrhichius	⏑ ⏑
3.	فَضْلُ Faḍlu	Trochæus	— ⏑
4.	فَضُولْ Faḍūl	Iambus	⏑ —
5.	فَضْلُنْ Faḍlun	Spondeus	— —
6.	فَضُولُ Faḍūlu	Amphibrachys	⏑ — ⏑
7.	فَضِلُنْ Fāḍilun	Anapæstus	⏑ ⏑ —
8.	مَفْضُولُ Mafḍūlu	Antibacchius	— — ⏑
9.	مَفْضُولُنْ Mafḍūlun	Molossus	— — —
10.	فَاضِلَتُ Fāḍilatu	Pæon primus,	— ⏑ ⏑ ⏑
11.	مَفَاضِلُ Mafāḍilu	„ secundus	⏑ — ⏑ ⏑
12.	فَضِلَاتُ Faḍilātu	„ tertius	⏑ ⏑ — ⏑
13.	فَضِلَتُنْ Fāḍilātun	„ quartus	⏑ ⏑ ⏑ —
14.	مُسْتَفْضِلُ Mustafḍilu	Ionicus major	— — ⏑ ⏑
15.	فَضِلَاتُنْ Faḍilātun	Ionicus minor	⏑ ⏑ — —
16.	فَاضِلَاتُ Fāḍilātu	Ditrochæus	— ⏑ — ⏑
17.	مَفَاضِلُنْ Mafāḍilun	Diambus	⏑ — ⏑ —
18.	مُفَاضِيلُ Mufāḍīlu	Antispastus	⏑ — — ⏑
19.	مُفْتَضِلُنْ Muftaḍilun	Choriambus	— ⏑ ⏑ —

a. It may be observed that the preceding list of metrical feet, regular and irregular, corresponds, very nearly, both as regards number and quality, with those in use among the Greeks and Romans of old. The Arabs, however, have neither the Tribrachys nor the Dactylus in their list, so far as I have been able to ascertain. This is the more surprising, as the greater part of the verbal roots in the language consists, *theoretically*, of three short syllables.

Of the Metres—الْبُحُورُ (plural of بَحْرٌ).

373. We shall now proceed to lay before the reader a Table of the Sixteen Standard Metres employed in Arabian verse. These, it may be observed, are wholly composed of perfect feet, and are thence called perfect metres; but, as we have shewn in the last paragraph, § 372, since there are a great number of imperfect feet, so there are numerous imperfect or secondary metres. Here again the distinction is whimsical and useless; for the great body of the poetry of the language, especially poems of any length, are found to admit of imperfect metre, probably because the perfect would prove too monotonous by long continuance. It would have occupied too much of our space to have inserted, in our Table, the translation of the Arabic names of the various metres; nor would it be of any great use if we did, for in most instances the aptness of the name is not very perceptible. We also in this Section dispense with giving the equivalent of the *nūnation* in all Arabic technical terms when printed in the Roman character. Of such terms, however, we shall make a sparing use, as our object is to explain clearly the principles of the *art*, not to enlarge upon its dry technicalities. We are nowise ambitious of

rivalling the "Rhetorician," whose "rules teach nothing but to name his tools."

a. The Arabs consider a verse to consist of two equal members; in fact, what we call a couplet is, with them, viewed as a single verse, which they call بَيْتْ *bait*, i.e. "a tent" or "a house;" as will be seen in the following extract (a little corrected) from Gladwin, viz., "It is generally allowed that a *bait*, or verse, cannot consist of less than two hemistichs; and each of these hemistichs is called مِصْرَاعْ *miṣrā'* or مِصْرَعْ *miṣra'*, a word which literally signifies "one of the two folds of a door;" and the resemblance between a distich and a door of two folds, consists in this, that in the same manner as with a door of two folds you may open or shut which you please without the other; and when you shut both together it is still but one door; so also of a distich, you may scan which of the hemistichs you please without the other, and when you read both together they will form but one verse. The first foot of the first hemistich, in a poetical composition, is called صَدْرْ *ṣadr*, and the last foot thereof عَرُوضْ *'arūḍ*. Of the second hemistich, the first foot is called اِبْتِدَاءْ *ibtidā*, and the last ضَرْبْ *ḍarb* or عَجْزْ *'ajz*. The intermediate feet of both have the general name حَشْوْ *ḥashw*. The meaning of *ṣadr* is the "first" or "chief," and *ibtidā* signifies "commencement;" the first beginning the distich, as the other does the second hemistich. The last foot of the first hemistich is called *'arūḍ*, as signifying the "pole of a tent;" for, as the pole is the support of the tent, so is the distich supported on this prop; and until this foot is determined, the hemistich is not complete, nor its measure known. The last foot of the second hemistich is called *ḍarb*, i.e. "of one kind," or "alike," it resembling the *'arūḍ* inasmuch as both are at the end of a hemistich. *Ḥashw* signifies, literally, "the stuffing of a cushion," and on account of their situation in filling up the interior of each hemistich the intermediate feet are so called."

TABLE OF ARABIAN METRES.

Class I.—*Hemistich of Four Feet, each Three and Four Syllables alternately.*

	NAME.	MEASURE.	AFFINITY.
1.	طَوِيلٌ *Tawīl*	Fāʿūlun, Mǎfāʿīlun, Fāʿūlun, Mǎfāʿīlun	⏑ – – | ⏑ – – – | ⏑ – – | ⏑ – – – |
2.	مَدِيدٌ *Madīd*	Fāʿīlātun, Fāʿīlun, Fāʿīlātun, Fāʿīlun	⏑ – – | – ⏑ – | – ⏑ – – | – ⏑ – |
3.	بَسِيطٌ *Basīṭ*	Mustafʿīlun, Fāʿīlun, Mustafʿīlun, Fāʿīlun	– – ⏑ – | – ⏑ – | – – ⏑ – | – ⏑ – |

Class II.—*Hemistich of Three Feet, each Five Syllables.*

	NAME.	MEASURE.	AFFINITY.
4.	وَافِرٌ *Wāfir*	Mǎfāʿīlǎtun, Mǎfāʿīlǎtun, Mǎfāʿīlǎtun	⏑ – ⏑ ⏑ – | ⏑ – ⏑ ⏑ – | ⏑ – ⏑ ⏑ – |
5.	كَامِلٌ *Kāmil*	Mǔtǎfāʿīlun, Mǔtǎfāʿīlun, Mǔtǎfāʿīlun	⏑ ⏑ – ⏑ – | ⏑ ⏑ – ⏑ – | ⏑ ⏑ – ⏑ – |

Class III.—*Hemistich of Four Feet, each Four Syllables.*

	NAME.	MEASURE.	AFFINITY.
6.	هَزَجٌ *Hazaj*	Mǎfāʿīlun, Mǎfāʿīlun, Mǎfāʿīlun, Mǎfāʿīlun	⏑ – – – | ⏑ – – – | ⏑ – – – | ⏑ – – – |
7.	رَجَزٌ *Rajaz*	Mustafʿīlun, Mustafʿīlun, Mustafʿīlun, Mustafʿīlun.	– – ⏑ – | – – ⏑ – | – – ⏑ – | – – ⏑ – |
8.	رَمَلٌ *Ramal*	Fāʿīlātun, Fāʿīlātun, Fāʿīlātun, Fāʿīlātun.	– ⏑ – – | – ⏑ – – | – ⏑ – – | – ⏑ – – |

CLASS IV.—*Hemistich of Three Feet, each Four Syllables.*

	NAME.		MEASURE.
9.	مُنْسَرِحْ	*Munsariḥ*	Mustafʿilun, Mafʿūlātu, Mustafʿilun
0.	خَفِيفْ	*Khafīf*	Fāʿilātun, Mustafʿilun, Fāʿilātun
1.	مُضَارِعْ	*Muḍāriʿ*	Mafāʿīlun, Fāʿilātun, Mafāʿīlun.
2.	مُقْتَضَبْ	*Muḳtaḍab*	Mafʿūlātu, Mustafʿilun, Mustafʿilun
3.	مُجْتَثْ	*Mujtathth*	Mustafʿilun, Fāʿilātun, Fāʿilātun
4.	سَرِيعْ	*Sarīʿ*	Mustafʿilun, Mustafʿilun, Mafʿūlātu

AFFINITY.

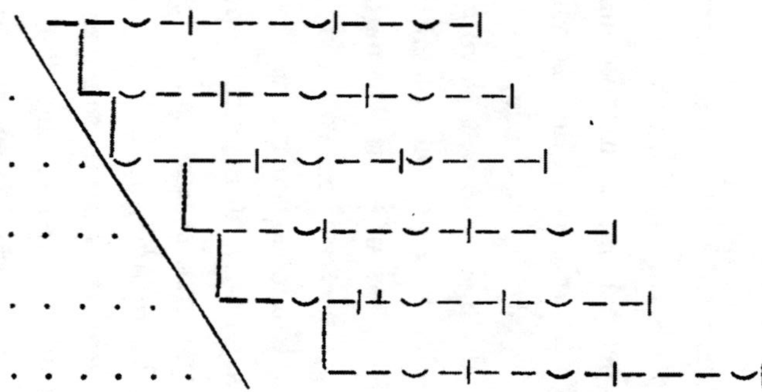

CLASS V.—*Hemistich of Four Feet, each Three Syllables.*

5.	مُتَقَارِبْ	*Mutaḳārib*	Fāʿūlun, Fāʿūlun, Fāʿūlun, Fāʿūlun
6.	مُتَدَارِكْ	*Mutadārik*	Fāʿilun, Fāʿilun, Fāʿilun, Fāʿilun

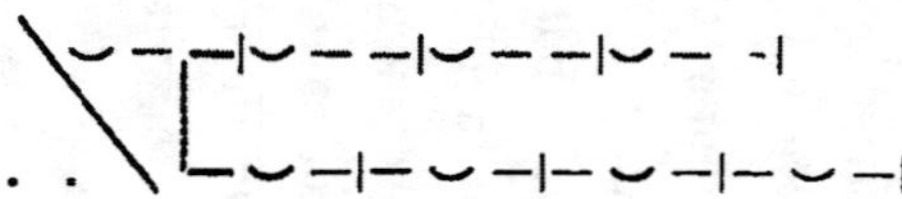

374. In the general treatment of the various metres I have adopted an entirely new plan of my own, which, I flatter myself, will be found far more perspicuous than the clumsy method followed by the native grammarians and their servile imitators in Europe. In the first place, I have adopted the Roman character throughout, which is a great saving of space. Secondly, I have carefully marked the quantities of the vowels, but only in those cases where there might possibly occur a mistake. For instance, when a vowel is followed by two consonants, or by a single consonant at the end of a word, as in the foot *Mustafḍilun*, it is quite superfluous to mark the quantities of the first, second, and fourth vowels, and to write the word *Mūstāfḍilūn*, or, still more absurdly, *Mūstūf ilŭn*, as we have seen it figure in some recent works on the subject. It would be equally superfluous to have marked the third vowel of this foot as short, because we at once see that it is followed by a single moveable consonant, and consequently it is short by rule (see § 369). Lastly, by our adopting the various modifications of the root فعل as our standard of measure, we are enabled to explain, in a satisfactory manner, the subject of Arabian Prosody, in accordance with its true principles.

a. If proof be required to shew the inadequacy of employing the modifications of the root فعل, in the Roman character, the reader will find it in the second vol. of De Sacy's Grammar, p. 618, where the eight Perfect feet are thus represented, viz., *Fă-oū-lōn*, *Mĕ-fā-ī-lōn*, *Mĕ-fā-ĭ-lĕ-tōn*, *Fā-ĭ-lā-tōn*, *Fā-ĭ-lōn*, *Mŏs-tăf-ĭ-lōn*, *Mŏ-tĕ-fā-ĭ-lōn*, and *Mĕf-oū-lā-tŏ*. The grand defect here is, that we have no representative of the nondescript consonant ع, which is altogether ignored;

the consequence is that the learner is not only *perplexed,* but utterly *misled.* The proper course would clearly have been, either to have eschewed the Roman character entirely, or to have employed a more appropriate Arabic root for the purpose of illustration.

375. With a view to exhibit, in the clearest manner, the affinity or relationship that holds between the various metres of each class, I have made use of the *straight line,* which leads *more directly to the point,* than the *circles* used by the Prosodians of the East. Let us, for instance, examine Class I.: where we see at a glance that, by taking away the first two syllables of the metre *Ṭawīl* from the *beginning* of the hemistich, and by transferring the same to the *end,* we have the metre *Madīd,* which comes next. In like manner, if we transfer the first three syllables of the *Madīd* from the beginning to the end of the hemistich, we have the metre *Basīṭ,* and so on with all the rest. In Class IV. I have slightly altered the usual arrangement, by placing the *Sarī'* metre at the end of the class, rather than at the beginning, as it is formed by transferring the first three syllables of the *Mujtathth* from the beginning of the latter to its close. We may further observe that all the metres of Class IV. consist only of two out of the four Epitriti feet of the ancients, variously arranged.

a. What we have here denominated the *Five Classes* of metres, are, by the Arabs, called the *Five Circles*; because they describe the relationship of the metres in each by means of circles, of which the reader may see specimens in p. 9 of Clerk, and in p. 147 of Freytag. The first circle they call the Discordant; the second, the Associated;

the third, the Extracted, its feet being taken from the first circle; the fourth they call the Resembling or Similar; and the fifth, the Concordant. The first two circles are peculiar to the Arabs; the rest are common to the Arabs and Persians, with this difference, however, that with the former the Hexametric form (See § 376) is preferred when they employ the third circle.

376. The student will bear in mind that throughout the foregoing Tables we have given only the first hemistich of each stanza or verse, the second hemistich being a mere repetition of the first; consequently every complete verse must consist of an even number of feet. A verse consisting of eight feet, as in the metres of Class I., is said to be مُثَمَّن *Muthamman* or Octameter; if it be of six feet, like those in Class IV. it is called مُسَدَّس *Musaddas* or Hexameter. Some of the metres are used in both forms, as we shall see hereafter; and some of the Hexametric metres, by dropping a foot in each hemistich become what is called مُرَبَّع *Murabba'* or Tetrameter.

377. We shall now proceed to offer a few brief and plain observations on such metres only as are of most frequent occurrence. These are the *Ṭawīl'*, the *Basīṭ*, the *Wāfir*, the *Kāmil*, the *Khafīf*, the *Sarī'*, the *Mutaḳārib* and the *Rajaz*. The remaining metres are of comparatively rare usage, especially among the older writers. We have already observed (§ 373), that we should make a sparing use of the technicalities of the "Ars Metrica." There are, however, a few terms, such as the *'Arūḍ*, the *Ḍarb*, and the *Ḥashw* (See § 373, *a*) which we must here employ for the sake of con-

ciseness. Those who have a taste for additional matters of this sort may consult Freytag, in whose copious work he will find at least three hundred of them, more or less.

Of the Metre Ṭawīl, or the Long.

Standard, *Faḍūlun, Mafāḍīlun, Faḍūlun, Mafāḍīlun,* (twice).

378. This is a favourite metre among the older Arabian poets. It is Octameter, and subject to one deviation (*ziḥāf*) in the last foot or *'Arūḍ* of the first hemistich, which may become *Mafāḍilun* instead of *Mafāḍīlun.* In the *Ḍarb* or final foot of the second hemistich it admits of two deviations, viz., *Mafāḍīlun* and *Mafāḍī* instead of *Mafāḍīlun.* Occasionally the intermediate feet or *Ḥashw* of each hemistich may deviate into *Mafāḍilun* and *Faḍūlu* respectively.

a. Of the seven famous Arabian poems called the *Mu'allaḳāt,* composed about, or a little previous to, the time of Muḥammad, the first three, viz., that of *Amru-l-Ḳais,* of *Ṭarafat,* and of *Zuhair,* are in the metre *Ṭawīl.* The *Mu'allaḳāt* are what we may call the "Competition Poems" of Arabia; and they derive their title from the circumstance of having had the high honour of being written in letters of gold, and suspended for public perusal in the portico of the temple of Mecca.

Of the Metre Basīṭ, or the Extended.

Standard, *Mustafḍilun, Fāḍilun, Mustafḍilun, Fāḍilun,* (twice).

379. This, like the preceding, is a favourite metre with the older poets. It admits of one deviation in the *'Arūḍ,* viz.,

Fāḍilun instead of *Fāḍilun*; and in the *Ḍarb*, it admits both *Fāḍilun* and *Faḍlun*, for *Fāḍilun*. By omitting the fourth foot in each hemistich, the verse becomes a Hexameter, in which case the *'Arūḍ* may be *Mustafḍil* instead of *Mustafḍilun*; and the *Ḍarb* may deviate from *Mustafḍilun* into *Mustafḍilān* or *Mustafḍil*. Finally, all the feet in this metre admit of several deviations. For instance, *Mustafḍilun* may, in addition to those we have mentioned, become *Mutafḍilun*, *Mutaḍilun*, or *Mutaḍilān*.

Of the Metre Wāfir, or the Exuberant.

Standard, *Mafāḍilatun, Mafāḍilatun, Mafāḍilatun*, (twice).

380. This metre is occasionally (though very rarely) employed as an Octameter by an additional *Mafāḍilatun* in each hemistich. Its general form, however, is Hexameter; in which case both the *'Arūḍ* and the *Ḍarb* generally admit of the deviation *Mafāḍil* instead of *Mafāḍilatun*. By withdrawing *Mafāḍilatun* from each hemistich of the Hexameter, it is occasionally employed as a Tetrameter; and in such case, the *Ḍarb* or last foot of the verse may deviate from *Mafāḍilatun* into *Mafāḍiltun*. The fifth poem of the *Seven Mu'allakāt*, by 'Amru the son of Kulthūm, is composed in the Hexametric form of this metre. The poet lived, in "the days of ignorance" as the Arabs express it, which means that he flourished before the time of Muḥammad.

Of the Metre Kāmil, or the Perfect.

Standard, *Mutafāḍilun, Mutafāḍilun, Mutafaḍilun*, (twice).

381. This metre, like the preceding, with which it is

closely allied, is employed occasionally as an Octameter; but most commonly as a Hexameter or Tetrameter. As a Hexameter it admits of one deviation in the *'Arūḍ*, viz., *Mutafā* for *Mutafāḍilun*. In the *Ḍarb* it may deviate from the regular foot into *Mutafā* or *Mutafāḍil*. The fourth of the *Mu'allakāt* by Labīd, and the sixth by 'Antarah, are composed in the Hexametric form of this metre.

Of the Metre Khafīf, or the Nimble.

Standard, *Fāḍilātun*, *Mustafḍilun*, *Fādilātun*, (twice).

382. This metre is of frequent occurrence both as a Hexameter and as a Tetrameter, the former being the more common. It admits of one deviation, both in the *'Arūḍ* and *Ḍarb* of the Hexameter, by dropping the last syllable of *Fāḍilātun*. In the Tetrameter, the *Ḍarb*, or last foot of the verse, may deviate into *Mutafḍil* in lieu of *Mustafḍilun*. The seventh and last of the *Mu'allakāt* by Ḥārith, the son of Ḥillazah, is composed in the Hexametric form of the *Khafīf*. This metre is also a great favourite with the Persian poets, who generally employ (as the Arabs sometimes do) *Mafāḍilun* instead of *Mustafḍilun*, as the middle foot of the hemistich.

Of the Metre Sarī', or the Rapid.

Standard, *Mustafḍilun*, *Mustafḍilun*, *Mafḍūlātu*, (twice).

383. This metre is a favourite with the earlier Arabian poets. It is employed only in the Hexametric form; and admits of several deviations both in the *'Arūḍ* and *Ḍarb* of

the verse. In the former, *Mafḍūlātu* may become *Mafḍūlā*, *Mafḍŭlā*, or *Mafūlā*; and in the latter it may deviate into *Mafḍulāt*, *Mafḍūlā*, or *Mafḍū*. With the Persian poets the Sarī' is of very frequent occurrence, only the last foot of the hemistich generally deviates into *Fāḍilāt*, *Faḍūlun*, *Fāḍilun*, or *Faḍ*, instead of *Mafḍūlātu*.

Of the Metre Mutaḳārib, or the Proximate.

Standard, *Faḍūlun*, *Faḍūlun*, *Faḍūlun*, *Faḍūlun* (twice).

384. This metre is generally employed as an Octameter, in which case the *Ḍarb* may deviate into *Faḍūl*, *Faḍū*, or *Faḍ*, instead of *Faḍūlun*. It is occasionally used as a Hexameter, in which form both the *'Arūḍ* and the *Ḍarb* admit of the deviation of *Faḍūlun* into *Faḍū*. As an Octameter it is a great favourite with the Persian poets who generally change the last foot of each hemistich into *Faḍūl*, *Faḍū*, or *Faḍal*.

Of the Metre Rajaz, or the Tremulous.

Standard, *Mustafḍilun*, *Mustafḍilun*, *Mustafḍilun*, *Mustafḍilun* (twice).

385. This is a favourite metre both with the Arabs and Persians, the former preferring the Hexametric form, as we intimated in § 375, *a*. It admits of several deviations in all the feet, in consequence of which it is almost as easy to compose in it as if it were plain prose; hence it is generally employed when didactic or scientific subjects of any length are treated of in verse. Of works of this nature we may mention the Alfiya (or Quintessence of Arabic Grammar), by Jamālu-d-

Dīn, commonly called Ibn Mālik. The *Rajaz* has another peculiarity in which it differs from the rest of the Arabian metres—viz., the first hemistich of each verse generally rhymes with the second as in our heroic metre; and the *Ḍarb* of each verse does not, as is usual, necessarily rhyme with that of the verse following, though there is no rule to the contrary. The deviations to which the standard foot *Mustafdilun* is liable are, *Mutafḍilun*, *Muftaḍilun*, and *Mutaḍilun*. In the *Ḍarb* or last foot of the second hemistich, *Mustafḍilun* may deviate into *Mustafḍil*. This metre is also a favourite with the poets of Persia who employ it both as an Octameter and as a Hexameter.

a. The eight metres which we have just noticed are those of most frequent occurrence among the oldest Arabian poets whose works have come down to us, such as the collection of poetical fragments entitled the Ḥamāsah, to which we may add the Mu'allaḳāt, already alluded to, and the Dīwān of 'Alī Bin Abī Ṭālib, the son-in-law of Muḥammad. Our limited space does not permit us to notice the remaining eight metres. Suffice it to say that they are all subject to some such deviations as we have above enumerated, chiefly in the *'Arūḍ* and *Ḍarb* of the verse, but occasionally deviations are to be met with in the *Ḥashw* or interior part of a verse. The classical student will at once perceive that most of the *Ziḥāfāt* or deviations of the Arabian verse, are similar in principle to those that occur in the Iambic metre of the Greek tragedians.

Of the Rhyme اَلْقَافِيَةُ (pl. اَلْقَوَافِي).

386. The rhyme of the Arabs agrees, at least, virtually, with that of other nations, viz., the last syllable of one verse

corresponds in pronunciation with the last syllable of the verse following. There is this peculiarity, however, in the poems of the Arabs, that with the exception of the species called مُزْدَوِج *muzdawaj*, "paired" or "wedded" (See § 390), the same rhyme is continued in the *Ḍarb* of each verse throughout the piece. When the verse ends with a consonant the rhyme is said to be مُقَيَّدَة *muḳaiyadah*, "fettered," and when it ends with a vowel, it is said to be مُطْلَقَة *muṭlaḳah*, "free." The last consonant of a verse constitutes the essential part of the rhyme, and is called the رَوِيّ *rawī*, "that which binds" or "unites." The species of poem called قَصِيدَة *ḳaṣīdah* (See § 389), may be further qualified by a relative adjective formed from the letter constituting the *rawī*. For example, if the *rawī* be the letter م *mīm*, with or without a vowel, the poem is called قَصِيدَةٌ مِيمِيَّة, and so on with regard to any other letter, with the exception of ا, و, and ي inert, when preceded by their homogeneous short vowels, in which case, the consonant bearing the short vowel is the *rawī*. When the last consonant of a verse is moveable by a short vowel, such vowel is theoretically lengthened, the same as if it were followed by the letter of prolongation with which it is homogeneous; and this easily accounts for what we have just stated respecting the letters ا, و, and ي, as not constituting the *rawī* of a verse; for virtually their presence does not affect the quantity of the final syllable.

Of the Different Kinds of Poems.

387. The poetical compositions of the Arabs, like those of other nations, are called by various names, conformable to their

subject, the manner of treating the subject, and their form. Of these the principal species are, the قِطْعَةٌ *ḳiṭ'ah*, the قَصِيدَةٌ *ḳaṣīdah*, and the مُزْدَوِجٌ *muzdawaj;* each of which we shall here briefly describe.

Of the قِطْعَةٌ *Ḳiṭ'ah* (pl. قِطَعٌ and مُقَطَّعَاتٌ).

388. This species of poem appears to have been extensively in use among the Arabs previous to the time of Muḥammad. The collection of ancient fragments of poetry called the *Ḥamāsah* is chiefly, if not entirely, of this form. The *Ḳiṭ'ah*, according to native writers, must consist of not fewer than two verses, or, as we should call them, couplets, nor does it admit of more than one hundred and seventy-five. The difference as to form, between the *Ḳiṭ'ah* and *Ḳaṣīdah* is merely this—that the two hemistichs of the first couplet do not necessarily rhyme in the *Ḳiṭ'ah*, but whatever may be the rhyme of the second hemistich of the first couplet, the same must be continued in the second hemistich of every succeeding couplet. In conclusion, we may observe, that both the *Ḳaṣīdah* and the *Ḳiṭ'ah* may be composed in any metre which the poet may choose; though those of most frequent occurrence are the seven metres we briefly noticed from § 378 to § 384, both inclusive.

Of the قَصِيدَةٌ *Ḳaṣīdah* (pl. قَصَائِدُ).

389. This kind of poem resembles the Idyllium of the Greeks. Its subjects, generally, are praise of great personages, living or deceased; satire; elegy; also moral and religious reflections. In the first verse, or as we should say, couplet, of the *Ḳaṣīdah*, the *'Arūḍ* must always rhyme with

the *Ḍarb*, and, as in the case of the *Ḳiṭ'ah*, that identical rhyme must continue in the second hemistich of each verse to the end of the poem. When the subject of the *Ḳaṣīdah* is panegyric, the poet generally finishes with a benediction or prayer for the health and prosperity of the person addressed, such as, "May thy life, health, and prosperity endure as long as the sun and moon revolve!" According to the author of the *Chār Gulzār*, a valuable treatise on Arabian and Persian Prosody, the *Ḳaṣīdah* must consist of not fewer than twenty-five couplets, nor must it extend to more than one hundred and seventy-five. This statement, however, appears to have been made without due consideration; for, in the first place, there are numerous *Ḳaṣīdahs* of fewer than twenty-five couplets. Secondly, the same author further states, that, among the Arabians, the *Ḳaṣīdah* seems to have been unlimited as to length, as they have sometimes made it exceed five hundred couplets. This last assertion, also, may be true, for ought I know to the contrary, but I have never yet seen a *Ḳaṣīdah* of this extreme length. The *Mu'allaḳāt*, or seven Arabian prize poems, suspended of old in the temple of Mecca, to which we formerly alluded, are all of the *Ḳaṣīdah* species.

a. There are two other species of poetical composition derived from the *Ḳaṣīdah*, which we may here briefly notice, viz., the رُبَاعِيّ *Rubā'ī*, and the غَزَل *Ghazal*. The *Rubā'ī*, as its name imports, consists of four hemistichs, of which the first, second, and fourth must have the same rhyme, but not necessarily the third. In fact if we take the first two stanzas out of the *Ḳaṣīdah* we have the *Rubā'ī*, which nearly corresponds with the epigram of the ancients both in its form and in the mode of its application. It is more especially employed in order to express the date of any event by the أَبْجَد mode of numeration. (See § 39.)

b. The *Ghazal* is a short poem consisting, at an average, of five to twelve stanzas. As in the *Kaṣīdah*, the first two hemistichs must rhyme, and that same rhyme is continued in the *Ḍarb* of each stanza to the end of the composition. The ordinary subjects of a *Ghazal* are extravagant descriptions of the beauty of a mistress, and the sufferings of a lover (from the cruelty of the former); to which we may add the commendation of wine and hilarity. From what we have just stated then, it will be obvious that the *Ghazal* differs in no respect from the *Kaṣīdah*, except in regard to length. In fact the fifth of the *Mu'allaḳāt*, by 'Amru the son of Kulthūm is to all intents and purposes a *Ghazal*, so far as the subject of it is concerned; it merely differs as to form. The *Rubā'ī* and the *Ghazal* are more in use among the Persian poets than they are among the Arabs.

Of the مُزْدَوِج *Muzdawaj, i.e. "paired."*

390. The term *Muzdawaj* (called by the Persians *Mathnawī*) is generally applied to compositions of greater extent than those we have already described. It is unrestricted as to length—from three couplets upwards to any number, according to the nature of the subject. It consists of a succession of stanzas or couplets, all of the same metre, and the second hemistich of each stanza must rhyme with the first; but the stanzas themselves do not necessarily rhyme with one another, as in the *Kiṭ'ah* and *Kaṣīdah*. The metre generally assigned to the *Muzdawaj* is the *Rajaz*, or some of its numerous modifications, as we intimated in § 385; hence such compositions are freqently denominated by the general term أُرْجُوزَةٌ (plur.

أراجِيز). The *Muzdawaj* in Arabic corresponds with the hexametric poems of the Greek and Latin, or with such of our own poems as are composed in the Iambic metre of ten syllables, with rhyme.

a. Most Arabian poems fall under one or other of the three general classes described from § 388-390. A poem, however, may have a still more restricted denomination, according to the subject of which it treats; thus, if the subject be eulogy, or the praise of any person, place, or thing, the composition is called مَدِيحٌ (pl. مَدَائِحُ). A satiric poem is called هِجَاءٌ or أُهْجِيَّةٌ (pl. أَهَاجِيُّ). An elegy is called رِثَاءٌ or مَرْثِيَةٌ (pl. مَرَاثٍ). A poem intended to be sung with musical accompaniment is called أُغْنِيَّةٌ (pl. أَغَانِيُّ). When poetical quotations are introduced into prose compositions, which is very frequently the case, the same are prefaced by the general terms شِعْرٌ "poetry," or نَظْمٌ "verse," etc., as we noticed in § 42, *a.*

Poetic Licence.

391. The poets of Arabia appear to have availed themselves of the *Licentia Vatum* much more freely than their tuneful brethren of Europe ever did, with the exception, perhaps, of the poets of modern Italy. The Arabs, like the Italians, may be said to possess a language peculiar to poetry, and not amenable to the strict grammatical rules that apply to plain prose. The principal licences that obtain in Arabian poetry may be classed under the following species; viz. 1. The shortening of long vowels in the middle or end of a word by suppressing the letters of prolongation. 2. By a contrary process, they may lengthen a short vowel either by adding to it the homogeneous letter of prolongation, or by doubling

the following letter according to certain rules. 3. They may, in certain triliteral words, altogether suppress the short vowel of the middle letter, and substitute *jazma* instead of it. 4. They may add a short vowel (generally a *kasra*) to certain verbal terminations, in a manner similar to what we stated respecting the symbol *waṣla*, § 36, *a*. Lastly, they take considerable liberties with the *nūnation* and other case terminations of the nouns, both in the singular, dual, and plural. All these peculiarities, however, I do not here enter into at greater length, for reasons mentioned in our concluding paragraph which immediately follows.

392. In conclusion, I have only to observe that my object in this last Section has been merely to explain the true and simple principles on which the prosody of the Arabs is founded. It would have occupied too much space in an elementary Grammar like the present to have treated the subject at greater length. The student who desires further information, however, may have recourse to one or other of the following works, viz., "Tractatus de Prosodia Arabica," Oxonii, 1661, 12mo. This Treatise is by Samuel Clerk, and is generally appended to a work by Edward Pocock, entitled "Carmen Tograi," etc. Clerk's work at first sight appears a little uncouth and repulsive, inasmuch as all the Arabic technical terms of the art are dignified with Latin terminations; but still a perusal of it will amply repay the student's labour. The best work, however, on Arabian Prosody is that of Dr. Freytag, entitled "Darstellung der Arabischen Verskunst," 8vo., Bonn, 1830, pp. 557. It treats the sub-

ject in a clear and satisfactory manner, illustrated throughout with numerous examples from the poets, fully pointed, and accompanied with translations. The only objection to it (if objection it be) is, that it is composed in German, a language not nearly so well known in this country as ours is throughout Germany.

a. Should the reader be possessed of the second edition of De Sacy's Grammar, a work now exceedingly scarce, he will find at the end of the second volume a very neat Treatise on Prosody. Professor Ewald, of Gottingen, also published in 1825 a small 8vo. volume on the same subject; but of the merits of this last it would be rash in me to express any opinion, as I never had sufficient perseverance to fathom that gentleman's Latinity, which differs very considerably from that of Cicero and Quintilian. So far as I can understand him, however, I am led to believe that he labours to make the metre of the Arabs square with that of the ancient Greeks and Romans. In order to effect this object, Professor Ewald is forced to set up, in every one of the sixteen metres, a *standard of his own*, which all preceding grammarians have considered as mere *deviations* from other estab. . d standards. Well, this is mere matter of careful investigation, whereupon my own experience does not authorise me to give anything like a positive opinion. If Prof. Ewald *can prove* that his standards of metre are the rule, and those of all others the exception, why then, he may well exclaim, once more, as he does rather prematurely in his preface, "*sublimi feriam sidera vertici.*" Till this proof, however, is established, I prefer following in the wake of the native grammarians.

THE END.

Published by

Facsimile Publisher
Ashok Vihar, Delhi-110052 (India)
Website: www.facsimilepublisher.com

Distributed by

Gyan Books Pvt. Ltd.
5, Ansari Road, Daryaganj, New Delhi-110002 (India)
E-mail: books@gyanbooks.com, Website: www.gyanbooks.com

2 222000 000394